J.K. LASSER'S™

1001 DEDUCTIONS AND TAX BREAKS 2022

J.K. LASSER'S™

1001 DEDUCTIONS AND TAX BREAKS 2022

Your Complete Guide to Everything Deductible

Barbara Weltman

Published by John Wiley & Sons, Inc., Hoboken, New Jersey.
Published simultaneously in Canada.

Library of Congress Cataloging-in-Publication Data is Available:

ISBN 978-1-119-83847-0 (paperback)
ISBN 978-1-119-83853-1 (ePDF)
ISBN 978-1-119-83854-8 (ePub)

Cover design: Wiley

SKY10030227_101821

Contents

Introduction

The COVID-19 pandemic triggered a number of changes in tax rules designed to help individuals cope financially with the economic fallout in the economy. Some changes are temporary, while others are permanent. The word "taxes" makes most people groan. There are good reasons for this response: First of all, the cost of paying your taxes annually can be a financial burden. You may feel taken to the cleaners every time you view your paycheck *after* withholding for federal income taxes (not to mention state income taxes as well as Social Security and Medicare taxes). And taxes are time consuming—to gather information, meet with a tax professional if you use one, or prepare and submit your own returns.

Second, it can cost you money to get your taxes done. The IRS says that nearly 60% of taxpayers use paid preparers for their returns. Of course, because more than 90% of individual income tax returns are completed by computer (through a paid preparer, with software, or FreeFile), the places where deductions and credits are entered on the return is not critical to you; it's effectively done automatically.

Third, the tax law is very complicated and changing all the time. There have been several major tax acts impacting 2021 returns. These include the Consolidated Appropriations Act, 2021, and the American Rescue Plan Act.

Fourth, you have to know what the tax rules are and can't claim ignorance to avoid taxes and penalties. Even if you use a tax professional or tax preparation software to prepare your return, you remain responsible for your taxes. The Tax Court has noted that using software is not an automatic excuse to avoid underpayment penalties.

How can you combat the feeling of dread when it comes to taxes? It helps to know that the tax law is peppered with many, many tax breaks to which you may be entitled. These breaks allow you to *not* report certain economic benefits you enjoy or to subtract certain expenses from your income or even directly from your tax bill. As the famous jurist Judge Learned Hand once stated (in the 1934 case of *Helvering v. Gregory* in the Court of Appeals for the Second Circuit):

Anyone may arrange his affairs so that his taxes shall be as low as possible; he is not bound to choose that pattern which best pays the Treasury. There is not even a patriotic duty to increase one's taxes. Over and over again the Courts have said that there is nothing sinister in so arranging affairs as to keep taxes as low as possible. Everyone does it, rich and poor alike, and all do right, for nobody owes any public duty to pay more than the law demands.

So get your tax affairs in order and legally reduce what you pay each year to Uncle Sam!

In getting a handle on how to do this by taking advantage of every tax break you may be entitled to without running afoul of the Internal Revenue Service (IRS), there are some simple rules to keep in mind. They include:

- You must report all of your income unless a specific law allows you to exclude or exempt it (so that it is never taxed) or defer it (so that it is taxed at a later time).

- You can claim deductions only when and to the extent the law allows. Deductions are referred to as a "matter of legislative grace"; Congress doesn't have to create them and does so only for some purpose (for example, to encourage economic activity or to balance some perceived inequity in the tax law).

- Tax credits are worth more than tax deductions. A credit reduces your tax payment on a dollar-for-dollar basis; a $1,000 credit saves you $1,000 in taxes. A deduction is worth only as much as the top tax bracket you are in. Suppose you are in the 24% tax bracket, which means this is the highest rate you pay on at least some of your income. If you have a $1,000 deduction, it is worth $240 (24% of $1,000) because it saves you $240 in taxes you would otherwise have to pay.

- In a number of cases, different deduction rules apply to the alternative minimum tax (AMT), a shadow tax system that ensures you pay at least some tax if your regular income tax is lower than it would have been without certain deductions.

Whether you prepare your return by hand, use computer software or an online solution, or rely on a professional, this book is designed to tell you how to get every tax edge you're entitled to. Knowing what to look out for will help you plan ahead and organize your activities in such a way that you'll share less of your hard-earned money with the government.

Tax-Favored Items

There are 5 types of tax-advantaged items receiving preferential or favorable treatment under the tax law:

1. *Tax-free income*—income you can receive without any current or future tax concerns. Tax-free income may be in the form of exclusions or exemptions from tax. In many cases, tax-free items do not even have to be reported in any way on your return.

2. *Capital gains*—profits on the sale or exchange of property held for more than one year (long-term). Long-term capital gains are subject to lower tax rates than the rates on other income, such as salary and interest income, and may even be tax free in some cases. Ordinary dividends on stocks and capital gain distributions from stock mutual funds are taxed at the same low rates as long-term capital gains.

3. *Tax-deferred income*—income that isn't currently taxed. Since the income builds up without any reduction for current tax, you may accumulate more over time. However, at some point the income becomes taxable.

4. *Deductions*—items you can subtract from your income to reduce the amount of income subject to tax. There are 2 classes of deductions: those "above the line," which are subtracted directly from gross income, and those "below the line," which can be claimed only if you itemize deductions instead of claiming the standard deduction (explained later).

5. *Credits*—items you can use to offset your tax on a dollar-for-dollar basis. There are 2 types of tax credits: one that can be used only to offset tax liability (called a "nonrefundable" credit) and one that can be claimed even if it exceeds tax liability and you receive a refund (called a "refundable" credit). Usually you must complete a special tax form for each credit you claim.

This book focuses on different types of tax-favored items: exclusions (tax-free income), above-the-line deductions that don't require itemizing, itemized deductions, tax credits, and other benefits, such as subtractions that reduce income. At the end of this Introduction you'll see symbols used to easily identify the type of benefit being explained.

Limits on Qualifying for Tax-Favored Items

In many cases, eligibility for tax benefits (including Economic Impact Payments), or the extent to which they may be claimed, depends on adjusted gross income (AGI) or modified adjusted gross income (MAGI).

Adjusted gross income is gross income (all the income you are required to report) minus certain deductions (called "adjustments to gross income"). Adjustments or subtractions you can make to your gross income to arrive at your adjusted gross income are limited to the following items:

Alimony payments for pre-2019 divorces and separation agreements

Archer Medical Savings Accounts (MSAs) (for accounts set up prior to 2008)

Business expenses of self-employed individuals

Capital loss deductions of up to $3,000

Charitable contributions up to $300 ($600 for joint filers) if you don't itemize personal deductions

Educator expenses up to $250

Employer-equivalent portion of self-employment tax

Forfeiture-of-interest penalties because of early withdrawals from certificates of deposit (CDs)

Health Savings Account (HSA) contributions

Individual Retirement Account (IRA) deductions

Jury duty pay turned over to your employer

Legal fees for unlawful discrimination claims

Net disaster loss if you don't itemize personal deductions

Net operating losses (NOLs)

Performing artist's qualifying expenses

Qualified retirement plan contributions for self-employed individuals

Rent and royalty expenses

Repayment of supplemental unemployment benefits required because of the receipt of trade readjustment allowances

Self-employed health insurance deduction

Simplified employee pension (SEP) or savings incentive match plan for employees (SIMPLE) contributions for self-employed individuals

Student loan interest deduction up to $2,500

Travel expenses to attend National Guard or military reserve meetings more than 100 miles from home

Figuring AGI may sound complicated, but in reality it's merely a number taken from a line on your tax return. For example, AGI is the figure you enter on line 11 of the 2021 Form 1040 or 1040-SR.

Modified adjusted gross income is merely AGI increased by certain items that are excludable from income and/or certain adjustments to gross income. *Which* items are added back varies for different tax breaks. For example, the MAGI limit on eligibility to claim the student loan interest deduction is AGI (disregarding the student loan interest deduction) increased by the exclusion for foreign earned income and certain other foreign income or expenses. All of these items are explained in this book.

Household income is a term in tax law used to determine eligibility for the premium tax credit to help pay for coverage purchased through a government marketplace. Household income is explained further in this book in connection with these tax rules.

Qualified business income. If you are an owner in a pass-through entity—a sole proprietorship, limited liability company, partners, or S corporation—you may be eligible for a qualified business income (QBI) deduction. QBI for purposes of this personal deduction is explained further in Chapter 14.

Taxable income. This is the amount of income remaining after subtracting deductions. Taxable income is the amount on which taxes are figured. Taxable income is also the threshold used for determining the QBI deduction explained in Chapter 14.

Standard Deduction versus Itemized Deductions

Every taxpayer, other than a dependent of another taxpayer, is entitled to a standard deduction. This is a subtraction from your income, and the amount you claim is based on your filing status. Table I.1 shows the standard deduction amounts for 2021. In 2018 (the most recent year for statistics), about 88% of all filers used the standard deduction.

TABLE I.1 Standard Deduction Amounts for 2021

Filing Status	Standard Deduction
Married filing jointly	$ 25,100
Head of household	18,800
Single (unmarried)	12,550
Qualifying widow(er) (surviving spouse)	25,100
Married filing separately	12,550

In addition to the basic standard deduction, certain taxpayers can increase these amounts. An additional standard deduction amount applies to those age 65 and older and for blindness. For 2021, the additional amount is $1,700 for individuals who are not married and are not a surviving spouse and $1,350 for those who are married or a surviving spouse.

Example

In 2021, you are single, age 68, and *not* blind. Your standard deduction is $14,250 ($12,550 + $1,700).

You cannot claim any additional standard deduction that applies to those 65 or older and/or blind if you choose to itemize deductions in lieu of claiming the basic standard deduction amount.

Individuals who do not itemize but suffer a net qualified disaster loss in a federally declared disaster area can effectively increase their standard deduction amount. Net qualified disaster losses are explained in Chapter 12.

Instead of claiming the standard deduction, you can opt to list certain deductions separately (i.e., *itemize* them). Itemized deductions include:

Medical expenses

Taxes

Interest payments

Gifts to charity (without regard to the dollar limit allowed for those claiming the standard deduction)

Casualty and theft losses in federally-declared disaster areas

Gambling losses

Estate tax payments on income in respect of decedents

Generally, claim the standard deduction when it is greater than the total of your itemized deductions. However, it may save overall taxes to itemize, even when total deductions are less than the standard deduction, if you are subject to the alternative minimum tax (AMT). ***The reason:*** The standard deduction cannot be used to reduce income subject to the AMT, but certain itemized deductions can.

In the past there was an overall limit on itemized deductions for high-income taxpayers. This limit does not apply for 2018 through 2025.

If a married couple files separate returns and one spouse itemizes deductions, the other must also itemize and cannot claim a standard deduction.

Impact of Deductions on Your Chances of Being Audited

Did you know that the IRS collects statistics from taxpayers to create profiles of average deductions? If you claim more than the average for your income range, the IRS's computer *may* select your return for further examination.

Tax experts agree that you should claim every deduction you are entitled to, even if your write-offs exceed these statistical ranges. Just make sure to have the necessary proof of your eligibility and other records you are required to keep in case your return is examined.

How to Use This Book

This book is tied to Form 1040, *U.S. Income Tax Return for Individuals*. It can also be used for Form 1040-SR, *Income Tax Return for Seniors;* a form specifically for seniors age 65 and older.

The chapters in this book are organized by subject matter so you can browse through them to find the subjects that apply to you or those in which you have an interest.

Each tax benefit is denoted by an icon to help you spot the type of benefit involved:

 Exclusion

 Above-the-line deduction

 Itemized deduction (a deduction taken *after* figuring adjusted gross income)

 Credit

 Other benefit (e.g., a subtraction other than an above-the-line or itemized deduction that reduces income)

For each tax benefit you will find an explanation of what it is, starting with the maximum benefit or benefits you can claim if you meet all eligibility requirements. You'll learn the conditions or eligibility requirements for claiming or qualifying for the benefit. You'll find both planning tips to help you make the most of the benefit opportunity as well as pitfalls to help you avoid problems that can prevent your eligibility. You'll see where to claim the benefit (if reporting is required) on your tax return and what records you must retain to support your tax position.

You'll find dozens of examples to show you how other taxpayers have successfully taken advantage of the benefit. Over the years, taxpayers have been able to write off literally thousands of items; not every one is listed here because space does not allow it. And you'll learn what *isn't* allowed even though you might otherwise think so. There are references to free IRS publications on a variety of tax topics that you can download from the IRS website (www.irs.gov) or obtain free of charge by calling 800-829-1040.

You'll also see key dates for various actions, such as filing returns, contributing to retirement plans, and reporting foreign financial accounts to the U.S. Treasury. For example, the deadline for filing 2021 federal income tax returns is April 18, 2022.

In the appendices, you'll find a listing of items that can be adjusted each year to reflect cost-of-living changes so you can plan ahead, as well as a checklist of items that are tax free, and a checklist of items that are not deductible.

Throughout the book you will find alerts to possible changes to come. For a *free* update on tax developments, look for the Supplement to this book in February 2022, by going to www.jklasser.com, as well as to my website, www .BigIdeasForSmallBusiness.com.

CHAPTER 1

You and Your Family

The nature of families is changing, and taxes have specific rules for them. Do the old clichés still ring true? Can two still live as cheaply as one? Are things really cheaper by the dozen? For tax purposes, there may be a penalty or bonus for being married versus single. And there are certain tax breaks for having a family.

This chapter explains family-related tax benefits, such as tax credits related to your children and the consequences of marital dissolutions. Economic impact payments (EIPs) in 2021 to individuals and dependents are explained in Chapter 12. For more information on these topics, see IRS Publication 501, *Dependents, Standard Deduction, and Filing Information*; IRS Publication 503, *Child and Dependent Care Expenses*; IRS Publication 504, *Divorced or Separated Individuals*; IRS Publication 596, *Earned Income Credit*; and IRS Publication 972, *Child Tax Credit*.

Marital Status

Whether you are married or single has a significant impact on your taxes. In some cases, being married results in a "marriage bonus," which means effectively averaging taxes when one spouse works and the other does not. In other cases, being married results in a "marriage penalty," which means that two working spouses earning about the same likely will pay higher total tax than if they were single. For some tax rules, a married couple has the identical tax break as a single individual, such as the $3,000 capital loss deduction against ordinary income and the $10,000 limit on itemizing state and local taxes, which is a distinct disadvantage for those who are married. For some tax rules, a married couple has double the tax break for singles, such as the ordinary loss deduction for so-called Section 1244 stock, so marital status makes no difference here.

Technically, there are a number of filing statuses that determine eligibility for various tax breaks:

- Married filing jointly
- Married filing separately
- Head of household
- Unmarried (single)
- Qualifying widow(er) with a dependent child. This filing status is also referred to as a surviving spouse.

You need to know which term applies to you. The terms are not further defined here and often cause confusion, so check IRS Publication 501 if you are unsure. Note that under federal tax law, the terms "husband," "wife," and "spouse" are gender neutral. The term "husband and wife" means two individuals lawfully married to each other. However, those in a civil union or domestic partnership are not married for federal income tax purposes.

Dependents

No personal or dependency exemptions can be claimed in 2018 through 2025. So if you had 4 exemptions in 2017 and deducted $16,200 ($4,050 × 4) in that year, your deduction in 2021 is zero. The suspension of exemptions seriously reduces write-offs for many taxpayers. Of course, because high-income taxpayers were subject to a phaseout of exemptions, they are not greatly affected by the suspension in the deduction for exemptions.

However, the concept of dependents has not been eliminated and continues to apply for various purposes. For example, for purposes of a child tax credit that may be claimed for a qualifying child or a dependent who is not a qualifying child, the concept of dependents continues to apply. The definition of dependent varies for certain purposes and is explained in each relevant tax break in this book. For example, the amount of income for a qualifying relative taken into account in determining dependent status in 2021 is $4,300.

Qualifying Child

The following is a brief explanation of a qualifying child and a qualifying relative (someone who is not a qualifying child):

A qualifying child must meet all of the following conditions:

- *Relationship test:* The child must be your son or daughter (natural, adopted, step, and in some cases foster) or a descendant of your sibling (e.g., niece or nephew).
- *Age test:* The child must be younger than you and either younger than 19 years old, be a "student" younger than 24 years old as of the end of the calendar year, or any age but permanently and totally disabled.
- *Residency test:* The child must live with you in the United States for more than half the year (special rules for noncustodial parents are explained later).
- *Joint return test:* The child cannot file a joint return unless doing so to claim a tax refund.
- *Support test:* The child does not provide more than half of his or her own support.

Multiple people claiming the child as a dependent. Where one parent has physical custody of the child, he or she can waive treating the child as a dependent to permit the noncustodial parent to do so. The waiver (annually or permanently) is made on Form 8332, *Release/Revocation of Release of Claim to Exemption for Child by Custodial Parent.* The form applies to some benefits (e.g., child tax credit) but not for other benefits (e.g., earned income tax credit, dependent care credit, head of household status).

Where 2 people are eligible to treat the child as a dependent, a "tie breaker rule" comes into play. Generally, the person with greater physical custody (determined by counting the nights that the child spends with each person) is determinative. However, when there's an even split, other rules are used to decide which person can treat the child as a dependent.

Qualifying Relative

This is a person who is not a qualifying child and who meets all of the following conditions:

- *Relationship test.* The person must be either related to you in a stated way (e.g., a child too old to be a qualifying child, grandchild, parent, certain in-laws, aunt, uncle, niece, or nephew) or a member of your household.
- *Support test.* You must provide more than half of the person's support for the year.
- *Gross income test.* The person must have a gross income below a set amount ($4,300 in 2021).

Child Tax Credit

The U.S. Department of Agriculture estimates that it costs a middle-class family over $233,610 to raise a child born in 2015 to age 18 (there are no newer statistics), but if you factor in inflation, the cost becomes $261,473). In recognition of this cost, the tax law allows you to claim a tax credit.

Benefit

You may claim a tax credit of up to $3,600 for a qualifying child from birth to under age 6 and $3,000 for age 6 but under 18. You may claim a $500 credit for a qualifying dependent (a person who is not a qualifying child). If the credit for a qualifying child that you are entitled to claim is more than your tax liability, you may be entitled to a refund under certain conditions.

The credit for a qualifying child is fully refundable if you (or your spouse if married filing jointly) meet certain conditions; the credit for a qualifying dependent is not refundable. From July 1, 2021, through December 31, 2021, the IRS paid one-half of the credit on an advanced basis (ratably each month) to you if you were eligible for the credit, unless you opted to forego the advance payments. These payments are reported to you on IRS Letter 6419 (sent in January 2022). The balance of the credit is claimed on your 2021 income tax return.

The advance payments were based on information the IRS had about you for 2020 (your income, dependents, filing status, residency). If there have been changes, you may have to repay any excess credit amounts you received (see *Pitfalls*).

Conditions

To claim the child tax credit, you must meet 2 conditions:

1. You must have a qualifying child or a qualifying dependent with a valid Social Security number.
2. Your income must be below a set amount. To have the credit treated as refundable, you must meet a residency test. This means you (or your spouse

if married filing jointly) have a principal place of abode in the U.S. for more than half of 2021 or are a bona fide resident of Puerto Rico for 2021.

QUALIFYING CHILD

You can claim the credit only for a "qualifying child." There are 5 tests for a qualifying child and you must meet all of them. A qualifying child who meets the 5 tests:

1. *Age test.* The child must be under age 18 by the end of the 2021. This age limit applies even if a child is disabled (but such an older child may be a qualifying dependent explained later).

2. *Residence test.* The child must have the same principal residence as you for more than half the tax year. There are some exceptions in certain cases for a child of divorced or separated parents, a kidnapped child, temporary absences, and for a child who is born or dies during the year.

3. *Support test.* The child does not provide more than half of his or her support.

4. *Social Security number.* No credit is allowed unless the child has a Social Security number. The Social Security number must be issued on or before the due date of your return. A Social Security card that is labeled "not valid for employment" (i.e., it is only good for purposes of receiving federal benefits, such as Medicaid) is not treated as a valid Social Security number for purposes of the child tax credit.

5. *Nationality.* The child must be a U.S. citizen or national, or a resident of the United States. The person can't be a resident of Canada or Mexico.

QUALIFYING DEPENDENT

You may claim the $500 nonrefundable child tax credit for a qualifying dependent. A "qualifying dependent" is a person who is not a qualifying child and who is viewed as a dependent (even though there is no dependency exemption). More specifically, a dependent is a qualifying relative. There are 5 tests for being a qualifying relative, all of which must be met:

1. *Relationship test.* The person must be your child (including adopted or step); your grandchild or great-grandchild; in-law (son, daughter, father, mother, brother, or sister); parent or stepparent; sibling (including step and half); and aunt, uncle, niece, or nephew if related by blood.

2. *Gross income test.* For 2021, this means having gross income exceeding $4,300.

3. *Support test.* You must provide more than half of the person's support for the year.

4. *Qualifying child test.* The person cannot be a qualifying child for you or any other taxpayer.

5. *Residency test.* The qualifying dependent must be a U.S. citizen, national, or resident of the United States. The person can't be a resident of Canada or Mexico.

MAGI LIMIT

You must have modified adjusted gross income (MAGI) below a set amount. The credit you are otherwise entitled to claim is reduced or eliminated if your MAGI exceeds a set amount. MAGI for purposes of the child tax credit means AGI increased by the foreign earned income exclusion, the foreign housing exclusion or deduction, or the possession exclusion for American Samoa residents.

The credit phases out in 2 stages: first for the amount above $2,000 and then for the remaining $2,000. The credit amount above $2,000 is reduced by $50 for each $1,000 of MAGI or a fraction thereof over the MAGI limit for your filing status. The phaseout begins if MAGI exceeds the limits found in Table 1.1. The remaining $2,000 credit phaseout limits are in Table 1.2.

Example

In 2021, a single parent with one qualifying child age 4 has MAGI of $100,000. The $3,600 credit is reduced to $2,350 (reduction is $1,250, which is $25,000 excess MAGI over the applicable threshold ÷ $50).

TABLE 1.1 Stage 1 Phaseout of the Child Tax Credit over MAGI Limits in 2021

Filing Status	MAGI Limit
Married filing jointly	$150,000
Head of household	$112,500
Single	$ 75,000

TABLE 1.2 Stage 2 Phaseout of Child Tax Credit over MAGI Limits in 2021

Filing Status	MAGI Limit
Married filing jointly	$400,000
Other filing status	200,000

ADDITIONAL CHILD TAX CREDIT

If you can't meet the residency test discussed earlier, you may still qualify for a child tax credit that exceeds your tax liability and is refundable to you. The basic child tax credit amount for those not meeting the residency test is $2,000; income limits apply. The refundable portion is limited to $1,400, but no more than either:

- 15% of earned income in excess of $3,000, or
- For those with 3 or more qualifying children, the excess if any of Social Security taxes over the earned income credit.

Planning Tips

The child tax credit and the credit for other dependents should be factored into income tax withholding from paychecks to enjoy the tax savings throughout the year. The amount of the child tax credit in 2022 will be lower unless Congress makes a change. But you may still file a new Form W-4 with your employer to factor in the applicable child tax credit into your withholdings for the year.

If you know you will become entitled to claim the credit (e.g., you expected the birth of a child), you may wish to adjust your withholding so that you don't have too much income tax withheld from your paycheck. Increase your withholding so that less income tax is withheld from your pay by filing a new Form W-4, *Employee's Withholding Certificate*, with your employer. There is a Tax Withholding Estimator at https://www.irs.gov/individuals/tax-withholding-estimator to help you complete Form W-4.

If you can't claim a credit for a qualifying child because the child doesn't have a valid Social Security number, you may be able to claim the credit for a qualifying dependent. For example, if there is another taxpayer identification number (e.g., Adoption Taxpayer Identification Number, or ATIN), you may be eligible for the $500 credit.

Pitfalls

If you had a change in income, dependents, filing status, or residency, you may have received more in advance payments of the child tax credit than what you are actually entitled to, based on 2021 income, dependents, filing status, and residency. You may have to repay some or all of the excess advance payments received.

- There's no repayment required if your modified adjusted gross income (MAGI) for 2021 does not exceed $40,000 for singles, $50,000 for heads of households, or $60,000 for joint filers as long as your principal place of abode was in the U.S. for more than half the year.

- There *may* be repayment if MAGI for 2021 is between $40,000 and $80,000 for singles, $50,000 and $100,000 for heads of households, or $60,000 and $120,000 for joint filers as long as your principal place of abode was in the U.S. for more than half the year. It depends on the "repayment protection amount," which is $2,000 multiplied by the number of children used to figure your advance payments minus the number of children used to figure the total credit amount on your 2021 return. If the number of children is the same, then the overpayment must be repaid (i.e., there is no repayment protection amount). If there is a repayment protection amount, then there is a reduction in what must be repaid.

- There's full repayment if MAGI is at least $80,000 singles, $100,000 for heads of households, or $120,000 for joint filers.

If you claim the foreign earned income exclusion to exclude income earned abroad up to the annual dollar limit ($108,700 in 2021), you cannot receive the refundable child tax credit.

For 2021 returns filed in 2022, the IRS is not permitted to issue tax refunds for the refundable child tax credit before mid-February 2022. As a result, refunds usually aren't received until the third or fourth week in February, even for returns submitted in January 2022.

Where to Claim the Credit

On page 1 of Form 1040 or 1040-SR, enter dependents for whom you are claiming a child tax credit or credit for other dependents, along with their Social Security numbers and relationship to you. The child tax credit—refundable and non-refundable amounts—as well as the additional child tax credit are figured on Schedule 8812 of Form 1040 or 1040-SR. The nonrefundable child tax credit or the credit for other dependents is entered on line 19 of the return. The refundable child tax credit or the additional child tax credit is entered on line 28 of the return.

Earned Income Credit

Low-income taxpayers are encouraged to work and are rewarded for doing so by means of a special tax credit, called the earned income credit. The earned income credit is the second-largest program, after Medicaid, that provides assistance to low-income people. The amount of the credit varies with income, filing status, and the number of dependents, if any. The credit may be viewed as a "negative income tax" because it can be paid to taxpayers even if it exceeds their tax liability.

TABLE 1.3 Maximum Earned Income Credit for 2021

Number of Qualifying Children	Maximum Earned Income Credit
No qualifying child	$ 1,502
1 qualifying child	3,618
2 qualifying children	5,980
3 or more qualifying children	6,728

Benefit ⊕

If you are a working taxpayer with low or moderate income, you may qualify for a special tax credit of up to $6,728 in 2021. The amount of the credit depends on several factors, including your adjusted gross income, earned income, and the number of qualifying children. Table 1.3 shows the maximum credit you may claim based on the number of your qualifying children, if any.

The credit is "refundable" because it can be received in excess of the tax owed.

Conditions

To be eligible for the credit, you must have earned income from being an employee or a self-employed individual. The amount of the credit you are entitled to claim depends on several factors.

QUALIFYING CHILDREN

You may claim the credit even if you have no qualifying child. But you are entitled to a larger credit if you have one qualifying child and a still larger credit for 2 or more qualifying children.

To be a qualifying child, the child must:

- Be a qualifying child as defined earlier in the chapter under the child tax credit
- Be under age 19 or under age 24 and a full-time student or permanently and totally disabled
- Live in your U.S. household for more than half the year
- Qualify as your dependent if the child is married at the end of the year
- Be a U.S. citizen or resident (or a nonresident who is married to a U.S. citizen and elects to have all worldwide income subject to U.S. tax)

EARNED INCOME

Earned income includes wages, salary, tips, commissions, jury duty pay, union strike benefits, certain disability pensions, U.S. military basic quarters and subsistence allowances, and net earnings from self-employment (profit from your

TABLE 1.4 Earned Income Needed for Top Credit in 2021

Number of Qualifying Children	Earned Income Needed for Top Credit
No qualifying child	$ 9,820
1 qualifying child	10,640
2 or more qualifying children	14,950

self-employment activities). Military personnel can elect to treat tax-free combat pay as earned income for purposes of the earned income credit.

Nontaxable employee compensation, such as tax-free fringe benefits or salary deferrals—for example, contributions to company 401(k) plans—is not treated as earned income.

Earned income does not include pensions and retirement plan distributions, long-term disability and military disability pensions, welfare, and Social Security benefits (for retirement or disability).

To qualify for the maximum credit, you must have earned income at or above a set amount. Table 1.4 shows the earned income you need to obtain the top credit (depending on the number of your qualifying children, if any).

For 2021, you may use your 2019 earned income to figure the credit if it was higher than your earned income in 2021.

ADJUSTED GROSS INCOME

If your adjusted gross income is too high, the credit is reduced or eliminated. Table 1.5 shows the AGI phaseout range for the earned income credit. This depends not only on the number of qualifying children, if any, but also on your filing status, as shown in the table.

JOINT RETURN

If you are married, you usually must file a joint return with your spouse in order to claim an earned income credit. However, this requirement is waived if your spouse did not live in your household for the last 6 months of the year or have a decree, instrument, or written agreement of separation and did not live with a spouse by the end of the year. In this case, assuming you paid the household

TABLE 1.5 AGI Phaseout Range for the Earned Income Credit in 2021

Number of Qualifying Children	Married Filing Jointly	Other Taxpayers
No qualifying child	$17,560–27,380	$11,610–21,430
1 qualifying child	$25,470–48,108	$19,520–42,158
2 qualifying children	$25,470–53,865	$19,520–47,915
3 or more qualifying children	$25,470–57,414	$19,520–51,464

expenses in which a qualifying child lived for the full year, you qualify as single for purposes of the earned income credit (using "other taxpayers" limits on AGI).

> ### Example
>
> You are married and file a joint return. You and your spouse have 1 qualifying child. In 2021, if your AGI is less than $25,470, your earned income credit is *not* subject to any phaseout. If your AGI is $48,108 or higher, you cannot claim *any* earned income credit; it is completely phased out. If your AGI is between these amounts (within the phaseout range), you may claim a reduced credit.

CHILDLESS INDIVIDUALS

For 2021, the minimum age for claiming the earned income credit, which had been 25, is reduced to 19. The minimum age for a full-time student is 24; it's 18 for a former foster child or homeless youth. The maximum age, usually 65, does not apply in 2021.

If you have a qualifying child who lacks a Social Security number, you may claim the earned income tax credit as if you were childless.

Planning Tips

The credit is based on a set percentage of earned income. However, you don't have to compute the credit. You merely look at an IRS Earned Income Credit Table, which accompanies the instructions for your return.

You can have the IRS figure your credit for you (you don't even have to look it up in the table). To do this, just complete your return up to the earned income credit line and put "EIC" on the dotted line next to it. If you have a qualifying child, complete and attach Schedule EIC to the return. Also attach Form 8862, *Information to Claim Earned Income Credit after Disallowance*, if you are required to do so as explained next.

If your child does not qualify as your dependent because of the tie-breaker rule (discussed earlier in this chapter), you may claim the earned income credit with no qualifying child. For example, a grandmother has a home in which her daughter and the baby (granddaughter) live. Under the tie-breaker rule, while the baby could be a qualifying child of the grandmother and mother, she is the daughter's qualifying child. The grandmother can claim the earned income tax credit with no qualifying child, assuming all other requirements for the credit are met. Alternatively, if the daughter foregoes the dependency exemption, the grandmother can claim it and the earned income tax credit, assuming that her AGI exceeds the daughter's AGI. In this instance, the daughter could claim the

earned income tax credit with no qualifying child, assuming all other requirements for the credit are met.

Pitfalls

You lose eligibility for the credit if you have unearned income over $10,000 in
2021 from dividends, interest (both taxable and tax free), net rent or royalty
income, net capital gains, or net passive income that is not self-employment
income.

   You lose out on the opportunity to claim the credit in future years if you neg-
ligently or fraudulently claim it on your return. (If you use a paid preparer, he or
she is required to perform to diligence before allowing you to claim the earned
income credit.) You are banned for 2 years from claiming the earned income
credit if your claim was reckless or in disregard of the tax rules. You lose out for
10 years if your claim was fraudulent. If you become ineligible because of neg-
ligence or fraud, the IRS issues a deficiency notice. You may counter the IRS's
charge by filing Form 8862, *Information to Claim Earned Income Credit after
Disallowance*, to show you are eligible.

   If the IRS accepts your position and recertifies eligibility, you don't have to
file this form again (unless you again become ineligible). For 2021 returns filed
in 2022, the IRS is not permitted to issue tax refunds for the refundable earned
income tax credit before February 15, 2022. As a result, refunds usually aren't
received until the third or fourth week in February, even for returns filed in
January 2022.

Where to Claim the Earned Income Credit

You can claim the earned income credit on line 27 of Form 1040 or 1040-SR.

Dependent Care Expenses

Many taxpayers must pay for the care of a child in order to work. According to the
World Population Review, the cost of child care in 2021 for an infant is $15,000
at a center. The tax law provides a limited tax credit for such costs, called the
dependent care credit. The amount of the credit you may claim depends on your
income. It may be as much as 50% of eligible expenses. Or, if your employer helps
with child care costs, you may exclude the payments from your income.

Benefit ⊕ ⊗

If you hire someone to care for your children or other dependents to enable
you to work or incur other dependent care expenses, you may be eligible for
a fully refundable tax credit of up to $8,000. More specifically, this credit is a
percentage of eligible dependent care expenses (explained later). The credit

percentage ranges up to 50%. However, no credit may be claimed if income is $440,000 or more (explained later).

If your employer pays for your dependent care expenses, you may be able to exclude this benefit from income up to $10,500 in 2021.

The maximum amount of expenses taken into account for the credit in 2021 is $8,000 for one qualifying dependent and $16,000 for 2 or more qualifying dependents. This limit doesn't need to be divided equally among them.

Example

A single parent has two children. She spends $12,000 for daycare for one and $6,000 for after-school daycare for the other. Because her total expenses do not exceed the limit of $18,000, she can take them all into account in figuring the dependent care credit for 2021.

In 2021, the credit is fully refundable.

Conditions for the Tax Credit

There are a number of conditions for claiming the dependent care credit; you must satisfy all 8 of them to claim the credit:

1. Incur the expenses to earn income.
2. Pay expenses on behalf of a qualifying dependent.
3. Pay over half the household expenses.
4. File a joint return if you are married.
5. Have adjusted gross income below a set amount.
6. Have qualifying expenses in excess of employer reimbursements.
7. Meet a residency requirement.
8. Report information about the child care provider.

INCUR THE EXPENSES TO EARN INCOME

The purpose of the dependent care credit is to enable you to work. This generally means that if you are married, you both must work, either full time or part time.

However, a spouse who is incapacitated or a full-time student need not work; he or she is treated as having earned income of $250 per month if there is one qualifying dependent or $500 per month if there are 2 or more qualifying dependents.

> **Example**
>
> You are a single mother and a full-time student with 1 child. You are treated as having earned income of $3,000 for the year ($250 × 12). You can use this income in figuring your credit, even though you didn't actually receive this income.

PAY EXPENSES ON BEHALF OF A QUALIFYING DEPENDENT

This is for your child under the age of 13, your incapacitated dependent of any age, or your spouse who is incapacitated.

If your child has his or her 13th birthday during the year, you can take into account expenses incurred up to this birthday.

Only certain types of child care expenses can be taken into account in figuring the credit. Qualifying expenses can be incurred in your home or outside the home (using a day care center). You cannot include amounts paid to you, your child who is under age 19 at the end of the year, your spouse, or any other person you can claim as a dependent.

EXAMPLES OF QUALIFYING EXPENSES

Babysitter

Day camp, including a specialty camp such as soccer or computers (but only the day cost of a sleep-away camp)

Day care center

Housekeeper (the portion of compensation allocated to dependent care)

Nursery school

Private school (The costs for first grade and higher do not qualify unless the child is handicapped, provided the child spends at least 8 hours per day in your home.)

Transportation, if supervised (so that it is part of care), such as to a day camp or after-school program not on school premises, but not the cost of personally driving a dependent to and from a dependent care center

You do not have to find the least expensive means of providing dependent care. For example, just because your child's grandparent lives in your home doesn't mean you must rely on the grandparent for child care; you can pay an unrelated person to babysit in your home or take your child to day care.

The expenses you incur for dependent care must be greater than any amount you exclude as employer-provided dependent care.

PAY OVER HALF THE HOUSEHOLD EXPENSES

You (and your spouse) must pay more than half of the maintenance expenses of the household.

FILE A JOINT RETURN IF MARRIED

Generally, to claim the credit you *must* file a joint return if eligible to do so. However, you can claim the credit even though you are still married if you live apart from your spouse for over half the year, you pay over half the household expenses for the full year, and your spouse is not a member of your household for the last 6 months of the year. In this case, you qualify to file as unmarried (single).

HAVE AGI BELOW SET LIMITS

The credit percentage scales down as adjusted gross income (AGI) rises. The same AGI threshold and percentages apply to singles and joint filers. For 2021:

- The maximum credit of 50% of eligible expenses applies for AGI up to $125,000.
- The credit rate is reduced by one percentage point for each $2,000 of excess AGI, resulting in a 20% credit when AGI is $183,000. The 20% credit applies for those with AGI between $183,000 and $400,000.

Example

You are single with one qualifying child and have eligible expenses of $8,000. Your AGI in 2021 is $132,000. Your credit percentage is 46% (50% – 4 percentage points having $7,000 AGI over $125,000, which rounds up to $8,000 excess). Your credit is $3,680 (46% of $8,000).

- The 20% rate is further by one percentage point for each $2,000 of excess AGI over $400,000.
- No credit may be claimed once AGI is $440,000 or more.

Example

Same as the example above except you have AGI of $420,000. Your credit rate is reduced from 20% to 10% (20% – 10 percentage points for having $20,000 of AGI over $400,000). Your credit is $800 (10% of $8,000).

MEET A RESIDENCY REQUIREMENT

To be eligible for the refundable credit for 2021, you must have your main home in one of the 50 states or the District of Columbia for more than half of the tax year. Your main home can be any location where you regularly live. Your main home doesn't need to be the same physical location throughout the taxable year. If you are temporarily away from your main home because of illness, education, business, vacation, or military service, you are generally treated as living in your main home during that time.

REPORT INFORMATION ABOUT THE DEPENDENT CARE PROVIDER

You must list the name, address, and employer identification number (or Social Security number) of the person you pay for dependent care. No employer identification number is required if payment is made to a tax-exempt charity providing the care.

If the person has not completed Form W-4, *Employee's Withholding Allowance Certificate*, as your household employee, you can obtain the necessary information by asking the provider to complete Form W-10, *Dependent Care Provider's Identification and Certification*, or by looking at a driver's license or other government-issued photo ID, business letterhead, or invoice. This may seem like a lot of bother and formality for a baby-sitter, but if you want to claim the credit, you must comply with this information-reporting requirement.

HOW TO FIGURE YOUR CREDIT PERCENTAGE BASED ON AGI

The amount of the credit you claim, if any, for 2021 depends on your AGI. The maximum credit of 50% of eligible expenses applies for AGI up to $125,000. The credit rate is reduced to 20% for AGI up to $185,000. The 20% rate is reduced starting with AGI of $400,000. No credit may be claimed once AGI is $440,000 or more.

Example

You have 1 qualifying child and adjusted gross income of $110,000. Your credit is 50% of your dependent care expenses up to $8,000, for a top credit of $4,000.

Conditions for the Exclusion

Benefits must be provided by your employer under a written plan that does not discriminate in favor of owners or highly compensated employees (for example, top executives cannot obtain greater benefits than you). The dollar limit on this benefit is $10,500 (or $5,250 if you are married and file separately).

The same limits apply to a flexible spending arrangement (FSA), which is an employer plan to which you contribute a portion of your pay to be used for dependent care expenses. This salary reduction amount is *not* currently taxable to you; it becomes tax-free income that you withdraw from the FSA to cover eligible expenses.

Planning Tips

If you have the option of making salary reduction contributions to your company's flexible spending arrangement (FSA) for dependent care expenses, decide carefully on how much to contribute each month. You can use the funds in the FSA only for dependent care expenses; you cannot, for example, use any of the funds for your medical expenses or other costs. Any funds not used up by the end of the year (or within the first two and a half months of the next year if your employer has a grace period) are forfeited; they do not carry over. The IRS has not ruled clearly about whether virtual daycare expenses qualify for the credit. However, if it can be shown that the cost was incurred to enable a parent to work, then it seems the expenses could be taken into account.

Pitfalls

If in the same month you and your spouse both did not work and were either full-time students or not physically or mentally capable of caring for yourselves, only one of you can be treated as having earned income ($250 or $500 as explained earlier in this chapter) in that month.

If you qualify to receive an exclusion, you must reduce the amount of eligible expenses used in figuring the credit by the amount of the exclusion.

Example

You have 1 child and receive reimbursement from your employer's plan for 2021 of $3,000. In figuring your tax credit (assuming you are eligible for the maximum credit), you can use only $1,000 of eligible expenses ($4,000 − $3,000). In essence, if your exclusion in 2021 is $4,000 for 1 child or $8,000 if you have 2 or more children, you cannot claim any tax credit.

If you participate in a dependent care FSA, distributions from the plan are treated as employer reimbursements. Like excludable benefits, distributions from FSAs reduce the amount of expenses you can use to figure the credit.

Check with the administrator of the dependent care FSA you participate in to learn about possible carryovers or using up contributions after the year is over.

If you pay someone to care for your dependent in your home, you are the worker's employer. You are responsible for employment taxes. For more information about these employment taxes, see IRS Publication 926, *Household Employer's Tax Guide*, at www.irs.gov.

Where to Claim the Tax Credit or Exclusion

You figure the credit and the exclusion on Form 2441, *Dependent Care Expenses*. The amount of the credit is entered on Schedule 3 of Form 1040 or 1040-SR.

If you owe employment taxes for a dependent care worker, you must file Form 1040 or 1040-SR and complete Schedule H, *Household Employment Taxes*, which is attached to the return. You include employment taxes you owe on Schedule 2 of Form 1040 or 1040-SR.

Adoption Costs

One out of every 25 families in the United States has an adopted child. Each year, more than 135,000 children are adopted in the United States, with costs as much as $40,000 or more. Taxpayers who adopt a child may qualify for a tax credit. The amount of the credit may or may not fully offset actual costs for the adoption. If an employer pays for adoption costs, a worker may be able to exclude this fringe benefit from income. And, there's a waiver of the 10% early distribution penalty for withdrawals from retirement plans up to $5,000 to pay adoption expenses (but the distribution itself is taxable).

Benefits

If you adopt a child, you may be eligible to claim a tax credit for the expenses you incur. The maximum credit is $14,440 per child in 2021. The credit is 100% of eligible adoption expenses up to this dollar limit. If you adopt a child that the state has determined as having special needs (e.g., a medical condition), the credit is $14,440 without regard to your actual adoption expenses. The credit, including one for a special needs child, is subject to income limits.

Example

In 2021, your income is $100,000; you pay $9,000 in attorney's and adoption agency fees to adopt a child who is not a special needs child (the adoption becomes final in 2021). You can claim a tax credit of $9,000 (100% of your eligible costs that do not exceed $14,440). If the child adopted is a special needs child, then the credit is $14,440, even though this is greater than the amount of actual adoption expenses.

If your employer pays or reimburses you for adoption expenses, you may exclude this benefit from your income; it is tax free to you if you meet eligibility conditions. The exclusion has the same dollar limit and income limits as the credit.

If a tax-exempt organization makes a payment to help pay adoption costs, the payment is not taxable. The payment is viewed as a gift to the recipient.

If you take withdrawals from your 401(k) plan to pay for adoption expenses, you are not subject to the 10% early distribution penalty even though you're under age 59½. However, the penalty waiver only applies to distributions up to $5,000 for the adoption of an individual (other than a child of the taxpayer's spouse) who is under age 18 or who has a physical or mental incapacity making the person incapable of self-support. The distribution is taxable, but can be recontributed to a retirement plan so that you can recoup any taxes paid on the distribution by filing an amended return.

Conditions

To claim the adoption credit or exclusion, 2 key conditions apply:

1. You must pay qualified adoption expenses.
2. Your modified adjusted gross income cannot exceed a set amount.

There is an additional condition for married persons; they must file jointly unless they are legally separated or live apart for the last 6 months of the year. This requirement applies even if only one spouse is adopting a child.

The determination of whether a child is a special needs child must be made by the state; a taxpayer cannot make this call on his or her own.

QUALIFIED ADOPTION EXPENSES

Qualified expenses include any reasonable and necessary expenses related to the adoption.

EXAMPLES OF QUALIFIED ADOPTION EXPENSES

Adoption agency fees

Attorney's fees

Court costs

Travel expenses while away from home (including meals and lodging)

Nonqualifying expenses include those related to your adoption of your spouse's child, expenses related to a surrogate parenting arrangement, expenses paid for adopting your spouse's child, expenses paid using funds received from a government program, and expenses that violate the law.

MODIFIED ADJUSTED GROSS INCOME LIMIT

To be eligible for the full credit or the exclusion, your modified adjusted gross income (MAGI) in 2021 cannot exceed the amount listed in Table 1.6.

Example

You adopt a child in 2021 and your MAGI is $266,660. You can only claim a credit of up to $7,200 (assuming the child is not a special needs child); half of the credit limit is phased out because of your MAGI.

Modified adjusted gross income for this purpose is AGI increased by the foreign earned income exclusion; the foreign housing exclusion or deduction; and the exclusion for income from Guam, American Samoa, Northern Mariana Islands, or Puerto Rico.

TABLE 1.6 MAGI Phaseout Range for the Adoption Credit in 2021

Credit Amount	MAGI
Full credit	Not more than $216,660
Partial credit	Over $216,660 but under $256,660
No credit	$256,660 or more

Planning Tips

The amount of the adoption credit cannot be more than your tax liability for the year. Tax liability for this purpose means your regular tax, plus your tentative alternative minimum tax (without regard to the foreign tax credit), dependent care credit, credit for the elderly or disabled, either education credit, child tax credit, or mortgage interest credit if any.

However, if the credit exceeds your tax liability, you can carry the excess credit forward for up to 5 years beyond the year in which the credit arose.

If your employer has an adoption assistance program but you aren't entitled to some or all of the exclusion (e.g., your MAGI is too high or your expenses exceeded the dollar limit), plan to pay tax on the amount your employer pays or reimburses you. The employer is *not* required to withhold income tax on these payments. Employer-paid expenses are reported on your Form W-2.

There are no income limits for using the penalty waiver for distributions from qualified retirement plans to pay adoption expenses.

Obtain a taxpayer identification number for the child if he/she does not have one. Use Form W-7A, *Application for Taxpayer Identification Number For Pending Adoption*, to obtain a temporary tax ID for a child in a domestic adoption who does not have or is unable to obtain his or her own Social Security number.

Pitfall

The year for which you are entitled to claim the credit depends on the type of child you are adopting.

CHILD WHO IS A U.S. CITIZEN OR RESIDENT

If you adopt or are adopting a child who is a U.S. citizen or resident, use Table 1.7 to see the year for which to claim the credit for payments you make.

FOREIGN CHILD

You can take the credit only if the adoption becomes final. Use Table 1.8 to see the year in which to claim the credit.

TABLE 1.7 Year to Claim the Credit for Adoption of a U.S. Citizen or Resident Child

When You Pay Expenses	When You Claim Credit
Any year before year the adoption becomes final (or falls through)	Year after year of payment
Year adoption becomes final (or falls through)	Year adoption becomes final (or falls through)
Any year after year adoption becomes final (or falls through)	Year of payment

TABLE 1.8 Year to Claim the Credit for Adoption of a Foreign Child

When You Pay Expenses	When You Claim Credit
Any year before year adoption becomes final	Year adoption becomes final
Year adoption becomes final	Year adoption becomes final
Any year after year adoption becomes final	Year of payment

Where to Claim the Adoption Credit, Exclusion, or Penalty Waiver

You figure the adoption credit on Form 8839, *Qualified Adoption Expenses*, which is attached to your return. The amount of the credit is entered on Schedule 3 of Form 1040 or 1040-SR.

To claim the credit, you must retain certain documents; they do not have to be attached to the return.

- For U.S. adoptions, attach a copy of the adoption order or decree.

- For adoptions finalized abroad, include the child's Hague Adoption Certificate, an IH-3 visa, or a foreign adoption decree translated into English. If the child's country of origin is not a party to the Hague Convention, then attach a copy of the translated decree or an IR-2 or IR-3 visa.

- If you adopt a special needs child, also attach the state determination of the child's special needs status certificate so you can claim the full $14,440, regardless of the adoption costs you paid.

Example

In 2020, you start the adoption process, hiring a lawyer and paying a retainer of $3,000. In 2020, the lawyer helps you work with an authorized adoption agency to which you pay a fee of $10,000 to adopt your daughter, a U.S. resident. The child is placed with you at that time. In 2021, you pay the lawyer an additional $4,000 and the adoption becomes final in this year. You may *not* claim any credit in 2020. In 2021, you may claim a credit up to $14,440, comprised of $13,000 [retainer and adoption fee] paid in 2020 and $1,610 of the $4,000 additional attorney's fee paid in 2021. The excess expenses of $2,390 [$4,000–$1,610]) are not carried over and cannot be used in the future.

If your employer paid or reimbursed you for qualified expenses, you must also complete this form to figure excludable benefits.

Distributions from qualified retirement plans for adoption expenses are reported to you on Form 1099-R and entered on line 5b of Form 1040 or 1040-SR. You must also file Form 5329 to claim the penalty exception.

Foster Care

Taxpayers who care for children in foster care and receive funds for expenses may not be taxed on those funds. Instead, they may be able to exclude the payments they receive from income.

Benefit

Exclusion for foster care payments. If you receive foster care payments to care for a child placed with you by a state or local agency or a tax-exempt foster care placement agency, you are not taxed on those payments. They are fully excludable; there is no dollar limit.

Qualified payments include payments for the provision of foster care. They also include difficulty-of-care payments to account for the additional care required for a child with physical, mental, or emotional handicaps. Payments under a state Medicaid Home and Community-Based Services Waiver (Medicaid waiver) program are treated as difficulty-of-care payments.

However, the exclusion for foster care payments is limited to payments received for 5 qualifying individuals who are over age 18. The exclusion for difficulty-of-care payments is limited to payments received for 10 qualifying individuals who are over age 18. There are no limits on the number of children age 18 or under for whom the exclusion may be claimed.

Deduction for out-of-pocket costs. See Chapter 6.

Condition

Foster care payments include only those made by a state or local government or qualified foster care placement agency for the care of a qualified foster child or a difficulty-of-care payment. Also, you and the foster child must live in the same home.

Planning Tip

If you are a foster care parent dealing with a private agency, make sure the placement entitles you to exclude payments received for the care of the child.

Pitfalls

Payments received from private agencies that are not tax-exempt entities, even though licensed by the state, are not excludable from income.

Payments made to a child's biological parent cannot be excluded, even if labeled "foster care payment" because such parent is never a foster parent.

Where to Claim the Exclusion

Foster care payments are not reported on the return if they are excludable. If you care for more than the allowable number of children over age 18, you must include the payments in income. Report this as "other income" on your return.

Child Support

Divorced or separated parents may be ordered by a court to make support payments for a child of the marriage. Even an unwed parent may be instructed to support his or her child. The recipient of child support payments, typically the parent with whom the child resides, is not taxed on these payments. (The parent making the payments cannot deduct them, but paying child support may entitle the parent to other tax write-offs discussed throughout this chapter.)

Benefit ⊗

Child support payments are not taxable to the child, nor to the parent who receives them on behalf of the child. There is no dollar limit to this benefit. It does not matter whether child support payments are made pursuant to a divorce decree or separation agreement made before 2019 or after 2018 (when the rules for alimony payments were changed).

Conditions

Payments for child support should be fixed. If they are set by a decree of divorce or separate maintenance or a separation agreement, they are considered to be fixed.

In addition, if payments made to a parent will be reduced or terminated upon a contingency related to the child, then those payments are treated as being fixed for child support. Contingencies for this purpose include:

- Reaching the age of majority (generally age 18 or 21, depending on the law in your state)
- Leaving school
- Marrying
- Entering military service
- Moving out of the custodial parent's home
- Starting to work and/or attaining a set income level

Planning Tip

If a parent is required to pay both alimony and child support under a pre-2019 divorce decree and makes a single payment that is less than the total amount due, the first dollars are considered tax-free child support. This is relevant if the alimony is pursuant to a divorce decree or separation agreement executed before 2021 under which alimony payments are deductible.

Example

Ed owes his former spouse $1,000 each month to cover alimony of $600 and child support of $400. Assume they were divorced several years ago. In March 2021, Ed pays only $500. Of this amount, $400 is treated as child support; $100 is treated as alimony.

Pitfalls

The parent who makes child support payments cannot deduct them. They are not considered to be part of deductible alimony payments where applicable (explained in the next section).

If a reduction in child support payments to a parent is not specifically tied to the child's age of majority but is scheduled to occur within 6 months before or after such date, the reduction is treated as if it was tied to the child. This means that the amount subject to reduction is viewed as child support and not as deductible alimony if a pre-2019 divorce decree or separation agreement is involved. The same rule applies if you are making payments on behalf of more than one child and there are at least 2 reductions, each of which is within a year of a child's reaching the age of majority.

If you are due a refund of federal income tax because you overpaid it through withholding or estimated taxes, you won't receive it if you are delinquent on your child support payments. The IRS is authorized to divert your refund to the parent owed the child support payments as long as the state provides notice to you and a procedure you can follow to contest this action.

Where to Claim the Exclusion

Child support payments received are not reported on the return.

Alimony

Taxpayers who are required by a court to make payments to a spouse or former spouse can deduct such payments if the divorce or separation agreement was executed before January 1, 2019. The payments may be called alimony, support, or spousal maintenance, depending on state law (called "alimony" here for convenience). The tax law, in most cases, imposes symmetry on the treatment of alimony so that the government effectively comes out even, as explained below.

Benefit 🔼

If you have a divorce or separation agreement executed before 2019, and you make payments to a spouse or former spouse for alimony, support, or spousal maintenance, you can deduct the payments if certain conditions are met. There is no dollar limit on this deduction. The deduction is claimed as an adjustment to gross income; you do not have to itemize your other deductions to write off alimony payments you make. But if you make payments pursuant to a divorce or separation agreement executed after December 31, 2018, you cannot deduct your payments.

Conditions

There are 4 conditions that must be met for payments made under a pre-2019 divorce decree or separation agreement to a spouse or former spouse to be considered alimony:

1. Amounts must be paid pursuant to a legal requirement, such as a court decree.
2. Payments must be made in cash.
3. You must live apart from your spouse or former spouse.
4. Your responsibility to make payments must terminate on the death of your spouse or former spouse.

Typically, alimony that is deductible by the payer is taxable to the recipient—the government effectively nets no additional tax revenue from the arrangement. But this symmetry is not required. If you meet all of the conditions, you can deduct your alimony payments even if your former spouse is not required to pay tax on them (for example, your former spouse lives abroad where alimony is exempt income).

PAYABLE UNDER A COURT DECREE

You can't deduct alimony under a pre-2019 divorce decree or separation agreement if you voluntarily make payments. You must either be ordered to do so under a decree of divorce, legal separation, or support or agree to make payments under a written separation agreement.

If the marriage is annulled and you are ordered to make payments, they can be treated as alimony if the other conditions are satisfied.

CASH PAYMENTS

You can deduct only payments under a pre-2019 divorce decree or separation agreement made in cash. But you don't necessarily have to make these payments directly *to* your spouse or former spouse. Payments made *on behalf of* your spouse or former spouse qualify for the deduction if required by the divorce decree or separation agreement. For example, if you are ordered to pay your former spouse's rent with a check directly to the landlord, you can treat the payment as alimony if the other conditions are met.

If you continue to own the home in which your former spouse resides (i.e., own it by yourself or jointly with your former spouse) and you pay the mortgage and other expenses, only some of these expenses qualify as deductible alimony—even if you are required to make the payments under the terms of a divorce decree or separation agreement. If you own the home, you benefit from the payment of the mortgage, real estate taxes, and other maintenance on the property and cannot deduct these payments. If you own the home jointly, only one-half of your payments can be treated as alimony because only one-half benefits your spouse or former spouse. (Of course, you can deduct mortgage interest and real estate taxes as itemized deductions as explained in Chapter 4.)

LIVING APART

To deduct payments under a pre-2019 divorce decree or separation agreement, you and your spouse or former spouse must not live in the same household. This means separate residences; merely having separate bedrooms in the same home is not good enough for payments to be treated as alimony.

However, payments made while you are preparing to leave can be deducted. There is a one-month limit so that only payments made within one month prior to your departure can be treated as alimony. If it takes you longer to move out, your earlier payments are not deductible.

PAYMENT RESPONSIBILITY ENDS ON DEATH

Your responsibility to make payments to your spouse or former spouse must end if that person dies in order for payments under a pre-2019 divorce decree or separation agreement to be deductible alimony. If your obligation to make payments continues beyond the recipient's death (for example, you must continue to pay until total payments reach a set amount), you cannot treat *any* of the payments as alimony (even those made before death).

Generally, the divorce decree should state that your obligation to make payments ends on the recipient's death. But this isn't necessary as long as this condition is part of the law in your state.

The fact that your estate continues to be liable for payments after your death does not prevent you from treating your payments as alimony.

Planning Tips

If you have a pre-2019 divorce decree or separation agreement, don't make voluntary payments if you want to deduct them. For example, don't make payments prior to a court order or separation agreement and don't voluntarily increase your payments. If you want to ensure that increased payments qualify as deductible alimony, you need to amend the court order or separation agreement to incorporate the change. If a pre-2019 divorce decree or separation agreement is changed or amended, the old alimony rules continue to apply unless the revised document specifically says that the new rules (i.e., that payments are not deductible by the spouse who pays or taxable to the spouse who receives) should apply.

Pitfalls

Payments made to someone who was never legally your spouse cannot be treated as alimony. For example, if you make payments to a domestic partner, you cannot deduct them even though they otherwise have all the earmarks of alimony.

Property settlements are not deductible.

Where to Claim the Deduction

The amount of deductible alimony payments is entered on Schedule 1 of Form 1040 or 1040-SR. There is no separate form or schedule to complete when deducting alimony. However, you *must* include the recipient's Social Security number on your return (to allow the IRS to cross-check whether the recipient reported the alimony as income) and the date of the divorce or separation agreement (to allow the IRS to see whether alimony is deductible).

ABLE Accounts

If you have a child who became disabled before age 26 or meets certain eligibility conditions, there is a special savings account that generally does not adversely impact eligibility for means-tested government programs (e.g., Medicaid). The account can be used on a tax-free basis for various disability-related expenses (including funeral and burial costs). See details in Chapter 2.

Medical Expenses

Covid-19 continued to be problematic in 2021 and brought medical care and its cost to the forefront. Rising premiums, increased co-pays, higher drug prices, and government mandates continue to be headline news. Fortunately, the tax law provides you with some relief for the high cost of medical care by allowing you to treat your medical expenses in special tax-advantaged ways, as explained in this chapter. There is no longer any federal tax penalty for failing to have minimum essential health coverage, which had previously been required by the Affordable Care Act. (A few states continue to have their own individual mandates.) You may also be able to enjoy tax-free benefits from employer-provided medical plans as well as tax-free coverage for COVID-19 testing and treatment.

To learn more about medical and dental expenses, see IRS Publication 502, *Medical and Dental Expenses*, IRS Publication 969, *Health Savings Accounts and Other Tax-Favored Health Plans*, and IRS Publication 974, *Premium Tax Credit*. A discussion of employer-paid sick leave is in Chapter 13.

Individual Mandate

The Affordable Care Act (ACA) had created an individual health coverage mandate that required individuals to have minimum essential health coverage or pay a penalty. The penalty was repealed and does not apply after 2018. While there is no federal individual mandate, most people want health coverage and the tax-advantaged ways to do this are coverd in this chapter.

Employer-Provided Health Insurance

Employers with 50 or more full time and full-time equivalent employees are required to offer affordable health coverage for their staff and dependents or pay a penalty. Most of these employers offer health coverage. What's more, many employers that are not required to provide coverage do so anyway. This means that many employees enjoy coverage through their employers at no cost to them; others pay a portion of coverage and the employers pay the rest. The value of employer-paid coverage is tax free, regardless of amount.

Benefit ⊗

The value or amount that an employer pays for premiums to cover you, your spouse, your dependent, and a child under the age of 27 is not taxable. There is no dollar limit on the amount of coverage you can receive on a tax-free basis.

Conditions

There are none; as long as you are an employee, your company-paid coverage is tax free to you. This is so even though the amount of this employee benefit is reported on your Form W-2.

Planning Tips

If both you and your spouse work and each is entitled to health coverage, compare the medical plans and choose the one that offers the better coverage. If you must contribute toward your coverage, but your spouse does not and can include you, it may be preferable to decline your employer's coverage so you can use your spouse's plan.

If you do not have a group health plan at work but your employer reimburses you for the premiums of individual coverage, the reimbursement may be tax free; see the discussion on Health Reimbursement Arrangements later in this chapter.

Pitfalls

While employer-paid coverage for spouses is tax free, this treatment does not apply to domestic partners. Employees are taxed on employer-paid coverage for their domestic partners.

If you are 65 and older and covered by an employer plan of a company with fewer than 20 employees, Medicare is your primary payer. Be sure to apply for Medicare within 3 months before and 3 months after you turn age 65 (7-month enrollment period) so that you have the right coverage.

Where to Report the Benefit

You do not have to report this tax-free fringe benefit. Even if your employer reports the value of the coverage on your W-2 form, this does not change the tax-free treatment of the benefit to you.

Premium Tax Credit

If you do not have coverage through an employer, Medicare, Medicaid, or certain other program but think you may have trouble paying for private insurance, you may be eligible for a tax credit to help pay for coverage if you purchase it through a government health care exchange. The credit is refundable (it can exceed the amount of taxes owed) and can even be applied toward premiums throughout the year.

Benefit ✚

If you have low or moderate income, you may qualify for the premium tax credit. It is an advanceable, refundable tax credit for eligible people who purchase coverage through a government health care exchange. The credit amount varies with household income for eligible taxpayers.

You can choose to have the credit paid in advance to your insurance company you've chosen from the exchange, or you can claim all of the credit when you file your tax return for the year. If you choose to have the credit paid in advance, you will have to reconcile on your tax return the amount paid in advance with the actual credit to which you are entitled.

Conditions

To qualify for the credit, all of the following conditions apply:

- You must obtain coverage through a government health care exchange (also called the Marketplace), such as HealthCare.gov.
- You must apply for the credit at the time you purchase your coverage by estimating household income, unless you are waiting until you file your return to claim the credit.
- If your employer offers coverage, it is not *affordable* to you.
- You are not eligible for a government program (e.g., Medicare, Medicaid, CHIP, or TRICARE).
- If you are married, you must file jointly, unless you are a domestic abuse victim and file separately.
- You are not someone else's dependent.

COVERAGE THROUGH AN EXCHANGE

Only coverage purchased through a government Marketplace ("exchange") can entitle you to the credit. If you buy identical coverage directly from the insurer, you do not qualify for the credit; you didn't get it through a government Marketplace. However, it is not necessary that you obtained the coverage online; you may have submitted paper returns or obtained coverage by telephone.

APPLY FOR THE CREDIT

The federal government does not automatically give you the credit. You must prove eligibility for the credit, either at the time you purchase your health coverage from an exchange or when you file your return.

HOUSEHOLD INCOME LIMITS

The credit amounts for individuals and families depends on having household income between 100% and 400% of the federal poverty line for their family size. For 2021 and 2022, those with household income above 400% of the federal poverty line qualify for the same credit amount as those at 400%. Household income has a special meaning for purposes of the premium assistance credit. It is modified adjusted gross income (MAGI) of everyone in your household (you, your spouse, and anyone claimed as a dependent). MAGI for this purpose is adjusted gross income plus any excluded foreign income, nontaxable Social Security benefits (including tier 1 Railroad Retirement benefits) (including benefits attributable to prior years received as part of a lump sum in the current year), and tax-exempt interest. It does *not* include Supplemental Security Income (SSI).

TABLE 2.1 Poverty Amounts in the Contiguous States and D.C.*

Household Size	Household Income
One individual	$12,760 (100%) up to $50,040 (400%)
Family of 2	$17,240 (100%) up to $68,960 (400%)
Family of 3	$21,720 (100%) up to $86,880 (400%)
Family of 4	$26,200 (100%) up to $104,800 (400%)
Family of 5	$30,680 (100%) up to $122,720 (400%)
Family of 6	$35,160 (100%) up to $140,640 (400%)
Family of 7	$39,640 (100%) up to $158,560 (400%)
Family of 8	$44,120 (100%) up to $176,480 (400%)
Family of more than 8	Add $4,480 for each additional person

*The guidelines are higher in Alaska and Hawaii; see https://aspe.hhs.gov/poverty-guidelines.

TABLE 2.2

Household Income Percentage of Federal Poverty Line	Initial Percentage	Final Percentage
Less than 150%	0.00%	0.00%
At least 150% but less than 200%	0.00%	2.00%
At least 200% but less than 250%	2.00%	4.00%
At least 250% but less than 300%	4.00%	6.00%
At least 300% but less than 400%	6.00%	8.50%
At least 400%	8.50%	8.50%

Eligibility for the credit depends on your household income relative to the federal poverty level, although those with household income above 400% of the federal poverty level may still claim a credit for 2021 and 2022. The 2021 credit is based on 2020 poverty amounts listed in Table 2.1. The amount of the credit depends on your household income as a percentage of the federal poverty line. Table 2.2 lists the percentage of household income you are required to pay of the premiums for coverage obtained from the government Marketplace in 2021. The percentage applicable to you is applied toward the second-lowest cost silver plan (or if there is only one silver plan available to you, then the cost of this silver plan); this is your tax credit.

Example

In 2021, a single individual (the only person in the household) has household income of $25,500. He is eligible for the premium tax credit (see Table 2.1). Because his household income is at least 200% but less than 250% (Table 2.2), his applicable percentage is 4.00%. Assuming the cost of the second-lowest silver plan available to him is $5,000 for the year, he's expected to contribute $1,020 (4% of $25,500). His credit amount is $3,980 ($5,000 − $1,020).

UNAFFORDABLE EMPLOYER COVERAGE

Even if your employer offers coverage, you may still be eligible for the premium tax credit. Coverage in 2021 is deemed "unaffordable" if premiums for self-only coverage (even if you have family coverage) exceed 8.5% of your household income (see the definition of household income under *household income limits* earlier). If your employer offers multiple health coverage options, the affordability test applies to the lowest-cost option available to you that also satisfies the minimum value requirement (i.e., the plan covers at least 60% of the expected total allowed costs for covered services). If your employer offers any wellness programs, the affordability test is based on the premium you would pay if you received the maximum discount for any tobacco cessation programs, and did not receive any other discounts based on wellness programs.

However, you cannot claim the credit if you enroll in an employer plan, even if it is unaffordable. If you receive reimbursement from your employer for individually-obtained coverage under a QSEHRA (discussed later in this chapter), there is a coordination of the reimbursement with the credit, so you can't receive a double benefit.

INFORMATION RETURNS

If you have coverage through a government marketplace (whether through a federal or state exchange), you'll receive Form 1095-A, *Health Insurance Marketplace Statement*.

Form 1095-A is relevant to the premium tax credit because the credit applies only to coverage obtained through the Marketplace. You use information on Form 1095-A to compute the credit on Form 8962, *Premium Tax Credit*. But you don't need the form to complete your return (i.e., if it's late and you want to file early, go ahead).

Planning Tips

If you are 26 or younger, you may obtain coverage through an employer plan of your parent.

If you got married during the year, file a joint return, and one or both of you have received the premium tax credit on an advance basis, there is an alternative way to compute the allowable credit amount given that household income has changed. Under the alternative computation (called the "year of marriage rule") you may reduce the amount of excess credit, if any, that must be repaid. The computation is complex, but it's illustrated in examples in Reg. §1.36B-4(b)(5) and in IRS Publication 974.

Plan now for coverage for 2022. Even though the individual mandate has been repealed, the premium tax credit continues to be available for eligible individuals who buy coverage through a government marketplace. Use your 2021 income, increases in the poverty amounts, and an increase in the percentage used to determine whether coverage is unaffordable to make projections for credit eligibility.

Pitfalls

You cannot claim the credit if you buy coverage directly from the insurer. This is so even if the coverage is identical to what is sold through the government Marketplace.

For 2020, there was no requirement to repay any excess advance premium tax credit. However, starting in 2021, this rule applies so that if there is a change during the year in your marital status, number of dependents, or household income that may work to increase or decrease the initial credit amount used on an advanced basis to pay insurance premiums, you'll have to reconcile this when you file your 2021 income tax return.

Where to Claim the Credit

Figure the credit on Form 8962, *Premium Tax Credit*. If you claimed the credit on an advanced basis when you signed up for coverage through the Marketplace, now determine whether the allowable credit is *more* or *less* than the amounts advanced during the year. Report the excess advanced premium tax credit repayment on Schedule 2 of Form 1040 or 1040-SR. Report the net premium tax credit on Schedule 3 of Form 1040 or 1040-SR.

Health Coverage Tax Credit

If you qualify for Trade Adjustment Assistance (TAA), you may be able to claim a refundable tax credit called the Health Coverage Tax Credit (HCTC) for a portion of your health insurance premiums for you and your family.

Benefit

If you qualify, the government pays a percentage of your health insurance premiums for coverage under any of the following:

- COBRA (Consolidated Omnibus Budget Reconciliation Act of 1986)
- A health insurance program offered to state employees or a comparable program
- A group health plan that is available through the employment of an eligible individual's spouse

The portion of health insurance premiums paid by the federal government is 72.5%. There is no dollar limit on the credit you can claim or any restrictions on claiming the credit because of your income level.

> ### Example
>
> You lose your job in June 2021 because of foreign competition and, as an eligible recipient, begin to pay health coverage starting July 1, 2021, and through the end of the year. The cost of the premiums is $4,000. You pay $1,100 (27.5% of $4,000); the government pays $2,900 (72.5% of $4,000).

CONDITIONS

To claim the credit, you must meet 2 conditions:

1. You are an eligible recipient ("eligible individual")
2. You pay for certain health coverage ("qualifying health coverage")

Eligible Individual.   To be an eligible individual, you must fall within either of 2 categories:

1. You are a worker who lost your job due to foreign trade competition. You must be treated as someone eligible to receive a trade adjustment allowance (TAA) or an alternative TAA.
2. You are a retiree age 55 or older receiving benefits from the Pension Benefit Guaranty Corporation (you are called a PBGC pension recipient). This means that to claim the credit in 2020, you must have been born before 1966.

You claim the credit if your spouse or dependent is an eligible individual. If you file a joint return, only one spouse has to meet the eligibility conditions. You cannot claim the credit if you can be claimed as another taxpayer's dependent.

Eligibility is determined on a month-by-month basis. You are eligible in a month if, as of the first day of the month, you meet the eligibility requirements. You may, for example, only be entitled to a credit for a portion of the year (the months in which you are an eligible individual).

You do not qualify if you are imprisoned under federal, state, or local authority.

As a practical matter, you don't have to determine whether you're an eligible individual; the government does this for you. It will send you Form 8887, *Health Insurance Credit Eligibility Certificate,* stating that you are an eligible TAA, alternative TAA, or PBGC pension recipient.

Qualifying Health Insurance.   Even if you are an eligible individual, you do not qualify for the credit if you have health coverage under Medicare Part A,

Medicare Part B, Medicaid, State Children's Health Insurance Program (S-CHIP), Federal Employees Health Benefit Plan (FEHBP), Tricare (for certain military personnel and their families), or any coverage if at least 50% is paid by your (or your spouse's) employer.

EXAMPLES OF QUALIFYING HEALTH INSURANCE

Certain state-sponsored health insurance if your state elects to have it apply.

COBRA (see later in this chapter).

Coverage under a group plan available through employment of your spouse.

Coverage under individual health insurance, provided you were covered during the entire 30-day period that ends on the date you separated from the employment that makes you an eligible individual.

Planning Tips

You can include as part of the credit any distributions taken from a Health Savings Account or Archer Medical Savings Account (discussed later in this chapter) to pay qualified health coverage.

You can claim the credit in advance of filing your tax return and are entitled to it even if you don't owe any taxes. As long as you obtain the proper certification, you pay only your required percentage of health insurance premiums, and the federal government pays the balance.

Of course, you cannot claim a tax credit on your tax return if the credit has been obtained on an advanced basis by means of government payment of your health insurance. The amount of the credit you claim on your tax return is reduced by the amount of the credit you receive in advance.

Looking Ahead

The Health Coverage Tax Credit is set to expire at the end of 2021. However, Congress many extend it; check the Supplement for any update.

Pitfalls

Even if you are an eligible individual, not all health insurance qualifies for the credit. Examples of nonqualifying health insurance (in addition to those listed earlier) include:

- Accident and/or disability insurance
- Automobile medical insurance
- Coverage for on-site medical clinics

- Coverage for only a specified disease or illness
- Coverage under a flexible spending arrangement (FSA)
- Credit-only insurance
- Hospital indemnity or other fixed indemnity coverage
- Liability insurance or a supplement to liability insurance
- Medicare supplemental insurance ("Medigap")
- Tricare supplemental insurance (for military personnel and their families)
- Workers' compensation or similar insurance

Check for enrollment requirements. State programs can require eligible individuals to enroll within a reasonable period after becoming qualified and deny enrollment for failure to make timely payments (and can restrict eligibility to state residents).

If you claim the credit, you cannot include the same premiums in determining your itemized medical deduction on Schedule A, your self-employed health insurance deduction, or tax-free distributions from any medical or health savings account. What's more, if you claim the premium tax credit for coverage obtained through a government Marketplace, you cannot use the health coverage tax credit; no double benefit is allowed.

Where to Claim the Credit

There are 2 ways to obtain the credit: by registering in advance so that a portion of the credit is applied toward your premiums (register by calling toll free 866-628-4282) or by claiming it on your tax return.

You figure the credit on Form 8885, *Health Insurance Credit for Eligible Recipients*. You claim the credit on Schedule 3 of Form 1040 or 1040-SR.

Itemized Medical Expenses

Medical care for most Americans today is very costly. Even those with insurance still pay out-of-pocket for many things, including copayments, noncovered procedures, and, often, the insurance premiums themselves. The tax law recognizes that medical costs, even though they are personal expenses, should be deductible if they exceed a set percentage of your income.

Benefit ⊜

If you itemize deductions (instead of claiming the standard deduction), you can write off medical expenses that are not covered by insurance, employer payments, or government programs to the extent they exceed 7.5% of adjusted gross income.

Example

Your adjusted gross income is $100,000. You have $12,000 of medical costs that are not covered by insurance. You can deduct $4,500—the first 7.5% ($7,500) is nondeductible.

There is no dollar limit on what you can deduct for medical expenses once you pass the AGI threshold.

Conditions

To be treated as qualified medical expenses, payments must be for the diagnosis, cure, mitigation, treatment, or prevention of disease, or any treatment that affects a part or function of your body.

Deductible expenses include those paid not only for yourself but also for a spouse and any qualifying dependent (a qualifying child or qualifying relative, as explained in Chapter 1).

Example

In 2021, you provide more than half of your mother's support, including the payment of all her medical expenses. Her gross income is $12,000, which is more than the $4,300 limit for a dependent. You can, however, include your payment of her medical expenses with yours when figuring your medical expense deduction.

Examples of Deductible Medical Expenses

PROFESSIONAL SERVICES

Annual physical

Chiropodist

Chiropractor

Christian Science practitioner

Dermatologist

Dentist

Full body electronic scans

Gynecologist

Neurologist

Nurse, including board, wages, and employment taxes on wages

Nurse's aide for an elderly person in need of supervision and assistance
Obstetrician
Ophthalmologist
Optician
Optometrist
Osteopath
Pediatrician
Physician
Physiotherapist
Plastic surgeon for medically necessary surgery
Podiatrist
Practical nurse
Psychiatrist
Psychoanalyst
Psychologist
Registered nurse
Surgeon
Telehealth services

DENTAL SERVICES

Artificial teeth
Cleaning teeth
Dental x-rays
Extracting teeth
Filling teeth
Gum treatment
Oral surgery
Orthodontia

EQUIPMENT AND SUPPLIES

Abdominal supports
Arches
Artificial eyes and limbs
Autoette
Back supports

Blood sugar test kit

Braces

Braille books and magazines

Contact lenses

COVID-19 home testing kit

Crutches, canes, and walkers

Elastic hosiery

Eyeglasses

Hearing aids and their batteries

Heating devices

Home exercise equipment for doctor-prescribed weight loss

Home pregnancy test

Invalid chair

Iron lung

Lactation equipment and supplies

Mattress to alleviate arthritic condition

Orthotics and orthopedic shoes (but only the excess over the cost of regular shoes)

Oxygen or oxygen equipment to relieve breathing problems caused by a medical condition

Personal protection equipment (PPE) for preventing the spread of COVID-19

Protheses

Reclining chair if prescribed by a doctor

Repair of special telephone equipment for someone who is hearing impaired

Sacroiliac belt

Seeing Eye dog and its maintenance

Splints

Telephone-teletype costs and television adapter for closed-caption service for someone who is hearing impaired

Television adapter to display the audio part of programs as subtitles for the hearing impaired

Truss

Wheelchair

Whirlpool baths prescribed by a doctor

Wig advised by a doctor as essential to the mental health of a person who lost all hair from disease

HOME IMPROVEMENTS

Air conditioner where necessary for relief from an allergy or for relieving difficulty in breathing

Cost of installing stair-seat elevator for a person with a heart condition

Fluoridation unit

Lead-based paint removal to prevent a child with lead poisoning from eating the paint (but not the cost of repainting the scraped area)

Ramps for wheelchair access

Swimming pool (the portion of the cost that does not increase the home's value)

INSURANCE

Blue Cross and Blue Shield

Contact lens replacement insurance

Health insurance premiums you pay to cover hospital, surgical, and other medical expenses (Health insurance paid by your employer is not deductible by you, but you aren't taxed on this benefit.)

Long-term care insurance to the extent permitted for your age (explained later in this chapter)

Medicare premiums

Medigap (supplemental Medicare insurance)

Membership in a medical service cooperative

Student health fee

MEDICINE AND DRUGS

Birth control pills

Insulin

Prescription drugs

Viagra if medically prescribed

TESTS

23andMe DNA testing (the portion of the cost related to medical information)

Blood tests

Cardiograms

COVID-19 home testing

Full body electronic scans

Metabolism tests

Spinal fluid tests

Sputum tests

Stool examinations

Urine analyses

X-ray examinations

TREATMENTS AND PROGRAMS

Abortion

Alcoholism inpatient treatment at a therapeutic center

Acupuncture

Blood transfusion

Breast reconstructive surgery following a mastectomy

Childbirth classes for expectant mothers

Childbirth delivery

Clarinet lessons advised by a dentist for the treatment of tooth defects

Convalescent home—for medical treatment only

Diathermy

Drug treatment center—inpatient care costs

Egg donor fees (including legal fees for preparation of a contract between the taxpayer and the donor)

Electroshock therapy

Fertility treatments, including in vitro fertilization and surgery to reverse prior sterilization

Health institute fees for exercises, rubdowns, and so on that are prescribed by a doctor as treatments necessary to alleviate a physical or mental defect or illness

Hearing services

Hospitalization

Hydrotherapy

Kidney donor's or possible donor's expenses

Laser eye surgery or keratotomy

Lifetime care (see "Continuing Care Facilities and Nursing Homes" section later in this chapter)

Long-term care costs for someone who is chronically or terminally ill

Navajo healing ceremony ("sings")

Organ transplant (including the costs of a donor or prospective donor)

Prenatal and postnatal visits

Psychotherapy

Radium therapy

Remedial reading for someone with dyslexia

Sex reassignment surgery for someone with gender identity disorder (GID)

Special school for a mentally or physically impaired person if the main reason for attendance is to use its resources for relieving the disability

Sterilization

Stop-smoking programs

Surgery to remove loose skin following 100-pound weight loss

Tutoring for severe learning disabilities

Umbilical cord blood banking services if needed to treat an existing or imminently probable disease

Vaccines

Vasectomy

Weight-loss program to treat obesity, high blood pressure, or other condition

TRAVEL

Ambulance hire

Autoette (auto device for handicapped person)

Bus fare to see doctors, obtain treatment (including attendance at AA meetings), or pick up prescriptions

Cab fare to see doctors, obtain treatment (including attendance at AA meetings), or pick up prescriptions

Car use to see doctors, obtain treatment (including attendance at AA meetings), or pick up prescriptions at 16¢ per mile for travel in 2021

Conference expenses (travel costs and admission fees) for medical conferences on an illness or condition suffered by you, your spouse, or dependent

Lodging to receive outpatient care at a licensed hospital, clinic, or hospital-equivalent facility, up to $50 per night ($100 per night if you accompany a sick child)

Train fare to see doctors, obtain treatment (including attendance at AA meetings), or pick up prescriptions

Due to COVID-19, you may have purchased masks, gloves, goggles, or other personal protective gear as well as hand sanitizers and additional cleaning supplies to disinfect surfaces. The IRS says these are deductible medical expenses because they prevent the spread of disease.

Planning Tips

Payments by credit card are deductible in the year of the charge (not in the year of paying the credit card bill), so year-end charges for unreimbursed expenses (such as prescription sunglasses) are deductible in the year of the purchase.

If you don't expect your medical expenses to be sufficient to exceed the AGI floor this year, hold off on elective procedures until next year. Then you can effectively bunch expenses (this year's and next year's) into one year to exceed the AGI floor.

Pitfalls

Not every expense of a medical nature is deductible. Here is a listing of instances where no deduction was allowed by the IRS:

- Antiseptic diaper services
- Bottled water purchased to avoid the city's fluoridated water
- Breast augmentation surgery for a male who undergoes sex reassignment surgery
- Burial, cremation, and funeral costs
- Child care so a parent can see a doctor
- Cosmetic surgery *unless* it is medically necessary (For example, a nose job to improve appearance is not a qualified medical expense, but one done following a car accident to repair a nose broken in the accident is a qualified expense.)
- Dancing lessons
- Ear/body piercing
- Hair transplant
- Health club and gym memberships for maintaining general good health or appearance
- Illegal drugs and controlled substances (e.g., laetrile) in violation of federal law
- In vitro fertilization costs incurred to enable a healthy man to have a woman carry his child

- Marijuana, even if prescribed by a doctor in a state permitting the prescription (it is contraband under federal law, but this could change so check the Supplement)
- Marriage counseling fees
- Massages recommended by a doctor to relieve stress
- Maternity clothes
- Menstrual supplies (e.g., tampons) (but these costs can be reimbursed by HSAs, FSAs, etc. explained later in this chapter)
- Nicotine patches and gums
- Nutritional supplements, including vitamins, and herbal supplements
- Organ donations (e.g., a kidney)
- Over-the-counter medicines without a doctor's prescription (although they can be reimbursed through HSAs, FSAs, and other plans discussed later in this chapter)
- Premiums on policies guaranteeing a specified income each week in the event of hospitalization
- Prescription drugs purchased abroad, such as from Canada (although there is an FSA exception in certain situations)
- Sex change operation
- Special foods or beverage substitutes (in lieu of what is normally consumed)
- Swimming lessons
- Tattooing
- Teeth-whitening treatment
- Toothpaste
- Umbilical cord blood banking services to treat a disease that might possibly develop in the future
- Veterinary fees (other than for service animals)
- Weight-loss program to improve general good health or appearance

When figuring the deductible portion of home improvements made for medical reasons, such as a swimming pool used to alleviate a medical condition, only the portion of the cost that does not increase the home's value is deductible. However, the cost of making improvements to accommodate a disability, such as installing ramps or widening doors, usually doesn't add any value to the home and is fully deductible.

Medical expenses are also deductible for purposes of the alternative minimum tax (AMT) to the same extent as for the regular tax.

Where to Claim the Deduction

Itemized medical expenses are reported in the first part of Schedule A of Form 1040 or 1040-SR. The total of all itemized deductions is then entered on line 12a of Form 1040 or 1040-SR.

RECORDKEEPING

Retain all canceled checks, doctors' statements, receipts, and other evidence of medical expenses you paid. If you are deducting car mileage for medical-related travel, keep a detailed record of the date and distance of each trip in a diary, logbook, or other record keeper.

Self-Employed Health Insurance Deduction

Self-employed individuals (owning more than 2% S corporation shareholders) cannot deduct their health insurance costs from their business income. This means that health insurance costs do not reduce net earnings from self-employment. But these individuals are permitted to deduct premiums as an adjustment to gross income (an "above-the-line deduction") even if they do not itemize other deductions.

Benefit ⬆

Self-employed individuals and shareholders owning more than 2% of S corporations can deduct all of their health insurance directly from gross income. Thus, the write-off can be taken even if other deductions are not itemized.

This deduction includes not only payments for normal medical care but also long-term care insurance. There is no dollar limit on this deduction.

Conditions

To qualify for this write-off, you and your spouse may not have any employer-subsidized coverage. This condition applies on a month-by-month basis.

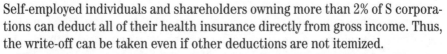

Example

If you (or your spouse) are eligible for employer-subsidized coverage in January but opt to pay your own coverage that month, you do not qualify for the deduction. But if, in February, you are no longer qualified under the employer plan, you can deduct your premium for this month.

Also, the deduction cannot exceed the net earnings from the business in which the medical insurance plan is established. These earnings may not be aggregated with earnings from other businesses. For S corporation shareholders, the deduction cannot be more than wages from the corporation (if this was the business in which the insurance plan was established).

Planning Tips

You can claim the deduction whether you buy the insurance through the business or individually, as long as you meet the conditions explained earlier. If you are an employee of an S corporation owned by your parent and are covered by a company health plan, you are treated the same as your parent: the premiums are taxable income to you, but you can deduct 100% of the premiums as an adjustment to gross income. In effect, you're treated like a self-employed person even though you are an employee of the corporation.

Premiums for Medicare Part B coverage for a self-employed individual can qualify for the above-the-line deduction. The IRS has yet to rule on whether COBRA coverage also qualifies as eligible coverage for purposes of this above-the-line deduction.

If you are paying for your medical insurance, you may wish to combine this with a Health Savings Account (explained later in this chapter).

Pitfalls

The deduction does not offset business expenses. In the case of S corporation shareholders owning more than 2% of the corporation, the shareholder can deduct his or her premiums from gross income only if the corporation pays the premiums or reimburses the shareholder for the premiums *and* includes the premiums as wages on the shareholder's Form W-2.

The self-employed health insurance deduction is a reduction to qualified business income for purposes of the 20% QBI deduction (see Chapter 14).

Where to Claim the Deduction

The self-employed health insurance deduction is claimed on Schedule 1 of Form 1040 or 1040-SR (whether or not you itemize other medical expenses).

Long-Term Care Coverage

Individuals who are suffering from chronic conditions such as Alzheimer's disease or are merely elderly and incapable of self-care (such as feeding and bathing themselves) require long-term care, either in their own homes or in nursing homes. According to a Genworth survey on costs for 2020 (the most recent year for statistics), the average annual cost of a nursing home stay in a private room is now $105,852 ($93,072 for a semiprivate room); it is $379,968 for a private room in Alaska. What's more, the cost of in-home care and adult daycare are also very high. These costs generally are *not* covered by Medicare or supplemental Medicare insurance. Only special insurance, called long-term care insurance, pays for long-term care. The tax law allows a portion of this special medical insurance to be deductible.

Benefit

You can deduct a portion of long-term care insurance premiums as a qualified medical expense (based on your age).

Benefits received under a long-term care policy generally are treated as tax-free income (the benefits are an exclusion from income).

Conditions

Since there are 2 benefits—a deduction for the payment of long-term care insurance premiums and an exclusion from income for benefits received under the policy—different conditions apply for each.

CONDITIONS FOR THE DEDUCTION

You can deduct only a portion of premiums based on your age. For 2021, the federal deduction is limited to the amounts shown in Table 2.3.

The premium limit is on a per-person basis.

Example

Both you and your spouse carry long-term care insurance. You are age 68 and your spouse is age 59. Your annual premium is $4,800 and your spouse's premium is $2,800. You can treat $6,210 ($4,520 for you and $1,690 for your spouse) of your total $7,600 premiums as a deductible medical expense if the sum of your medical expenses exceeds 7.5% of your AGI.

CONDITIONS FOR THE EXCLUSION

The exclusion from income for benefits received under the policy applies only to qualified long-term care services provided to a person who is chronically ill and that are necessary for medical or personal care and are provided under a plan of care prescribed by a licensed health care practitioner. You are chronically ill if a licensed health care practitioner certifies that within the past 12 months you meet *either* of these conditions:

- You are unable for at least 90 days to perform at least 2 activities of daily living without substantial assistance, due to loss of functional capacity. Activities of daily living include eating, toileting, transferring, bathing, dressing, and continence.

TABLE 2.3 Deductible Long-Term Care Premiums for 2021

Age by Year-End	Deduction Limit
Age 40 or younger	$ 450
Age 41–50	850
Age 51–60	1,690
Age 61–70	4,520
Age 71 or older	5,640

- You require substantial supervision for your safety due to severe cognitive impairment.

If the policy pays your long-term care expenses, you can exclude these payments.

Benefits paid under an indemnity-type contract are fully excludable to the extent they cover long-term care expenses. If you receive benefits under a per diem contract, there is a per-day dollar limit on what you can exclude. For 2021, the exclusion is $400 per day, even if your actual expenses are less.

Planning Tips

Since the average annual cost of a nursing home now is $105,852 for a private room ($93,072 for a semiprivate room), you might want to carry long-term care coverage to pay some or all of this cost if it arises. The younger you are when you purchase the policy, the smaller your annual premiums will be (they are fixed at the time of purchase and generally do not increase thereafter).

Long-term care insurance may be available as an employee fringe benefit under your company's cafeteria plan. If you opt for this coverage, you are not taxed on this benefit.

If you add a long-term care rider to a life insurance or annuity contract, the premiums are not deductible when payments for long-term care are a charge against the cash surrender value of the life insurance policy. If there isn't such a charge, then the premiums for the long-term care portion are deductible subject to the limitations discussed earlier.

Many states allow more generous deductions or credits, even if you receive no benefit at the federal level. In New York, for example, there is a 20% tax credit, with no age or dollar limitation.

And some states have long-term care insurance partnerships, which are programs that encourage individuals to buy long-term care insurance while offering special state benefits. These benefits allow you to keep certain assets while qualifying for Medicaid for long-term care once you exhaust your insurance coverage. You can find a list of states offering these partnerships from the American Association for Long-Term Care (www.aaltci.org/long-term-care-insurance/learning-center/long-term-care-insurance-partnership-plans.php).

Commercial annuities can offer a long-term care rider. Such annuities usually cost from 35% to 50% more than stand-alone annuities.

Pitfall

Since long-term care insurance usually pays a fixed dollar amount and, hopefully, you won't need long-term care for many years to come, it can be difficult to know how much insurance to carry. Consider including a cost-of-living rider to adjust your dollar coverage for inflation.

Where to Claim the Deduction and/or Exclusion

The deduction for long-term care insurance premiums is treated like other deductible medical expenses. Generally, they are included with your other itemized medical expenses (up to your allowable dollar limit). However, if you are self-employed, you can include this amount with your other medical insurance claimed as part of the self-employed health insurance deduction, which is an adjustment to gross income.

If you receive benefits under a long-term care policy that are fully excludable, you do not have to report anything on your return. But if you are limited in what you can exclude (as explained earlier), excess benefits are reported as "other income" on Schedule 1 of Form 1040 or 1040-SR.

Flexible Spending Accounts for Health Care

Companies are increasingly forced to make employees pay for some or all of their medical expenses. But they can assist them by creating special arrangements, called flexible spending accounts (health FSAs), that enable employees to pay for medical expenses on a pretax basis. This means employees can dedicate some of their wages to special accounts used for medical expenses. Amounts put into these accounts are not currently taxed. The maximum amount you can contribute to an FSA in 2021 is $2,750. The limit for 2022 will be adjusted for inflation; check the Supplement for an update.

Benefit

Businesses can set up flexible spending accounts (FSAs) to allow employees to pay for expenses not covered by insurance on a pretax basis. At the start of the year employees agree to a salary reduction amount as their contribution to the FSA. These amounts are not treated as taxable compensation and are not subject to Social Security and Medicare (FICA) taxes. Employees then use these amounts any time during the year to pay for medical costs, including health insurance premiums or other expenses not covered by insurance, such as orthodontia and prescription eyeglasses.

For purposes of health FSAs, reimbursable medical expenses include prescription medications and insulin, as well as over-the-counter medications (no prescription is necessary), personal protective equipment (PPE) to prevent the spread of COVID-19, and menstrual products.

Conditions

The plan can set the limits on how much you can commit to the FSA each year up to the dollar limit allowed for the year (e.g., $2,750 for 2021). It may be fixed as a percentage of your compensation (e.g., up to 6%). Ask your plan administrator for details on your contribution limits and the deadline for signing up each year (just because you were in the FSA this year does not automatically cover you for next year; you may be required to complete the same paperwork all over again).

> **Note**
>
> Due to COVID-19, you may make mid-year elections (e.g., elect or revoke participation in FSAs; change your contributions) in 2021. Any change is prospective only.

Planning Tips

You can tap into your annual contribution at any time during the year (even before you have fully paid into the FSA).

> **Example**
>
> In January you agree to contribute $1,800 for the year, which is $150 each month, to your company's FSA. In February, when you have contributed only $300, you pay a dental bill of $1,500 that is not covered by insurance. You submit the paid bill to your plan administrator and receive the full reimbursement of $1,500.

Your employer can adopt an approved grace period. Usually, the grace period cannot extend past March 15 of the following year. But due to COVID-19, a plan with a grace period may allow all unused amounts from 2021 to be used through December 31, 2022.

Instead of a grace period, the plan may allow for a carryover of unused amounts to the following year. Usually the carryover is capped at a limited amount, but due to COVID-19, the carryover is more generous. Any unused contribution for 2021 (up to the annual contribution limit of $2,750) can be carried over to 2022. Assuming the plan allows for a carryover, it does not impact your annual contribution.

An employer can transfer funds in an FSA to an employee's Health Savings Account (HSA). The limit on the transfer is the lesser of the account balance on the date of transfer or on September 21, 2006. This is a one-time opportunity.

Reservists called to active duty can take penalty-free withdrawals from their FSAs for any purpose (not just medical).

Pitfalls

FSAs operate on a use-it-or-lose-it basis subject to the grace period or limited carryover discussed earlier. If you contribute more than your covered medical expenses for the year and cannot use it up in the contribution year or grace period (if applicable) and cannot take advantage of the carryover, you can't get the money back. Don't agree to a salary reduction amount in excess of what you reasonably expect to use for medical expenses. You were able to, adjust your 2021 contribution mid-year if the plan allowed it (it is uncertain whether this rule will apply in 2022, so be cautious in determining your annual contribution).

FSAs cannot pay for any expenses that would not qualify as a deductible medical expense (other than for over-the-counter medications and menstrual products). For example, FSAs cannot be used to pay for cosmetic surgery (unless it is medically necessary—for example, to correct a birth defect) or for a breast pump (which is helpful to a nursing mother but does not treat or mitigate a medical condition).

If you leave the job before using up your FSA contributions for the year, you usually have to spend the unused amount within a time fixed by the plan (usually by the end of the month in which the employment ends). However, for 2021, you may be reimbursed for unused amounts. And, if you opt for COBRA (see later in this chapter), then FSA funds can continue to be used through the end of the year (and through the grace period if applicable); no additional contributions can be made to the FSA after termination of employment.

Where to Claim the Benefit

Since this benefit is an exclusion from income, you do not have to report anything on your return. Compensation reported on your Form W-2 is reduced to the extent of your FSA contributions.

However, you are required to account to the FSA administrator in order to receive payments from the plan. For example, you may be asked to submit a paid bill for prescription sunglasses in order to receive reimbursement from the FSA, and the bill must be submitted within a certain period after incurring the expense. Talk to your plan administrator for rules on how to obtain reimbursements from the plan.

Health Reimbursement Arrangements

Companies are continually looking for ways to reduce their health care costs for employees. In the past, companies had set up health reimbursement accounts (HRAs) to help employees pay for medical costs, but the Affordable Care Act threw the legitimacy of these plans into question. An employee could use funds in his or her account within the plan to pay for medical costs without being taxed when funds were contributed or when they were withdrawn for approved medical expenses. Employers may offer various types of HRAs and reimbursements are tax free.

Individual Coverage HRAs

Your employer may choose to reimburse you for your individually-obtained health coverage. You don't contribute to this arrangement, although your employer can set up a salary reduction arrangement for you to pay premiums in excess of the reimbursements. This option, called an ICHRA, is available only if your employer does not have traditional group health coverage. The reimbursement amount is fixed by your employer. Again, use the reimbursements to pay some or all of the premiums on health coverage you buy privately (on or off the government marketplace) or for Medicare. Depending upon the terms of your employer's plan, reimbursements can also be used to pay unreimbursed medical costs. These include amounts listed as itemized medical expenses earlier in this chapter. You are not taxed on the reimbursements.

Planning Pointers

You must substantiate your premium payments as required by your employer. This may include signing a statement attesting to coverage or providing other proof of coverage.

You are permitted once a year to opt out of the ICHRA if you find that the coverage isn't affordable. You can then obtain coverage through a Marketplace and use the premium tax credit (discussed earlier in this chapter) for premium payments.

Pitfall

You can be reimbursed only for eligible medical expenses (i.e., those that would be deductible by itemizers), assuming the plan allows for reimbursements of expenses other than insurance premiums. You cannot, for example, be reimbursed for vitamins and other health supplements.

Where to Claim the Benefit

Since this benefit is an exclusion from income, you do not have to report anything on your return.

Excepted Benefit HRAs

This option, called an EBHRA, is a supplement to an employer's group health coverage to pay for co-payments, deductibles, other amounts not covered by insurance, and excepted benefits (e.g., dental and vision care). Reimbursements, which are tax free, cannot be made to cover health insurance premiums other than COBRA, short-term limited duration insurance, and dental and vision care. The dollar limit is fixed by the government annually ($1,800 in 2021). The 2022 limit will be in the Supplement to this book.

Planning Pointers

You must substantiate your payments as required by your employer. This may include signing a statement attesting to coverage or providing other proof of coverage.

Unused amounts may be carried forward to the next plan year.

Pitfall

Reimbursements cannot be used to pay health insurance premiums.

Where to Claim the Benefit

Since this benefit is an exclusion from income, you do not have to report anything on your return.

QSEHRAs

Small businesses can offer Qualified Small Employer Health Reimbursement Arrangements (QSEHRAs), which are plans that enable employers to reimburse employees for their individually obtained health coverage on a tax-free basis. This benefit is paid entirely by employers; no employee salary reduction contributions are made. It is an alternative to the Individual Coverage HRA discussed earlier in this chapter.

Benefit ⊗

The value of the reimbursement received from your employer is not includible in gross income. This is so even though it may be reported on your Form W-2.

Conditions

There are several conditions for the exclusion to apply:

- Your employer must be a "small employer" (fewer than 50 full time/full-time equivalent employees) and not have any other group health plan.
- You must submit proof to your employer that you obtained health coverage.
- The amount of the annual reimbursement for 2021 is capped at $5,300 for self-only coverage or $10,700 for family coverage.

Planning Tip

While the Tax Code does not specify that reimbursement can cover an employee's cost under a spouse's plan through the spouse's employer, the IRS suggested in informal advice in 2015 that this could be possible. More IRS guidance is needed on this point.

Pitfalls

You cannot claim a premium tax credit for your coverage paid with QSEHRA reimbursements, even though your income is low enough that you'd otherwise qualify for it. If you claim the credit, the QSEHRA benefit is reduced dollar for dollar.

If you don't have coverage for the full year, the dollar limit for reimbursement is prorated. For example, if you have family coverage from July through December 2021, your exclusion is limited to $5,350 (half of the $10,700 annual limit).

Benefits under a QSEHRA do not have to be given to an employee who has not completed 90 days of service, is under age 25, or is a part-time or seasonal employee. If you are in any of these categories, check with your employer about reimbursements for your premiums.

Where to Claim the Benefit

Since this benefit is an exclusion from income, you do not have to report anything on your return.

Health Savings Accounts

Individuals who are covered by health insurance policies with high deductibles may be eligible to contribute money to a special savings account, called a Health Savings Account (HSA). HSAs have become a way to obtain needed health coverage now on an affordable basis. In 2020 (the most recent year for statistics), there were over 30 million people who had HSAs. HSAs can be obtained individually or through an employer if such a benefit is offered. Many employers are

TABLE 2.4 Health Savings Account Contribution Limits for 2021

Your Age	Self-Only Plan	Family Plan
Under age 55	$3,600	$7,200
55 or older	$4,600	$8,200*

* If both spouses are age 55 or older and contribute to add an additional $1,000, they must have separate HSAs.

offering these accounts along with high-deductible health insurance (defined later), either as an employee's health care choice or the only option available.

Contributions to the account are tax deductible. Earnings on the account are not subject to immediate tax. If withdrawals are made to pay for medical expenses, they are fully tax free. Otherwise, withdrawals are taxable and subject to a 20% penalty unless taken when age 65 or older or disabled. Spouses who inherit an account can roll over the funds tax free.

Benefit ⊗ ⬆

If you have a "high-deductible" health insurance policy (defined in the "Conditions" section), you can contribute to a special savings account. Benefits to HSAs include:

- Contributions within set limits are deductible as an adjustment to gross income (you do not have to itemize deductions to claim this benefit). See Table 2.4 for 2021 limits. The limits for those under age 55 can be indexed for inflation (the limits for 2022 are in the *Planning Tips*); the additional contribution limit for those age 55 and older remains at $1,000.
- Interest or other earnings in the account are tax deferred.
- Withdrawals used to pay medical costs are tax free.

Conditions

To contribute to an HSA, you must meet 2 conditions:

1. You are not covered by Medicare.
2. You are covered by a high-deductible health plan (HDHP). Healthcare.gov has a filter to help you identify high-deductible health plan options on the government Marketplace.

MEDICARE

HSAs are designed to cover individuals who do not qualify for Medicare. Therefore, you are ineligible for an HSA once you are enrolled in Medicare. Since

TABLE 2.5 2021 High-Deductible Policy Limits

	Self-Only Coverage	Family Coverage
Annual deductible at least	$1,400	$2,800
Limit on out-of-pocket expenses	$7,000	$14,000

determination of eligibility is made month by month, you may be qualified for a deduction for the portion of the year before you are covered by Medicare.

QUALIFYING HIGH-DEDUCTIBLE HEALTH INSURANCE

You must have a high-deductible health plan (HDHP) for at least all of December in 2021. This can be an insurance policy that you have obtained personally or coverage provided by your employer. The determination of whether you have such coverage is made on the first day of the month.

A high-deductible policy is one that falls within certain limits. (See Table 2.5.) An HDHP can pay for certain preventive services (listed in the examples that follow) without failing to be an HDHP. For, an HDHP may also cover the cost of testing and treatment for COVID-19 as well as telehealth services without any required deductible.

At present, insurance plans offered in certain states that provide male sterilization and contraception services with no deductible or a deductible below the minimum deductible for HDHPs are permissible for 2021 even though this technically conflicts with federal law.

You cannot have any other health coverage, other than accident insurance, dental care, disability coverage, disease-specific coverage (such as cancer insurance), long-term care, vision care, and workers' compensation.

Like individual retirement accounts (IRAs), contributions to HSAs can be made up to the due date for the return (without extensions). For example, contributions for 2021 can be made up to April 18, 2022.

Tax-Free Withdrawals

Only account distributions used to pay qualified medical expenses are tax free. Qualified medical expenses include:

- Any expense that could be claimed as an itemized medical deduction (see the section earlier in this chapter)
- Child and adult immunizations
- COBRA premiums

- Menstrual products
- Obesity weight-loss programs
- Over-the-counter medications (no prescription is necessary)
- Periodic health evaluations, such as annual physicals
- Personal protective equipment preventing the spread of COVID-19 (e.g., masks, hand sanitizer, sanitizing wipes)
- Premiums for long-term care insurance
- Routine prenatal and well-child care
- Screening services, such as those listed
- Tobacco cessation programs

Examples of Screening Services Treated as Medical Expenses for HSAs

CANCER SCREENING

Breast cancer (e.g., mammogram)

Cervical cancer (e.g., Pap smear)

Colorectal cancer

Oral cancer

Ovarian cancer

Prostate cancer (e.g., prostate-specific antigen [PSA] test)

Skin cancer

Testicular cancer

Thyroid cancer

HEART AND VASCULAR DISEASES SCREENING

Abdominal aortic aneurysm

Carotid artery stenosis

Coronary heart disease

Hemoglobinopathies

Hypertension

Lip disorders

INFECTIOUS DISEASES SCREENING

Bacteriuria

Chlamydial infection

COVID-19

Gonorrhea

Hepatitis B virus infection

Hepatitis C

Human immunodeficiency virus (HIV) infection

Syphilis

Tuberculosis infection

MENTAL HEALTH CONDITIONS AND SUBSTANCE ABUSE SCREENING

Dementia

Depression

Drug abuse

Family violence

Problem drinking

Suicide risk

METABOLIC, NUTRITIONAL, AND ENDOCRINE CONDITIONS SCREENING

Anemia, iron deficiency

Dental and periodontal disease

Diabetes mellitus

Obesity in adults

Thyroid disease

MUSCULOSKELETAL DISORDERS SCREENING

Osteoporosis

OBSTETRIC AND GYNECOLOGIC CONDITIONS SCREENING

Bacterial vaginosis in pregnancy

Gestational diabetes mellitus

Home uterine activity monitoring

Neural tube defects

Preeclampsia

Rh incompatibility

Rubella

Ultrasonography in pregnancy

PEDIATRIC CONDITIONS SCREENING

Child developmental delay

Congenital hypothyroidism

Lead levels in childhood and pregnancy

Phenylketonuria

Scoliosis, adolescent idiopathic

PREVENTIVE CARE PAYABLE BY HDHPs for those diagnosed with specified conditions

Angiotensin converting enzyme (ACE) inhibitors for congestive heart failure, diabetes, and/or coronary artery disease

Anti-resorptive therapy for osteoporosis and/or osteopenia

Beta-blockers for congestive heart failure and/or coronary artery disease

Blood pressure monitor for hypertension

Inhaled corticosteroids for asthma

Insulin and other glucose-lowering agents for diabetes

Retinopathy screening for diabetes

Peak flow meter for asthma

Glucometer for diabetes

Hemoglobin Alc testing for diabetes

International normalized ratio (INR) testing for liver disease and/or bleeding disorders

Low-density lipoprotein (LDL) testing for heart disease

Selective serotonin reuptake inhibitors (SSRIs) for depression

Statins for heart disease and/or diabetes

VISION AND HEARING DISORDERS SCREENING

Glaucoma

Hearing impairment in older adults

Newborn hearing

Planning Tips

It is up to you to keep track of medical costs so that you can prove withdrawals from your HSA were used to pay qualified expenses. The financial institution with which you have your account won't ask you for any substantiation on your part. Neither will your employer if the account is set up through your company.

HSAs can be funded by a one-time transfer by an employer from a flexible spending account (FSA) or by a health reimbursement arrangement (HRA), to an employee's HSA or an IRA rollover. Transfers from FSAs and HRAs are limited (as explained earlier in this chapter). Rollovers from IRAs are not currently taxed.

HSAs can be funded by means of a direct deposit of a tax refund. Be sure to designate whether the refund is being used to fund a 2021 or 2022 contribution where possible.

Example

If you expect a refund for 2021 taxes and plan to contribute to an HSA, file your return early enough so that the IRS has time to process it and transfer your refund directly to the HSA (you must provide account information to make the transfer possible). Alternatively, use a 2021 refund to make a contribution to an HSA for 2022 if eligible to do so for that year.

Funds in the HSA can be used for retirement savings. Since there is no tax on earnings that the account is building up, the healthier you stay (and the less you need to use account funds for medical bills), the more you'll have in retirement to use for any purpose. While the withdrawals will be taxed, there is no penalty on withdrawals for nonmedical purposes once you reach age 65.

Planning ahead for 2022, the contribution limits for HSAs are $3,650 for self-only coverage and $7,300 for family coverage. The parameters for a high deductible health plan in 2022 are a minimum deductible of $1,400 and maximum out-of-pocket limit of $7,050 for self-only coverage ($2,800 and $14,100 respectively for family coverage).

Pitfalls

If you take withdrawals to pay nonmedical expenses, the distribution is taxed as ordinary income, regardless of your age. In addition, if you are under age 65, you are also subject to a 20% penalty (unless you are disabled). Taxable income treatment and the 20% penalty applies if the IRS levies on the HSA to cover back taxes, even though the withdrawal is involuntary. There is no 20% penalty on distributions because of the account owner's death.

If you have a separate prescription drugs benefit plan that has no deductible (only copayments for each prescription), you cannot be an eligible individual for HSA purposes.

If you receive a retroactive lump sum from Social Security because you begin taking benefits after your full retirement age, keep in mind that you'll also be automatically enrolled in Medicare retroactively. This means that any contributions made to your HSA during that retroactive period are "excess contributions" (contributions for the portion of the year prior to the Medicare coverage are permissible). Excess contributions are subject to a 6% excise tax until the excess amount, plus earnings on it, are withdrawn from the account.

If you inherit an HSA and are not a surviving spouse of the account owner, you must take a complete distribution of the account and include all of the funds in your income. Check to see if you qualify for a deduction for federal estate tax on the HSA (see Chapter 15).

Where to Claim the Benefits

The deduction is figured on Form 8889, *Health Savings Accounts (HSAs)*. The deduction is then claimed on Schedule 1 of Form 1040 or 1040-SR.

If your employer contributes to an HSA on your behalf, this is a tax-free fringe benefit; no reporting is required.

Archer Medical Savings Accounts

Self-employed individuals and small employers had been able to set up Archer Medical Savings Accounts (MSAs) to save money for their health insurance costs by combining a "high-deductible" medical insurance policy with this special savings plan. The opportunity to set up new MSAs expired at the end of 2007, so contributions for 2021 can be made only to MSAs set up before 2008. If they have a policy that falls within parameters set by the tax law, then they (or their employees) can contribute a fixed amount to an IRA-like account. Contributions are deductible, earnings are not currently subject to tax, and withdrawals for medical purposes are tax free (i.e., contributions and earnings on contributions used to pay medical costs are never taxed). Archer MSAs are an alternative to HSAs for eligible taxpayers, although HSAs usually are more favorable.

Benefit

If you are self-employed or an employee of a small employer with a "high-deductible" health insurance policy (defined in "Conditions" section), you can contribute to a special savings account that can be tapped to cover unreimbursed medical expenses. There are several benefits to Archer MSAs:

- Contributions within set limits are deductible (or tax free if made by your employer).
- Interest or other earnings in the account are tax deferred.
- Withdrawals used to cover medical expenses are tax free.

TABLE 2.6 2021 Limits on Deductibles and Out-of-Pocket Expenses

Type of Coverage	Minimum Annual Deductible	Maximum Annual Deductible	Maximum Annual Out-of-Pocket Expenses
Individual (self-only policy)	$2,400	$3,600	$4,800
Family	$4,800	$7,150	$8,750

Conditions

You must be self-employed or an employee of a "small employer" covered by a "high-deductible" health insurance policy. A small employer is an employer who had on average 50 or fewer employees during either of the 2 preceding calendar years. If the business is new, then the employer is treated as a small employer if it reasonably expects to employ 50 or fewer workers. If a business made contributions to an Archer MSA this year, it can continue to be treated as a small employer as long as it had no more than 200 employees each year after 1996.

A high-deductible policy is one that falls within certain limits on deductibles and out-of-pocket expenses required to be paid (other than premiums) before the policy kicks in. (See Table 2.6.)

Example

In 2021, you are self-employed and have a self-only health insurance policy with an annual deductible of $2,400 and a limit on out-of-pocket expenses of $4,800. You had set up an MSA in 2006 and have been funding it annually. Assuming you meet other conditions, you have a high-deductible plan and can fund your Archer MSA in 2021.

You (or your spouse) cannot have any other health plan that is not a high-deductible plan. But coverage under certain other health plans will not prevent you from being able to fund an Archer MSA. Other coverage you may have *in addition* to a high-deductible plan includes insurance covering accidents, disability, dental care, vision care, long-term care, benefits related to workers' compensation, a specific illness or disease, or a fixed amount per day or other period of hospitalization.

Assuming you meet the conditions for claiming a deduction, the amount is limited to 65% of your annual deductible for self-only coverage or 75% of your annual deductible for family coverage.

Example

In 2021, you are self-employed and have a health insurance policy for family coverage with a $6,800 annual deductible (which is more than the minimum deductible of $4,800 but less than the maximum deductible of $7,150 in 2021). In 2021, you can contribute $5,100 to an Archer MSA ($6,800 × 75%) (assuming the account was set up prior to 2008 and the out-of-pocket expense limit does not exceed $8,750 in 2021).

If you have coverage for only part of the year, you must prorate the deduction.

Example

Same facts as in the preceding example but you end coverage on June 30, 2021, and maintain it for the balance of the year. You can contribute $2,550 to an Archer MSA ($6,800 × 75% ÷ 12 months × 6 months).

Contributions for 2021 must be made no later than April 18, 2022.

Planning Tips

You can roll over funds in an Archer MSA tax free to a Health Savings Account. This may be advisable because of the extensive availability of financial institutions offering HSAs compared with limited Archer MSA options.

You can fund an Archer MSA for 2021 or 2022 via a direct deposit of your 2021 tax refund. Just provide the IRS with the account information and your refund will be transferred directly to your account.

You can use an Archer MSA to provide retirement income. Money can be withdrawn for any purpose penalty-free after you attain age 65.

Pitfalls

If you are self-employed, you cannot contribute more than your net earnings from self-employment. Thus, if you have a loss year, you cannot fund an Archer MSA.

Example

You are 65 years old and, because you have stayed healthy, the funds in your account have accumulated to $10,000. You can withdraw this money to take a vacation. While you'll owe income tax on the withdrawal (because you are not using the funds for medical reasons), you are not subject to the 20% penalty (explained next).

If you withdraw funds from an Archer MSA for other than medical expenses before attaining age 65, the funds are subject to a 20% penalty unless you are disabled (or die).

WHEN YOU DIE

If you have an Archer MSA, you can name your spouse as the beneficiary of the account. Your spouse becomes the owner of the account when you die. If you designate any other person as your beneficiary, the account ceases to be an Archer MSA on your death and the funds remaining in the account are taxable to the beneficiary as income. If there is no designated beneficiary, the balance of your account is included as income on your final tax return.

Where to Claim the Benefits

The deduction is figured on Form 8853, *Archer MSAs and Long-Term Care Insurance Contracts*. The deduction is then claimed on Schedule 1 of Form 1040 or 1040-SR.

If your employer contributes to an Archer Medical Savings Account on your behalf, this is a tax-free fringe benefit; no reporting is required.

REPORTING INCOME

Withdrawals are reported to you (and the IRS) on Form 1099-SA, *Distributions from an HSA, Archer MSA, or Medicare Advantage MSA*. Funds withdrawn for anything other than medical expenses are taxable as ordinary income. Report the income on Schedule 1 of Form 1040 or 1040-SR as other income.

If you owe a 20% penalty on withdrawals for nonmedical purposes before age 65, you report the penalty on Schedule 2 of Form 1040 or 1040-SR.

ABLE Accounts

Federal law enables states to create special accounts called Achieving a Better Life Experience (ABLE) accounts, which are designed to ease the financial burden of families with disabled children. At present, ABLE accounts are live in 42 states and the District of Columbia, likely with more to follow. These accounts generally do not adversely impact eligibility for means-tested government programs (e.g., Medicaid can continue regardless of the amount of assets in the account).

Benefit

Contributions to an ABLE account are not tax deductible. However, earnings grow on a tax-deferred basis and withdrawals for qualified disability purposes are tax free.

The maximum contribution amount in 2021 is $15,000 per beneficiary. The contribution limit can be increased under certain circumstances if it's made by the designated beneficiary before 2026. Contributions can also be made by rolling over funds in a 529 plan, subject to the annual contribution limit.

Conditions

An ABLE account must be set up in the state in which the disabled child resides unless that state contracts with another to facilitate such an account. The beneficiary of the ABLE account must be either:

- Receiving Social Security disability payments on account of blindness or a disability that occurred before age 26
- Certified by a doctor that he or she is blind or disabled due to an impairment that began before age 26 and that is expected to result in death or last (or has lasted) for at least 12 months

The beneficiary can have only one ABLE account at a time.

Distributions from an ABLE account are excludable only if used for qualified disability expenses, which include:

- Assistive technology
- Education
- Employment training
- Funeral and burial expenses
- Health
- Housing
- Personal support services
- Prevention and wellness
- Transportation

Planning Tips

Investment choices can be changed up to 2 times per year. And contributions may entitle the beneficiary to claim the retirement savers credit (see Chapter 5).

A family that has been thinking of setting up a supplemental needs trust for a disabled child should consider whether an ABLE account can meet the family's objectives. Discuss the situation with a knowledgeable attorney.

ABLE account programs are active in all but a handful of states. Check the map at the ABLE National Resource Center at www.ablenrc.org/ state-review for information on your state. However, you do not have to open an account in your state; there is no residency requirement for having an ABLE account.

Pitfalls

While assets in an ABLE account do not prevent eligibility for Supplemental Support Income (SSI), once the account balance reaches $100,000, SSI benefits are suspended (but not terminated).

A distribution is comprised of a return of contributions (which are not taxed) and a receipt of earnings (which are taxed). This is figured on a pro rata basis. In addition, there is a 10% penalty on the taxable amount of the distribution (regardless of the beneficiary's age).

Where to Claim the Benefit

You do not report contributions you make to an ABLE account on your return (remember, they are not deductible).

COBRA Coverage

The Consolidated Omnibus Budget Reconciliation Act of 1986, or COBRA for short, imposed a new requirement on certain employers who maintain health insurance coverage for workers: allow workers who leave the job to continue their company coverage for a period of time (at the workers' expense). The opportunity to continue under the company's health plan means that terminated workers and other eligible people pay for medical insurance at group rates.

Benefits ⊜ ⊗

Under federal law, if you work for a company that regularly employs 20 or more workers and has group health insurance, you are entitled to continue under the employer's group plan even if you leave employment (voluntarily or are laid off for any reason other than gross misconduct) or your hours are reduced below the level entitling you to employer-paid coverage. This is referred to as COBRA continuation coverage, or simply COBRA. Your state may have its own "mini-COBRA" law, which may expand your rights (contact your state insurance department for details). Thus, even if the employer has fewer than 20 employees, state law may extend COBRA rights to employees and former employees. And there is a special second COBRA election period for certain qualifying individuals. April 1, 2021, through September 30, 2021, employers had to pay the cost of this coverage for certain employees (see Chapter 13).

Being eligible for and electing COBRA coverage gives you 2 key benefits:

1. Health insurance at an affordable group rate.
2. A deduction for premium payments if you itemize your medical expenses. (The IRS has not yet ruled on whether you can deduct COBRA coverage as an adjustment to gross income if you are self-employed, although some experts argue that you can.)

You can continue COBRA coverage for up to 18 months or until you become eligible under a new employer's plan, you qualify for Medicare, or you fail to make your COBRA payments (there is usually a 30-day grace period). The coverage period can be extended to 29 months if you become disabled within the first 60 days of COBRA coverage. Your family can retain COBRA coverage for up to 36 months if their eligibility results from your death.

You usually must pay the full cost of coverage, plus up to 2% as an administrative fee (102% of the premiums). But you enjoy the group term rates, which may be less than what you could purchase on your own. Your payment of premiums under COBRA is a deductible medical expense (explained earlier).

If you are a displaced worker, you may be able to claim a tax credit for your COBRA premiums, as explained earlier in this chapter.

Conditions for Coverage

If your employer is subject to COBRA, you must notify the employer about a qualifying event and opt for coverage within 60 days of that event (no extensions are granted). A qualifying event includes:

- You terminate employment (voluntarily or involuntarily, as long as you are not terminated for fraud or other gross misconduct).
- Your parent has health insurance through his or her employer and you attain the age at which you no longer qualify (generally through age 26).
- Your spouse has health coverage through his or her employer and you divorce your spouse.

SECOND COBRA ELECTION PERIOD

To qualify, you must be receiving trade adjustment allowance (TAA) benefits (or would be but for the requirement that you first exhaust unemployment benefits), you lost health coverage because of termination of employment that resulted in TAA eligibility, and you did not elect COBRA during the regular COBRA election period.

Planning Tips

Before opting for COBRA, see if there are less costly health insurance options. For example, if your spouse is working, his or her employer may offer less expensive health coverage. Or you may be able to buy coverage through a professional or trade association or through the government Marketplace that is less expensive than COBRA.

If you obtain COBRA coverage with the federal subsidy, even if the subsidy is taxable to you, there is still a cost savings.

If you received COBRA premium assistance from your employer or former employer from April 1, 2021, through September 1, 2021, this benefit is not taxable to you.

Pitfalls

COBRA may not be less costly than coverage you could obtain on an individual basis. You can reduce your current level of coverage under COBRA, but you can't increase it. For example, if you had dental coverage but now wish to eliminate it (and the expense) under COBRA, you can do so. But if you didn't have dental coverage, you can't add it under COBRA.

COBRA does not apply to long-term care insurance. You may be able to pick up the long-term care policy individually when you leave employment, but your employer is not required to offer you this coverage through COBRA.

If you leave employment and are at least 65 years old, Medicare is your primary carrier so apply for coverage. This is so even if you opt for COBRA coverage for medical costs not covered by Medicare.

Where to Claim the Deduction

COBRA payments are treated as a deductible medical expense (see earlier in this chapter).

Medicare

In 1965, Congress introduced a federally sponsored health insurance program as part of the Social Security Act. This program, called Medicare, is designed primarily to provide those age 65 and older with affordable comprehensive health coverage. Today, the program has grown to afford seniors various types of coverage options, from fee-based services to managed care programs. More than 60 million Americans are now covered by Medicare.

Benefit

If you are age 65 or older, are under age 65 and disabled for at least 2 years, or have end-stage renal disease, you are entitled to participate in Medicare. Your monthly premiums (whether paid directly by you or withheld from your Social Security benefits check), as well as your copayments and deductibles under Medicare, are qualified medical expenses that are deductible to the extent your total exceeds 7.5% of adjusted gross income (see the general rules on deducting medical expenses, including medical insurance, discussed earlier in this chapter). You are not taxed on the benefits you receive through Medicare. If you are self-employed, you can treat your Medicare premiums as self-employed coverage. This is 100% deductible as an adjustment to gross income; no itemizing is required.

If your Medicare premiums are being withheld from Social Security benefits, the amount of your annual Medicare premiums is reported to you in the description of the amount in box 3 of Form SSA-1099, *Social Security Benefit Statement*.

Part A, which covers hospitalization, is free (those who did not work a sufficient number of quarters can pay for this coverage). Part B, which covers doctors' charges and certain other expenses, requires you to pay a monthly premium. The premium is subtracted from your Social Security benefits if you are collecting benefits. Both Part A and Part B have certain copayments or deductibles for your covered medical expenses.

There is a Medicare prescription drug plan called Part D. Once you reach the coverage gap (which used to be called the "donut hole") of $4,130, the maximum payment for both brand-name and generic drugs is capped at 25%. After paying $6,550 in covered drug costs in 2021 (referred to as the "catastrophic coverage stage"), co-payments for additional drugs drop considerably for the rest of the year.

Certain low-income beneficiaries qualify for additional assistance to pay for prescription drugs in what is called the Extra Help program, which is estimated to be worth about $5,000 per year. To be eligible for partial Extra Help, beneficiaries enrolled in Medicare Part D must have an annual income in 2021 below $19,320 if single or $26,130 if married and not be eligible for any other prescription drug coverage (including outpatient prescription drug coverage through Medicare managed care plans). Beneficiaries cannot have savings and resources (excluding a home, car, personal possessions, and a burial plot) exceeding $14,790 if single or $29,520 if married and living together for Extra Help in paying for prescription drugs. More modest income and asset limits apply for full Extra Help. Details on the Medicare drug program can be found at www.medicare.gov or through the Medicare Rights Center at https://bit.ly/2NxzsZq.

Conditions

To be eligible for free coverage under Part A, you (or your spouse) must have at least 40 quarters of Medicare-covered employment. If you don't have the necessary number of quarters, you can pay for this coverage.

Part B is available to just about anyone age 65 or older (there are no minimum work requirements).

Part D is available to all Medicare beneficiaries.

Planning Tips

Medicare coverage generally isn't automatic; you must apply for it if you haven't yet applied for Social Security benefits. You should contact your local Social Security office to apply for Medicare 3 months before the date you reach your full retirement age so that coverage can start on time.

If you have been collecting Social Security benefits before your full retirement age (e.g., starting at age 62), you do not have to apply when you near full retirement age; enrollment in Medicare Part A (hospitalization insurance) in this case is automatic and free; however, you must then decide whether to also elect Medicare Part B (health insurance). Alternatively, you can enroll in Medicare Advantage (Part C), which provides the same coverage as Parts A and B (and in most cases Part D as well).

If you opt for traditional fee-for-service Medicare (rather than some managed care program within Medicare), you may want to purchase supplemental Medicare insurance ("Medigap" coverage). Medigap premiums are deductible as a qualified medical expense (explained earlier in this chapter).

Pitfalls

If you claim the standard deduction (including the additional amount for being age 65 or older), you cannot deduct your Medicare Part B payments since you do not itemize deductions.

If your modified adjusted gross income in 2019 was above a certain amount for your filing status, you are subject to surcharges on your Medicare premiums. For example, the "standard" premium for Part B coverage in 2021, the premium paid by most beneficiaries, is $148.50 per month (compared with $144.60 per month on average for 2020). Those who fall within a "hold harmless" definition pay a lower monthly premium for 2021. But Tables 2.7 and 2.8 (one for Part B and one for Part D) show the 2021 surcharges and total premiums for higher-income taxpayers, which are based on modified adjusted gross income (MAGI) in 2019.

The Medicare surcharges for 2022, based on MAGI for 2020, will be included in the Supplement.

If you wait too long to apply for Medicare Part B, your monthly premium will be increased. To obtain the lowest possible premium, you *must* apply either

TABLE 2.7 Part B Premiums for 2021

2019 MAGI for Joint Filers	2019 for Other Filers*	Total Monthly Part B Premium for 2021
Up to $176,000	Up to $88,000	$148.50 unless held harmless
$176,001 to $222,000	$88,001 to $111,000	$207.90
$222,001 to $276,000	$111,001 to $138,000	$297.00
$276,001 to $330,000	$138,001 to $165,000	$386.10
$330,001 to $749,999	$165,001 to $499,999	$475.20
$750,000 or greater	$500,000 or greater	$504.90

*Married persons filing separately for 2019 who did not live apart for the entire year are subject to a monthly premium for 2021 of $475.20 if 2019 MAGI was over $88,000 through $411,999, or $504.90 if 2019 MAGI was $412,000 or more.

TABLE 2.8 Part D Premiums for 2021

2019 MAGI for Joint Filers	2019 for Other Filers*	Total Monthly Part D Premiums for 2021
Up to $176,000	Up to $88,000	Plan premium (no surcharge)
$176,001 to $222,000	$88,001 to $111,000	$12.30 + plan premium
$222,001 to $276,000	$111,001 to $138,000	$31.80 + plan premium
$276,001 to $330,000	$138,001 to $165,000	$51.20 + plan premium
$330,001 to $749,999	$165,001 to $499,999	$70.70 + plan premium
$750,000 and higher	$500,000 and higher	$77.10 + plan premium

* Married persons filing separately for 2019 who did not live apart for the entire year are subject to a monthly premium for 2021 of $70.70 if 2019 MAGI was over $88,000 through $411,999, or $77.10 if 2019 MAGI was $412,000 or more.

within a 7-month window extending from 3 months before to 4 months after your 65th birthday, or, if still employed and covered at work where employer coverage is your primary coverage (there are more than 20 employees at the company), within 8 months after that ends.

If you did not sign up for Medicare Part D but were eligible to do so, and you do not have other "creditable coverage" (e.g., employer or other coverage that is at least as good as Medicare), you are penalized 1% per month for each month you delay.

Example

If you wait 15 months to sign up beyond the deadline, you pay 15% of the premium as a penalty when you enroll. If the premium is normally $40 per month, you'd pay $46 per month ($40 plus 15% penalty). The penalty percentage continues for the rest of your life.

Where to Claim the Deduction

You deduct premiums as well as your copayments and deductibles as itemized medical expenses (see earlier in this chapter). You must complete Schedule A and attach it to Form 1040 or 1040-SR.

Continuing Care Facilities and Nursing Homes

Elderly and infirm individuals may require round-the-clock care because of their age or condition. Comprehensive programs in special living arrangements are now used to care for these individuals. A portion of the cost may qualify as a deductible medical expense.

Benefit

Advanced age and/or chronic illness may require ongoing daily treatment. Payments for nursing homes, convalescent homes, and sanitariums may be treated as deductible medical expenses. The deduction generally is not limited to the portion covering medical care; it also includes lodging and meals if confinement is primarily for the purpose of medical treatment.

If the main reason for admission is not medical care, you can still treat the portion of monthly fees allocable to medical care as a deductible medical expense. Typically, this applies to fees to continuing care facilities—the portion of the fees for medical care is deductible but the portion covering lodging and meals is not.

Conditions

Admission to the facility must be *primarily* for medical treatment to deduct all charges and fees. You can prove this by showing that:

- Entry was on or at the direction of a doctor.
- Attendance or treatment at the facility has a direct therapeutic effect on the condition suffered by the patient.
- Attendance at the facility is for the treatment of a specific ailment and not merely for general good health.

Planning Tip

Generally, prepayments for future care are not currently deductible medical expenses. However, you can claim a current deduction if you can show there is a current obligation to pay and you can establish the portion of the prepayment allocated to medical care.

Example

You and your spouse enter a retirement home that requires the payment of an entrance fee of $50,000, plus monthly payments of $1,000, to cover your accommodations, meals, and medical care for life. The home estimates for you that 10% of the entrance fee and 15% of the monthly fee are used for medical care. If you leave the home, you are entitled to a refund of a portion of the founder's fee. On these facts, you can treat 10% of the entrance fee and 15% of the monthly fee paid in the year as deductible medical expenses.

Pitfall

If you claim the standard deduction (including the additional amount for being age 65 or older), you cannot deduct your payments for continuing care facilities or nursing homes since you do not itemize deductions. As a practical matter, however, if you are a resident in such a facility for a full year, the cost will generally result in a large enough medical deduction to warrant itemizing your deductions in lieu of claiming the standard deduction, even with the additional amount for age.

Where to Claim the Benefit

See itemized medical expenses earlier in this chapter.

Accelerated Death Benefits

Whoever thought that life insurance could be beneficial to the person insured? Today, policies intended to provide death benefits to heirs may be used for lifetime assistance to the insured under special circumstances. The proceeds receive the same tax-free treatment as death proceeds in certain circumstances.

Benefit ⊗

If you own a life insurance policy with cash value and become terminally or chronically ill, you may be able to tap into that cash value on a tax-free basis to pay medical and other personal expenses.

There are 2 ways in which to use a life insurance policy to provide you with current cash on a tax-free basis:

1. Tap into the policy's cash surrender value under an accelerated death benefit clause if the policy contains such an option.
2. Sell the policy to a viatical settlement company (a company in the business of buying policies under these conditions).

Conditions

You must be terminally or chronically ill to qualify for the exclusion. You are considered to be terminally ill if a physician certifies that you suffer from an illness or physical condition that is reasonably expected to result in death within 24 months of the date of certification.

You are considered to be chronically ill if a licensed health care practitioner certifies that within the past 12 months you meet *either* of these conditions:

- You are unable for at least 90 days to perform at least 2 activities of daily living without substantial assistance, due to loss of functional capacity. Activities of daily living include eating, toileting, transferring, bathing, dressing, and continence.
- You require substantial supervision for your safety due to severe cognitive impairment.

LIMITS FOR THE CHRONICALLY ILL

While *all* payments received by someone who is terminally ill are fully excludable (whether or not such amounts are used for medical care), limits apply to those who are chronically but not terminally ill. The same limits for benefits received under a long-term care policy apply for this purpose. Thus, if accelerated death benefits are not more than the daily dollar limit ($400 in 2021) and do not exceed actual long-term care costs, they are fully excludable. But any excess amounts are taxable.

Planning Tip

To the extent you use accelerated death benefits for medical expenses, you reap a double tax benefit: The funds are tax-free income to you, and you can treat the payments you make as deductible medical expenses if you itemize your deductions.

Pitfall

To the extent you use your life insurance policy while you are alive, there is that much less for your beneficiaries after your death. If you have other options to cover your expenses, you might weigh your current needs against your beneficiaries' needs after your death in deciding whether to use accelerated death benefits.

Where to Claim the Benefit

If benefits are fully excludable, they are not reported. However, if a chronically ill person receives benefits in excess of the limit ($400 per day in 2021), such amounts are reported as other income on Schedule 1 of Form 1040 or 1040-SR.

Decedent's Final Illness

There are no special deductions for someone who dies. But the tax law provides opportunities on the timing of deductions for the deceased. Those handling the affairs of a person who has died can choose how to handle medical deductions for optimum tax savings.

Benefit

Payments of medical expenses for a deceased spouse or dependent can be deducted as a medical expense in the year they are paid, even if this is before or after the person's death.

A decedent's personal representative (executor, administrator, etc.) has a choice of how to treat medical expenses—as an itemized deduction on the decedent's final income tax return (to the extent provided) or as a deduction on the estate tax return. Of course, if the decedent's estate is too small to require the filing of an estate tax return, there is no real choice; the expenses should automatically be treated as a deduction on the decedent's income tax return.

If the personal representative of a decedent's estate pays medical expenses within one year of death, an election can be made to treat the expenses as if they were paid by the decedent in the year the services were provided rather than the year in which they were paid. This may entitle the personal representative to file an amended return for the decedent for a prior year.

Example

In 2020, the decedent received treatment for a condition that eventually resulted in her death on May 1, 2021. At the time of death, payment for this treatment was outstanding. Assuming her personal representative pays any of her unreimbursed cost in February 2021, the personal representative may file an amended return for the decedent for 2020 to include the payment along with the decedent's other deductible medical expenses.

Condition

The decision on when and where to claim the decedent's medical expenses is made by the personal representative—the executor, administrator, or other person empowered by a court to act for the estate. This person can override a decision by a surviving spouse.

Planning Tip

Generally, if the decedent leaves an estate large enough to be subject to estate tax, it usually is preferable to claim the deduction on the estate tax return because the estate tax rate is 40%. What's more, *all* of the medical expenses can be deducted on the estate tax return; there is no AGI floor for this purpose.

Of course, given the federal estate tax exemption of $11.7 million per person in 2021, most people who die in this period will not have any federal estate tax, so the costs of a final illness will probably be deducted on the final income tax return.

Pitfall

If the personal representative opts to deduct medical expenses on the decedent's income tax return, the portion that is not deductible because of the applicable percentage of AGI cannot be claimed on the estate tax return.

EXAMPLES OF NONDEDUCTIBLE EXPENSES FOR A DECEDENT

Burial fees

Cremation costs

Funeral expenses

Perpetual care for a grave or mausoleum

Where to Claim the Benefit

If the personal representative opts to deduct eligible medical expenses on the decedent's income tax return, a statement must be attached to the return agreeing *not* to claim the expenses as a deduction on the decedent's estate tax return.

Medical Insurance Rebates

Insurance companies must spend a set portion of premiums (called a medical loss ratio) on health services. If they fail to do so by overspending on salaries and other administrative costs, they are required to rebate premiums (in the form of cash or premium reductions) to policyholders. Private insurers were expected to pay out about $2.1 billion to consumers in 2021 as rebates on their 2020 coverage. Not everyone receives a rebate, but if you do, it may be tax free or taxable to you.

Benefit ⬒

If you claimed the standard deduction, any rebate is fully tax free. If you itemized deductions, the rebate is taxable to you according to the tax benefit rule (the same rule for tax refunds applies to medical insurance rebates so you can use Worksheet 16.1 to figure your taxable amount). Similarly, if you are self-employed and claimed a deduction for premiums from gross income, the rebate is taxable.

If, under an employer plan, you paid premiums through a salary reduction contribution using pretax dollars, the rebate is treated as additional compensation to you in 2021. If you used after-tax dollars, the rebate is taxed according to the tax benefit rule.

Where to Report the Rebate

If you determine that the 2020 rebate received in 2021 is taxable, do *not* amend your 2020 return. Instead report the taxable portion as "other income" on Schedule 1 of your 2021 Form 1040 or 1040-SR.

Education Costs

No one doubts the importance of education—for ourselves, our children, and our grandchildren—but obtaining it can be pricey. According to the Scholarship Workshop, the average cost of one year in a public university (in-state) for 2021–2022 is $46,770 and for a private college is $100,946, and the cost of higher education is increasing at 7% annually (compared with an overall inflation rate of about 2.25% for 2021). Fortunately, the tax law provides many incentives to help you save for education and to pay for it on a tax-advantaged basis. There has also been COVID-19-related relief with respect to student loan repayments and other measures related to education costs.

This chapter explains the tax deductions, credits, and other breaks you can claim with respect to education costs. For more information, see IRS Publication 970, *Tax Benefits for Education*.

FAFSA Submissions

If you want to apply for federal financial aid for yourself or your child, you must complete the Free Application for Federal Student Aid (FAFSA). The information on the application is based on your federal income tax return. The U.S. Department of Education made certain changes designed to ease the application process.

The deadline for submission is October 1 each year. In addition, the information on the application can be based on the *prior*-prior year's information (two years prior), instead of the prior year's information. This allows tax information from the prior-prior year to be readily available.

Example

The FAFSA form for aid in the 2022–2023 school year is based on your 2020 federal income tax return, which is filed no later than October 15, 2021 (assuming you obtained a filing extension).

You can retrieve your tax return information from the IRS electronically through Fafsa.ed.gov if you e-filed your tax return. While this option has been available for a while, the new submission deadline makes it easier for you as well as more students and their parents to use the option.

Employer-Paid Education Assistance

Companies want an educated workforce. Some are willing to underwrite the cost of additional education for their employees. The tax law not only allows companies to deduct the costs they pay on behalf of workers for higher education, but also workers can enjoy this fringe benefit tax free up to a set dollar amount each year. Education assistance includes payments toward employees' education loans.

Benefit ⊗

If your employer pays or reimburses you for the cost of higher education, you are not taxed on payments up to $5,250 annually. If the courses are job-related, there is no dollar limit to the exclusion from income for this employer-paid fringe benefit. This fringe benefit is not subject to Social Security and Medicare (FICA) taxes.

If you work for an educational institution and receive tuition reductions, such benefit may be excludable (see Conditions, next).

If your employer pays your student loan debt directly or reimburses you for it, you aren't taxed on up to $5,250 per year.

Conditions

Different conditions apply to employer-paid education under an education assistance plan and tuition reduction if you work for a college or university.

EMPLOYER-PAID EDUCATION

Employer-paid education must be furnished under an employer's education assistance plan that does not discriminate in favor of owners or highly paid employees.

The courses need *not* be job-related to qualify for the limited exclusion of $5,250 annually. For example, if you are currently a programmer and your employer pays for accounting courses, you can still exclude the benefit.

There is no dollar limit on the amount you can exclude from income if you meet the following 3 conditions:

1. The courses relate to your current job.
2. The courses do not qualify you for a new profession.
3. You have already met the job's minimum education standards.

For example, if you are a programmer who takes more programming courses, the value of this benefit is fully excludable.

TUITION REDUCTION

If you work for an educational institution, you are not taxed on tuition reductions for you, your spouse, and your dependents (as well as widows or widowers of deceased or former employees) if:

- The courses are undergraduate courses. However, if you are a graduate student who is a teaching or research assistant, you aren't taxed on tuition reduction as long as it is in addition to regular pay for your teaching or research activities.
- The benefit is *not* payment for teaching or other services. However, if you receive a scholarship under the National Health Services Corps Scholarship Program or the Armed Forces Health Professionals Scholarship Program, you can exclude any reduction despite your service requirements.

If you are eligible for tuition reduction, the benefit is not limited to courses taken at the school in which you work. You can exclude from your income the value of courses you take at any school covered by a tuition reduction agreement (area colleges and universities typically have reciprocal class agreements).

STUDENT LOAN REPAYMENT

Your employer's payment of up to $5,250 annually toward your student loan debt obtained to pay tuition and other expenses that would be tax free if the employer had originally paid them (as explained earlier) is not taxable. The payment may be made by the employer directly to the lender or as a reimbursement to you for your payments. Such student loan assistance can be done annually. This tax break is scheduled to expire at the end of 2025 unless Congress extends it.

Planning Tip

If you are seeking a job and plan to pursue college or graduate courses while working or have student loan debt to repay, look for a company with an educational assistance plan. The value of this benefit can be substantial to you if you use it fully and should be factored into the salary being offered for the position.

Example

You are in the 24% tax bracket and in 2021 your employer pays for courses totaling $5,000. If you had to pay for these courses yourself, you would need to earn an additional $6,200 in income to have the funds to pay for the courses yourself.

Pitfalls

Generally, you must attain a certain course grade for your employer to pay for the education. Make sure you understand what you must do to obtain reimbursement or have your course fully paid by your employer.

You cannot use any benefit received under an employer's plan as the basis for claiming a second tax benefit. For example, if your employer pays $2,000 for a course you take, you cannot claim an education credit for this amount.

Or if your employer pays for a student loan, you cannot deduct interest paid on that loan (explained later in this chapter).

Where to Claim the Exclusion

If employer-provided education assistance is excludable from income, it is not reported on your return. You may find the amount of employer-paid education benefits reported on your Form W-2 for information purposes only; it is not added to your compensation.

Scholarships, Fellowships, and Grants

According to some estimates there are about 1.7 million scholarships available each year. This money is available through government programs, nonprofit organizations, and corporations that support education. Grants are made on the basis of need, scholastics, or special talents (such as athletics or music). The tax law enables you to receive this money on a tax-free basis under certain circumstances.

Benefit ⊗

If you are enrolled in a degree program at a school and receive a scholarship, fellowship, or grant, you can exclude the portion of the grant for tuition, course-related fees, books, supplies, and equipment. There is no dollar limit on this exclusion.

If you receive a Fulbright award, it is fully taxable (unless you can claim the foreign earned income exclusion explained in Chapter 13).

Condition

For tax-free treatment to apply, the grant must be for study in a degree program. A degree program includes:

- Primary and secondary school
- College or university degree programs
- Full-time or part-time scholarships for study at a school that provides an education program acceptable for full-time credit toward a degree or offers a program of training to prepare students for employment in a recognized occupation

Planning Tips

For education planning purposes, obtaining a scholarship, fellowship, or grant is the best way to finance learning. The award doesn't cost you anything and doesn't have to be repaid. Explore carefully any grants to which you, a spouse, or a dependent may be entitled.

Stipends and non-tuition fellowship payments for graduate and postdoctoral students, which are not treated as taxable compensation, can be treated as such for purposes of making IRA contributions.

Pitfalls

Scholarship amounts for room, board, and incidental expenses are taxable.

If you are a graduate student who receives payment (a stipend) for teaching, doing research, or providing other services as a condition of the grant, you are taxed on the payment. Such amount is reported on Form W-2 and is subject to income tax withholding.

Generally, no exclusion can be claimed if receipt of a federal grant is conditioned on your performing services in the future. For example, if you receive a scholarship that requires you to teach for at least 3 years as a condition of the grant, you cannot exclude this grant from your income.

Where to Claim the Exclusion

If the grant is excludable from income, you do not have to report it on your return.

If the grant is partially taxable (for example, you are not a degree candidate and so are taxed on the portion of the grant for housing), you report this as other income on Schedule 1 of Form 1040 or 1040-SR. If you are a graduate student receiving a stipend for services, such amounts are reported as wages directly on Form 1040 or 1040-SR.

American Opportunity Credit

The tax law allows you to claim a limited tax credit, called the American opportunity credit, when you pay for higher education. The credit applies whether you pay out-of-pocket from savings or borrow the money. You may claim the credit each year you qualify for it.

Benefit

If you meet certain conditions and do not claim the lifetime learning credit discussed later, you can claim the American opportunity credit for higher education costs of up to $2,500 per student (100% of the first $2,000 of costs, plus 25% of the next $2,000 of costs). Thus, for example, if you have twins who are freshmen in college, you can qualify for a credit of up to $5,000.

In 2021, 40% of the credit is refundable in most situations (it can be repaid to you even though it is more than your tax liability).

Conditions

To claim the American opportunity credit, you must meet all 5 of these conditions:

1. Payments relate to the first 4 years of higher education.
2. Payments are made on behalf of an eligible student.
3. Payments are made to an eligible institution.
4. Payments cover qualified higher education costs.
5. Your modified adjusted gross income is not above a set limit.

FIRST 4 YEARS OF HIGHER EDUCATION

The credit applies for only the first 4 years of college or other postsecondary school. Thus, if a student takes 5 or more years to earn a college degree, the American opportunity credit applies only for study during the first 4 years of higher education.

Example

Your child started college in September 2018. Assuming you qualify, you can claim an American opportunity credit for tuition in 2021 because your child is still within the 4-year limit.

ELIGIBLE STUDENT

The credit may be claimed for you, your spouse, or your dependent for whom you claim an exemption on your return. The student must be enrolled for at least one academic period (a semester, trimester, or quarter) during the year.

No credit may be claimed if the student has a federal or state felony drug conviction on his or her record.

ELIGIBLE EDUCATIONAL INSTITUTION

Only payments to an eligible institution entitle you to claim the credit. This includes any accredited public, nonprofit, or proprietary postsecondary institution eligible to participate in the student aid programs administered by the U.S. Department of Education. Thus, enrollment in a foreign educational institution probably will not entitle you to claim this tax credit. Ask your school if it is eligible, or check www.studentaid.ed.gov.

Enrollment must lead to a degree, certificate, or other recognized educational credential.

QUALIFIED HIGHER EDUCATION COSTS

Qualified expenses include *only* tuition, related fees, and books, supplies, and required equipment. Related fees can include, for example, a student activity fee paid to the institution if it is required for all students and no portion of it covers personal expenses. Hobby or sports courses and noncredit courses do not qualify for the credit *unless* they are part of the student's degree program.

The following costs do *not* qualify for the credit:

- Any expenses paid with tax-free educational assistance
- Room and board (even if they are required to be paid to the institution as a condition of enrollment)

- Medical expenses
- Transportation
- Insurance
- Personal living expenses

The cost of a computer may qualify for the credit if it is needed for attendance at the school. Otherwise, it is viewed as a personal expense for which the credit cannot be taken.

As a practical matter, the institution furnishes the student with an information return showing qualified tuition and related expenses paid for the year. The return, Form 1098-T, *Tuition Payments Statement*, for 2021 is issued by January 31, 2022, and usually you need to have received the form in order to claim the credit.

If you prepay expenses for an academic period that begins within the first 3 months of 2022, you can include this amount when figuring your 2021 credit. You cannot choose to take the credit for the prepayment in 2022.

Example

In December 2021 you pay tuition for your child for the semester beginning February 2022. You can include the tuition payment as part of qualified expenses in figuring your 2021 credit.

MAGI LIMIT

The ability to claim the credit depends on your modified adjusted gross income (MAGI). MAGI for this purpose is adjusted gross income increased by the foreign earned income exclusion and other foreign items.

If your MAGI is below a phaseout range, then the full credit can be claimed; a partial credit is allowed for those with MAGI within the range. No credit can be claimed if MAGI exceeds the range. Table 3.1 shows the phaseout ranges for 2021.

TABLE 3.1 2021 MAGI Phaseout Range for Education Credits

Filing Status	MAGI
Married filing jointly	$160,000–180,000
Other filing status*	$ 80,000–90,000

*No credit may be claimed by married persons filing separately.

Planning Tips

You can claim the credit even though eligible expenses are paid with the proceeds of a loan. You can also claim the credit if eligible expenses are paid by someone other than you, your spouse, or your dependent, such as the student's grandparent. The payment is treated as having been made by the student, and as your dependent (even though no dependency exemption is deductible in 2021), this entitles you to claim the credit if you are otherwise eligible to do so.

As the parent, if you pay the expenses but your MAGI is too high to permit you to claim the credit, you can waive your right to do so. This will allow your child to claim the credit on his or her own return (assuming the child has tax liability and can benefit from the credit). Your child can claim the credit even though you pay the expenses.

Pitfalls

The credit must be coordinated with other education tax benefits you may be qualified to use. You can claim the credit in the same year in which you receive distributions from a Coverdell education savings account (ESA) or 529 plan. However, the expenses on which you base the credit cannot be the same expenses used to figure the tax-free portion of the distributions.

If you claim a credit and in a later year (after you have filed the return and claimed the credit) receive a refund of an amount that was used to figure the credit, you must recapture some or all of the credit. This means you must repay some or all of the credit. You treat the recaptured amount as additional tax liability for the year of recapture. Do not amend the return on which the credit was claimed.

> **Example**
>
> In 2021, you take an American opportunity credit of $2,500 based on $4,000 of tuition costs. In 2022, your child receives a grant reimbursing him for tuition of $1,000. You must recapture $250 (25% of $1,000). You report this recapture as "other income" on your 2022 return.

You cannot claim the credit for expenses that are paid by tax-free scholarships, fellowships, grants, veterans' educational assistance, or employer-provided educational assistance.

Where to Claim the Credit

The American opportunity credit is figured on Form 8863, *Education Credits*. The refundable portion of the credit is then entered on line 29 of Form 1040 or 1040-SR. The nonrefundable portion of the credit is entered on Schedule 3 of Form 1040 or 1040-SR.

Lifetime Learning Credit

The tax law allows you to claim a limited tax credit, called the lifetime learning credit, when you pay for higher education and do not claim the American opportunity credit. The credit applies whether you pay out-of-pocket from savings or borrow the money. You may claim the credit each year you qualify for it.

Benefit

If certain conditions are met, you can claim a credit of up to $2,000 on your return for the payment of qualified higher education costs for you, your spouse, or your dependent. In contrast to the American opportunity credit, which is a per student credit, the lifetime learning credit is per taxpayer. So if you have 3 children in college, your lifetime learning credit for the year is limited to $2,000 (assuming you qualify to claim it).

Unlike the American opportunity credit, which applies only for the first 4 years of higher education, the lifetime learning credit can be claimed for any higher education, including graduate-level courses.

Conditions

Most of the conditions for the lifetime learning credit are the same as those for the American opportunity credit detailed earlier, unless otherwise noted here. Thus, the same planning tips and pitfalls also apply.

The ability to claim the lifetime learning credit depends on your modified adjusted gross income (MAGI). For 2021, the limits for this credit are the same as the limit applicable to the American opportunity credit. If your MAGI is below a phaseout range, then the full credit can be claimed; a partial credit is allowed for those with MAGI within the phaseout range. No credit can be claimed if your MAGI exceeds the range. Table 3.1 earlier in this chapter shows the phaseout ranges for 2021.

ELIGIBLE STUDENT

There is no ban on claiming the lifetime learning credit for a student who has a felony drug conviction on his or her record, as there was for claiming the American opportunity credit.

HIGHER EDUCATION

Unlike the American opportunity credit, which can be claimed only for courses leading to a degree, the lifetime learning credit can be claimed for one or more courses at an eligible educational institution that are part of a postsecondary degree program or part of a nondegree program taken to acquire or improve job skills. In other words, the student does not need to be pursuing a degree or other recognized educational credential.

There is no limit on the number of years for which the lifetime learning credit may be claimed.

Planning Tip

Since the lifetime learning credit cannot be claimed for a student for whom an American opportunity credit is claimed, decide which credit produces the greater tax savings. Usually, this is the American opportunity credit because there is a higher credit limit ($2,500 versus a $2,000 limit for the lifetime learning credit). However, once a student is beyond 4 years of college, then there is no choice; only the lifetime learning credit can be claimed.

Pitfalls

The same pitfalls applicable to the American opportunity credit apply to the lifetime learning credit. Thus, you must receive Form 1098-T before claiming the credit.

Where to Claim the Credit

The lifetime learning credit is figured on Form 8863, *Education Credits*. The credit is then entered on Schedule 3 of Form 1040 or 1040-SR.

Work-Related Education

Americans are always trying to better themselves. If you are self-employed, you may be eligible to deduct your education costs. In the past, employees, such as teachers taking courses toward an advanced degree or a data processor learning the latest technology, could deduct education costs as a miscellaneous itemized deduction. However, no miscellaneous itemized deduction for employees is permissible for 2018 through 2025. If you are self-employed (e.g., you are a web designer and take a course on a new technology), you may be able to deduct the cost as a business expense.

Benefit ⊗

If you pay for education related to your current line of work, you may be able to deduct your expenses.

If you qualify for the deduction by meeting all of the conditions, you claim the deduction as a business expense if you are self-employed. There is no dollar limit on this deduction.

Conditions

To deduct education expenses, you must meet all 5 of these conditions:

1. You are self-employed.
2. You already meet the minimum job requirements for your work (as set by your employer or state law).
3. The courses maintain or improve your skills or you are required by your employer or by law to take the course to keep your current salary or position.
4. The courses do not lead to a new line of work.
5. You pay for eligible education expenses.

SELF-EMPLOYED

You cannot deduct the cost of courses taken before you start to work.

Working for only a short period of time before beginning an MBA program may not establish you in a trade or business. For example, the Tax Court denied a deduction for the costs of an MBA to an individual who graduated from college in 2007 and started the MBA program in 2009 after holding only short-term positions, none of which required or even related to an MBA.

MINIMUM JOB REQUIREMENTS

You must meet the minimum work requirements based on a review of your employer's standards, the laws and the regulations of your state and the standards of your profession or business.

If work requirements change after you start your trade or business, any courses you take to meet the new standards are deductible.

> **Example**
>
> You graduated from college with a degree in physical therapy and set up your own practice. Then state law is changed to require physical therapists to complete at least one year of graduate school to retain certification. You can deduct the cost of the additional year of schooling because you had already met your initial minimum job requirements.

MAINTAIN OR IMPROVE SKILLS REQUIRED BY LAW

General education courses are not deductible. The courses must be designed to keep you up to date and qualified.

Courses that give you a specialty *within* your current line of work are deductible.

EXAMPLES OF DEDUCTIBLE COURSES

- Accounting manager who obtains an MBA.
- Attorney in practice who takes LLM courses to obtain a master's degree in taxation.
- Continuing education courses by professionals.
- Dentist who takes courses in orthodontics. This postgraduate schooling improves professional skills as a dentist.
- Practicing psychiatrist who takes courses at an accredited psychoanalytic institution.
- Psychiatrist who takes personal therapy sessions.

NOT A NEW LINE OF WORK

If the courses enable you to follow a new line of work, they are not deductible.

EXAMPLES OF NONDEDUCTIBLE COURSES

- Software engineer who obtained an executive MBA.
- Law school (even by someone who intends to continue in his or her original line of work, such as accounting).
- Nurse who takes courses that qualify him to become a physician's assistant.
- NASA engineer who obtained a pilot's license (even though this helped with his engineering activities).

ELIGIBLE EDUCATION EXPENSES

If you qualify for the deduction, it is not limited to the cost of tuition and fees as is the case with many other types of education tax breaks. The deduction applies not only to the cost of courses but also to:

- Books and supplies.
- Local transportation expenses to and from the course, including bus, subway, or train fares. If you use your car, you can deduct mileage at the rate of 56¢ per mile in 2021, plus parking and tolls.
- Lodging, meals, and transportation. If you attend courses out of town, you can deduct away-from-home expenses. The deduction for meals is limited to 50% of actual cost.

Planning Tip

Monitor developments in Congress to see whether the itemized deduction for employee education costs is restored.

Pitfall

When taking continuing education courses or seminars for your work as a self-employed individual, be sure to retain proof of attendance and the costs involved.

Where to Claim the Deduction

As a self-employed person, you deduct the expenses directly as a business expense on Schedule C of Form 1040 or 1040-SR.

Student Loan Interest

Millions of students must borrow money to pay for their education. Repayment of student loans runs between 5 and 30 years. Fortunately, the tax law allows interest on student loans to be deductible each year within limits.

Benefit ⬆

If you pay interest on student loans, you may be able to deduct up to $2,500 of interest as an adjustment to gross income (if your actual interest payment is more than $2,500, your deduction is limited to that amount). There is no limit on the number of years you can claim this deduction; as long as you continue to pay off the loan, you can deduct your interest if eligible to do so.

If the loan is canceled, you may qualify for tax-free treatment on the debt forgiveness (explained later in this chapter).

If your employer pays your student loan (interest and principal) up to $5,250 under an educational assistance plan, you are not taxed on this benefit (explained earlier in this chapter).

Conditions

There are a couple of conditions for claiming a deduction for student loan interest as an adjustment to gross income. You must meet both:

1. The loan must be a qualified loan.
2. Your modified adjusted gross income cannot exceed a set limit (there is a partial deduction allowed if MAGI falls within a phaseout range).

LOAN QUALIFICATIONS

To be treated as a student loan for which interest is deductible, the loan must have been taken out solely to pay qualified education expenses. Qualified education expenses relate to a qualified educational institution (virtually all accredited public, nonpublic, and proprietary postsecondary institutions are eligible educational institutions). Qualified education expenses include:

- Tuition and fees
- Room and board
- Books, supplies, and equipment
- Other necessary expenses (including transportation to and from school)

You cannot deduct interest on a loan from a related person or made under a qualified employer plan. Related persons include:

- Spouses
- Siblings and half-siblings
- Parents
- Grandparents
- Children
- Grandchildren
- Certain corporations, partnerships, trusts, and exempt organizations

The loan must be for you, your spouse, or your dependent (in the year you take out the loan). The loan must be taken for an eligible student, who is enrolled at least half-time in a degree program.

You must be legally obligated to make payments on the loan. For example, if your child took out the loan and you are now helping her make the payments, you cannot deduct the interest because you are not the borrower (you are not

TABLE 3.2 2021 Phaseout Ranges for Student Interest Deduction

Filing Status*	MAGI
Unmarried (single), head of household, and surviving widow(er)	$ 70,000–85,000
Married filing jointly	$140,000–170,000

*You cannot claim the deduction if you are married filing separately.

legally responsible for the loan). However, your child can deduct the interest even if you make the payments (as long as your child is not your dependent).

If the loan is a revolving line of credit (e.g., credit card debt), interest qualifies as student loan interest only if funds on the line are used solely to pay qualified education expenses.

MAGI LIMITS

You can claim the full deduction if your modified adjusted gross income is below the phaseout range. A partial deduction is permitted if your MAGI is within the phaseout range. No deduction can be claimed if your MAGI exceeds the phaseout range, which is adjusted annually for inflation. Table 3.2 shows the 2021 phaseout ranges for claiming the student interest deduction.

> **Example**
>
> You are single and graduated from college in May 2021. You start to pay back your loans, paying interest in 2021 of $800. You can deduct this amount in full if your MAGI is under $70,000. If, however, you landed your dream job and earned $85,000 or more in just the 7 months remaining in 2021, you cannot deduct any of your student loan interest because your MAGI is above the limit for your filing status.

Planning Tips

If a student has taken the loan and parent, grandparent, or anyone else pays the debt, the student is treated as having made the payment and can take the student loan interest deduction (as long as the student is not a dependent and has MAGI below the threshold amount). In some instances, the cancellation of student loans can be tax free (usually the cancellation of debt is taxable). This is explained later in this chapter.

If you employer reimburses you for student loan debt under an educational assistance plan (explained earlier in this chapter), this is a tax-free fringe benefit. But you may not deduct the interest that is part of the repayment.

Repayment of student loans under federal loan programs was paused at least through January 31, 2022. A 0% interest rate was applied during this suspension.

Pitfalls

You cannot claim a double benefit for the same interest deduction. For example, if you take out a home equity loan to pay your child's college expenses, you cannot claim a student interest deduction if you deduct the mortgage interest as an itemized deduction. It is, of course, more favorable to treat the interest as student loan interest to the extent possible.

If your employer helps to pay your student loan debt and this does not fall under an educational assistance plan, this is taxable compensation to you.

If you have your federal student loan repayments paused, you may not deduct the interest that hasn't yet been paid.

Where to Claim the Deduction

The deduction is claimed on Schedule 1 of Form 1040 or 1040-SR. No special form or schedule is required.

Interest on U.S. Savings Bonds

The first savings bonds, series A, were issued in 1935 at 75% of face value in denominations of $25 to $1,000, paying 2.9% accrued interest, and were sold through the U.S. Post Office. Since then savings bonds have become a permanent investment vehicle. Today, savings bonds can be purchased only online through TreasuryDirect.gov. Sales of savings bonds have dropped dramatically since the Treasury eliminated over-the-counter sales at banks, and interest rates on these savings bonds in recent years were very modest. Nonetheless, if you happen to be holding these bonds and decide to cash them in to pay for higher education costs, you may be eligible to receive the interest tax free.

Benefit ⊗

If you redeem U.S. savings bonds to pay for qualified higher education costs or to contribute to a 529 plan or Coverdell education savings account, you are not taxed on the interest as long as your modified adjusted gross income (MAGI) is below a set amount. There is no dollar limit to this benefit; if you qualify you can exclude from income all of the interest received on the redemption of the bonds.

Conditions

Assuming you have not been reporting interest on the savings bonds annually but deferring it, you can claim the exclusion if you meet all 4 of these conditions:

1. Eligible bonds.
2. Eligible taxpayer.
3. MAGI limit.
4. Qualified use of redemption proceeds.

ELIGIBLE BONDS

The exclusion applies only to series EE bonds issued after 1989 or series I bonds. You cannot claim the exclusion when redeeming older EE bonds or E bonds.

ELIGIBLE TAXPAYER

You must be the purchaser of the bond and hold it in your name or the joint name of you and your spouse. You must have been at least 24 years old when you purchased the bonds.

No exclusion can be claimed for interest on bonds held in the child's name or in the joint name of you and your child.

If you are married, you must file jointly to claim the exclusion.

MAGI LIMIT

To claim a full or partial exclusion you cannot have modified adjusted gross income (MAGI) over a fixed dollar limit (which is adjusted annually for inflation). MAGI for this purpose means AGI increased by the redeemed interest, the deduction for student loan interest, foreign earned income exclusion and other foreign items, and the exclusion for employer-paid adoption.

Table 3.3 shows the phaseout range for 2021. If your MAGI is below the start of the phaseout range, you can claim a full exclusion. If your MAGI is over the phaseout range, no exclusion can be claimed, even if all of the other conditions are met. If your MAGI is within the phaseout range, you can claim a partial exclusion.

Example

In 2021, you are married filing jointly with MAGI of $139,800. You redeem bonds with interest of $5,000, and you use all of the redemption proceeds for qualified higher education expenses. You can exclude $2,500 of the $5,000 interest because your MAGI is in the middle of the phaseout range.

TABLE 3.3 2021 Phaseout Ranges for Savings Bond Interest Exclusion

Filing Status*	MAGI
Unmarried (single) and head of household	$83,200–98,200
Married filing jointly and surviving widow(er)	$124,800–154,800

*No exclusion can be claimed if you're married and file separately.

QUALIFIED USE OF REDEMPTION PROCEEDS

The proceeds must be used only for a qualified purpose:

- Paying higher education costs (tuition and fees for a college, university, or vocational school that meets federal financial aid standards). The higher education expenses can be for you, your spouse, or a dependent.
- Funding a 529 plan or a Coverdell education savings account.

If the proceeds from the redemption exceed the amount used for a qualified purpose, you can exclude a portion of the interest based on the ratio of expenses (or funding) to the redemption amount.

Example

In 2021, you redeem bonds worth $10,000, using $5,000 to pay your child's qualified higher education costs. Interest on the bonds is $3,000. Since half of the proceeds were used for qualified expenses, half of the interest, or $1,500, is eligible for the exclusion (assuming the other conditions are met).

Planning Tips

If you are holding EE or I savings bonds and want to know how much they are worth today, you can check their redemption values at www.savingsbonds.gov.

The U.S. Treasury has changed the way in which interest on Series EE bonds is computed. Rather than adjusting the interest semiannually, these bonds now pay a fixed rate until redemption or maturity. As a result, Series I bonds may be a better option because their interest rate still adjusts semiannually for inflation.

You can purchase I bonds via a direct deposit of your tax refund into a TreasuryDirect account used for this purpose. Just provide the IRS with the account information, and your refund will be transferred directly to your account. Bonds can be purchased only in multiples of $50; there is a $5,000 limit on purchases using a tax refund.

Interest on savings bonds is *never* subject to state income tax (such interest is always exempt).

Pitfalls

You cannot use this exclusion to pay college expenses for your grandchild *unless* the grandchild is your dependent in the year in which the bonds are redeemed.

You cannot claim the exclusion if you are married and file a separate return from your spouse.

Where to Claim the Exclusion

If you claim the exclusion, you must complete Form 8815, *Exclusion of Interest from Series EE and I Bonds Issued after 1989*, and attach it to your return.

Coverdell Education Savings Accounts

Is the high cost of a prep school or college in your child, niece or nephew, or grandchild's future? If you decide to help save for this expense, consider doing so using a tax-advantaged savings account, called a Coverdell education savings account (ESA), designed for this purpose.

Benefit

You may be able to contribute up to $2,000 annually to a savings account for each beneficiary. The account is called a Coverdell education savings account (ESA) (it used to be called an education IRA). The account can have multiple contributors, but no more than $2,000 can be placed in the account for any one year.

Earnings on contributions accumulate tax deferred. If withdrawals from the account are used to pay qualified education expenses, the earnings become tax free.

Conditions

There are a couple of conditions for funding a Coverdell education savings account as well as for taking tax-free distributions.

1. For purposes of contributions, they can be made only on behalf of an eligible beneficiary (defined next) by a contributor whose modified adjusted gross income does not exceed set limits. Contributions must be made in cash, not property.
2. For purposes of tax-free distributions, funds must be used only for eligible expenses.

ELIGIBLE BENEFICIARY

Generally, a beneficiary is a person who is under the age of 18 at the time the contribution is made. Thus, for example, if a beneficiary attains the age of 18 on July 1, 2021, contributions can be made through June 30, 2021.

TABLE 3.4 MAGI Phaseout Ranges for Coverdell ESA Contributors

Filing Status	MAGI Phaseout Range
Married filing jointly	$190,000–220,000
Other taxpayers	$ 95,000–110,000

A beneficiary can also be a special needs person over the age of 18. A special needs beneficiary is one who requires additional time to complete his or her education because of a physical, mental, or emotional condition. This would include, for example, a person with a learning disability.

MAGI FOR CONTRIBUTORS

There is no familial requirement for contributors. Anyone can make a Coverdell education savings account contribution on behalf of an eligible beneficiary, as long as the contributor meets MAGI limits. Contributions can even be made by the beneficiary herself.

In order to contribute the full $2,000 to a Coverdell education savings account, your modified adjusted gross income cannot be more than a set limit. MAGI for this purpose means adjusted gross income increased by the foreign earned income exclusion, the foreign housing exclusion or deduction, the exclusion for income from American Samoa, or the exclusion for income from Puerto Rico.

A reduced contribution limit applies if your MAGI falls within a phaseout range. No contribution can be made if your MAGI exceeds the phaseout range, which is not adjusted annually for inflation. The MAGI phaseout range for Coverdell ESA contributors may be found in Table 3.4.

Example

In 2021, you are a single parent with MAGI of $80,000. You can make a $2,000 contribution on behalf of your 12-year-old child. But if your MAGI is between $95,000 and $110,000, only part of the $2,000 may be contributed (you figure the limit using a worksheet provided in IRS Publication 970).

CASH CONTRIBUTIONS

Contributions must be made in cash; you cannot contribute property to a Coverdell ESA. If you own stocks or mutual funds, you must sell the property and invest the proceeds. You may incur a capital gain on the sale of property.

ELIGIBLE EXPENSES

Coverdell education savings accounts can be used for education in grades K–12 and/or for higher education without any dollar limit. Primary and secondary school can be public, private, or religious school.

The range of eligible expenses for which tax-free withdrawals can be made is quite broad. Just about anything related to education is a qualified expense.

EXAMPLES OF ELIGIBLE ELEMENTARY AND SECONDARY SCHOOL EXPENSES

Academic tutoring

Books

Computer and peripheral equipment; software only if it is predominantly educational in nature

Extended day programs required or provided by the school

Internet access

Special services for a special needs beneficiary

Supplies

Transportation

Uniforms

EXAMPLES OF ELIGIBLE HIGHER EDUCATION EXPENSES

Books, supplies, and equipment

Room and board

Tuition and fees

Planning Tips

You can open a Coverdell education savings account at any bank or other financial institution that has received IRS approval to offer Coverdell ESAs. You can then select the investments you prefer, from certificates of deposit to stocks and mutual funds (to the extent available from the institution you select).

Just like IRA contributions, contributions to Coverdell ESAs can be made up to the due date of the return for the year to which they relate. However, obtaining a filing extension does not extend the deadline for making contributions.

Example

Contributions for 2021 may be made only up to April 18, 2022, even if the contributor and/or the beneficiary has obtained a 6-month filing extension.

You can turn taxable custodial accounts into tax-free Coverdell education savings accounts by using the funds in the custodial account for contributions. However, only cash contributions are permitted to a Coverdell education savings account, so investments in the custodial accounts must first be sold so that the proceeds can be contributed.

Example

Junior has $5,000 in a custodial account that owns shares in a mutual fund, the earnings from which are reported annually as taxable income to Junior. He can opt to sell $2,000 from the mutual fund in his custodial account each year and contribute the proceeds to a Coverdell education savings account of which he is the designated beneficiary (assuming he meets the age and MAGI limits). The account can own shares in the same mutual fund, but now the earnings become tax deferred and, if funds are withdrawn for qualified expenses, they become tax free.

You can change accounts from one financial institution to another by means of a tax-free rollover. You may not be satisfied with the service or investment options you have at one financial institution and can switch by means of a rollover to another financial institution.

You can move money in a Coverdell ESA between certain beneficiaries on a tax-free basis. The amount withdrawn from a Coverdell ESA can be rolled over to the same or a new designated beneficiary who is a member of the original beneficiary's family (listed in the next section). The rollover must be completed within 60 days. There are no tax consequences to naming a new designated beneficiary (as long as such beneficiary is permissible).

You can fund contributions to a Coverdell ESA by means of a direct deposit of a tax refund. For example, say you are owed a refund on your 2021 return. Use the refund to contribute to a Coverdell ESA (assuming you meet eligibility requirements) by filing the return early enough for the IRS to process it and electronically transfer the refund to the Coverdell ESA by April 18, 2022, for a 2021 contribution (you can also use the 2021 tax refund to make a 2022 contribution if your income allows it and the beneficiary will not have aged out of eligibility).

Anyone who receives a military death gratuity or payment under the Servicemen's Group Life Insurance (SGLI) program can contribute this amount to a Coverdell ESA; the usual contribution limit and MAGI limit do not apply in this case.

Pitfalls

While distributions can be used to pay for primary and secondary school expenses, they cannot be used for home schooling.

If you contribute more than $2,000 on behalf of a beneficiary within one year, the excess amount is subject to a 6% excise tax (this is a penalty). The penalty is paid by the beneficiary (not the contributor). But the penalty can be avoided by withdrawing the excess contribution, plus any earnings on the contribution, before the beginning of the 6th month following the year of the contribution (e.g., by May 31, 2022, for 2021 contributions).

Example

In 2021, Aunt Mary contributes $2,000 to a Coverdell ESA for Amy. Unaware of Aunt Mary's contribution, Uncle Ed also contributes $2,000 to a Coverdell ESA for Amy in 2021. Amy can avoid the 6% excise tax on the excess $2,000 contribution by withdrawing it, plus any earnings, by May 31, 2022. (Whether she chooses to give it back to Aunt Mary or Uncle Ed or split it between them is up to Amy.)

The 6% excise tax continues to apply each year in which excess contributions (and earnings on excess contributions) remain in the Coverdell ESA.

Taxable distributions, which are withdrawals made to pay for noneligible expenses, are not only taxed as ordinary income but are subject to a 10% additional tax. However, the 10% penalty does not apply to distributions that meet any of these conditions:

- Distributions are made to a beneficiary or to the estate of a designated beneficiary on or after the death of a designated beneficiary.
- Distributions are made because the designated beneficiary is disabled.
- Distributions are made because the designated beneficiary received a tax-free grant or educational assistance allowance that equals or exceeds the distribution.
- Distributions are taxable only because the qualified expenses are reduced by expenses taken into account in figuring an education credit.

Withdrawals from a Coverdell ESA can be made in the same year in which an education credit is claimed. However, the same expenses cannot be used for both benefits.

Withdrawals from both a Coverdell ESA and a 529 plan are permitted in the same year. But if total withdrawals exceed qualified higher education expenses, the expenses must be allocated between the Coverdell ESA and 529 plan to figure the taxable portion of the withdrawals. Generally, the allocation is based on the ratio of the Coverdell ESA withdrawals to the total withdrawals.

Example

In 2021, Henry begins college and withdraws $800 from a Coverdell ESA and $3,200 from a 529 plan to pay $3,000 of eligible expenses. Of the $800 withdrawn, $600 is tax free: $800 Coverdell ESA withdrawal ÷ $4,000 total withdrawals = 0.2; 0.2 × $3,000 qualified expenses = $600.

Funds remaining in the account become taxable to the beneficiary within 30 days of attaining age 30 (or within 30 days of death if the beneficiary dies before age 30). The 30-year age limit does not apply to a special needs beneficiary (defined earlier).

However, tax on the earnings in the account can be avoided if the balance in the account is transferred to another eligible beneficiary within 60 days of attaining age 30 (or death if earlier). An eligible beneficiary for this purpose includes members of the beneficiary's family:

- Spouse
- Child or stepchild
- Grandchild
- Brother, sister, half-brother, or half-sister
- Niece or nephew
- Parent or stepparent
- Grandparent
- In-laws and the spouses of any of the listed relatives

Where to Claim the Exclusion

Contributions to a Coverdell education savings account are not reported on the return of the contributor or the beneficiary. Similarly, withdrawals that are not taxable are not reported on any return.

If contributions are subject to the 6% excise tax, the beneficiary figures the excise tax in Part V of Form 5329, *Additional Taxes on Qualified Plans (Including IRAs) and Other Tax-Favored Accounts*, and reports it on Schedule 2 of Form 1040 or 1040-SR.

If withdrawals from a Coverdell ESA are taxable, they are reported on the beneficiary's return as "other income" on Schedule 1 of Form 1040 or 1040-SR.

If they are also subject to the 10% additional tax, this amount is figured in Part II of Form 5329, *Additional Taxes on Qualified Plans (Including IRAs) and Other Tax-Favored Accounts*.

Qualified Tuition Programs (529 Plans)

You can help save for the higher education expenses of your child or grandchild using a tax-advantaged account called a 529 plan. The 529 plan is a qualified tuition program offering federal (and in some cases state) tax incentives for savings.

Benefit ⊗

There are 2 types of qualified tuition programs (QTPs): a prepayment plan under which payments are guaranteed to cover (or partially cover) tuition, regardless of tuition increases, and a savings-type plan in which the funds you will have available to pay for education depend on the investment performance of your account. From a tax perspective, however, both types of plans are governed by the same tax rules under Section 529 of the Internal Revenue Code (hence the name "529 plans"), and both types of plans have the same benefits and conditions.

While contributions to qualified tuition programs do not generate a federal income tax deduction or credit, the long-term benefits are considerable:

- Earnings within the plan are tax deferred.
- If funds in the plan are used to pay qualified education costs, they are tax free (the earnings on the contributions are never taxed in this case).
- Unused amounts can be transferred tax free to another beneficiary if the original beneficiary does not go to college or otherwise need the funds.

There may be state income tax breaks for the contributions to qualified tuition programs as well. For example, if you are a resident in New York, you can deduct contributions to the New York 529 College Savings Program up to $5,000 per taxpayer per year on your New York state income tax return. Of the states with income taxes, only the following do not offer a deduction or credit for contributions: California, Delaware, Hawaii, Kentucky, New Jersey, and North Carolina (Massachusetts offers a deduction only through 2021).

Conditions

Most conditions and requirements are fixed by each state's own 529 plan. However, for tax purposes, there are a couple of key conditions to obtaining all of the benefits under a qualified tuition program:

1. Contributions can be made only to qualified tuition programs. There are no federal tax limits on annual or total contributions to a 529 plan. These limits are fixed by each state's unique program (e.g., California's plan has a $529,000 cap per beneficiary in 2021 and no contributions can be made once the plan reaches this cap).
2. Distributions can be withdrawn only for qualified expenses.

QUALIFIED TUITION PROGRAMS

Contributions can be made only to state plans and IRS-approved private college/university plans. A personally devised plan, even one that mimics the investment strategies of the state plans, does not entitle you to these benefits.

At present, all states offer savings-type plans and nearly 2 dozen have prepaid tuition plans.

QUALIFIED EXPENSES

For distributions from qualified tuition programs to be tax free, they must be used only to pay for qualified expenses. For higher education purposes, these include tuition, fees, books, supplies, computers and technology (e.g., Internet access), and room and board (if the student is enrolled at least half time). Withdrawals from a 529 plan to pay for a computer, Internet access, or the like are not for qualified expenses, so they are taxable. There is no set dollar limit on these expenses, including room and board. Thus, any reasonable amount for room and board (including expenses of off-campus housing) can qualify.

Qualified expenses also include costs associated with registered apprenticeships, even though these are not considered "higher education." And qualified expenses include student loan repayments up to a set limit. This is $10,000 in a lifetime for the beneficiary and the same for each of the beneficiary's siblings.

For 2018 through 2025, funds in 529 plans can be used for tuition at private or religious primary and secondary schools (grades K–12) up to $10,000 annually. The dollar limit applies per student, so if a student is a beneficiary of more than one 529 plan, only $10,000 can be used annually for the student without any federal income tax on the distribution.

Planning Tips

The terms and conditions of qualified tuition programs vary considerably from state to state. You can learn about the investment options, fees, and other rules on state 529 plans at www.savingforcollege.com. For details on the private 529 plan created by a consortium of private colleges and universities (nearly 300 schools participate), go to www.privatecollege529.com.

If you plan for your child to attend your alma mater on a legacy basis, ask the school whether it offers or plans to offer a tuition prepayment plan.

For purposes of the federal financial aid formula, funds in 529 plans are not considered to be the assets of the student.

Qualified tuition programs can be used effectively for estate planning purposes. For example, a wealthy grandparent can reduce the size of his or her estate while funding an education savings plan for a grandchild with little or no gift tax cost. If you plan to make sizable contributions in one year, you can elect to treat the contributions as made equally over 5 years. This will entitle you to apply the annual gift tax exclusion, which is $15,000 in 2020 ($30,000 for married persons making joint gifts), 5 times to avoid or reduce gift tax.

Example

In 2021, when the annual gift tax exclusion is $15,000 per beneficiary, you contribute $75,000 (or $150,000 per couple) to a state savings plan for your grandchild. Since you can treat the $75,000 as having been made ratably over 5 years, there is no taxable gift in this transfer. The transfer is fully offset by the annual gift tax exclusion ($15,000 × 5).

If the contribution exceeds this limit, the excess amount is treated as a gift in the year the contribution is made.

Amounts in a 529 plan can be transferred to a new beneficiary or rolled over tax free within 60 days of a distribution. There is a limit of one transfer or rollover per year. However, a beneficiary can be changed without making a transfer or rollover; the new name is substituted for the old one on the same account. This option applies only if the new beneficiary is a member of the old beneficiary's family, which includes:

- Child or grandchild
- Stepson or stepdaughter
- Sibling or stepsibling
- Parent or grandparent
- Stepparent
- Aunt or uncle
- Niece or nephew
- Son-in-law, daughter-in-law, father-in-law, mother-in-law, brother-in-law, or sister-in-law
- The spouse of any relative on this list
- First cousin

In the case of a savings-type 529 plan, if the account declines in value from the amount contributed, the loss may be recognized when all of the funds in the account are distributed. The IRS says that the loss is treated as a miscellaneous itemized deduction on Schedule A of Form 1040 or 1040-SR, which is deductible to the extent total miscellaneous itemized deductions exceed 2% of adjusted gross income, but cannot be deducted in 2021 due to the suspension of this deduction. Some tax experts believe that the loss is simply claimed as an ordinary loss. This theory has yet to be tested in court.

You can change investment selections once a year, and whenever there is a change in beneficiary.

For 2018 through 2025, amounts in a 529 plan can be rolled over tax free to an ABLE account if the ABLE account beneficiary or this designated beneficiary's family member is the beneficiary of the 529 plan. Any amount rolled over counts toward the overall limit on annual contributions to an ABLE account. Because such rollover is counted, it probably isn't a good idea to do it and instead fund the ABLE account; this maximizes the overall savings for the beneficiary.

Funds within 529 plans offer asset protection in case of bankruptcy. Contributions to the plan made at least one year but less than 2 years before filing for bankruptcy are protected up to $5,000. Contributions made 2 years or more before filing for bankruptcy are fully protected (no dollar limit applies). All contributions made within one year of filing for bankruptcy are at risk.

Pitfalls

If funds are withdrawn from a 529 plan and *not* used for qualified education expenses, earnings on the distribution are taxable. For example, if part of a distribution is used for spending money or travel expenses, the earnings on this portion of the distribution are taxable.

Example

If $25,000 is withdrawn and $20,000 is used for qualified expenses while $5,000 is used for spending and travel money, earnings on the $5,000 portion of the distribution are taxable.

In addition, the portion of the distribution representing earnings on contributions is subject to a 10% penalty. However, both the tax and the penalty on a refund made by the institution (e.g., because the student receives a scholarship) can be avoided by redepositing the funds in the 529 plan within 60 days of receipt.

Withdrawals from a 529 plan can be made in the same year in which an education credit is claimed, but the same expenses cannot be used for both benefits.

If withdrawals are made from a 529 plan and Coverdell ESA in the same year and the total withdrawal exceeds qualified education expenses, a portion of the withdrawal is taxable. How to figure the taxable portion was explained earlier in the Coverdell Education Savings Accounts section, under "Pitfalls."

The permissible distribution up to $10,000 annually for primary and secondary school tuition does not apply to home schooling expenses. And be sure to check on the state income tax treatment of distributions for primary and secondary school tuition (some states are taxing them).

Where to Claim the Exclusion

Contributions to qualified tuition programs are not reported on the return of the contributor or the return of the beneficiary.

Distributions from qualified tuition programs are not reported if they are tax free. To figure the tax-free portion of distributions, you can use a worksheet for this purpose in IRS Publication 970. For any year in which distributions are made, the 529 plan must send you (and the IRS) an information return, Form 1099-Q, *Qualified Tuition Program*. For distributions in 2021, the form must be issued no later than January 31, 2022.

ABLE Accounts

If you have a disabled child or are under age 26 and meet certain eligibility conditions, you can have a special savings account that generally does not adversely impact eligibility for means-tested government programs (e.g., Medicaid). The ABLE account is similar to a 529 savings plan (discussed earlier in this chapter), but differs in several ways. An ABLE account can be used on a tax-free basis for education and job training, as well as other qualified disability expenses. And funds can be transferred up to a limited amount from a 529 plan to an ABLE account on a tax-free basis, as explained earlier in this chapter. See details in Chapter 2.

Seminars

You've seen the ads: Attend a seminar to learn all about this subject or that. While some seminars are free of charge, others can cost hundreds or even thousands of dollars. From a tax standpoint, the cost of seminars is deductible only under limited circumstances.

Benefit 🔃

Work-related seminars may be deducted if the conditions for work-related education discussed earlier in this chapter are met.

No deduction can be claimed for seminars on self-improvement that are not work-related. No deduction can be claimed for investment seminars.

Where on the Return to Claim the Deduction

See work-related education for self-employed individuals discussed earlier in this chapter.

Educational Travel

Travel was severely curtailed in 2020 by COVID-19, but picked up somewhat in 2021. Saint Augustine said, "The world is a book, and those who do not travel read only a page." Taxwise, the cost of travel usually is a nondeductible personal expense. But there are exceptions for which the cost of travel may be deductible.

Benefit

They say travel is broadening (a century ago, wealthy young men and women used to "take the grand tour" as a coming-of-age lesson). From a tax perspective, however, a deduction for educational travel is extremely limited. As a general rule, no deduction can be claimed for educational travel. However, this ban does not apply to overseas courses and lectures, the cost of which may qualify for a work-related education deduction for a self-employed individual.

Conditions

To be deductible as work-related education, travel must meet all of the conditions discussed earlier in this chapter.

Planning Tip

Overseas courses need not be taken for credit to qualify for a deduction. For example, an English teacher who took a course on Greek myths in Greece taught by university professors was allowed a deduction for her travel expenses and course registration fees even though she did not take the courses for credit (this case arose when employees were able to deduct education costs as miscellaneous itemized deductions.).

Pitfall

No deduction can be claimed for travel that is merely beneficial. For example, an architect who travels to Europe to view cathedrals there cannot deduct the cost of the trip as an education expense.

Where to Claim the Deduction

See work-related education for self-employed individuals discussed earlier in this chapter.

Cancellation of a Student Loan

It's been estimated that outstanding student loan debt totals more than $1.71 trillion. If you are facing mountains of debt from student loans and have opted to get out from under by taking a particular job, you may be able to not only have your loans canceled, but have them canceled without any tax cost to you.

Benefit

Normally, the cancellation of a loan results in taxable income to the borrower. But under certain conditions, the cancellation of a student loan can be tax free. There is no dollar limit to this benefit.

> **Example**
>
> You take out a government loan to obtain your teaching license. The loan is forgiven if you work for 5 years as a teacher on a Native American reservation. This debt forgiveness is *not* income to you if you complete the required years of work.

Conditions

You can exclude the debt forgiveness on your student loan from income if you are required to work for a set period of time in a certain profession (e.g., nursing, medicine, law, or education) for any of a broad class of employers.

The loan must have been made by a qualified lender, which includes:

- The government (federal, state, or local government or an agency of the government)
- A tax-exempt public benefit corporation
- An educational institution if the loan is made under an agreement with the government or a tax-exempt public benefit corporation or under a program designed to encourage students to serve in occupations or areas with unmet needs

There is another way in which the cancellation of student loan debt is not taxable. For discharges in 2018 through 2025, there is no income from the cancellation of this debt on account of the death or total and permanent disability of the student. Loans eligible for this tax-free discharge are those made by a qualified lender listed above as well as a private education loan (Section 140(7) of the Consumer Protection Act).

Planning Tips

Make sure you fully understand your work obligation in order to secure tax-free treatment for cancellation of your student loan.

Due to COVID-19, the U.S. Department of Education provided repayment deferrals of certain federal student loans at least through January 1, 2022. The interest rate during this suspension period is 0%. If borrowers choose to make repayments during this period, 100% of the payments are applied toward principal. This suspension period does not apply to loans from private lenders or to certain federal student loans (e.g., Perkins Loans) owned by private lenders.

Pitfalls

If you satisfy only part of the required work and a portion of the loan is forgiven anyway, you must include that portion in income.

Don't assume that filing for bankruptcy will erase your student loan debt. A discharge for student loan debt in bankruptcy may be allowed for undue hardship. And an appellate court also allowed a discharge under a new interpretation of the bankruptcy law.

Where to Claim the Benefit

If the loan forgiveness is tax free, you do not report anything on your return. If cancellation of your student loan is not tax free, you must include the debt forgiveness in income on your return. Report it as other income on Schedule 1 of Form 1040 or 1040-SR. Generally, debt forgiveness that is not tax free is reported to you (and to the IRS) on Form 1099-C, *Cancellation of Debt*.

Penalty-Free Withdrawals from IRAs

Distributions can be taken from an IRA before age 59½ if the funds are used to pay qualified higher education costs for yourself, your spouse, or dependent. The Tax Court has said that funds used to buy a computer are *not* a qualified expense where its use is not required for any course and access to computer-posted course syllabi can be done through school computers in the library.

Withdrawals can be taken penalty-free only in the year in which you pay the expenses.

Government Reimbursements

If you have a disabled child who cannot receive adequate education in your school district and you are reimbursed by your school district for the costs of special education, you are *not* taxed on this reimbursement. Since federal law requires schools to provide special education, you are treated as if you incur the costs on behalf of the school district.

Internships and Apprenticeships

If you're paid while learning on the job, your wages are includible in gross income, but the value of your training is not taxable. The U.S. Department of Labor estimates that the value of training through a registered apprenticeship program is $40,000 to $150,000.

As mentioned earlier in this chapter, distributions from 529 plans can be taken tax free to cover the costs of registered apprenticeship programs.

COVID-19-Related Grants

Emergency financial aid grants made by a federal or state agency, Indian tribe, higher education institution, or scholarship-granting organization (including a tribal organization) to undergraduate and graduate students because of an event related to the COVID-19 pandemic are not taxable. They are treated as qualified disaster relief payments.

However, because they are not taxable income, they cannot be the basis on which to take any deduction or credit, such as the American opportunity credit or the lifetime learning credit.

Your Home

Home ownership is part of the American dream. According to the U.S. Census Bureau, 65.4% of Americans owned their own homes in the second quarter of 2021. There are many reasons that we want to own rather than rent a home—for example, as a way to build up equity. And with COVID-19 causing many individuals to work from home, having a good place to do it has meant being a homeowner for many individuals. But there are also sound tax reasons favoring home ownership. Certain expenses of home ownership are deductible. And when you sell your home, some or all of your profit may be tax free. If you had problems with your mortgage or lost your home to foreclosure, there may be special tax breaks for you.

This chapter explains the tax breaks you can claim with respect to your home. Disaster losses that can befall your home, and the deductions you can claim for them, are explained in Chapter 12. The home office deduction for using a portion of your home for business is explained in Chapter 14. Work-related moving expenses (other than for military personnel) are not deductible for 2018 through 2025.

For more information, see IRS Publication 521, *Moving Expenses*; IRS Publication 523, *Selling Your Home*; IRS Publication 530, *Tax Information for First-Time Homeowners*; IRS Publication 936, *Home Mortgage Interest Deduction*; and IRS Publication 4681, *Canceled Debts, Foreclosures, Repossessions, and Abandonments*.

Mortgages

Mortgages are a way to leverage yourself into home ownership: The bank or other lender (called the mortgagee) lends you the funds needed to buy your home over and above your out-of-pocket investment. You become the mortgagor and each month repay a portion of the principal (the money you borrowed), plus interest. While your repayment of principal is *never* deductible, you may be able to deduct your interest payments.

Benefit 🖁

Interest on your home mortgage may be fully deductible as an itemized deduction. There is no dollar limit on the amount of interest you can deduct annually, but there are limits on the size of the mortgage on which the interest is claimed. The mortgage interest rule applies to both fixed and adjustable rate mortgages.

The amount of acquisition indebtedness on which interest is deductible depends on when the loan was obtained:

- For loans obtained before October 14, 1987: No loan limit. As a practical matter, most of these old mortgages have been fully repaid by now.
- For loans obtained after October 13, 1987, and before December 16, 2017: $1 million.
- For loans obtained after December 15, 2017: $750,000.

The limits apply to your main home and one other residence. If unmarried co-owners jointly own a home, each can use the applicable limit on acquisition indebtedness. For example, if a brother and sister bought a home together on

May 1, 2017, with a $2 million mortgage, each can deduct interest on $1 million of the loan. In effect, the limit applies per residence(s).

A special limitation applies to distressed homeowners, as explained later.

Conditions

For interest to be fully deductible, you must meet 4 conditions:

1. Acquisition indebtedness (which is usually a mortgage used to buy or build your home) cannot exceed the limits explained earlier.
2. The debt must be secured by the residence.
3. You deduct interest on no more than 2 residences.
4. You are personally obligated for repayment of the debt.

ACQUISITION INDEBTEDNESS

Acquisition indebtedness is usually a mortgage obtained to buy, build, or substantially improve a home (subject to the 2-residence limit). If you use the funds to construct your home, only interest paid during the 24-month period starting with the month in which construction begins is deductible. Interest paid before or after this 24-month period is not acquisition indebtedness; it is treated as nondeductible personal interest.

Example

In May 2021, you buy land to build your dream home and obtain a construction loan in June. Construction begins in September 2021, and the home is completed in June 2022. On your 2021 return, you may deduct interest on the loan starting with interest in September 2021, the month in which construction began. Since the home is completed within 24 months, interest for January 2022 through the end of construction is deductible on your 2021 return.

If a loan is taken out within 90 days after construction is completed, it may still qualify in full as acquisition indebtedness. It qualifies as acquisition indebtedness to the extent of construction expenses incurred within the last 24 months before the completion of the home, plus expenses through the date of the loan.

Example

Same as the preceding example, except that in July 2021 you refinance the loan. Since the loan is obtained within 90 days after building completion, it qualifies as acquisition indebtedness, and interest is deductible.

How much renovation is required to be considered a substantial improvement to the home? There is no clear rule. Generally, if you add a room, convert an attic, garage, or basement to living space, or renovate a kitchen, you can safely treat interest on the loan as acquisition indebtedness. Just about any type of capital improvement that adds to the basis of your home constitutes a substantial improvement; a repair is not a capital improvement, and a loan to make repairs is not acquisition indebtedness.

A home for this purpose isn't limited to a single-family dwelling. It also includes a condominium or cooperative unit, houseboat, mobile home, or house trailer as long as it has sleeping, cooking, and toilet facilities.

DEBT SECURED BY THE HOME

The loan must be secured by your main or second home in order for interest on the loan to be deductible. "Secured" means that the loan is recorded in your city, town, or county recording office or the loan satisfies similar requirements under your state's law that gives the lender the right to foreclose against your home if you fail to repay the loan.

TWO-RESIDENCE LIMIT

A deduction for mortgage interest is limited to 2 residences: your main home and a second residence. If you have more than 2 homes, you can select which of the additional homes to designate as your second residence for interest deduction purposes. Obviously, it pays to designate the home with the larger interest payments (assuming the total amount of debt on the two homes does not exceed your applicable dollar limit discussed later). You can change your designation from year to year.

If a married couple files jointly, they can designate a second residence as a home even if it is owned or used by one of them. But if they file separately, each spouse generally may deduct interest on debt secured by one home unless they agree in writing to allow one spouse to deduct interest on the main home plus a second residence.

If you rent out a home during the year but use it for personal (nonrental) purposes for more than 14 days or 10% of the rental days, you can treat the home as a personal residence for which the interest is deductible. In counting rental days, include any days that the home is held for rental. In counting personal days, include any days your home is used by close family members.

Example

In addition to your main home, you own a beachfront condominium that you rent out through a rental agency 2 weeks each year at the start of the summer season. You spend the balance of the summer at your unit, so your personal use is sufficient for your home to be treated as a personal residence despite the rental. You can designate your condo as your second residence and deduct interest on the mortgage on the condo.

PERSONAL LIABILITY

To deduct interest on a home mortgage you must be personally obligated for its repayment. If, for example, you are financially unable to obtain a mortgage so your parents help you out by obtaining the loan, you cannot deduct mortgage interest (even if you pay the lender directly rather than repaying your parents). Only they can deduct the interest.

One case did allow a homeowner to deduct interest on a loan obtained by a brother because the homeowner had a poor credit rating, but the facts in the case were unique; the homeowner was contractually obligated to his brother to pay off the mortgage.

DOLLAR LIMIT

The amount treated as acquisition indebtedness on which interest can be deductible is the total amount of such debt on your principal residence and designated second home. As explained earlier in this chapter, the time the mortgage is taken determines the dollar limit of the loan on which interest is deductible.

For loans obtained before October 14, 1987, there is no loan limit; most of these loans have already been fully repaid. For loans obtained after October 13, 1987, and before December 16, 2017, the dollar limit is $1 million. And for loans obtained after December 15, 2017, the dollar limit is $750,000.

Example

In January 2021, you take out a $500,000 mortgage to purchase a main home. The loan is secured by the main home. In February 2021 you take out a $250,000 loan to purchase a vacation home. The loan is secured by the vacation home. Because the total amount of both mortgages does not exceed $750,000, all of the interest paid on both mortgages is deductible. However, if you took out a $250,000 home equity loan on the main home to purchase the vacation home, then the interest on the home equity loan (explained later in this chapter) would not be deductible.

If the total amount of acquisition indebtedness exceeds the applicable dollar limit, then only a percentage of the interest is deductible based on this formula:

$$\frac{\text{Applicable dollar limit}}{\text{Total acquisition indebtedness}} \times \text{Interest payment}$$

Example

In January 2021, you take out a $500,000 mortgage to purchase a main home. The loan is secured by the main home. In February 2021, you take out a $500,000 loan to purchase a vacation home; the loan is secured by the vacation home. Total interest paid in 2021 is $60,000. Because the total amount of both mortgages exceeds $750,000, your deductible interest is: $45,000 ($750,000/$1,000,000 x $60,000).

DISTRESSED HOMEOWNERS

A distressed homeowner is someone who is at risk of foreclosure because of delinquent mortgage payments. Such a homeowner may obtain certain mortgage assistance, such as a reduction or suspension of payments or a loan modification to reduce the outstanding balance (and in turn, the amount of monthly payments). The IRS has created a safe harbor for determining the amount of mortgage interest a distressed homeowner can claim. The safe harbor runs through 2021 (unless this is extended). More specifically, such a homeowner may deduct the lesser of:

- Actual home mortgage interest payments to the mortgage servicer or the state housing finance agency (HFA)
- Amounts shown on Form 1098 for mortgage interest received, real property taxes, and mortgage insurance premiums (if otherwise deductible by the homeowner). States may issue Form 1098-MA, *Mortgage Assistance Payments*, in lieu of Form 1098.

Planning Tips

Think hard about the type and amount of mortgage you want to take out when you buy your home. Once you have purchased your home, additional financing generally doesn't qualify as acquisition indebtedness.

If you refinance home acquisition debt, the refinanced amount is treated as home acquisition debt, but only up to the amount of the balance of the old mortgage principal just before the refinancing. If you take out equity by refinancing for a higher amount than the outstanding balance and don't use the funds to substantially improve the home securing the debt, then only interest on the refinanced amount is deductible.

Example

Your home today is worth $500,000 and the remaining balance of your old mortgage is $200,000. If you refinance for $350,000 and use $50,000 of the proceeds to buy a personal car, take a vacation, and pay off some credit card debt, you can deduct interest on only $300,000 ($200,000 of acquisition indebtedness and $100,000 of home equity debt).

When you sell your home, look at the settlement papers to determine the interest charged up to the date of sale so that you don't overlook any interest deduction you may be entitled to claim.

Pitfalls

You cannot deduct your interest if you claim the standard deduction; you must itemize deductions to claim this benefit.

You cannot deduct mortgage fees that you paid to obtain the loan, such as the cost of an appraisal, a credit report, or loan assumption fees. But points paid to obtain the mortgage may be deductible, as discussed later.

You cannot deduct interest on mortgage assistance payments made on your behalf under Section 234 of the National Housing Act.

The IRS has a good idea about what your initial mortgage was because the outstanding mortgage balance at the start of the year and the loan origination date are reported by the lender to the IRS and you on Form 1098.

A married person filing separately has an interest deduction limit on borrowing up to one-half the applicable dollar limit for acquisition indebtedness (e.g., $500,000 for pre-December 16, 2017, mortgages; $375,000 for post-December 15, 2017, mortgages), even if the other spouse does not claim *any* mortgage interest deduction.

Where to Claim the Deduction

You deduct home mortgage interest on Schedule A of Form 1040 or 1040-SR. The amount of mortgage interest is reported annually to you by the lender on Form 1098, *Mortgage Interest Statement*, or for distressed homeowners, Form 1097-MA, *Mortgage Assistance Payments*.

Mortgage Interest Tax Credit

The government's policy is to encourage home ownership. To help low-income people become homeowners, the government offers certain assistance, including the opportunity to claim a tax credit for mortgage interest.

Benefit ✚

Even better than deducting your mortgage interest, you may be eligible for a tax credit of up to $2,000 of home mortgage interest paid through mortgage interest certificates. These certificates are issued to certain homeowners as a means of encouraging home ownership. The credit may be claimed regardless of whether you itemize your personal deductions or claim the standard deduction.

If you received a mortgage credit certificate from your state or local government in connection with the purchase or renovation of your main home, you may be entitled to claim a tax credit with respect to your mortgage interest. The amount of the credit is the percentage shown on your mortgage credit certificate multiplied by the lesser of:

- Interest you paid during the year on your actual loan amount
- Interest you paid on the loan amount shown on your mortgage credit certificate

The credit cannot be more than $2,000 if the percentage shown on your mortgage credit certificate is 20% or more.

You must reduce your deduction for home mortgage interest by the amount of any credit you claim.

Conditions

You can claim this tax credit only if you meet 2 conditions:

1. You have received a mortgage credit certificate from your state or local government ("qualified mortgage credit certificate").
2. Your home meets certain requirements ("qualified home").

QUALIFIED MORTGAGE CREDIT CERTIFICATE

Qualified mortgage interest certificates are issued by a state or local government or agency under a qualified mortgage credit certificate program designed to help low- and moderate-income people become homeowners. You qualify for the credit only if you receive a qualified mortgage credit certificate (MCC). Certificates issued by the Federal Housing Administration, the Department of Veterans Affairs, and the Farmers Home Administration as well as Homestead Staff Exemption Certificates do not qualify.

QUALIFIED HOME

The home must be your main home. The value of your home cannot exceed a certain value:

- A value of 90% of the average area purchase price
- A value of 110% of the average area purchase price in certain targeted areas

Planning Tips

If you are thinking about buying a home but do not know if you can afford the payments, you may be able to swing a deal if you qualify for this type of government assistance. For information about special financing programs, visit the U.S. Department of Housing and Urban Development at www.hud.gov/buying/insured.cfm.

To find out whether you are eligible for a mortgage credit certificate, contact your local housing or redevelopment agency or ask your local real estate agent for information.

If you qualify for the credit and it exceeds your tax liability without regard to other tax credits, you do not lose the credit. Instead, you can carry the excess amount forward to be used in a future year if you are also eligible for the credit in that year.

If you refinance your mortgage, you do not lose your eligibility to claim the credit if your certificate is reissued and the reissued certificate meets 5 conditions:

1. It must be issued to the original holder of the existing certificate for the same property.
2. It must entirely replace the existing certificate (you cannot retain any portion of the outstanding balance of the existing certificate).
3. The certified indebtedness on the reissued certificate cannot be more than the outstanding balance on the existing certificate.
4. The credit rate of the reissued certificate cannot be more than the credit rate of the existing certificate.
5. The reissued certificate cannot result in a larger amount of interest than is otherwise allowable under the existing certificate for any year.

Pitfalls

You must reduce your deduction for home mortgage interest by the amount of the credit.

If you own your home jointly with a person who is not your spouse, you must divide the credit between the two of you according to your respective ownership interests. If you each own a 50% interest in the home, then you are each entitled to one-half of the credit.

If you buy a home using a mortgage credit certificate and sell it within 9 years, you may have to repay some of the credit.

Where to Claim the Credit

You figure the credit on Form 8396, *Mortgage Interest Certificate*, and enter the amount of the credit on Schedule 3 of Form 1040 or 1040-SR.

If you are subject to recapture of the credit because you sold your home within 9 years of using the mortgage credit certificate, you must complete Form 8828, *Recapture of Federal Mortgage Subsidy*. You report the recaptured amount on Schedule 2 of Form 1040 or 1040-SR.

Home Equity Loans

Equity is the amount of money you would receive, over and above any outstanding mortgage, if you were to sell your home today. Equity is built up in 2 ways: by paying down a mortgage on the home and by appreciation in property values. As your equity increases, you may be able to tap into it *without* selling the home by using a home equity loan. This loan may be the only loan on the property or it may be a second or even third loan in addition to any other home mortgage.

No deduction is allowed for interest on a home equity loan in 2018 through 2025. This is so regardless of when the loan was obtained. However, if the funds are used to buy, build, or substantially improve your main home or second home and the loan is secured by the home, the interest is deductible subject to the overall limit on acquisition indebtedness discussed earlier in this chapter.

Example

In May 2021, you took out a home equity loan to pay off credit card debt and take a vacation. No interest on this loan is deductible in 2021. However, if you used the funds to add a room to your main home and the total amount of your mortgage plus home equity loan does not exceed $750,000 (the applicable limit for post-December 15, 2017, loans), then all the interest is deductible.

Points

"Points" are additional charges for acquiring a loan. Each point is 1% of the loan amount. In general, the more points you pay, the lower your interest rate on the loan. Points generally are deductible; the only question is *when* they can be deducted.

Benefit

When you take out a mortgage, you may pay points to the lender. Points paid to obtain a home mortgage are deductible as part of your itemized interest deduction. However, points in some cases are deductible in full in the year in which they are paid while in other cases they must be amortized (deducted ratably) over the term of the loan.

Conditions

First determine whether the payment qualifies as "points" (defined next). Then see if the points can be deducted in full in the year of payment or must be deducted over the term of the mortgage.

IMMEDIATE DEDUCTIBILITY

If the loan is taken to buy, build, or substantially improve your main home, you may deduct the points in the year of payment if you meet the following conditions:

- Points are charged for interest and not for services performed by the lender. The designation of the payment, as points, loan origination fees, or otherwise, is not controlling of the tax treatment; it is the purpose for which the money is charged that governs whether you can treat points as interest.

- The loan is secured by your main home. If the loan relates to a second home, you cannot fully deduct the points in the year of payment.

- The charging of points is an established business practice in the geographical area in which you are located.

- The amount of points is computed as a percentage of the loan and specifically earmarked on the loan closing statement as points, loan origination fees, or loan discount.

- You pay the points directly to the lender. Points withheld from the loan proceeds used to buy your main home are treated as having been paid directly to the lender. Points withheld from loan proceeds used to substantially improve your main home are not immediately deductible; you must pay the points with other funds to secure a full deduction in the year of payment. Points paid by the seller are not treated as paid directly to the lender but rather are viewed as an adjustment to the purchase price of the home.

DEDUCTIBLE OVER THE TERM OF THE LOAN

As long as the payments meet the definition of points (e.g., are not fees for services performed by the lender), but cannot be deducted in full in the year of payment (or you opt not to deduct them in full), they are deducted over the term of the loan.

Example

In January 2021, you pay points of $3,600 to obtain a 30-year mortgage for your vacation home. You must amortize the points over 360 months and can deduct $10 per month each year until you've deducted all of the points or pay off the mortgage.

The following are situations in which you amortize the points rather than fully deduct them in the year of payment:

- To buy a second home.
- To substantially improve your main home but the points are withheld from the mortgage.
- To refinance an existing mortgage.
- To buy your main home but you elect to amortize the points.

Planning Tips

If you pay points to buy your main home, you are not required to deduct them in full in the year of payment. You can opt to amortize them over the term of the loan. You may wish to make this election if you can't benefit from the deduction in the year of payment. This might occur if you buy your home late in the year and your total itemized deductions do not exceed your standard deduction amount. Another reason to opt to amortize is if your acquisition indebtedness (plus points) in the year you paid the points is over your applicable dollar limit for purposes of deducting mortgage interest.

When you are financing a mortgage and are faced with the option of paying higher interest with little or no points or a lower interest rate but some or substantial points, which option should you select? The answer usually depends on how long you plan to remain in the home (how long you will be paying the mortgage). To help you make this decision based on your circumstances, use a mortgage points calculator (you can find one at www.dinkytown.net/java/MortgagePoints.html).

Pitfall

If you refinance your loan with a new lender and have been amortizing points over the term of a previous loan (for example, this is your second or third refinance), be sure to deduct the remaining balance of the unamortized points.

Example

In January 2017, when rates had declined below your original mortgage rate, you refinanced your outstanding balance for a new 15-year mortgage, paying $1,800 in points. In July 2021, you refinance again. On your 2021 return, be sure to deduct the unamortized points of $1,260: $1,800 ÷ 180 months = $10 per month; 4 years, 6 months × $10 = $540; $1,800 − $540 = $1,260.

Where to Claim the Deduction

You deduct points along with your home mortgage interest on Schedule A of Form 1040 or 1040-SR. There is a separate line on Schedule A to list your points if they are not included on Form 1098 with your other home mortgage interest.

Prepayment Penalties

It costs a lender money to make a loan, which it expects to recoup through interest collected during the term of the loan. But if a borrower pays off a loan within a short time of obtaining it (generally under 2 years), the lender has not had time to recoup its lending costs. To protect the lender against a quick payoff, prepayment penalties may be owed. The prepayment penalties are spelled out in the mortgage note at the time of obtaining the mortgage. From the borrower's perspective, the tax law looks favorably on prepayment penalties, allowing them to be deductible if certain conditions are met.

Benefit

If you pay off your mortgage or home equity debt before you are required to, there may be a prepayment penalty as specified in your mortgage papers. Prepayment penalties are treated as deductible interest. They are a set amount of interest: for example, 6 months of interest on 80% of your outstanding loan balance if you pay off the mortgage before a set term (usually one to 2 years). For the rules on deducting interest on your home or second home, see earlier in this chapter.

Conditions

There are no special conditions to meet for deducting prepayment penalties. Simply refer to the rules discussed earlier in this chapter on how to treat mortgage interest.

Planning Tip

Think ahead. When taking out a mortgage, check whether there are any potential prepayment penalties. You may be able to get the lender to delete these from the loan agreement. This is important because you may have to relocate before you had planned and do not want to incur this needless cost.

Pitfall

Don't sign any mortgage loan agreement before finding out if there are prepayment penalties. One common scam by unscrupulous lenders is nondisclosure of prepayment penalties, which can run as much as 6 months of interest on up to 80% of the outstanding loan balance. Such a high penalty can keep you locked into a mortgage when you otherwise could have refinanced for a lower mortgage rate.

Where to Claim the Deduction

Assuming that the prepayment payment penalty is deductible, you claim it with your home mortgage interest on Schedule A of Form 1040 or 1040-SR. The amount of mortgage interest is reported annually to you by the lender on Form 1098, *Mortgage Interest Statement*.

Late Payment Penalties

Under the terms of a loan, if a payment is late for any reason the borrower may owe additional amounts called late payment penalties. There are different types of late payment penalties: a flat fee, such as $50, charged without regard to the amount of the late payment or how long it is outstanding, and a percentage fee, fixed with regard to the late payment. The percentage fee continues to be assessed each month that a payment remains delinquent. Only late payment penalties qualifying as "interest" may be deductible.

Benefit

If you are late in making a payment, you may be charged a penalty by the lender. Generally, penalties for delinquent payments are treated as deductible interest, which can be written off if you itemize your deductions.

Example

Your monthly mortgage payment is $1,000, which is subject to a 2% late payment penalty. Due to unexpected financial reverses, you fail to make your payment for June, July, and August. In September, you're back on your feet and pay up all outstanding amounts, including the late payment penalties of $120 (June payment: 2% of $1,000 × 3 months; July payment: 2% of $1,000 × 2 months; August payment: 2% of $1,000 × 1 month). Since the late payment penalties are an interest charge, they are deductible.

Condition

Late payment penalties are treated as deductible interest as long as they are not imposed for a specific service provided by the lender. If they are a flat charge imposed regardless of how late the delinquency may be, they are viewed as a nondeductible service charge rather than as deductible interest.

Planning Tip

Even though late payment penalties can be deductible, you should try to avoid them if possible. The deduction does not fully offset your payment. One way to do so is to arrange for mortgage payments to be debited automatically from your checking account.

Pitfall

Being late on making your mortgage payments can cost you more than late payment penalties. Being late can adversely affect your credit rating and hurt your ability to obtain a loan or even get a job within 2 years or so of the late payment. Usually if your payment is no more than 30 or 60 days late, it likely won't seriously affect your FICO score if it occurs only once or twice, although it may stay on your credit report for about 2 years. However, if you are 90 days late even once, your credit rating will suffer; the late payment will stay on your credit report for up to 7 years.

Where to Claim the Deduction

Assuming that the late payment penalty is deductible, you claim it with your home mortgage interest on Schedule A of Form 1040 or 1040-SR. The amount of mortgage interest is reported annually to you by the lender on Form 1098, *Mortgage Interest Statement*.

Mortgage Insurance

If you put less than 20% down to purchase your home, you may be required to carry private mortgage insurance (PMI) or mortgage insurance from a government agency on the shortfall to protect the lender from a default. The cost of PMI typically runs from 0.6% to 0.8% of the loan amount. Payments of mortgage insurance may result in a tax deduction.

Benefit

Premiums for PMI paid can be deducted as mortgage interest by those with adjusted gross income below a threshold amount. There is no dollar limit on the amount of the deduction for this expense.

Conditions

To qualify for this itemized deduction, 2 conditions must be met:

1. The insurance must be first obtained after 2006 and through 2021. This insurance is available through commercial insurers as well as through federal loan programs such as the Veterans Administration (VA), the Rural Housing Administration (RHA), and the Federal Housing Administration (FHA).
2. To claim the full deduction, your adjusted gross income cannot exceed $100,000 ($50,000 for married persons filing separate returns). Any deduction is reduced by $1 for each dollar in excess of the AGI limit; no deduction is allowed if AGI exceeds $109,000 ($54,500 for married persons filing separate returns).

Planning Tip

PMI may be a way to help you buy a home even though you haven't yet saved the full down payment.

Once the equity in your home, from making payments on your mortgage as well as appreciation in property value, reaches 20%, cancel the mortgage insurance.

Pitfall

There is no downside to claiming this deduction if it is extended. But even so, if your acquisition indebtedness is above your applicable dollar limit, you won't be able to deduct your PMI unless it's amortized. Of course, this isn't likely for those with AGI below the limit applicable for deducting PMI.

Where to Claim the Deduction

The deduction is reported on Schedule A of Form 1040 or 1040-SR.

Looking Ahead

The deduction for mortgage insurance expires at the end of 2021 unless it's extended by Congress. Check the Supplement for any update.

Reverse Mortgages

Homeowners who are at least 62 years old and have little or no mortgage left on their primary residence can access the equity that has built up in their home over the years by obtaining a reverse mortgage. As the name implies, you receive money from a lender but do not have to repay it immediately; usually repayment is postponed until you move from your home or die. Proceeds of the mortgage can be made to you in a lump sum, as monthly payments, or as a line of credit that you can draw on to the extent needed.

Benefit

Proceeds received from a reverse mortgage are tax free. There are no dollar limits on the amount that is tax free, but there are limits on how much of a reverse mortgage you can obtain, based on your age, the current interest rate, and the appraised value of your home.

Conditions

To qualify for a reverse mortgage, you must be at least 62 years old and own a primary residence. There are no income limits on eligibility.

Planning Tip

To learn more about reverse mortgages from the U.S. Department of Housing and Urban Development (HUD), go to www.consumer.ftc.gov/articles/0192-reverse-mortgages.

Pitfall

Even though interest accrues on funds borrowed under a reverse mortgage, no deduction can be claimed until repayment is made.

Where to Claim the Benefit

You do not have any tax reporting with a reverse mortgage when you obtain the loan proceeds. You report (and deduct) interest only when you actually pay it. Reporting rules on mortgage interest are explained earlier in this chapter.

Cancellation of Mortgage Debt

During the subprime mortgage debacle more than a decade ago, thousands of Americans lost their homes. During the pandemic, millions of homeowners stopped paying their mortgages, but whether this ultimately led to foreclosures and loan forgiveness was unclear at the time of publication. Keep in mind that the CARES Act allowed homeowners with mortgages backed by Fannie Mae or Freddie Mac to ask for reduced or suspended mortgage payments for up to 12 months without fees or penalties, with similar relief available to mortgages backed by the Department of Veterans Affairs.

Homeowners are usually personally liable for the amount of the mortgage, even though the lender can foreclose, sell the home, and use the sale proceeds to pay down the debt. Unfortunately, the borrower may still owe money on the loan after foreclosure (the home sale may not cover what's due). Generally, when the lender forgives a portion of the outstanding mortgage, a practice that lets the borrower off the hook, this debt forgiveness is considered to be ordinary income for tax purposes. However, under a special law, forgiven debt on a main home may not be taxable.

Benefit ⊗

If you are not personally liable on the mortgage debt, then forgiveness of debt does not result in any income. There are more than a dozen states with anti-deficiency laws that make the forgiven debt to a homeowner not recourse and, therefore, nontaxable.

If you are personally liable on the debt, forgiveness is treated as tax-free income within the limits that follow.

Conditions

There are 2 conditions for tax-free treatment:

1. The forgiven debt must have been used to buy, build, or substantially improve your main home and the debt must have been secured by the home. If a debt has been refinanced, the amount qualifying for this tax break is limited to the mortgage principal immediately before the refinancing.
2. The limit in 2021 on qualifying debt is $750,000 ($375,000 for a married person filing separately).

Planning Tip

Debt forgiveness can apply to a so-called short sale, which occurs when the amount of the outstanding debt is greater than the value of the home (what a lender would realize if the home were sold). The short sale avoids the need for foreclosure. Also, some lenders will work with a homeowner to reduce the mortgage balance or change the terms of the loan so the homeowner can stay in his or her home. If there is any cancellation of debt, it can be tax free to the same extent as cancellation related to a foreclosure.

Pitfalls

The tax break on forgiven debt does not apply to a second home, rental property, or business property. You may still have to recognize gain if the home was foreclosed upon and the amount realized on the sale is greater than your basis in the home. The fair market value of the property (reported to the borrower in

Box 7 of Form 1099-C, *Cancellation of Debt*) is treated as the amount realized on the sale. If you sell your home at a loss, you cannot deduct the loss; it is a nondeductible personal loss.

However, if any part of the mortgage is forgiven in conjunction with the sale, the resulting income can be excluded if the conditions stated earlier apply.

Where to Claim the Benefit

Forgiven debt is reported to you by the lender on Form 1099-C. To claim the exclusion, complete Form 982, *Reduction of Tax Attributes Due to Discharge of Indebtedness* (instructions to the form point out the specific lines applicable to home mortgage debt forgiveness). There is no income from debt cancellation to report on the return; just attach the completed Form 982 to the return.

Penalty-Free IRA Withdrawals for Home-Buying Expenses

If you thought IRAs were for retirement only, you'd be wrong. The tax law lets you tap into your IRA for certain special reasons without incurring any penalty (although withdrawals are subject to tax). One of those reasons is to buy a home.

Benefit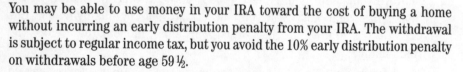

You may be able to use money in your IRA toward the cost of buying a home without incurring an early distribution penalty from your IRA. The withdrawal is subject to regular income tax, but you avoid the 10% early distribution penalty on withdrawals before age 59½.

Condition

You can withdraw only up to $10,000 free from penalty from your IRA. This is a once-in-a-lifetime opportunity. If you have already used this break to buy a previous home, you can't use it again.

You must spend the $10,000 on qualified first-time home-buying expenses, such as a down payment to purchase a home. These are expenses used to buy, build, or rehabilitate a main home for yourself, your spouse, child, grandchild, or ancestor (parent or grandparent) of you or your spouse. Such person cannot have had an ownership interest in a principal residence within 2 years before the purchase, construction, or renovation of the new home.

Planning Tip

Use this tax break only as a last resort. Once you withdraw the funds from the IRA and spend them on home-buying expenses, you cannot replace the funds in your retirement savings account. In effect, you lose the opportunity to build up your retirement savings.

Pitfalls

If you take a withdrawal from your IRA with the intention of using the money to buy a home but the sale falls through, you become taxed on the money unless you redeposit it back in the IRA. You have 120 days from your initial withdrawal to redeposit the funds. And, if you're under age 59½, the distribution is also subject to a 10% penalty.

When a couple is buying a home together, each must be a first-time home-buyer for the penalty exception to apply.

Where to Claim the Benefit

If you take money from your IRA, you must file Form 5329, *Additional Taxes on Qualified Plans (Including IRAs) and Other Tax-Favored Accounts*. You report total early distributions from your IRA. You can then subtract those exempt from the 10% penalty because you used them for qualified first-time home-buying expenses. You must indicate which exception to the 10% penalty you are relying on (a number is assigned to each exception, and these numbers are listed in the instructions to this form).

Real Estate Taxes

Property owners are charged real estate taxes to cover government services related to the property. Local property taxes may include city, town, and/or county taxes; school taxes; and even other charges (such as fire or sewer district taxes). Fortunately, the tax law allows property owners to deduct these taxes as an itemized deduction, subject to an overall limit on the deduction for state and local taxes.

Benefit ⊜

Your burden of paying local property taxes, including city, town, and/or county taxes and school taxes, can be eased somewhat by deducting your payments.

If you itemize deductions, you can deduct real estate taxes you pay on your main home and any other home you own. There are no limits on the number of homes for which you can claim the deduction. However, the deduction for all state and local taxes, referred to as SALT (real estate taxes, income or sales taxes, and personal taxes) is capped at $10,000 ($5,000 for married persons filing separately). (Congress is considering a change to the SALT cap. Check the Supplement for any update.) The deduction for real estate taxes on your residence and vacation homes is claimed as an itemized deduction (you cannot use this benefit if you claim the standard deduction).

If you pay real estate taxes on a rental property, it is deductible against your rental income, regardless of whether you itemize your personal deductions.

Conditions

You must be the owner of the home so that you are obligated for the payment of the tax. If you buy the property at a tax sale, you cannot start to deduct property taxes until you receive title to the property under state law (typically following a redemption period).

If you pay the seller's unpaid back taxes when you purchase the home, you cannot deduct this payment as your taxes. You can add the payment to your basis in the home used for figuring gain or loss when you sell it.

In the year that property is sold, real estate taxes must be allocated between the buyer and the seller. (Generally this allocation is reflected in your closing papers.)

- The seller can deduct taxes for the portion of the year through the day before the date of sale.
- The buyer can deduct taxes for the portion of the year commencing with the date of sale.

Generally, if you rent rather than own your home, you cannot deduct the portion of the rent that the landlord uses to pay the property taxes. However, in Hawaii you can do so if the lease runs for 15 years or more. Also, as a tenant in California you can deduct your payments if you have your name placed on the tax rolls and agree to pay the tax directly to the taxing authority.

Planning Tips

Consider prepaying an upcoming tax bill before the end of the year to increase your current deductions. For example, you can pay your January 2022 property tax bill in December 2021 to increase your deductions for 2021, assuming this does not put you over the SALT cap explained earlier (and likely obtain a discount for paying early).

If you are self-employed and claim a home office deduction, part of the real estate taxes is taken into account in figuring that deduction. But because of the SALT cap, there are certain computational complications (see Chapter 10).

Ask your city or town whether you qualify for any property tax reductions or rebates. Some areas provide them on the basis of age (reduction for seniors), veteran status, or for some other reason. Some locations even suspend real estate taxes for seniors entirely until the home is sold (e.g., when the owner dies or relocates). Generally, a reduction or rebate is not automatic; the homeowner must apply for it. The amount saved because of a property tax reduction or rebate is *not* treated as income; it merely lowers the amount you pay for real estate taxes and, in turn, the amount of your itemized deduction for real estate taxes.

Pitfalls

If you make payments to the lender that are held in escrow and disbursed to the taxing authority, you can only deduct real estate taxes when the lender makes the disbursements (not when you pay the lender).

If the title to your home is in the name of one spouse and the other spouse pays the real estate tax bill, the deduction can be claimed only if you file a joint return. Since the party paying the tax isn't the legal owner of the home, the tax may not be deducted on a separate return.

Special assessments by homeowners associations for the purpose of maintaining common areas or special assessments by municipalities for certain government services (water, sewage, or garbage collection) are not deductible as real estate taxes.

Do not prepay real estate taxes if you itemize and are subject to the alternative minimum tax (AMT). Since taxes are not deductible for AMT purposes, prepaying them can trigger or increase your AMT liability. You effectively lose the benefit of claiming the deduction.

If you receive a homestead tax credit from your state based on a percentage of your real estate taxes, the IRS says that the credit is treated for federal tax purposes as a reduction in your state income tax. This limits the amount of state income tax you can claim as an itemized deduction on your federal income tax return; it doesn't change your deduction for real property taxes.

Some states have tried to create workarounds for the SALT limit using charitable contribution deductions. The IRS has nixed the charitable contribution workaround (see Chapter 6).

Where to Claim the Deduction

You deduct your payment of real estate taxes on your residence and vacation homes as an itemized deduction on Schedule A of Form 1040 or 1040-SR. You deduct real estate taxes on rental properties on Schedule E of Form 1040 or 1040-SR.

In the year you sell property, if your share of real estate taxes is paid in advance by the buyer, the lender or real estate broker will generally include this information on Form 1099-S, *Proceeds from Real Estate Transactions*. But this form is not required to be filed for all sales, so you should keep track of this information (check your settlement papers).

Each year that you own property you do *not* receive any official information return notifying you of the amount of taxes you paid during the year. As a practical matter, if you make payments to a commercial lender to cover real estate taxes, your annual tax payments will be detailed in a year-end statement sent to you by the lender.

Cooperative Housing

Cooperative housing, also called a co-op, is a form of home ownership. You become a tenant-stockholder in a cooperative housing corporation (CHC) that owns and runs a multiunit housing complex. Your shares entitle you to exclusive use of your housing unit, plus access to common areas. There are tax breaks unique to this form of home ownership.

Benefits

You may experience 2 levels of deductions—one that is allocated to you from the CHC and the other that you obtain through your direct payments. For example, you may incur 2 interest deductions—one for your share of interest on debt of the CHC (e.g., for common areas) and one for the purchase of your unit that you financed through a bank. This section discusses only your allocated deduction; deductions for your direct payments are included in other sections of this chapter (e.g., home mortgage interest).

Condition

The only condition for claiming a deduction for CHC expenses allocated to you is ownership of shares in the CHC.

Planning Tip

Tenant-stockholders in cooperative housing corporations are usually treated the same in the tax law as homeowners of condominiums and single-family homes.

Pitfalls

While a tenant-shareholder of an apartment in a cooperative housing corporation can deduct his/her share of the co-op's real estate taxes, a federal appeals court has decided that these taxes are *not* deductible for purposes of the alternative minimum tax (AMT). Even though the AMT rules do not specifically bar a deduction, these taxes are treated in the same manner as if the taxes had been paid directly by the owner of a single-family home. There had been speculation that coop owners could skirt the SALT cap. However, an IRS letter to a Congressional office said that the limit on deducting state and local taxes applies to taxes allocated to coop owners and deducted on their returns.

Where to Claim the Deduction

You claim a deduction for your share of the CHC's mortgage interest and real estate taxes allocated to you on Schedule A of Form 1040 or 1040-SR as a "Miscellaneous Itemized Deduction," which is deductible in 2021 because it is not subject to the 2%-of-AGI limitation.

The CHC should provide you with Form 1098, *Mortgage Interest Statement*, to show your share of these expenses.

Minister's Housing Allowance

Members of the clergy of any recognized faith or denomination who receive assistance with their housing costs, through free use of a home or payments toward these living costs, may qualify for a tax break. Their housing allowance, sometimes referred to as a parsonage allowance, may be a nontaxable fringe benefit of their job. An estimated 44,000 ministers, rabbis, imams, priests, and others take advantage of this tax break.

Benefit

You are not taxed on the rental value of a home provided to you by your religious institution—this is tax-free income to you. If you receive an allowance for housing, you can exclude the amount used to pay rent, make a down payment to buy a house, or make mortgage payments, or for utilities, real estate taxes, or repairs to the home. There is no dollar limit on this exclusion.

Conditions

You must be a duly ordained minister and acting in that capacity. A rabbi or cantor is treated as a minister for purposes of this exclusion. Retired ministers can qualify for the exclusion if the housing allowance is made in recognition of past services. A minister acting as a teacher or an administrator of a parochial school or seminary qualifies for the exclusion if the school is an integral part of a church organization.

Church officers who are not ordained cannot qualify for the exclusion. Ordained ministers who are working as executives of nonreligious organizations cannot claim the exclusion even if they perform religious duties. For example, a minister-administrator of an old age home not under church authority could not claim the exclusion.

The religious institution (e.g., church or local congregation) must designate the part of your compensation that is the housing allowance. This designation must be made in advance of the payments to you. Designation can be made in an employment contract, minutes, a resolution, or a budget allowance.

Planning Tip

If you pay mortgage interest and/or real estate taxes, you can claim deductions for these payments even if you finance them with the tax-free housing allowance. You must itemize your deductions to write off mortgage interest and real estate taxes on your home, as explained in this chapter.

Pitfalls

Even though the housing exclusion is not subject to income tax, it is treated as self-employment income for purposes of Social Security and Medicare taxes. If you use a church-provided home tax free, figure the rental value for purposes of self-employment taxes at what you would pay for similar quarters in your area, including utilities and garage or parking space, if any.

Claiming the housing allowance can have an adverse impact on your business deductions. The portion of business deductions allocable to the tax-free housing allowance is not deductible.

> **Example**
>
> Your salary as a minister is $25,000. You also receive a $25,000 housing allowance. Your work-related expenses are $6,000. You can deduct only $3,000. Since half of your income is tax free, only half of the expenses are deductible.

Where to Claim the Exclusion

If you can exclude the benefit, you do not have to report anything on your return. If you receive an allowance in excess of the amounts used for housing expenses, you must include the excess as part of your salary reported on Form 1040 or 1040-SR.

Home Sale Exclusion

Homeowners are highly favored under the tax law. Not only can they deduct certain costs of home ownership, such as mortgage interest and property taxes, but they can also receive tax-free income when they sell their homes. A special rule permits a limited amount of gain from the sale of a main home to escape federal income tax. And this tax break can be used over and over again within certain limits. Home sales in 2021 soared, with many realizing substantial profits, some or all of which may be sheltered by the home sale exclusion.

Benefit ⊗

If you sell your home for a profit, you may avoid tax on some or all of your gain as long as you meet certain conditions. More specifically, you do not pay any tax on a gain up to $250,000 from the sale of your home ($500,000 on a joint return or by a surviving spouse if the sale is within 2 years of the other spouse's death) if you owned and used the home as your main residence for at least 2 of the 5 years preceding the date of sale. The amount you exclude is tax-free income to you.

Conditions

To be eligible to use the full exclusion amount of $250,000 ($500,000 on a joint return or for a surviving spouse), you must meet all 3 conditions:

1. The home must be your main home ("principal residence").
2. You owned your home for at least 2 years prior to the sale.
3. You used your home as your main home for at least 2 years prior to the sale.

If you acquired your home in a tax-free exchange, the ownership and use periods must be 5 full years (instead of 2 of 5 years) before qualifying for the exclusion.

If you are a member of the uniformed services, Foreign Service, or intelligence community, or are a Peace Corps volunteer, you can elect to suspend the 5-year testing period for the ownership and use tests for up to 10 years.

MAIN HOME

Your main home is the one in which you primarily dwell. If you own 2 or more homes, you must determine which one is your primary residence. This determination is usually based on which one you live in for the greater part of the year. However, this isn't a bright line test; you can use other factors to show that the home you used less of the time is your main home. Such factors include:

- Where you work or own a business
- Where your family members reside
- The address you use for your federal and state income tax returns
- The address you use for your bills and correspondence
- Where you have your driver's license and voter registration
- The location of religious institutions and clubs you belong to

Your main home isn't limited to a single-family dwelling. You can treat as your main home a mobile home, trailer, houseboat, or condominium apartment used as your primary residence. Even stock in a cooperative housing corporation is subject to this rule as long as you live in the cooperative apartment or house as your main home.

If you change the title to your home, you don't necessarily lose the opportunity to claim the exclusion.

- If you transfer ownership of your home to a grantor trust, one in which you are treated as the owner of the trust and report all of the trust's income on your personal tax return, the trust can use the exclusion provided you meet the ownership and use tests.

- If you transfer ownership of your home to a single-member limited liability company, again, the LLC can use the exclusion provided you meet the ownership and use tests. The LLC is treated as a "disregarded entity" for tax purposes so you report all of the LLC's income on your personal tax return.

- If you divorce and the title to the home is changed from your spouse's name or joint name to your name alone, you can include the period of your spouse's ownership in meeting the ownership test.

- If you are a surviving spouse, you can use the $500,000 exclusion amount if you sell the home within 2 years after your spouse's death. But if you sell in a later year, you are limited to the $250,000 exclusion.

OWNERSHIP TEST

You must own your home for at least 2 years in the aggregate prior to the date of sale. This means that you owned the home for a full 24 months or 730 days (365×2) during the 5-year period that ends on the date of sale. The periods of ownership and use need not be continuous or identical.

If you are married and file a joint return, only one spouse is required to meet the ownership test to qualify for the exclusion as long as both satisfy the use test.

USE TEST

You must use your home as your primary residence for at least 2 years in the aggregate prior to the date of sale. This means that you lived in the home for a full 24 months or 730 days (365×2) during the 5-year period that ends on the date of sale. The periods of ownership and use need not be continuous or identical.

Example

In November 2017, you purchased your home and lived there until September 2019, when you took a 1-year sabbatical overseas. You returned to your home in September 2020 and lived there until you sold the home in December 2021. You meet the use test because you lived in your home for 26 months (10 months before the sabbatical and 16 months after it).

Temporary absences (for example, a 3-week vacation) are ignored. This is true even if you rent out your home while you are away.

If a homeowner becomes incapacitated before meeting the 2-year use test and resides in a licensed care facility, the full home sale exclusion can be used as long as the homeowner used the home for at least one year prior to moving from the home and meets the 2-year ownership test.

PARTIAL EXCLUSION

Even if you sell before meeting the full 2-year ownership and use tests, you may be eligible to use a prorated exclusion amount for the period of your ownership and use. A partial exclusion is allowed if you sell early because of:

- *Change in jobs.* If you relocate for a new job or a new business (if self-employed), you automatically are treated as having a qualified change in jobs if the distance test used for the moving expense deduction (explained later in this chapter) is met. The distance between your new job location and your former home must be at least 50 miles greater than the distance between your old job location and your former home. If your spouse, co-owner, or person who resides with you has a change of jobs, you can qualify for the exclusion.

- *Health reasons.* The change must be medically motivated (for example, your doctor recommends a change so you can receive medical or personal care for an illness or injury). A change that is merely beneficial to your health (for example, moving to a warmer climate) isn't viewed as a health reason for purposes of using the partial exclusion. Again, the health of your spouse, co-owner, or person who resides with you can be taken into account in determining your eligibility for the partial exclusion.

- *Unforeseen circumstances.* If you are forced to sell because of events beyond your control, you can use the partial exclusion. Such events include, but are not limited to: Your home is destroyed through acts of war or terrorism, someone in your household dies or goes on unemployment benefits, you become unable to pay basic living expenses because of a change in employment (e.g., being furloughed for 6 months) or self-employment, there is a legal divorce or separation, you have multiple births resulting from the same pregnancy, you must have a larger home to meet adoption agency requirements, you received death threats at the current address, you must leave a senior retirement home so your young grandchild can live with you, you must move to a home that can accommodate your paralyzed mother's disability, you are forced to sell because of pressure from neighbors, you experience excessive airport noise that was not disclosed by the seller, or you become part of a blended family or have additional children that cannot be accommodated in your current home.

Planning Tips

If you have owned your home for a long time and paid down the mortgage, your gain may exceed your exclusion amount. You can minimize your gain by adding to the basis of your home any capital improvements you've made to it.

EXAMPLES OF CAPITAL IMPROVEMENTS

Addition of a deck, garage, porch, or room

Appliances

Duct work

Fencing

Heating and cooling systems

Kitchen and bathroom modernization

New roof

Paving the driveway

Retaining wall

Satellite dish

Security system

Septic system

Smart home features (LED lighting, smart locks)

Soft-water system

Storm doors and windows

Walkway

Well

Wiring upgrade

If you subdivide your property, selling off vacant land separately from the parcel on which the home is situated, you can claim the exclusion for the sale of the vacant land and the sale of the home provided they occur within 2 years of each other. However, only one exclusion amount applies to both sales.

Example

You are single in 2021 and subdivide your property and sell the vacant land for a profit of $100,000 (you must allocate the basis in your home between the vacant land and the parcel with the home to determine your gain on the sale of each parcel). You can exclude this gain on your 2021 return. In 2022, you sell the parcel containing your home for a profit of $200,000. You can exclude $150,000 of this $200,000 gain on your 2022 return (you already used $100,000 of the exclusion on your 2021 return). You must report and pay tax on the remaining $50,000 profit.

If you have been claiming a home office deduction for a portion of the home, you can still apply the exclusion to the home office portion as long as both the personal and business portions are part of the same dwelling.

You can use the exclusion over and over again. As long as you meet the 2-year ownership and use tests for each residence, you can avoid tax on gains from each one. One exclusion can be claimed every 2 years.

If your home is destroyed by a casualty, and insurance proceeds exceed the basis of your home, resulting in a taxable gain, the transaction may qualify as a home sale for purposes of the home sale exclusion. The damage to the home must be sufficient to constitute a "destruction."

Pitfalls

The home sale exclusion applies only to "qualified use" of a residence. "Non-qualified use" includes any period after December 31, 2008, in which the home is not used as a principal residence. Thus, if you stop using the home as your main home and use it only as vacation property, or if you rent it out, gain related to this period does not qualify for the home sale exclusion. Temporary absences are not treated as nonqualified use; they're disregarded.

If you have been claiming a home office deduction for a portion of your home, you must recapture depreciation you have claimed for the office after May 6, 1997. This is so even though you can use the exclusion for gain on this part of the home. "Recapture" means you pay tax on all the depreciation claimed after May 6, 1997, at the rate of 25% (assuming your tax bracket is at or above this rate). Home office deduction rules are discussed in Chapter 14.

You must reduce the basis of your home by the amount of any energy credit claimed.

Example

If you claimed a $1,500 nonbusiness energy property tax credit in 2010 for installing new storm doors and windows, you must subtract $1,500 from the basis of your home. The same is true if you never took the nonbusiness energy credit before and now claim a $500 tax credit in 2021 for adding attic insulation.

If you fail the 2-year ownership and use test, you cannot claim a partial home sale exclusion based on unforeseen circumstances merely because a job promotion, house appreciation, or winning the lottery enables you to buy a bigger home.

Where to Claim the Exclusion

If your gain is fully excludable, you do not have to report the sale of your home on your return. If, however, some of the gain is taxable because it exceeds the exclusion amount (or all of your gain is taxable because you opt *not* to use the exclusion), you report the sale on Form 8949, *Sales and Other Dispositions of Capital Assets*, which is carried over to Schedule D and then to Form 1040 or 1040-SR.

You can use a worksheet in IRS Publication 523 to figure your gain and whether any portion of the gain is excludable.

Moving Expenses for Active Duty Military Personnel

According to Pew Research Center, 22% of Americans moved in 2020, most because of COVID-19. It's estimated that individuals will move 11.7 times during their lives. The American Moving and Storage Association says the average cost of an interstate move is about $4,300 while it's only $2,300 intrastate (both assuming 7,400 pounds). The cost of a move may be even higher—$13,000 or more (depending on distance and the amount of furniture and household goods to be moved). From a tax perspective, for 2018 through 2025, you can deduct your moving costs only if you are in the armed services and meet certain requirements.

Benefit 🔼 ✖

If you are member of the U.S. Armed Forces, you can deduct your moving expenses as an adjustment to gross income, even if you don't itemize your other personal expenses. If you are reimbursed or receive an allowance for moving expenses, you are not taxed on these payments. There is no dollar limit on this benefit.

Deductible amounts include amounts paid to pack, crate, and move your household goods and personal effects. Storage and insurance costs can be treated as deductible expenses for any period within 30 days after the items were moved from your old home but before they were delivered to your new home. If you are stationed overseas, there is no limit on storage and insurance costs while you work at your overseas location. The cost of connecting or disconnecting household appliances is a deductible moving expense, but the cost of installing a telephone in your new home is not deductible.

Deductible amounts also include travel expenses for you and members of your household.

EXAMPLES OF DEDUCTIBLE TRAVEL EXPENSES FOR THE MOVING DEDUCTION

- Lodging en route from the old home to the new home. Include the cost of lodging before you depart for one day after your old residence is unusable as well as lodging for the day of arrival at your new location before you move into your home. However, the cost of meals is not deductible.

- Transportation from the old home to the new home. You and members of your household do not have to travel together; simply add up the costs for each person. If you drive, you can figure your cost for moving in 2021 at 16¢ per mile.
- The cost of moving your pets. Pets are viewed as household items, not as members of your family.

Condition

To be treated as a deductible expense (or to qualify for an exclusion for reimbursement or an allowance for moving expenses), you or your spouse must be on active duty and the move must be because of a military order and incident to a permanent change of station.

Planning Tip

Even if you can deduct your moving costs, it still makes sense to keep them as low as possible. When planning a move, to get a rough idea of moving costs, get an estimate using a calculator from Moving.com (https://www.moving.com/movers/moving-cost-calculator.asp). Be sure to get several binding quotes from reputable moving companies before contracting with one of them. Finally, put everything you agree to in writing and include adequate insurance for loss, breakage, and other damage. Learn about moving, including how to insure the move, in *The Moving Guide* from MovingGuru (www.movingguru.com).

Pitfalls

Even if you are in the military and move because of a military order, not every move-related expense is deductible.

EXAMPLES OF NONDEDUCTIBLE MOVING EXPENSES

- Any part of the purchase price of a new home
- Car registration tags
- Driver's license
- Expenses of buying or selling a home
- Expenses of getting or breaking a lease (lease cancellation fee)
- Home improvements to sell your home
- Losses from disposing of club memberships
- Meal expenses
- Mortgage penalties (but they may be deductible as an itemized mortgage interest expense as explained earlier in this chapter)
- Premove house-hunting expenses

- Real estate taxes (but they may be deductible as an itemized expense)
- Refitting of carpets and draperies
- Security deposits forfeited
- Storage charges except those incurred in transit and for foreign moves
- Temporary living expenses

Where to Claim the Deduction

If your employer (the federal government) pays your moving costs and you are eligible to exclude this benefit from your income, you do not report them on your return.

If you deduct your expenses, figure the deduction on Form 3903, *Moving Expenses*, which you attach to your return. Enter the deductible amount on Schedule 1 of Form 1040 or 1040-SR.

Energy Improvements

Homeowners can claim various tax credits for making certain energy-saving improvements. In view of currently high energy costs, consider taking advantage of tax breaks to save money on taxes and energy costs.

Benefit ⊕

There are 2 tax credits that a homeowner may claim for making certain energy improvements to the home. These include a 10% credit for adding qualified energy efficiency improvements (called the nonbusiness energy property credit) and a 26% credit for solar energy and fuel cell power plants.

Conditions

The law requires that these improvements meet certain energy-saving standards and cannot exceed certain dollar limits. Different requirements apply to energy improvements and to solar energy and fuel cell power plants.

The qualified improvements must be made to an existing home, not a home that is being constructed. The home must be your principal residence and not vacation property.

NONBUSINESS ENERGY PROPERTY IMPROVEMENTS

To qualify for the 10% nonbusiness energy property credit, energy improvements must meet or exceed the criteria set for January 1, 2009, building standards and must be installed in your main home in the United States. Exterior windows, exterior doors, and skylights must meet Energy Star program requirements. You can rely on a manufacturer's certification in writing that a product is qualified residential energy property. Don't attach the certification to your return, but keep it with your records.

ELIGIBLE ITEMS

These include:

- Insulation systems that reduce heat loss/gain
- Exterior windows (including skylights)
- Exterior doors
- Metal roofs treated with special paint (meeting applicable Energy Star requirements) and certain asphalt roofs
- Advanced main air-circulating fan
- Qualified natural gas, propane, or oil furnace or hot water heater

These items are listed in the law, but they are not the only ones to qualify for the credit; other items meeting certain energy standards can also qualify. It is up to the manufacturer to obtain certification for its products. For example, certification has been obtained for a qualifying wood or pellet stove, fireplace, and fireplace insert by various manufacturers. Other items meeting certain energy standards include central air conditioners. To date, there has been no certification for LED lighting for purposes of this personal tax credit.

LIMITATIONS

The credit is 10% of the cost of expenditures, up to a maximum credit of $500.

Special limits. Certain expenditures are capped at low dollar amounts, so the $500 cap may not apply to them:

- $300 for approved electric and geothermal heat pumps; central air-conditioning systems; and natural gas, propane, or oil water heaters
- $200 for new windows
- $150 for a natural gas, propane, or oil furnace or hot water boiler
- $50 for an advanced main air-circulating fan

Lifetime limit. The $500 limit for the credit must be reduced by any nonbusiness energy property credit claimed after 2005.

SOLAR POWER AND FUEL CELLS

To qualify for the 26% residential alternative energy credit, solar panels, solar water heating equipment, a geothermal heat pump, a small wind property, or a fuel cell power plant must be added to your main home in the United States.

Looking Ahead

The nonbusiness energy credit expires at the end of 2021 unless Congress extends it; check the Supplement. The solar tax credit is scheduled to drop to 22% in 2023 and no credit for homeowners thereafter.

In general, a qualified fuel cell power plant converts a fuel into electricity using electrochemical means, has an electricity-only generation efficiency of more than 30%, and generates at least 0.5 kilowatts of electricity.

You can claim one credit equal to 26% of the qualified investment in a solar panel and another equivalent credit for investing in a solar water heating system.

Additionally, you are allowed a 26% tax credit for the purchase of qualified fuel cell power plants. The credit may not exceed $500 for each 0.5 kilowatt of capacity.

Planning Tips

How can you know whether improvements to your home will qualify for these tax credits? Obtain a manufacturer's certificate that the item has been approved by the IRS as qualifying for the credit. You can find helpful information at www.EnergyStar.gov.

The residential alternative energy credit can be claimed even for expenditures made with funds obtained from subsidized energy financing. The value of any subsidy provided by a public utility is excluded from gross income, but this must be used to reduce the basis of the energy improvement for purposes of figuring the credit.

Low- and middle-income homeowners who receive payments from the state to help pay for energy-efficient boilers and furnaces are not taxed on these payments (the state is not required to report them on Form 1099).

If you can't fully use the credit for alternative energy improvements in the current year, you can carry the unused credit forward; there is no limit on this carryforward period.

Check with your utility company to learn whether there are any grants or rebates for making energy improvements to your home.

Pitfalls

Not every energy-saving measure qualifies for a credit. For purposes of the energy improvements credit, insulated vinyl siding does not qualify. For purposes of the solar or fuel cell power plant credit, no part of either system can be used to heat a pool or hot tub.

You must reduce the basis of your home by the amount of any energy credit claimed. For example, if you claim a $500 tax credit in 2014 for installing new storm doors, you must subtract $500 from the basis of your home.

Where to Claim the Credits

You figure the credit on Form 5965, *Residential Energy Credits*. The credit is then entered on Schedule 3 of Form 1040 or 1040-SR.

ABLE Accounts

If you have a disabled child or are under age 26 and meet certain eligibility conditions, you can have a special savings account that generally does not adversely impact eligibility for means-tested government programs (e.g., Medicaid). An ABLE account can be used on a tax-free basis for housing, as well as other qualified disability expenses. See details in Chapter 2.

Disaster Rules for Casualties to Your Home

These special rules are explained in Chapter 12.

COVID-19 Emergency Assistance

If you received government assistance to pay your rent, utilities, or home energy expenses under Section 501 Emergency Rental Assistance authorized by the Consolidated Appropriations Act, 2021, you are not taxed on this assistance. This is so, whether payments were made to you and you used them for rent, utilities, and/or home energy expenses or the payments were made directly to your landlord and/or utility companies.

Home Office Deduction

If you work from home as a result of the pandemic, you may be eligible to claim a home office deduction. This write-off includes personal expenses that would not otherwise be deductible, such as utilities and home repairs. This deduction, which is limited to self-employed individuals, including independent contractors, in 2018 through 2025, is explained in Chapter 14.

Retirement Savings

Your Social Security benefits alone, or even retirement benefits derived from employer contributions to retirement plans on your behalf, won't provide you with the financial security you want for your retirement years. You need to save so that you'll have the assets to generate income after you stop working. Fortunately, the tax law provides important incentives to encourage your personal savings in special retirement accounts. You may be able to write off your savings (contributions) as well as qualify for special treatment when you start drawing from these savings. Retirement plans in 2021 continue to feel the impact of changes made by the SECURE Act, the CARES Act in response to COVID-19, and other legislation.

There are many different types of retirement plans that you may be able to use to save for your future. Contributions are subject to limits; if your income is high enough, it may bar you from contributing to some plans but not to others.

This chapter explains the tax breaks you may be entitled to when you save for retirement using tax-advantaged ways. If you are an employer, you may be eligible for a tax credit for starting a qualified retirement plan for your business. This credit is explained in Chapter 14.

For more information, see IRS Publication 560, *Retirement Plans for Small Business*; IRS Publication 575, *Pension and Annuity Income*; IRS Publication 590-A, *Contributions to Individual Retirement Arrangements (IRAs)*; IRS Publication 590-B, *Distributions from Individual Retirement Arrangements (IRAs)*; and IRS Publication 4333, *SEP Retirement Plans for Small Businesses*.

Traditional IRAs

The Employee Retirement Income Security Act of 1974 (referred to as ERISA) created individual retirement accounts (IRAs) to enable taxpayers to save for their own retirement largely because company pensions could no longer be relied upon for retirement income. With an IRA, the government effectively contributes to your retirement savings by permitting a tax deduction for contributions if certain conditions are met. The tax savings are the government's contribution. For example, if you are in the 32% tax bracket, the government contributes almost one-third of your contributions to a traditional (deductible) IRA—your tax savings from the total contribution amount; you only have to come up with about two-thirds of the contribution.

Benefit

If you work as an employee or have net earnings from self-employment, you can contribute to an IRA. The contribution limit for 2021 is $6,000, or $7,000 if you are age 50 or older by the end of 2021, as long as you earn at least this dollar amount.

Example

If you are single, under age 50, and earn at least $6,000, you can make a full contribution. If you work part-time and earn only $2,000, your contribution is limited to $2,000.

If you have a spouse who does not work for compensation, you can contribute to an IRA for your spouse based on your own earnings. The IRA for a nonworking spouse is called the Kay Bailey Hutchison Spousal IRA. The same dollar limit of $6,000 (or $7,000 if age 50 by the end of 2021) applies to a spousal IRA. This means that if you have sufficient earnings and both you and your spouse are under age 50, you may contribute up to $12,000 ($6,000 for yourself and $6,000 for your spouse) for 2021.

If you do not participate in another qualified retirement plan, such as a 401(k) plan, or if you do participate but your income is below a set amount, you can deduct your contributions. The deduction is claimed as an adjustment to gross income; you claim it regardless of whether you itemize your other deductions.

Earnings on IRA contributions build up on a tax-deferred basis (no tax is owed annually on the earnings of an IRA). However, you are required to take certain withdrawals from the IRA starting at a certain age (70½ for those attaining this age before 2020; 72 for those attaining age 70½ after 2019). If you fail to take these required amounts (called required minimum distributions or RMDs, which are not discussed further in this book), you may be subject to a whopping 50% penalty of the amount you should have taken.

Conditions for Making Contributions

There are 2 conditions for making a contribution:

1. Earned income
2. Cash contributions

EARNED INCOME

Earned income for purposes of making IRA contributions means taxable wages (including tips, commissions, bonuses, and jury duty fees) and net earnings from self-employment. Earned income for purposes of making IRA contributions also includes taxable alimony and tax-free combat pay. Earned income also includes stipends and non-tuition fellowship payments to graduate and postdoctoral students.

You must earn the income. If you live in a community property state where one-half of your spouse's earnings is viewed as income, you cannot use your share of your spouse's income as the basis for making your IRA contribution.

Earned income does *not* include:

- Conservation Reserve Program (CRP) payments even though they are reported as income for self-employment tax purposes.

- Deferred compensation, pensions, or annuities.
- Investment income, such as dividends or interest.
- Income earned abroad for which the foreign earned income exclusion has been claimed.
- Partnership income from a business for which you do not provide services that are a material income-producing factor.
- Social Security benefits.
- Unemployment compensation.

CASH CONTRIBUTIONS

All contributions must be made in cash (which includes payments by check). If you currently own investments that you want to use as your contributions, you must first liquidate them. Your IRA can then reacquire the same investments (provided they are not prohibited investments discussed later).

Condition for Claiming a Deduction

Just because you meet all the conditions for making an IRA contribution does not mean that you can claim a deduction for the contribution. Even if you qualify to make contributions, there is an additional condition in order to deduct your contributions.

To deduct contributions you must not participate in another qualified retirement plan or if you are an active participant in a qualified retirement plan, your modified adjusted gross income (MAGI) cannot exceed a phaseout range. The deduction amount phases out for MAGI within the phaseout range. No deduction can be claimed if MAGI exceeds the phaseout range. MAGI for this purpose is adjusted gross income, increased by exclusions for interest on U.S. savings bonds used for higher education, employer-paid adoption assistance, and foreign earned income as well as deductions for interest on student loans. Table 5.1 shows the phaseout ranges for 2021.

TABLE 5.1 2021 MAGI Phaseout Range for Active Participants Deducting IRA Contributions

Filing Status*	MAGI
Married filing jointly	$105,000–125,000
Other taxpayers (other than married filing separately)	$ 66,000–76,000

* A married person filing a separate return has a zero limit so that no deduction can be claimed if the person is an active participant.

If one spouse is an active participant, the other spouse is permitted to make a deductible IRA contribution only if the couple's MAGI is below a set limit. For 2021, the MAGI limit in this case is $198,000. The nonactive participant's spouse's contribution is reduced when the couple's MAGI exceeds $198,000; it is fully phased out when MAGI reaches $208,000.

Planning Tips

You have until the deadline for filing the return to make an IRA contribution. For example, you have until April 18, 2022, to make an IRA contribution for 2021. But even if you obtain a filing extension, you do not gain any additional time to make your annual contribution.

Just because you have more time to act doesn't mean it's a good idea to delay. The earlier in the year you make your contribution, the sooner you begin to earn tax-deferred income. For example, if you make your 2021 contribution on January 15, 2021, rather than on April 18, 2022, you gain an additional 15 months of tax-deferred investment buildup in the IRA.

You can help your child jump-start his or her retirement savings by providing the funds for an IRA contribution. As long as your child has earned income (e.g., from a part-time or summer job), you can make a gift of the contribution amount to your child.

The basic IRA contribution limit can be increased for inflation in $500 increments, so check the Supplement for any changes for 2022. The additional limit for those age 50 and older remains at $1,000.

If, in the course of a marital dissolution, an IRA is awarded to a spouse or former spouse, the IRA owner can avoid tax on the transfer by retitling the account in the spouse's name or making a direct trustee-to-trustee transfer. A distribution followed by a transfer to the spouse is taxable to the owner.

Pitfalls

IRAs are designed to be long-term investments for you. Don't make contributions if you know you'll need the funds within a short time (say, this year or next); early withdrawals may trigger a tax penalty and possibly an investment-related penalty (such as bank charges for cashing in a certificate of deposit before maturity). Early distribution penalties and the exceptions to them are discussed next.

Also, use care in figuring how much you can put into the IRA each year and how much you may be required to withdraw annually. Again, there are penalties for putting in too much or taking out too little under certain circumstances (discussed later).

You cannot treat reinvestments in your IRA as additional contributions and claim a deduction for them. Dividend reinvestments are merely investment returns on your contributions.

EARLY DISTRIBUTION PENALTIES

If you need funds from your IRA before you retire, you may be subject to a 10% early distribution penalty. This penalty applies if you take money out before age 59 ½, unless you meet one of the following exceptions to the penalty:

- You become disabled (or die and your heirs take out the money).
- You take the money in a series of substantially equal periodic payments. This essentially means you take withdrawals in even amounts for at least 5 years or until you attain age 59 ½, whichever is later.
- You use the money to pay medical expenses exceeding 10% of your adjusted gross income.
- You are unemployed and receiving unemployment benefits for at least 12 consecutive weeks (or if you had been self-employed, you would have received such benefits due to lack of work).
- You use the money to pay higher education expenses (this exception to the 10% penalty is explained more fully in Chapter 3).
- You take out no more than $10,000 and use it to pay first-time home-buying expenses (this exception to the 10% penalty is explained more fully in Chapter 4).
- The IRS places levies on your IRA for back taxes.
- You are a reservist called to active duty.
- You pay birth or adoption expenses up to $5,000.

There is no exception to the early distribution penalty for withdrawals on account of financial hardship (e.g., to pay your mortgage in order to keep your home out of foreclosure). There is no exception to the penalty for paying income taxes, even if this is done to avoid a levy on the IRA (which is a penalty exception).

EXCESS CONTRIBUTIONS PENALTY

If you are an active participant who contributed to an IRA but after the close of the year you find out your AGI is too high for a deductible contribution, you have several options to correct the contribution and avoid a 6% excise tax on excess contributions. The 6% excise tax applies each year until you correct the excess contribution.

You can treat the contributions as nondeductible IRA contributions. Alternatively, you can withdraw the excess contribution (plus any earnings on it) by the due date of your return (plus extensions). If you miss this deadline, you can limit the tax penalty to one year by withdrawing the excess by December 31 of the year following the year of the contribution.

Example

In 2021, you are 48 years old and an active participant in a qualified retirement plan. You anticipate your AGI for the year to be low enough to make a deductible IRA contribution. You contribute $5,500 to your IRA on November 15, 2021, intending to take a deduction for it on your 2021 return. In December you receive unexpected income (e.g., a year-end bonus, a large distribution from a mutual fund) that makes your AGI exceed the limit for making a deductible contribution in 2021. You can treat the contribution as a nondeductible IRA for 2021. You can withdraw the contribution (and earnings on it) by April 18, 2022, and avoid the penalty. You can withdraw the contribution (and earnings on it) by December 31, 2022; you'll owe the penalty for 2022.

If you contribute to an IRA but later determine that your income prevents you from claiming the IRA deduction reported on your return (for example, you are an active plan participant and a later IRS audit increases your MAGI above the phaseout range), you are subject to a 6% excise tax, called an excess contributions penalty. This tax continues to apply every year in which the excess contribution (and earnings on such contribution) remains in the IRA.

You can, however, designate that the excess contribution be treated as your IRA contribution in a subsequent year.

Example

In 2021, you deduct your $6,000 IRA contribution on your return. In 2023, the IRS audits your return and increases your MAGI to an amount that makes your contribution nondeductible. You were not eligible for a deductible contribution in 2022 but can make a fully deductible contribution in 2022. Designate the 2021 contribution as your 2023 deductible contribution to limit the 6% penalty to 2021 and 2022.

PENALTY FOR INSUFFICIENT WITHDRAWALS

Usually, starting in the year in which you attain the specified age (70½ for those attaining this age before 2020; 72 for those attaining age 70½ after 2019), you must take required minimum distributions (RMDs). If you don't take RMDs, you can be subject to a 50% penalty on the amount you failed to take.

While RMDs were suspended for 2020 due to COVID-19, they must begin or resume in 2021 to avoid the 50% penalty. RMDs that must commence or resume in 2021 are based on IRS tables found in IRS Publication 590-B. Use the table in Appendix C that fits your situation:

- If you inherited an IRA from an owner who died before 2020 (and you are not a spouse who made a rollover to your own IRA), then you must take RMDs based on Table I in Appendix C or use a 5-year rule. If you inherit an IRA from someone dying after 2019, special rules apply (explained later in this chapter).
- If you are married and the beneficiary of your IRA is your spouse, who is more than 10 years younger than you, use Table II.
- For IRA owners that do not have a spouse more than 10 years younger use Table III (uniform lifetime).

Looking Ahead

Starting in 2022, new life expectancy tables will be used to figure RMDs. These new tables reflect longer life expectancies, which translate into smaller RMDs. If you are the owner of the account or a beneficiary commencing RMDs in 2022, simply use the new tables to calculate the 2022 distribution amount.

Nonspouse beneficiaries of an IRA owner who died before 2020 or who are eligible designated beneficiaries of an IRA owner who died after 2019 or a Roth IRA owner who died after 2019, will be able to make a one-time "reset" to determine their 2022 distribution, which impacts subsequent distributions as well.

You are not limited, however, to RMDs and can withdraw more or all of the funds in the account at any time.

Special rule for IRAs inherited after 2019. Unless you meet an exception below, if you are a designated beneficiary, you cannot "stretch" distributions using the Uniform Table and, instead, must draw out the entire account no later than the end of the 10th year following the year of the owner's death. Certain "eligible" designated beneficiaries are permitted to continue taking RMDs under the old rules, as follows:

- A surviving spouse
- A child of the account owner who has not reached the age of majority. A minor child of an account owner who is a beneficiary may calculate distributions based on his or her remaining life expectancy until reaching the age of majority (18 in most states), at which point the remaining account balance must be distributed within 10 years
- An individual who is disabled
- A chronically ill individual
- An individual who is not more than 10 years younger than the account owner (e.g., a sibling who inherits an IRA)

If the account owner dies before the required beginning date and does not designate a beneficiary or designates a trust as beneficiary, the account balance must be distributed within 5 years ("5-year rule"); the 10-year rule does not apply.

INVESTMENT LIMITATIONS

You can invest your IRA contributions in a wide array of investment vehicles, including certificates of deposit, stocks, bonds, and mutual funds. You can even invest in real estate if you avoid self-dealing and other prohibited transaction rules.

However, the law places certain limits on the types of things you can invest in. If you opt to invest in a prohibited vehicle, you are treated as having taken a distribution; you are taxed on the amount and, if under age 59 ½, subject to a 10% penalty. You are prohibited from putting your IRA money into collectibles, which include:

- Antiques
- Art works
- Coins (other than state-issued coins or certain U.S. minted gold, silver, or platinum coins)

- Gems
- Guns
- Metals (other than gold, silver, platinum, or palladium bullion held by your IRA trustee)
- Stamps

Technically, you are permitted to own realty in an IRA. However, you must do so through a self-directed IRA that permits such investment, and you cannot mortgage the property (IRAs are barred from any borrowing, as explained later).

Also, even though there is no law preventing you, it makes no sense to put IRA money into tax-exempt municipal bonds. Since the IRA is already tax deferred, you don't gain any benefit from the tax-free interest on the bonds. And when you take distributions from the IRA, they will all be treated as ordinary income (even though the underlying investment producing the earnings was tax-exempt bonds).

It may also be advisable to avoid foreign investments because foreign taxes paid from the IRA do not qualify for a deduction or credit; they only reduce the funds within the account. Another type of investment you may want to avoid is a master limited partnership (MLP). If you invest IRA funds in an MLP, you may have reportable income even though you haven't taken any distribution. When the MLP has unrelated business taxable income (UBTI) over $1,000 from operations or the sale of units, you have to file Form 990-T, *Exempt Organization Business Income Tax Return*, for your IRA and pay required taxes. There are also basis adjustments as well as other complications for MPL losses in your IRA.

The IRS has not yet ruled on whether cryptocurrency (e.g., bitcoin) is a collectible for IRA purposes. There are companies offering self-directed IRAs that allow you to invest in cryptocurrency, but caution is advised until the IRS has weighed in.

BORROWING LIMITATIONS

You are prohibited from borrowing from your IRA or using it as collateral for a loan. If you do borrow from your IRA, the amount borrowed or used as collateral is treated as a taxable distribution to you (and can be subject to penalty if you are under age 59½). If you take a loan from the IRA, the value of the entire account as of the first day of the year in which the loan is taken is includible in your income. If you pledge part of the account, that part of the account is includible in your income.

But you can have access to the funds for a short time without any adverse tax consequences. You can take a distribution and use it for 60 days; as long as the funds are replaced by the end of 60 days, there is no taxable distribution.

ACCOUNT LOSSES

If your investments turn out to be unsound and you lose money, you generally can't deduct the loss. For example, if you put $6,000 of your IRA money into a mutual fund that declines in value to $800, you cannot deduct your $5,200 loss, even if the IRA sells the fund.

The only way to deduct a loss with respect to an IRA is if you made nondeductible IRA contributions and then liquidate all of your IRAs or spend all of the funds. In this case, if the total amount you receive is less than what you contributed to the nondeductible IRA, you can theoretically claim a loss on your return for the year of liquidation or account depletion. However, since such loss is a miscellaneous itemized deduction (not a capital loss), the write-off can't be claimed; miscellaneous itemized deductions subject to the 2%-of-AGI floor are barred through 2025.

Where to Claim the Deduction

You deduct your IRA contribution on Form 1040 or 1040-SR. However, because the receipt of Social Security benefits in a year in which an IRA contribution is made can impact the deductible amount, there is a special worksheet in IRS Publication 590 for figuring the IRA deduction in this case.

If you are treating the contribution as a nondeductible IRA, you must complete Form 8606, *Nondeductible IRAs*. The purpose of this form is to help you keep track of nondeductible contributions so that when distributions are later taken, you won't pay tax on these after-tax contributions.

If you are subject to the 10% penalty on early withdrawals from the IRA, you must file Form 5329, *Additional Taxes on Qualified Plans (including IRAs) and Other Tax-Favored Accounts*, and enter the penalty on Schedule 2 of Form 1040 or 1040-SR.

Roth IRAs

Roth IRAs (named after U.S. Senator William Roth, who sponsored the law) are an alternative personal retirement savings account that debuted in 1998. While these accounts offer no immediate tax break since contributions are not deductible, they offer long-term tax savings.

Benefit ⊗

You can contribute a limited amount to a special type of retirement savings account that allows you to build up tax-free income. (Contribution limits for Roth IRAs are the same as for deductible IRAs discussed earlier in this chapter.)

While there is no current tax deduction for your contributions, you have access to your contributions and can withdraw them at any time tax free (after all, you made those contributions with after-tax dollars). But you can also withdraw earnings on those contributions tax free after 5 years if certain conditions discussed later are met.

CONVERSION

You can also convert your existing traditional IRA to a Roth IRA; there is no dollar limit on the amount you can convert. You must pay income tax on the account, just like you would if you had taken a distribution. But there's no 10% early distribution penalty if you are under age 59 ½ as long as the funds remain in the Roth IRA for at least 5 years. Income from 2021 conversions is reported in full on 2021 returns.

Conditions for Making Roth IRA Contributions

To be eligible to make contributions to a Roth IRA, you must meet 2 conditions:

1. You must have earned income (as explained earlier under traditional IRAs).
2. Your modified adjusted gross income (MAGI) cannot exceed a set limit.

MAGI LIMIT

Your MAGI in 2021 cannot be more than $125,000 if you are unmarried, or $198,000 if you are married filing jointly. A partial contribution is allowed if your MAGI is between $125,000 and $140,000 if you are unmarried, or $198,000 and $208,000 if you are married filing jointly. No contribution is permitted if your MAGI exceeds $140,000 if you are unmarried, or $208,000 if you are married filing jointly. Married persons filing separately have a phaseout range of zero to $10,000; no Roth IRA contribution can be made if MAGI is $10,000 or more.

Example

You are single, age 40, with MAGI in 2020 of $75,000. You can contribute up to $6,000 to a Roth IRA in 2021. If your MAGI is over $140,000, no contribution is allowed, even if your company doesn't have any qualified retirement plan. If your MAGI falls within the phaseout range, you can make a partial contribution. You figure your allowable limit using Worksheet 5.1, adapted from IRS Publication 590-A.

WORKSHEET 5.1 Reduced Roth IRA Contribution Limit for 2021

1. Enter your MAGI.	1. _____

2. Enter:
  • $198,000 if you file a joint return or are a qualifying widow(er).
  • $0 if you are married filing a separate return and you live with your spouse at any time during the year.
  • $125,000 for all other taxpayers.
	2. _____

3. Subtract line 2 from line 1.	3. _____

4. Enter:
  • $10,000 if you file a joint return or are a qualifying widow(er).
  • $15,000 for all other taxpayers.
	4. _____

5. Divide line 3 by line 4. Enter the result as a decimal (carried to 3 places). If the result is 1.000 or more, enter 1.000.	5. _____

6. Enter the lesser of:
  • $6,000 ($7,000 if 50 or older), or
  • Your taxable compensation.
	6. _____

7. Multiply line 5 by line 6.	7. _____
8. Subtract line 7 from line 6. Round the result up to the nearest $10. If the result is less than $200, enter $200.	8. _____
9. Enter contributions for the year to other IRAs.	9. _____
10. Subtract line 9 from line 6.	10. _____
11. Enter the lesser of line 8 or line 10. *This is your reduced Roth IRA contribution limit.*	11. _____

This MAGI limit applies whether or not you participate in another qualified retirement plan.

There is no age limit for making Roth IRA contributions. As long as you continue working, you can continue to put money into a Roth IRA (assuming your MAGI is below the limit).

Conditions for Converting a Traditional IRA or 401(k) to Roths

If you want the opportunity for your retirement savings to build up on a tax-free basis, consider converting your existing IRA, 401(k), or similar plan account to a Roth IRA or convert your 401(k) to a designated Roth account that is part of that plan. There are no adjusted gross income limits on eligibility to convert to a Roth IRA.

You can choose to convert some or all of your retirement plan account or IRAs at a time. Consider the impact that additional income from the conversion will have on the amount of Social Security benefits to be included in income if you receive such benefits or whether the additional income puts you into a higher tax bracket, and subjects you to additional Medicare Parts B and D premiums. You must report all of the resulting income on your 2021 return.

Conversions from traditional 401(k) plans to a designated Roth account (if the plan allows for such conversions) are called in-plan rollovers. However, they are essentially the same as conversions to Roth IRAs. The conversion amounts are currently taxable, with no early distribution penalty even if you are under age 59 ½ at the time of the conversion. But once you make an in-plan rollover, it cannot be undone.

You cannot convert your required minimum distribution for the year; you must take it and then convert from the amount remaining in your account.

Conditions for Tax-Free Income Withdrawals

You can withdraw earnings on your contributions tax free after 5 years if you meet *any* of the following 3 conditions:

1. You are over age 59 ½.
2. You become disabled.
3. You withdraw no more than $10,000 and use the money for qualified first-time home-buying expenses. (Qualified first-time home-buying expenses are explained in Chapter 4.)

For contributory Roth IRAs, the 5-year period runs from the first day of the year to which your contributions relate. For example, if you contribute $6,000 to a Roth IRA for 2021 on April 18, 2022, the 5-year period commences on January 1, 2021. For Roth IRAs established through conversions, the 5-year period used to determine whether the 10% penalty applies if you are under age 59 ½ at the time of the conversion, the period starts on the first day of the year in which the conversion is made.

Example

On April 15, 2017, you contributed $4,000 to a Roth IRA for 2016. If you are at least 59 ½ in 2021, you can now withdraw the earnings you have built up in the account completely tax free—no income tax and no early distribution penalty. The 5-year period began on January 1, 2016. If, instead, you converted the Roth IRA on April 15, 2017, the 5-year period would have begun on January 1, 2017.

Planning Tips

The deadline for 2021 Roth IRA contributions is April 18, 2022. This is the same deadline for traditional IRAs discussed earlier in this chapter.

Assuming your income gives you the option of choosing between making a deductible IRA contribution or a nondeductible Roth IRA contribution, which alternative makes more sense for you? In most cases, choosing to make the Roth IRA contribution is wiser because the value of the IRA deduction you are forgoing is much smaller than the value of receiving tax-free income from the Roth IRA in the future.

Example

You are eligible to make either a deductible IRA contribution or a Roth IRA contribution. Assuming you are in the 24% tax bracket, a $6,000 deduction to a deductible IRA would save you $1,440 this year. But let's also assume that a $6,000 contribution can quadruple in the next 25 years to $24,000 (of which $18,000 is earnings on your contribution). If you opt for the Roth IRA, then when you withdraw the funds (assuming you are over age 59½), you won't pay any income tax on the earnings—a $4,320 tax savings if you are still in the 24% tax bracket.

Survivors of military personnel who died from injuries on or after June 17, 2008, can contribute the proceeds from Servicemembers' Group Life Insurance (SGLI) to a Roth IRA without regard to the annual contribution limit and without regard to the MAGI limit. This contribution is treated as a rollover contribution and must be made no later than one year after receipt of the SGLI proceeds.

Should you convert an existing traditional IRA or 401(k) plan account to a Roth IRA? There is no fixed answer; it depends on your situation. Factors to consider are your age (the younger you are, the longer you will have to build up tax-free income, but there is no age limit on making a conversion); your income (the more modest your income, the less the tax on the conversion); and whether you have the funds to pay the tax resulting from the conversion. If you decide you want to convert your 401(k) or similar account to a Roth IRA, be sure to do so using a direct rollover (the plan administrator will transfer the funds directly to your Roth IRA) so you avoid the mandatory 20% withholding tax that applies to qualified retirement plan distributions.

Contributions you make to a designated Roth account within a 401(k) plan have no impact on your ability to contribute to a Roth IRA. For example, say in 2021, you contribute $19,500 to a designated Roth account 401(k) within your employer's plan (you're not 50 years old or older). You can also contribute $6,000 to a Roth IRA (assuming your income does not exceed the limits).

Making a Roth IRA conversion for the year does not automatically prevent you from also making a Roth IRA contribution if you are otherwise eligible to do so. Of course, income resulting from the conversion can impact your eligibility by increasing your MAGI.

This decision to convert isn't an all-or-nothing proposition. You can convert part of your IRA to a Roth IRA. In fact, you can do this every year in which you are eligible to make a conversion.

Pitfalls

You should have the cash on hand to pay the tax resulting from the conversion. If you convert part of an IRA and use part of it to pay the tax, the portion used to pay the tax cannot later be placed in the Roth IRA. In effect, you lose out on an important retirement savings opportunity. What's more, if you are under age 59 ½, the portion used to pay the tax is subject to a 10% penalty.

Example

In 2021, when you are 40 years old, you opt to convert your $100,000 IRA to a Roth IRA. Assuming you are in the 24% tax bracket, the conversion costs you $24,000. If you use $24,000 of the $100,000 to pay the tax, then you have only $76,000 in your Roth IRA. And the $24,000 not converted to the Roth IRA is subject to a 10% penalty, for an additional tax of $2,400.

Don't confuse a Roth IRA with a Roth 401(k) (called a designated Roth account). The rules for a designated Roth account are separate and distinct from the rules for a Roth IRA.

Where to Claim the Benefit

You do not report contributions you make to a Roth IRA on your return (remember, they are not deductible).

If you convert your traditional IRA to a Roth IRA, you must report the income resulting from the conversion on Form 1040 or 1040-SR. If you use a portion of your IRA to pay the tax on the conversion and are subject to the 10% penalty on this amount, you must file Form 5329, *Additional Taxes on Qualified Retirement Plans (Including IRAs) and Other Tax Favored Accounts*, and enter the penalty on Schedule 2 of Form 1040 or 1040-SR.

If you make excess contributions to the Roth IRA (by contribution or conversion), you are subject to a 6% excise tax and must file Form 5329, *Additional Taxes on Qualified Plans (Including IRAs) and Other Tax-Favored Accounts*. Enter the excise tax on Schedule 2 of Form 1040 or 1040-SR.

IRA Rollovers

IRAs are highly portable—they can be transferred from one investment company to another with no immediate tax consequences if certain conditions are met. This allows taxpayers to move accounts from a bank to a mutual fund or from one brokerage firm to another.

Benefit

You can transfer funds from one IRA to another without any current tax. There are no dollar limits on the amount you can roll over each year.

There are 2 ways in which to make the transfer:

1. *Direct transfers*. You can instruct the custodian or trustee of your IRA to transfer funds directly to the custodian or trustee of another IRA.
2. *Distribution and reinvestment*. You can take a withdrawal of funds from your IRA and replace the funds within 60 days.

Conditions

The transfer method you use determines the conditions you must meet to achieve tax-free treatment.

DIRECT TRANSFERS

You instruct the custodian or trustee of your IRAs to complete the action; you cannot receive any funds that are part of the transfer. There is no time requirement for your fiduciaries to complete the transaction. There is no limit on the number of direct transfers you can make each year.

DISTRIBUTION AND REINVESTMENT

You must complete the transaction within 60 days. Generally, the IRS cannot extend this period. But you may qualify for a waiver of the 60-day deadline in limited circumstances detailed later under "Pitfalls."

You are permitted to make only one rollover per 12-month period (this rule is called the one-rollover-per-year rule even though technically it's a 12-month period). This rule applies per taxpayer, so only one rollover can be made within the period, regardless of how many separate IRA accounts you may have.

Note: Regardless of which method you select, rollovers are handled separately from annual contributions to IRAs and Roth IRAs. Thus, for example, you may make a rollover even if you also make a deductible IRA contribution for the year.

Planning Tips

You can use funds in your IRA as a short-term loan. While borrowing against an IRA is not permitted, you can take a distribution and avoid current tax if you replace the funds within 60 days.

> **Example**
>
> In early February 2021 you were out of work and didn't have money to pay the rent, so you used funds from your IRA for this purpose. Later in March 2021, you received an Economic Impact Payment and used some of it to replace your IRA withdrawal. Because you did this within 60 days, it is not treated as a taxable distribution.

You may want to roll your IRA over to a company retirement plan, such as a 401(k) plan. This may make sense for several reasons. Company investment options may entail lower fees than what you pay if you invest through a personal IRA. If you are nearing age 72 (the age for which RMDs must commence for those born after 1949) and still working for a company that has a qualified retirement plan deferring required minimum distributions (RMDs) until actual retirement, ask whether it accepts rollovers from your IRA. If so, you may want to take advantage of the opportunity to add to your company's retirement plan and delay RMDs until you retire. (This strategy does not work for anyone who owns 5% or more of the company.) And, the 401(k) may allow you to borrow from the plan, which is something you can't do with an IRA (although it isn't the best thing to do with a 401(k) if building up retirement savings is your goal).

If you try to complete the rollover on time but outside events prevent you from doing so, you may be able to obtain an extension to the 60-day limit. The limit is automatically extended if the account is frozen, if you are serving in a combat zone, are in a federal disaster area, or a victim of terrorist or military action. The limit is also extended if you meet all of the following conditions:

1. You were not previously denied a waiver request for a rollover by the IRS.
2. Your reason for missing the 60-day deadline is one of the following:
   - Your financial institution made an error.
   - You misplaced the distribution check and never cashed it.
   - You deposited the distribution in an account you thought was an eligible retirement plan.
   - Your principal residence was severely damaged.
   - A member of your family died.

- A member of your family was seriously ill.
- You were incarcerated.
- You were subject to restrictions imposed by a foreign country.
- There was a postal error.
- The distribution was made on account of an IRS levy and the proceeds have been returned to you.
- The party making the distribution delayed providing information required by the receiving plan or IRA despite your best efforts to obtain it.
- The distribution was made to a state unclaimed property fund.

3. You complete the rollover as soon as practical. There is a 30-day safe harbor, which means doing so within 30-days after the occurrence of the condition that prevented the rollover.

If you qualify for this self-certification, send a written letter to the plan administrator or IRA trustee stating that you satisfy the conditions for relief. There's a sample letter for this purpose in the Appendix to Revenue Procedure 2016–47.

Even if you can't use the self-certification process, you may still obtain relief for missing the 60-day rollover deadline in some situations. For example, the Tax Court allowed more time for a person suffering from depression to complete a rollover.

Pitfall

If you take a distribution and plan to reinvest within 60 days, make sure to watch the calendar closely. If you miss the deadline by even one day (and don't qualify for relief explained earlier), the entire distribution becomes taxable to you.

Where to Claim the Benefit

IRA rollovers that are distributed to you are reported to you (and the IRS) on Form 1099-R, *Distributions from Pensions, Annuities, Retirement or Profit-Sharing Plans, IRAs, Insurance Contracts, Etc*.

You must report the distribution on line 4a on page 1 of Form 1040 or 1040-SR, but if you successfully completed the transfer within 60 days, enter only zero on line 4b of Form 1040 or 1040-SR.

401(k) and Similar Plans

Pensions used to be the responsibility of employers, but for the past quarter of a century that responsibility has shifted to employees. To make it easier for employees to pay for their own retirement savings, the tax law has created special retirement plans. Companies set up the plans, but employees fund them (in whole or in part) by contributing a portion of their salary each year. Employees decide how their contributions are to be invested by selecting from a menu of investment options provided by the employer. The tax law encourages employee contributions by allowing them to escape immediate taxation.

Benefit ●

If you are eligible to participate in your employer's 401(k) or similar plan, you can agree each year to contribute a portion of your salary as your contribution to the plan. You can change your contribution from year to year; you may also be able to reduce it within a year. Depending on your employer's plan, you may be automatically enrolled and then have the opportunity to change the default contribution made by you (you can even opt out entirely from contributing) or be offered the opportunity to participate and make contributions within the limits discussed later.

Your contribution is called an elective deferral or salary reduction amount. This amount is *not* treated as compensation to you for the year; you do not pay income tax on your elective deferral (you do pay Social Security and Medicare taxes on the elective deferral).

Example

If your wages this year are $45,000 and you contribute $8,000 to your company's 401(k) plan, only $37,000 of your wages for purposes of income taxes is reported on your Form W-2; you only pay income taxes on $37,000 this year.

Note: Contributions to a designated Roth account within a 401(k) plan are not treated as elective deferrals; they must be made with after-tax contributions. A designated Roth account is similar but not identical to a Roth IRA.

Conditions

Eligibility requirements to make elective deferrals are spelled out in your company's plan. You should receive a summary of the plan from your employer and be given an opportunity to designate your elective deferrals for the year (typically within a month or so before the start of a new year or upon becoming eligible to participate in your company's plan).

ELECTIVE DEFERRAL LIMITS

The law fixes the *maximum* elective deferral limits for each year. Your plan may place other restrictions or limits on how much you can contribute annually to the plan.

The law allows you to contribute up to 100% of your earnings to the plan, up to a dollar limit on contributions. For 2021, the dollar limit is $19,500 (or $26,000 if you are age 50 or older by the end of 2021).

Example

In 2021, you are 28 years old and earn $30,000. Your maximum contribution, assuming you can afford to make it, is $19,500 (although your plan may restrict contributions to a percentage of your compensation).

Planning Tips

If you are pressed for funds and find it difficult to take full advantage of the elective deferral opportunity, at least contribute what is necessary to obtain your employer's matching contribution if available. Your employer's matching contribution is, in effect, "free money" to you, and it would be unwise to ignore it.

Example

In 2021, you are permitted under the plan to contribute $19,500 through elective deferrals. Your employer will match 50% of your contributions up to 6% of your compensation. If you earn $30,000, you must contribute at least $3,600 to obtain your employer's top contribution on your behalf of $1,800.

If you are self-employed and have no employees, you can set up a solo 401(k) to maximize your retirement plan contributions. You effectively make both employee and employer contributions (even though you are self-employed). This means you can contribute a total of up to $58,000 ($64,500 if you are age 50 or older by the end of 2021).

401(k) plans can offer a designated Roth option. If your plan allows it, you can choose to make after-tax contributions to a designated Roth account so that withdrawals can become tax free (like withdrawals from Roth IRAs). Contributions to a traditional and/or designated Roth cannot exceed the annual limit (which is $19,500, or $26,000 for those age 50 or older by December 31, 2021).

You can choose to split your contribution between a regular 401(k) and a designated Roth account—for example, $10,000 to a regular 401(k) and $9,500 to a designated Roth account; total contributions cannot exceed annual limits.

Keep in mind that taxes are only the tail that wags the investment dog. If you have a 401(k), be sure to monitor investment performance as well as fees for investment choices to optimize your retirement savings.

Pitfalls

Once you have made your elective deferral contributions, access to your money is limited by the terms of the plan and the tax law. Generally, you can't receive the funds until you retire from the company. However, you may be permitted to withdraw funds. There is a 10% penalty for distributions before age 59 ½ unless a penalty exception applies. Exceptions include:

- Death
- Disability
- Series of substantially equal periodic payments
- Payments under a qualified domestic relations order (QDRO)
- Payment of unreimbursed medical expenses exceeding your applicable AGI threshold
- Separation from service during or after the year you become age 55 (age 50 for public safety employees)
- Certain distributions to qualified military reservists called to active duty
- Birth or adoption expenses up to $5,000 IRS levy
- Qualified disaster-related distribution made before February 26, 2021 (a disaster distribution is explained later in this chapter)

You may be able to borrow from the plan or take a "hardship distribution." Plan loans are discussed in Chapter 11; hardship distributions are discussed later in this chapter.

Even though you are not taxed on your elective deferral amount (it is subtracted from your taxable compensation), such amount is still subject to Social Security and Medicare (FICA) taxes, which are withheld from your pay.

Where to Claim the Benefit

You do not have to report anything on your tax return. You will note that your elective deferral amount is subtracted from your pay so that only the reduced amount is reported as taxable compensation to you on Form W-2, which you then report as wages on Form 1040 or 1040-SR.

Self-Employed Retirement Plans

In 1962, self-employed individuals for the first time were given the opportunity to set up tax-qualified retirement plans similar to those available to corporations. Initially referred to as HR 10 plans (after the number of the tax bill creating them) or Keogh plans (after the senator sponsoring the bill), these plans have evolved over the years into the same retirement savings plans as are open to corporations. The tax law today calls them self-employed retirement plans.

Benefit ⬆

If you are a sole proprietor or independent contractor and have a profitable year, you can contribute to a qualified retirement plan. There are 2 main types of plans:

1. *Defined contribution plan*. The funds you have on retirement are based solely on what you've contributed and how well your investments have performed. A profit-sharing plan is a defined contribution plan.
2. *Defined benefit plan*. At retirement, you receive a pension based on your earnings (each year before retirement your contribution is determined by an actuary to be sufficient to pay this pension at a specific age, assuming a certain return on your investments).

You claim a deduction for your contribution. For a defined contribution plan in 2021, you can deduct 25% of compensation or $58,000, whichever is less. However, for self-employed individuals, net earnings from self-employment (the figure on which contributions are based) must be reduced by the contribution itself, so that the effective contribution rate is only 20% (not 25%). Also, you must reduce your net earnings from self-employment by the employer equivalent portion of your self-employment taxes. It may sound complicated to figure your allowable deduction, but you can use Worksheet 5.2, adapted from IRS Publication 560, to guide you (if you use tax preparation software, this is done automatically for you).

For a defined benefit plan, your deduction is based on what is actuarially required to fund the promised pension. You need the actuary to tell you what your contribution is, based on plan assumptions (e.g., at what age you expect to retire).

WORKSHEET 5.2 Figuring Your 2021 Contribution to a Defined Contribution Plan

1. Enter your net earnings from self-employment.	1. _____
2. Enter your deduction for self-employment tax (employer equivalent portion of the tax).	2. _____
3. Subtract line 2 from line 1.	3. _____
4. Enter your effective contribution rate (no more than 20%).	4. _____
5. Multiply line 3 by line 4.	5. _____
6. Multiply $290,000 by your actual contribution rate (no more than 25%).	6. _____
7. Enter the smaller of line 5 or line 6.	7. _____
8. Contribution dollar limit.	8. $58,000
9. Enter the smaller of line 7 or line 8. *This is your contribution.*	9. _____

Conditions

There are many conditions for starting and maintaining a qualified retirement plan. Some are highly complex and well beyond the scope of this book. But here are some things to watch out for:

- The plan must be set up by the extended due date of your return.

Example

In 2021, you are self-employed and profitable. You want to contribute to a profit-sharing plan for the year. You have until April 18, 2022, (or later if you obtain a filing extension) to set up and contribute to the plan.

- You must cover employees if they meet certain requirements. This raises the cost of having a plan. But you deduct contributions on behalf of your employees from your business income, reducing your net earnings from self-employment.
- You *may* have to file an annual information return with the U.S. Department of Labor. Generally, all qualified plans must file an information return, even if you are the only plan participant. However, if assets at the end of the plan are no more than $250,000, you don't have to file anything if you (or you and your spouse) are the only participants. A simplified annual return is used for plans covering fewer than 25 participants.

Example

In 2021, you have net earnings from self-employment (your profits on Schedule C) of $80,000 and your plan sets a contribution limit of 25%. Assume you did not defer any part of self-employment tax for 2021. Your contribution for 2021 on your behalf is $14,870, figured as follows:

1. Enter your net earnings from self-employment.	1.	$80,000
2. Enter your deduction for self-employment tax (employer equivalent portion of the tax).	2.	5,652
3. Subtract line 2 from line 1.	3.	74,348
4. Enter your effective contribution rate (no more than 20%).	4.	20%
5. Multiply line 3 by line 4.	5.	$14,870
6. Multiply $290,000 by your actual contribution rate (no more 20%, which is the plan contribution limit of 25%).	6.	57,000
7. Enter the smaller of line 5 or line 6.	7.	14,870
8. Contribution dollar limit.	8.	$58,000
9. Enter the smaller of line 7 or line 8. *This is your contribution.*	9.	$14,870

Planning Tip

You may want to consult with a benefits expert to help you decide which type of retirement plan is best for you, based on your profitability, age, the nature of your business, and other factors, including your desire to optimize contributions.

Pitfalls

Be aware that deductible contributions to your account claimed as an adjustment to gross income on your personal return is a reduction to qualified business income (QBI). The deduction reduces your QBI deduction (see Chapter 14).

Having a qualified retirement plan means you are subject to annual reporting requirements referred to earlier; the government wants to know some details about your plan.

Generally, for the 2021 plan year, you must file Form 5500-EZ, *Annual Return of One Participant (Owners and Their Spouses)*. But you are exempt from filing if you have a one-participant plan (the only participant is you or your spouse) and plan assets at the end of the year do not exceed $250,000. However, a return must be filed for the final year of a plan, even if assets are below the $250,000 limit.

If you are required to file, you cannot download the form from the Internet like most other tax forms because Form 5500-EZ is a scannable form that must be obtained by mail or at an IRS office. Usually it is sent to you automatically if you have filed one in the past; otherwise, you can request one from the IRS by calling 800-829-FORM. One-participant plans may file Form 5500-SF electronically in place of a paper-only Form 5500-EZ.

Either way, the form usually must be filed under the ERISA Filing Acceptance System (EFAST2) (www.efast.dol.gov). The form is due by the last day of the seventh month following the close of the plan year (e.g., August 1, 2022, because July 31 is a Sunday for the 2021 year of a calendar-year plan). You can obtain an automatic extension to October 17, 2022 (the same extended due date for federal income tax returns on extension) by filing Form 5558, *Application for Extension of Time To File Certain Employee Plan Returns*. If you obtain an automatic extension of time to file your 2021 income tax return, then you don't have to file Form 5558; you get an automatic extension for your Form 5500-EZ to October 17, 2022, as long as you and your plan have the same taxable year (retain a copy of Form 4868 used to obtain the income tax filing extension with your records for your qualified retirement plan).

If you are delinquent in filing Form 5500-EZ, you may obtain relief from penalties that would otherwise apply. Follow the steps in Revenue Procedure 2015–32.

Where to Claim the Benefit

You deduct contributions to the plan for your employees on Schedule C (such contributions are a business expense). You deduct your own contributions on Schedule 1 of Form 1040 or 1040-SR.

SEPs

A simplified employee pension (SEP) is a type of IRA that any business, whether self-employed or incorporated, can use for retirement savings. It is "simplified" because it is easy to set up and there are few administrative requirements (for example, there is no annual reporting to the government as is the case with most other company-sponsored retirement plans). The business sets up the plan and makes tax-deductible contributions to participant accounts.

Benefit 🔼

If you are self-employed (sole proprietor, independent contractor, partner, or limited liability company member) and have a profitable year, you can make deductible contributions to a simplified employee pension plan, or SEP. This is a type of IRA to which you can contribute more to than a traditional IRA. The same rules that apply to sole proprietors also apply to partners and LLC members.

You claim a deduction for the contribution on your behalf as an adjustment to gross income (not as a business expense). For 2021, the top deduction is 25% of your compensation or $58,000, whichever is less. Compensation if you are self-employed means your net earnings from self-employment, reduced by the employer equivalent portion of self-employment tax and by the contribution for yourself; your effective percentage rate becomes 20% in this case.

Example

In 2021, you are a consultant (sole proprietor) and have net earnings from self-employment of $50,000 (after reduction for the employer equivalent portion of self-employment tax). Your maximum deductible contribution is $10,000 ($50,000 × 20%).

Unlike qualified retirement plans, there is no annual reporting requirement for SEPs.

Conditions

You must meet 2 conditions to deduct your SEP contributions:

1. You must have profits if you are self-employed or receive a salary if you are an S corporation.
2. You must include your employees within the plan if they (1) are at least age 21, (2) earn more than $650 in 2021, and (3) have worked for you at least 3 of the past 5 years. If they are included in the plan, you must make contributions on their behalf based on their compensation.

Even though a SEP is a type of IRA, you can continue to make contributions on your behalf regardless of age as long as you continue to work. However, you must still commence your required minimum distributions at the set age (e.g., 72 if you attained age 70 ½ after 2019), even though you are still working. You cannot postpone taking distributions until retirement because you own more than 5% of the business.

Planning Tips

You can set up and contribute to a SEP up to the extended due date of your return.

Example

You are an independent contractor in 2021. You can set up and make your contributions to a SEP through April 18, 2022, or if you obtain an automatic 6-month filing extension for your 2021 return, to October 17, 2022.

You can convert a SEP to a Roth IRA if you meet the eligibility requirements discussed earlier in this chapter. Conversion allows all future earnings on the money to become tax free when you take withdrawals from the Roth IRA (but you must now pay a tax on the converted amount).

Pitfall

You cannot contribute to a SEP if you also have a self-employed qualified retirement plan; you must choose which plan is more favorable to you. Excess contributions are subject to the same penalties discussed earlier under IRAs.

Where to Claim the Benefit

You deduct contributions to the plan for your employees on Schedule C (such contributions are a business expense). You deduct your own contributions on Schedule 1 of Form 1040 or 1040-SR. No special form or schedule is required to figure your deduction.

SIMPLEs

Savings incentive match plans for employees, or SIMPLEs, are a type of retirement plan that allows businesses to share the cost of funding retirement savings. The company sets up the plan and employees are given the option of contributing, within set limits, a portion of their salaries to the plan. The company must make certain contributions according to a formula fixed by the tax law. The reason this type of retirement plan is SIMPLE lies in the ease of setting it up and administering it.

Benefit ⬆

If you are self-employed or a shareholder in a corporation, the business can set up a SIMPLE plan that allows you (and your employees) to make elective deferrals (salary reduction contributions) to the plan. Such amounts are excluded from your income. As an employer, you must contribute a set amount for each plan participant; you deduct your employer contribution as a business expense.

Whether you are the owner of the business or merely a rank-and-file employee, you can make elective deferral contributions to the plan. Like

401(k) plans discussed earlier, the portion of your compensation that you treat as your elective deferral is not included in your income for the year. (Limits on elective deferrals and required employer contributions are explained next under "Conditions.")

Earnings on contributions build up on a tax-deferred basis.

A SIMPLE can be set up as either a SIMPLE-IRA or a SIMPLE-401(k) plan. For purposes of the following discussion, only the SIMPLE-IRA, the more popular type, is examined.

Conditions

There are only 2 key conditions for setting up a SIMPLE plan:

1. You must be a "small employer." You must have had 100 or fewer employees who received $5,000 or more in compensation from you in the preceding year. If you set up the plan but in a later year exceed the 100-employee limit, you have 2 more years to continue the SIMPLE plan; after 2 years, you no longer qualify for a SIMPLE plan because you are no longer a small employer. You can also set up a plan if you are self-employed (even though you don't have any employees).

2. You do not maintain any other qualified plan. If, for example, you already have a profit-sharing plan, you can't also have a SIMPLE plan.

ELECTIVE DEFERRAL LIMIT

Whether you are the owner of the business or just an ordinary employee who is eligible to participate, you can agree to contribute a portion of your annual compensation to the SIMPLE plan. Your contribution, or elective deferral amount, is limited in 2021 to $13,500, or $16,500 if you are age 50 or older by the end of 2021. However, your contribution cannot exceed 100% of your compensation.

Example

In 2021, you are under age 50; you can contribute $13,500 whether your wages are $13,500, $30,000, or even $100,000. You can contribute up to 100% of your compensation, but no more than $13,500.

REQUIRED EMPLOYER CONTRIBUTION

Like other retirement plans, you must meet certain nondiscrimination requirements; your plan cannot favor you as the owner and other highly paid employees. However, SIMPLE plans don't have any complicated nondiscrimination formulas. Instead, if you make the required employer contribution on behalf of each employee who is eligible to participate, your plan is viewed as nondiscriminatory.

You must adopt one of these 2 contribution formulas and make contributions accordingly:

1. Employer matching contribution on a dollar-for-dollar basis
2. Nonelective contributions of 2% of compensation

In an employer matching contribution arrangement, you match employee contributions on a dollar-for-dollar basis up to 3% of employee compensation. If an employee does not make an elective deferral, you do not have to contribute anything on behalf of the employee.

Example

Your employee makes an elective deferral contribution to the SIMPLE of $5,000. Her annual compensation is $40,000. You must contribute $1,200 on behalf of this employee (matching her contribution of $5,000 up to 3% of $40,000).

Example

You make an elective deferral of $13,500, the maximum permitted in 2021. Your compensation is $460,000. Your matching contribution in this case is $13,500 (matching your contribution of $13,500, which is less than 3% of $460,000 [$13,800]).

If the formula requires nonelective contributions of 2% of compensation, these contributions must be made without regard to any employee elective deferrals. Thus, even if the employee makes no elective deferral, you must still contribute 2% on the employee's behalf if the employee is eligible to participate in the SIMPLE plan. No more than $290,000 of compensation can be taken into account in figuring nonelective contributions.

Example

Your employee makes an elective deferral contribution to the SIMPLE of $5,000. Her annual compensation is $40,000. You must contribute $800 (2% of $40,000).

> ### Example
>
> You make an elective deferral of $13,500, the maximum permitted in 2021. Your compensation is $300,000. Your nonelective contribution in this case is $5,800 (2% of $290,000).

Planning Tips

SIMPLEs may enable you to make the largest contribution possible (compared with self-employed retirement plans and SEPs) if your self-employment income is modest. SIMPLEs may also be the most cost-effective plan to use if you have employees. Discuss your retirement plan options with a benefits expert.

If you have made contributions to a SIMPLE-IRA, you can convert it to a Roth IRA (see earlier in this chapter). But you must wait at least 2 years following the contribution to make the conversion or be subject to a 25% early distribution penalty if you are under age 59½.

The basic limit ($13,500) and the additional limit for those age 50 and older ($3,000) can be adjusted annually for inflation.

Pitfalls

Distributions from SIMPLE-IRAs before age 59½ are subject to a higher early distribution penalty than the penalty imposed on traditional IRAs. Instead of the usual 10% early distribution penalty, you may be subject to a penalty of 25% for distributions within 2 years of SIMPLE-IRA participation if you are under age 59½.

Where to Claim the Deduction

You deduct contributions to the plan for your employees on Schedule C of Form 1040 or 1040-SR (such contributions are a business expense). You deduct your own contributions on Schedule 1 of Form 1040 or 1040-SR. You do not have to complete any form or schedule to claim the deduction.

Retirement Saver's Credit

A worker's wages just don't seem to stretch far enough to pay the bills *and* save for retirement. The tax law tries to encourage those having the most difficulty—low-income taxpayers—to make retirement plan contributions by offering a special tax credit. Those qualifying for this credit also enjoy other tax benefits from making the contributions, such as a deduction for IRA contributions. This is one of the few instances in the tax law where you get to "double dip" with a tax deduction or exclusion, plus a tax credit, for the same action (your retirement plan contribution). At the end of the road, taxpayers taking advantage of these breaks have not only enjoyed current tax savings but have also built up their personal retirement savings.

Benefit ⊕

If you contribute to a retirement plan through your company or to an IRA, you may be eligible to claim a tax credit of up to 50% of contributions up to $2,000, for a top credit of $1,000. This credit is in addition to any other benefit to which you may be entitled, such as salary reduction for a 401(k) plan contribution or a deduction for an IRA contribution.

Conditions

There are 3 conditions for claiming the retirement saver's credit. In order to claim the credit you must:

1. Have qualified retirement savings contributions for the year
2. Be an eligible individual
3. Have adjusted gross income below a set amount

QUALIFIED RETIREMENT SAVINGS CONTRIBUTIONS

Retirement savings can come from several sources; you total your contributions to all of the following:

- IRA contributions (whether they are deductible or nondeductible)
- Roth IRA contributions
- Elective deferrals (salary reduction contributions) to 401(k) plans, 403(b) annuities, or 457 plans
- Voluntary contributions to any qualified retirement plan of your employer
- ABLE account contributions through 2025

You must reduce your qualified contributions and elective deferrals by distributions included in your income that you receive from any qualified retirement plan of your employer or from a deferred compensation plan of your employer (if your employer is a state or local government or tax-exempt organization). You must also reduce your qualified contributions and elective deferrals by distributions from Roth IRAs during the 5 years following your contributions to such accounts or from a rollover to a Roth IRA. You must include not only distributions in the current year, but also those made in the 2 preceding years and in the period after the year for which you are figuring the credit up to the due date of the return (including extensions).

You want to claim the retirement saver's credit for 2021. In determining your eligible contributions and elective deferrals for 2021, you must look to distributions taken in 2019 and 2020, plus any distributions you take in 2021 and up to April 18, 2022, (assuming you file your return by this deadline).

You don't have to reduce your qualified contributions and elective deferrals by the following distributions:

- Amounts treated as loans from a qualified plan
- Excess contributions
- Deductions for dividends paid on certain employer securities
- Contributions returned to you before the due date of your return
- IRA accounts rolled over to a Roth IRA

ELIGIBLE INDIVIDUAL

To be eligible to claim the credit you must:

- Be at least 18 years old by the close of the year. Thus, even though someone who is 14 can contribute to an IRA, he or she isn't old enough to claim this credit.
- Not be claimed as a dependent on another taxpayer's return.
- Not be a full-time student (someone who is enrolled full time for at least 5 calendar months during the year).

MAGI LIMIT

To claim the top credit, your modified adjusted gross income must be below a set amount. If your MAGI is more modest, you may be entitled to a smaller credit. No credit can be claimed if your MAGI in 2021 exceeds a set limit, detailed in Table 5.2. MAGI for this purpose is your adjusted gross income increased by the foreign earned income exclusion, the foreign housing exclusion, or the exclusion for income from U.S. possessions or Puerto Rico.

Example

In 2021, you are single with MAGI of $32,000. Your elective deferral to your company's 401(k) plan for the year is $3,000. You may claim a tax credit of $200 (10% of $2,000, the maximum contribution taken into account in figuring the credit).

TABLE 5.2 MAGI Limits in 2021 for Retirement Saver's Credit

Modified Adjusted Gross Income						Applicable Percentage
Joint Return		Head of Household		All Others		
Over	Not Over	Over	Not Over	Over	Not Over	
$ 0	$39,500	$ 0	$29,625	$ 0	$19,750	50%
39,500	43,000	29,625	32,250	19,750	21,500	20
43,000	66,000	32,250	49,500	21,500	33,000	10
66,000		49,500		33,000		0

Planning Tip

The credit can be claimed in addition to other benefits that contributions entitle you to. For example, even though you excluded your 401(k) plan contributions from income, you can still claim the credit with respect to those same contributions. Similarly, even though you deducted your IRA contributions, you can also base the credit on the same contributions.

Pitfalls

Even though you meet all conditions for claiming the credit, you may lose out on the opportunity to use it if you claim certain other credits that offset your tax liability. The retirement saver's credit cannot be in excess of your regular tax liability, plus your alternative minimum tax liability, reduced by the sum of all credits to which you may also be entitled other than the child tax credit, the adoption credit, and the foreign tax credit. You cannot receive a refund from the retirement saver's credit, and you cannot carry forward the unused amount to a future year.

Lower-income individuals who qualify for the 50% credit may not have sufficient tax liability to use the entire credit (even assuming they can afford to make retirement plan contributions).

Example

A married couple has MAGI of $35,000, so they are entitled to a maximum credit of $1,000 ($2,000 x 50%). However, their tax liability is only $990 (10% of [$35,000 MAGI − $25,100 standard deduction]).

Where to Claim the Credit

You figure the credit on Form 8880, *Credit for Qualified Retirement Savings Contributions*, which you attach to the return. You enter the amount of your credit on Schedule 3 of Form 1040 or 1040-SR.

Custodial/Trustee Fees

Having an IRA isn't necessarily free—there may be charges for maintaining an account with a brokerage firm or mutual fund that acts as the IRA's custodian or trustee. Some firms charge only for trades that you make in the account, while others charge a flat management fee based on the value of assets in the account (e.g., 1% or more; lower for "robo advisers" providing computerized plans but no investment advice). These fees are not deductible in 2018 through 2025. This is so even if the fees are separately billed and you pay them with funds outside of your IRA.

Employer-Paid Retirement Planning Advice

Retirement planning is a difficult and confusing subject. Employees nearing the end of their careers often must make important decisions regarding their company retirement plans and their personal retirement savings in order to maximize their retirement income and minimize their taxes. Companies may step in to assist these employees by bringing in outside professional assistance to provide retirement planning advice. Employees taking advantage of this expertise may enjoy the fringe benefit tax free.

Benefit ⊗

You are not taxed on the value of retirement planning advice you (and your spouse) receive through your employer. You can exclude this benefit from your income. There is no dollar limit on what you can exclude.

Conditions

This fringe benefit must be provided to you by your employer on a nondiscriminatory basis (i.e., the benefit cannot be limited to owners and highly paid employees). Whether the benefit is discriminatory is something determined by your employer, not by you.

The tax-free benefit is limited to employer-paid retirement education services that you can use to make more informed investment decisions for your retirement plan contributions as well as decisions regarding distributions upon termination of employment. You may not exclude the value of related services, such as tax-preparation, accounting, legal, or brokerage services.

Planning Tip

Many companies are now offering free online investment information related to their retirement plans; take advantage of any advice offered.

Pitfall

There is no downside to taking full advantage of any advice and information your employer offers you. If, however, you believe the advice you have received is not suitable or helpful, then talk to your own retirement-planning adviser.

Where to Claim the Benefit

Since the benefit is not included in your income, you do not have to report it on your return or complete any form or schedule to claim it.

Charitable Transfers of IRA Distributions

There is a special tax break that allows those age 70 ½ and older to make tax-free transfers from their IRAs to a public charity. Technically, the transfer is called a qualified charitable distribution (QCD). It is a way to benefit your favorite charities while obtaining a tax break (the exclusion from income for the transfer).

Benefit

You may exclude up to $100,000 per year for a direct transfer from your IRA to a public charity. You can make such transfers year after year if you desire. The contribution can count toward your required minimum distribution (RMD) for the year.

Example

Your RMD for 2021 is $6,680. You instruct your IRA custodian to transfer $6,500 to the American Red Cross. Of the $6,680 RMD, $6,500 is tax free; the balance is taxable as ordinary income.

Conditions

There are 4 conditions for a QCD:

1. You must be at least age 70 ½.
2. You must be the owner of the IRA (i.e., not a beneficiary who inherited the IRA).
3. The distribution must be from a qualified account. This is a traditional or Roth IRA (although there is no tax motivation for making a QCD from a Roth IRA), or a SEP or SIMPLE-IRA that is not ongoing (i.e., no current contributions are being made). It does not include accounts in other types of qualified retirement plans, such as 401(k)s.

4. The funds must be transferred to a qualified charity by December 31. This is a public charity. Donor-advised funds and supporting organizations are not eligible recipients for a QCD.

Planning Tips

If you made nondeductible contributions to your IRA, a special rule treats amounts distributed to charities as coming first from taxable funds, instead of proportionately from taxable and nontaxable funds, as would be the case with regular IRA distributions.

If you want to make a QCD, contact your IRA custodian or trustee to determine what steps you must take. Some financial institutions require an IRA owner to submit written instructions for a QCD; others will make a transfer based on oral instructions. Be sure that the transfer identifies you to the charity (or you should notify the charity about the transfer so it knows it came from you).

The age for the QCD has not changed even though the age for RMDs has increased for those who attained age 70½ before 2019.

Pitfalls

A QCD can only be made from an IRA or a Roth IRA (although there is no tax reason to transfer funds from a Roth IRA). You cannot make a QCD from IRA-like retirement plans, such as a SIMPLE-IRA or a SEP-IRA, that you're still funding.

You cannot take a charitable contribution deduction for a QCD. The tax benefit is the exclusion from income for the IRA transfer. You may not take a QCD for any amount that is not includible in gross income.

> **Example**
>
> On December 23, 2021, an individual, age 75, directs the trustee of his IRA to make a distribution of $25,000 directly to a qualified charitable organization. The total value of the IRA is $30,000 and consists of $20,000 of deductible contributions and earnings and $10,000 of nondeductible contributions (basis). The QCD is $20,000 (deductible contributions and earnings).

If you make deductible IRA contributions after age 70½, they reduce the QCD.

> **Example**
>
> An individual, who was over age 70½ in 2020, made a deductible IRA contribution of $7,000. In 2021, the individual makes a QCD of $25,000. The maximum amount excludable is $18,000 ($25,000 − $7,000).

Where to Claim the Exclusion

You will receive Form 1099-R reporting your QCD, denoted as a distribution the taxation of which is undetermined. It's up to you to report it correctly on the return. The full amount of the QCD is shown on Line 4a of Form 1040 or 1040-SR. Do not enter any of these amounts on Line 4b of Form 1040 or 1040-SR, but write "QCD" next to that line.

Qualified Longevity Annuity Contracts

A qualified longevity annuity contract (QLAC) is an annuity contract purchased from an insurance company with funds from a qualified retirement plan or IRA (other than a Roth IRA). The QLAC is a special limited option for postponing required minimum distributions and ensuring retirement income for life.

Benefit ⊕

The value of the QLAC is excluded from the account balance used to determine required minimum distributions.

Conditions for a QLAC

There are 3 conditions for continued deferral on funds within the QLAC:

1. A maximum investment.
2. A limit on the deferral period.
3. A bar to any commutation benefit, cash surrender value, or other feature as well as a bar to any benefits payable after death.

MAXIMUM INVESTMENT

There is a dollar limit and a percentage limit on how much can be invested in a QLAC.

- For contracts entered into in 2021, the limit that can be transferred from an IRA or qualified retirement plan to the QLAC is capped at $135,000, the same limit as in 2020 (future adjustments to this limit will be made in increments of $10,000). This is a lifetime limit. If you bought a QLAC when the cap was lower (e.g., $125,000 in 2014–2017; $130,000 for 2018–2019), you can add to your existing policy (up to the new limit) or obtain a separate QLAC from another insurer for the additional amount.
- The percentage limitation is an amount equal to the excess of 25% of your account balance under the qualified plan or traditional IRA (including the

value of any QLAC held under the qualified plan for you or in a traditional IRA) as of that date over the sum of (1) the premiums paid before that date on the contract, and (2) the premiums paid on or before that date on any other contract intended to be a QLAC and that is held or was purchased for you under the qualified plan or in the traditional IRA. Your account balance means the last valuation date preceding the date of the premium payment, with certain adjustments.

DEFERRAL PERIOD

When going into a QLAC, you can specify the beginning annuity date (e.g., age 75). But the contract must provide that distributions begin no later than the first day of the first month after your 85th birthday.

BAR TO OTHER DISTRIBUTIONS

The only benefits payable to you from the QLAC are annuity payments commencing at the annuity starting date. So, once you commit to a QLAC, that's it.

However, if you die on or after the annuity starting date and have a surviving spouse, a life annuity can be paid to the surviving spouse where the annuity payment is not in excess of 100% of the annuity payment that is payable to you. If you die before the annuity starting date, the annuity for the surviving spouse is permitted to exceed 100% of the annuity payment that would have been payable to you to the extent necessary to satisfy the requirement to provide a qualified preretirement survivor annuity. The annuity to the surviving spouse must commence no later than it would for you. Other rules apply for non-spouse beneficiaries.

Instead of a life annuity payable to a beneficiary, a QLAC can permit the return of premiums after your death. The refund of premiums to the beneficiary is limited to what you paid minus any annuity payments you already received.

Planning Tip

A QLAC isn't for everyone, so think whether one makes sense for your situation. Factor in your health (and your family's health history) to project your longevity. Also consider your concerns about outliving your income and having insufficient Social Security benefits to sustain you past age 85.

Pitfalls

Once you buy it, your funds are locked in until the annuity commences. If you need the money for any reason, you're out of luck.

While the QLAC protects you from stock market downturns, you can't benefit from any upswings; your future payouts are locked in up front.

As with any annuity or similar investment product, there are investment fees involved that reduce your investment return.

Where to Report the QLAC

Information about QLACs—your annuity starting state, total premiums, and the fair market value of the QLAC at the end of the year—are reported to you on Form 1098-Q, *Qualified Longevity Annuity Contract Information*. But information about distributions from QLACs is reported on Form 1099-R. The taxable amount of QLAC payments are reported on Line 4d of Form 1040 or 1040-SR.

Hardship Distributions from Retirement Plans

Hardship distributions are distributions that a qualified retirement plan can make to you under special circumstances without losing its qualified status. Generally, the distributions are treated as any other distributions (e.g., taxable and, if under age 59 ½, subject to a 10% penalty unless some other penalty exception applies).

Special Rules for COVID-19 and Disasters

Things happen that may be devastating to individuals. COVID-19 is one example; federal disasters is another. Fortunately, there is some relief when it comes to using funds in qualified retirement plans and IRAs.

COVID-19-Related Relief

As a result of the pandemic, several tax breaks were created in 2020 to give tax-favored access to funds in qualified retirement plans. For 2021, some of these breaks continue to affect taxes.

Plan loans. COVID-19-related loans had a higher borrowing limit. These loans must begin to be repaid in 2021. Check with the plan administrator to determine repayment terms.

Distributions. COVID-19-related distributions taken from a qualified retirement plan or IRA in 2020 were subject to a 3-year income spread. Unless you opted to report the distribution in full on your 2020 return, one-third of the 2020 distribution must be reported as 2021 income.

There is an option to repay these distributions in order to maintain retirement savings. There is a 3-year period in which to replace the funds or deposit equivalent amounts in another retirement plan or IRA. If you recontribute funds, you file an amended return to recoup the taxes that have been paid on the amounts you've included in income.

> ### Example
>
> You received a coronavirus-related distribution in 2020 and chose to include the distribution amount in income over a 3-year period (2020, 2021, and 2022). In 2022, you choose to repay the full amount to an eligible retirement plan in 2022. You need to file amended federal income tax returns for 2020 and 2021 to claim a refund of the tax attributable to the amount of the distribution that you included in income for those years. You are not required to include any amount in income in 2022.

You must file Form 8915-F, *Qualified Disaster Retirement Plan Distributions and Repayments*, to report a repayment.

Disaster Relief

Relief similar to that provided for COVID-19 applies for any federally-declared disaster on or after January 1, 2020, through February 25, 2021. Loans and distributions subject to these special rules apply to those taken from December 27, 2020, through June 25, 2021. Check the Supplement for an extension of these rules for later disasters.

Repayment of loans during the incident period (the time of the disaster) are delayed automatically from the first day of the incident period to 180 days after the last day of the incident period. This automatic extension applies only to those with a principal residence located in the qualified disaster area at the time of the qualified disaster and only if the individual sustained an economic loss as a result of the qualified disaster.

Charitable Giving

Americans are very generous people. Aside from the good feeling you get from following your philanthropic nature, the tax laws reward you for making donations. Americans donated $471.44 billion to charities in 2020 (according to estimates by Giving USA 2021) and about 25% did volunteer work for charities.

This chapter covers the basic rules for claiming charitable contribution deductions, including the limits on different types of contributions and the substantiation required to support the deductions. This chapter also contains a record keeper that you can use to track your cash contributions throughout the year.

For more information, see IRS Publication 526, *Charitable Contributions*; IRS Publication 561, *Determining the Value of Donated Property*; IRS Publication 1771, *Charitable Contributions—Substantiation and Disclosure Requirements*; IRS Publication 3833, *Disaster Relief: Providing Assistance through Charitable Organizations*; and IRS Publication 4303, *A Donor's Guide to Vehicle Donations*.

Cash Donations

Donations by cash, check, or credit card to charities or government bodies are deductible within set limits if certain conditions are met. The impact of this deduction is that Uncle Sam becomes your partner in making contributions. For example, if you are in the 32% tax bracket, the government is effectively making almost $\frac{1}{3}$ of your contribution through the tax savings you enjoy from the donation.

Benefit

You can deduct the cash donations you make to public charities, private foundations other than nonoperating private foundations, and the government. Usually, you can annually write off your cash donations up to 60% of your adjusted gross income (AGI), if you itemize your deductions. However, for 2021, instead of the 60% limit you can elect to deduct cash donations to the extent of 100% of AGI. There is no dollar limit on your annual deduction; you are merely limited by your AGI. For those claiming the standard deduction, there is a limited dollar amount of contributions that can be deducted in 2021.

For those who itemize, donations made in prior years in excess of percentage cap based on your AGI can be carried forward for up to 5 years. Despite the 100%-of-AGI cap on cash donations in 2021, carryforwards from years in which a 50% or 60% of AGI limit applied are limited and cannot be used up to 100% of AGI in 2021.

Example

In 2021, you donate $50,000 cash to charity and itemize your deductions. You deduct $50,0000.

Example

In 2021, you have an itemized charitable contribution carryover of $50,000 from a donation you made in 2019 that exceeded the 60%-of-adjusted-gross-income limit applicable that year and did not itemize in 2020. In 2021, if you itemize deductions, you may deduct $50,000, to the extent of 60% of your AGI. If your AGI in 2021 is $80,000, you can deduct only $48,000 of the carryover (60% of $80,000). The balance of $12,000 is carried forward to 2022.

Conditions

To claim a deduction for your cash contributions to charity, you must meet all 3 conditions:

1. Donations must be made to a qualified charity.
2. You cannot deduct donations exceeding your adjusted gross income if you itemize or $300 ($600 on a joint return) if you claim the standard deduction.
3. You must have proof of your donations.

QUALIFIED CHARITY

Just because a charity calls itself one does not mean it is tax-qualified; it must receive IRS approval to be a tax-exempt organization to which contributions are tax deductible. The charity must be a domestic nonprofit organization, trust, community chest, fund, or foundation that is operated exclusively for one of the following purposes:

- Charitable purposes
- Fostering amateur sports competition
- Prevention of cruelty to children or animals
- Religious purposes
- Scientific, literary, and educational purposes

Other organizations or places to which you can make tax-deductible contributions are:

- Domestic fraternal groups operating under a lodge system
- Domestic nonprofit veterans' organizations or auxiliary units
- Legal services corporations set up under the Legal Services Corporation Act

- Nonprofit cemetery and burial companies (as long as voluntary contributions benefit the whole cemetery and not merely your plot)
- U.S. government; government of a U.S. possession, state, city, or town; or Indian tribal government

Certain well-known charities, such as the American Red Cross, the United Way, the Boy Scouts and Girl Scouts, and the Salvation Army, are clearly authorized to accept tax-deductible contributions. Some charities may be less known, and the IRS warns taxpayers to beware of scams that pop up following disasters, such as the COVID-19 pandemic and the Surfside building collapse. If you have any question about an organization's status, ask about its status or check with the IRS, which maintains an online database in IRS Publication 78, *Cumulative List of Organizations*, at www.irs.gov/charities-non-profits/exempt-organizations-select-check.

Once you determine that an organization is eligible to receive a tax-deductible contribution, you may want to check whether the organization is worthy. You can see how much of your contribution goes to the purpose you intend versus being used for administrative costs (e.g., advertising, salaries) of the organization at Charity Navigator at www.charitynavigator.org, GuideStar at www.guidestar.org, or Better Business Bureau Give.org at www.give.org.

AGI LIMIT

Your deduction if itemizing usually is limited to 60% of your adjusted gross income (AGI), a tax concept explained more thoroughly in the introduction to this book, but the AGI limit for 2021 is 100% of AGI if elected, after taking into account all other charitable contributions for the year.

Note: There are some organizations to which donations are limited to 30%, but this is not the usual case. To find out more about so-called "30% charities," see IRS Publication 526, *Charitable Contributions*, at www.irs.gov.

DEDUCTION FOR NON-ITEMIZERS

If you claim the standard deduction instead of itemizing, you can deduct charitable contributions made in 2021 up to $300. The limit applies per taxpayer, so joint filers can deduct up to $600. It applies only to cash donations.

SUBSTANTIATION

You must have proof of your donations in the event your return is questioned. The tax law is very specific about the type of proof (called substantiation in the tax law) that is recognized by the IRS.

Donations in *any* amount must be substantiated by a written acknowledgment from the charity or a bank statement. Formerly, you may have deducted cash donations to the weekly collection plate or the Salvation Army's red kettle during holiday time; such unsubstantiated donations are no longer allowed. Organizations that accept weekly cash donations may make arrangements to substantiate these donations, such as providing you with a monthly acknowledgment of total donations for the period.

Charitable donations through payroll deductions are treated as substantiated by a variety of means, including pay stubs, W-2 forms, or other written statements from an employer.

If the donation is more than $75, get a disclosure statement from the charity stating the value of any benefit received from the organization. Donations of $250 or more require a written acknowledgment from the charity; a canceled check is not enough proof in this case. More details on this statement may be found later in this chapter.

EXAMPLES OF DEDUCTIBLE CONTRIBUTIONS

- Checks payable to charity
- Collection plate contributions substantiated by the charity
- Credit card donations
- Rebates applied through credit card programs
- Withholding from wages for charitable purposes
- License plate fee above the normal plate cost if the state gives the extra amount to a qualified charity
- Voluntary contributions to a qualified charity made in the space provided on your state income tax return (you effectively make the donation by increasing your state income tax payment or reducing your state income tax refund)

Planning Tips

You can use the record keeper at the end of this chapter to track your total distributions for the year. Be sure to obtain substantiation for all donations.

TIMING ISSUES

You can deduct contributions made up to the last day of the year. In making year-end contributions, keep these points in mind:

- Contributions by credit card are deductible in the year you charge them, not in the year you pay your credit card bill. If you charge the gift by December 31, 2021, it is deductible in 2021 even though you pay the credit card company in 2022.

- Contributions by check that are mailed before December 31 are deductible in the year of mailing even though the charity receives the check and cashes it in the following year.
- A pledge to make a charitable contribution is not deductible until you pay the pledge.
- Contributions made through a pay-by-phone bank account are not deductible when you make the call but rather as of the payment date on the bank statement.

If you have not received a written acknowledgment from the charity by the deadline for filing your return, obtain a filing extension. This will allow you to meet substantiation requirements.

AGI PLANNING

Generally, tax planning dictates that you try to *reduce* your adjusted gross income to boost your deduction for medical expenses as well as eligibility for certain exclusions and credits. But if you make sizable donations and itemize your deductions, you may not want or need to adopt strategies to reduce your AGI. By claiming your charitable deduction, you effectively reduce or eliminate the tax on your income.

Example

In 2021, you donate $50,000 in cash to a charitable organization and are itemizing your deductions. Your AGI is $100,000 so the contribution is fully deductible. You can try to reduce your AGI to reduce your tax bill, but if you have a carryover of charitable contributions from 2020, don't reduce your AGI below an amount that will allow you to use it completely.

Pitfalls

Despite your generous nature and good intentions, you can easily slip up on technicalities that can prevent you from claiming a deduction. For example, an owner of a nationally well-known tax preparation company donated stock to charity. Since the value of the donation was never in question, he never bothered to obtain a qualified appraisal as required by the tax law. This tax-savvy taxpayer lost out on a sizable deduction for his stock donation because he overlooked a basic requirement for claiming it and the IRS caught him.

NONQUALIFIED ORGANIZATIONS

An organization may seem like a charity and still not be one. Don't assume that a hospital or school is automatically qualified to accept deductible donations. If it is operated for profit, your contributions are not deductible.

You may not deduct donations to foreign charities unless allowed by international treaties (for example, donations to charities in Mexico and Canada can be deductible). However, a domestic charity set up to distribute funds abroad may be a qualified organization under the rules discussed earlier.

Other organizations that are nonqualified include:

- Sororities and fraternities.
- Civic leagues, chambers of commerce, business leagues, or labor unions. However, you may be able to treat contributions to these organizations as deductible business expenses (see Chapter 14).
- Professional associations of attorneys, doctors, and accountants. However, some unrestricted gifts to state bar associations may be deductible (the bar association reports to you the portion of annual dues treated as charitable contributions).
- Foreign organizations other than certain Canadian, Israeli, or Mexican charitable organizations.
- Homeowners' associations.
- Political organizations and candidates.

OTHER NONDEDUCTIBLE DONATIONS

If you claim the standard deduction, you cannot deduct charitable contributions in 2021 in excess of $300 ($600 on a joint return). This is so regardless of the amount of your generosity.

Even if you itemize, you cannot deduct a donation you make directly to an individual, no matter how worthy the person is. For example, suppose your neighbor's house was severely damaged by a fire and you give your neighbor $1,000 to help him through the days following the fire. Your generosity does not warrant a tax deduction.

You cannot deduct a qualified charitable distribution from your IRA (discussed later in this chapter). You cannot deduct donations made on your behalf that are based on the purchases you make; these charitable contributions are made at no additional cost to you. For example, the 0.5% donations made through AmazonSmile or the donations (3% on average) through iGive based on your purchases are not deductible by you.

If you donate unused frequent flyer miles to Make-a-Wish Foundation, you cannot deduct them. According to the charity, frequent flyer miles are "a gift or an award from the corporation to the individual" (which means a taxpayer has no basis in them on which to figure a deductible amount).

EXPIRATION OF CARRYOVER

Unlike other carryovers in the tax law that run indefinitely, the carryover of excess charitable contributions is limited to 5 years. If you have such carryovers, don't let the 5 years expire causing you to waste potential write-offs. Consider realizing sufficient income to allow you to use up your carryovers. And don't elect to use the 100% of AGI limit for cash donations in 2021 or you'll lose the carryover.

Where to Claim the Deduction

If you itemize your deductions, report your charitable deduction for your cash donations on Schedule A of Form 1040 or 1040-SR. If you make only cash donations, you do not need any additional form or schedule other than Schedule A to report your charitable contributions. If you don't itemize, the deduction for cash donations up to $300 ($600 on a joint return) is claimed on line 12b of Form 1040 or 1040-SR.

Appreciated Property Donations

The government encourages donations of appreciated property held for more than one year by allowing tax deductions at the property's value (rather than limiting them to the donor's cost or other tax basis) as long as certain conditions are met. Even though cuts in the tax rates diminish the value of such contributions from a tax-savings perspective, philanthropic-minded individuals can still enjoy considerable tax breaks while benefiting their favorite causes.

Benefit

You can claim a charitable contribution deduction *and* avoid capital gains by donating appreciated property to charity. As long as the property has been held for more than one year, the charity is qualified, and other conditions are met, the donation is based on the property's value.

Example

You own stock you bought years ago for $2,000 that is now worth $10,000. If you donate it to a tax-exempt organization, you can claim a charitable contribution deduction of $10,000, the current value of the stock. What's more, you don't have to pay capital gains tax on your $8,000 of appreciation ($10,000 − $2,000), which would have cost you $1,200 ($8,000 × 15%). If you are in the 24% tax bracket, your deduction saves you $2,400 in taxes ($10,000 × 24%). Your total savings from your generosity is $3,600 ($1,200 capital gains tax saved plus $2,400 tax savings from the deduction).

Donations of appreciated property are limited to 30% of your adjusted gross income for the year, in most cases. Donations in excess of this limit can be carried forward for up to 5 years.

Donations of appreciated property that do not meet the conditions listed next are deductible only to the extent of your cost. In the case of donations of tangible personal property that do not meet the conditions, donations are based on basis (generally, cost) rather than value, but can be claimed up to 60% of your adjusted gross income.

Conditions

To claim a deduction for the value of the property you donate to charity, you must meet all 4 conditions:

1. The property must be held long-term ("holding period").
2. If the property is tangible personal property, such as artwork, cars, and equipment, the charity must put the property to use in its exempt purpose ("tangible property used in the charity's exempt purpose").
3. The property cannot be "ordinary income property" (which is property that would generate ordinary income rather than capital gain if it were sold instead of donated).
4. You must comply with substantiation requirements.

Remember that donations to only a qualified charity produce a tax deduction for you. Which organizations are qualified charities, and which are not, is discussed earlier in the chapter under "Cash Donations."

HOLDING PERIOD

To meet the long-term holding period, you must own the property for more than one year prior to the date of the donation.

TANGIBLE PROPERTY USED IN THE CHARITY EXEMPT PURPOSE

If you give property other than securities or real estate, you are giving tangible personal property. Items commonly donated in this category include works of art, books, antiques, furniture, equipment, and collectibles.

Use of the property in the charity's exempt purpose means that the use serves a function related to the charity's exemption. For example, if you donate art to a school and the school displays the work in the library or school museum so that students can study it, the property is being used in the charity's exempt purpose.

If the charity sells the property you donate, you don't meet the related use test even though the proceeds certainly serve the charity's exempt purpose. The tax law treats the sale as an unrelated purpose (see "Planning Tips" for protection).

PROPERTY IS NOT ORDINARY INCOME PROPERTY

If you donate appreciated property that would produce ordinary income if it were sold rather than donated, you cannot deduct the property's value; your donation is limited to your cost. Examples of ordinary income property include inventory, stock in trade, farm crops, and works of art, books, and memoranda donated by the person who created them. For example, businesses, whether or not incorporated, can claim an enhanced charitable contribution for donations of their food inventory.

SUBSTANTIATION REQUIREMENTS

If the total deduction claimed for your property donations is more than $500, you *must* attach Form 8283, *Noncash Charitable Contributions*, to your return.

If you make a donation exceeding $5,000 (one item or a collection), you must obtain a written appraisal for your donation. An appraisal is also required for a donation of used clothing or a household item valued at over $500 that is not in good used condition or better. The appraisal is summarized on the form.

You do not need a written appraisal if the donation is:

- Publicly traded securities—you simply use the market value on the date of the donation.
- Nonpublicly traded stock (stock in a private corporation) if valued at $10,000 or less. You do need an appraisal if the value exceeds this amount.

In addition to obtaining the appraisal, the charity must acknowledge on Form 8283 that it received your donation (so leave enough time to obtain this acknowledgment before filing your return).

If you donate art valued at $20,000 or more, you must attach the written appraisal to the return, along with a color photo or slide, if the IRS asks for it.

If you are required by the tax law to obtain an appraisal for your property donation, you must use a qualified appraiser (a person with the right credentials). Obtain the appraisal no earlier than 60 days before you make the donation. You must have the appraisal in hand by the time you file your return (including extensions).

Planning Tips

If you are concerned that the charity may sell the tangible property you donated, which would limit your deduction to your cost, ask the charity for a letter stipulating that it has no immediate intentions of selling. Then your deduction for the value of the property would be protected even if the charity later changes its intentions and sells your donation.

Donations of collectibles can yield even greater tax savings than donations of securities. The reason: Gain on a sale of collectibles is taxed up to 28%, compared with a top 15% (or 20% for those essentially in the top tax bracket) rate of gain from a sale of securities. Donations avoid the capital gains tax entirely.

ELECTION TO CHANGE AGI LIMIT

If you qualify to deduct the market value of your property, you can elect to reduce the gift by its appreciation and instead use a 50% AGI limit (instead of the 30% AGI limit that is usually required). This election makes sense when there is little appreciation on the property, and opting to reduce the deduction by appreciation still gives you a greater write-off.

> **Example**
>
> You donate stock valued at $100,000 that cost you $90,000. Your AGI is $180,000. If you do nothing, your deduction for your $100,000 is limited to $54,000 (30% of $180,000). But if you make the election to reduce the deduction by its appreciation so that it is limited to your cost of $90,000, you can deduct it in full; your limit in this case is 50% of AGI or $90,000.

You make the election simply by attaching your own statement to your return explaining that you are making the election; no special IRS form or schedule is required. But you can't change your mind later unless your election was based on a material mistake; you can't change your mind simply because you later reconsider the situation and prefer to carry forward the unused deduction that you could have claimed.

IRS APPRAISAL

If you are donating very expensive works of art valued at $50,000 or more, you can protect your deduction from IRS questioning by obtaining an advance valuation of the art from the IRS's Art Advisory Panel. If the IRS agrees to give you this advance valuation, you'll receive an IRS Statement of Value (SOV) that you attach to your return to support your deduction. There is a fee of $7,500 for one to 3 items, and $400 for each additional item, and obtaining an SOV can take as long as a year. The good news is that an SOV avoids hassles with the IRS over valuation later on. But the bad news is that if you don't agree with the SOV, you are left with no alternative but to litigate the issue (you still must attach it to your return, even if you claim a higher deduction than the SOV).

Pitfalls

Donations of appreciated property can produce important tax savings for you, but here are some things to watch out for.

PENALTY FOR OVERVALUATIONS

Valuing property isn't an exact science. When making charitable donations, you hope that the property is valued as highly as possible to boost your deduction. But don't be too generous in your estimations; substantial overvaluations of charitable donations resulting in a tax underpayment exceeding $5,000 can lead to a penalty.

- If the value claimed is 200% or more of the correct value (and results in an underpayment exceeding $5,000), the penalty is 20% of the underpayment.
- If the value claimed is 400% or more of the correct value (and results in an underpayment exceeding $5,000), the penalty is 40% of the underpayment.

Example

You donate an oil painting to charity and estimate that its value is $35,000. In truth, it is actually worth only $10,000. Since the value claimed is more than 200% of the correct value and your valuation results in your underpaying tax by more than $5,000, you are subject to a 20% penalty of the resulting underpayment of tax. In this case, for example, if you had been in the 28% tax bracket, there would have been a $7,000 underpayment ([$35,000 − $10,000] × 28%) so your penalty would be $1,400 ($7,000 × 20%). If you had valued the painting at $40,000, your penalty would have been 40% of the underpayment.

The penalty is applied on an item-by-item basis. So, for example, if you donate 2 objects, overvaluing one item and undervaluing the other, you cannot offset the undervaluation by the overvaluation.

DONATIONS OF PROPERTY THAT HAS DECLINED IN VALUE

If you donate property that meets all of the conditions discussed, your tax deduction is based on the value of the property, even if you paid more for it. In effect, you get no benefit from the loss in value.

Unless the charity has a specific need for your item, it is advisable to sell the property rather than donate it if you can claim a tax deduction for your loss (for example, the property is investment property on which a capital loss can be claimed). You can then donate the proceeds so that the charity receives the same benefit. But selling the property will allow you to take a tax loss on the sale.

> **Example**
>
> You own stock you paid $10,000 for years ago. It is now worth $2,000. If you donate the stock, your deduction is limited to $2,000. If you sell the stock and donate the proceeds, the charity receives the same $2,000. However, you can claim a tax loss of $8,000 ($10,000 − $2,000). You can use this loss to offset your capital gains and then up to $3,000 of your ordinary income; excess capital losses can be carried forward indefinitely and used in future years.

This strategy, however, does not apply to personal (noninvestment or non-business) items, such as your personal car, because you cannot take a capital loss deduction on their sale.

APPRAISALS AND ADDITIONAL COSTS

You may have costs over and above the property you're donating. There may be appraisal costs for determining the value of the donation so you know how much to deduct. There may be packing, shipping, and insurance costs to send donated items to a charitable organization. These costs are not deductible in 2018 through 2025 due to the suspension of the miscellaneous itemized deduction subject to the 2%-of-adjusted-gross-income floor.

Where to Claim the Deduction

Like cash donations if you itemize deductions, you report property donations on Schedule A of Form 1040 or 1040-SR.

But you may also have to complete Form 8283, *Noncash Charitable Contributions*, as explained earlier under "Substantiation."

Used Clothing and Car Donations

Clothing that no longer fits, appliances and sporting equipment that are no longer used, and cars being replaced may be of great benefit to someone else. The tax law rewards donations of these items to charities that can put them to continued good use by permitting a tax deduction for those who itemize if certain conditions are met.

Benefit

Your old clothing, linens, toys, cars, and other items can be of benefit to others. Consider donating them to charity and taking a tax deduction for your efforts. A deduction of these items is generally subject to the 50% of adjusted gross income limit. This means that donations of these items are included along with your cash contributions to determine your annual limit.

Conditions

The items must be donated to a qualified charity (see the explanation of a qualified charity under "Cash Donations" earlier in this chapter).

You cannot claim a deduction if you donate items directly to an individual, no matter how much in need that person may be. For example, if a fire destroys a neighbor's home and you provide your neighbor with clothing and other items, you cannot claim a charitable contribution deduction for your generosity.

For donations of used clothing and household items, no deduction can be claimed unless the items are in "good used condition or better." However, if a single item is appraised at over $500, it can be deducted even though it is not in good used condition (although condition certainly affects its value).

Special substantiation rules apply to donations of cars, boats, and planes valued at over $500. You must obtain a written acknowledgment, Form 1098-C, *Contributions of Motor Vehicles, Boats, and Airplanes*, within 30 days of the date of contribution or the date that the organization sells the vehicle without using it in any significant way (e.g., driving a car to deliver meals to the needy for one year). If the organization sells the vehicle without using it in a significant way in its charitable activities or making any improvements to the vehicle, your donation is limited to the sale proceeds that the organization receives from a sale. Information about the sale is provided to the IRS. Use of Form 1098-C is mandatory for these donations; a thank-you letter from the charity is no substitute.

If you value a car over $250 but not over $500 and the charity sells it, you can deduct the actual fair market value (you are not limited to the sales proceeds). But if you value the car over $500 and the charity sells it for less than $500, your maximum deduction is $500. For example, if you value the car at $650 and the charity sells it for $450, you can deduct $500.

Planning Tips

Don't know what your used items are worth? Here are some resources you can turn to for help:

- Used cars: Kelley Blue Book at https://kbb.com provides free online prices for used cars, based on the vehicle's mileage, condition, and other factors.
- Used clothing and household items: The Salvation Army's Valuation Guide at https://satruck.org/Home/DonationValueGuide is a free online guide to valuing used clothing, appliances, furniture, and other household items. The Valuation Guide for Goodwill Donor at https://goodwillnne.org/donate/donation-value-guide is another free online guide.
- Used computers, smartphones, and other electronics: Gadget Value at www.gadgetvalue.com provides values for old PCs.

In one case, a court allowed a donation for used clothing valued at $25 per bag.

There are some apps to help with valuation, such as TurboTax's ItsDeductible Donation Tracker and Donation Assistant by Tax Act, which are free. There are also a number of apps, such as IDonatedIt, that you can use for valuation purposes (check the fees for using an app). You can use your smartphone to take photos of the donated items to keep with your records.

Pitfalls

Don't expect the charity to provide you with a valuation of your donation. It's up to you to assess the value of the items you donate; the charity merely confirms that you actually made the donation.

Don't include in the amount of your charitable contribution any appraisal fees or the cost of packing and shipping you incur when making property donations. These expenses are not deductible due to the suspension of miscellaneous itemized deductions between 2018 and 2025.

Where to Claim the Deduction

For information about where to claim a deduction for your donation, see the rules under "Appreciated Property Donations" earlier in this chapter, including the rules on substantiation and filing Form 8283, *Noncash Charitable Contributions*. Also attach Form 1098-C, *Contributions of Motor Vehicles, Boats, and Airplanes*, if you donated such an item valued at over $500.

Intellectual Property Donations

If you give a patent, a certain copyright, or other intellectual property to charity, you can not only deduct the initial contribution, but can also claim deductions in future years for a percentage of the income that the charity derives from the property.

Benefit ⊜

You can claim an itemized deduction for donations of intellectual property to charity of:

- The fair market value of the donation in the year of the donation for intellectual property that you did not create (or, for self-created property, the amount that would have been ordinary income had you sold it rather than donated it).

- A percentage of the income derived from the property for up to 10 years following the year of the donation. The percentage is based on Table 6.1 (the table runs for 12 years because of the potential for a donee to have a fiscal year or a short tax year).

TABLE 6.1 Deduction for Income from Intellectual
Property Donations

Year Ending after Date of Contribution	Applicable Percentage
1st	100%
2nd	100
3rd	90
4th	80
5th	70
6th	60
7th	50
8th	40
9th	30
10th	20
11th	10
12th	10

Conditions

At the time of the donation, you must tell the charity that you intend to claim the additional deductions. This is done by providing the charity with your personal written statement of your intention to treat the contribution as a qualified intellectual contribution. This statement must also describe the property and the date of the donation.

Planning Tip

The additional deduction applies to all types of intellectual property donated after June 3, 2004. This includes not only patents and certain copyrights, but also trademarks, trade names, trade secrets, know-how, certain software, and certain applications or registrations of this property.

Pitfall

The additional deductions can be claimed for up to only 10 years following the year of the intellectual property donation.

If the life of the property is shorter than 10 years, you cannot claim additional deductions beyond this life.

The additional deduction does not apply to donations of intellectual property to a private foundation other than an operating private foundation.

Where to Claim the Deduction

Each year the charity informs you (and the IRS) of the income derived from your donation on Form 8899, *Notice of Income from Donated Intellectual Property*.

To claim a charitable contribution deduction, complete Schedule A of Form 1040 or 1040-SR. You may also have to complete Form 8283, *Noncash Charitable Contributions*, as explained earlier in this chapter under "Substantiation Requirements" for appreciated property donations.

Real Estate Donated for Conservation Purposes

Real estate development has gobbled up open spaces and turned them into houses, shopping malls, and office buildings. But the government wants to encourage the maintenance of green spaces and does so by permitting tax deductions for donations of certain property interests for this purpose.

Benefit ⊜

Certain donations of partial interests in real property to government agencies or publicly supported charities for exclusively conservation purposes may entitle you to a deduction. Such donations include:

- Your entire interest in real property other than retained rights to subsurface oil, gas, or other minerals. For example, you own land and donate it to your town, retaining these mineral rights.

- A remainder interest in real property. For example, you own land. You keep the right to use it for the rest of your life, giving your town the remainder interest in the property. You do this by deeding the remainder interest to the town.

- An easement, restrictive covenant, or similar property restrictions granted in perpetuity (meaning forever). For example, you own property but give your town an easement limiting the use of a portion of it for a bird sanctuary forever. Even if you later sell the property, the new owner must continue to respect the easement and keep the use as a bird sanctuary.

Conditions

Only donations for qualified conservation purposes entitle you to a deduction. Qualified conservation purposes include:

- The preservation of land areas for outdoor recreation, education, or scenic enjoyment.

- Preservation of historically important land areas or structures.

- Protection of plant, fish, and wildlife habitats or similar natural ecosystems.

For a conservation easement contribution that relates to a building in a registered historic district, there is a $500 filing fee if the claimed deduction is more than $10,000. This payment is accompanied by Form 8283-V, *Voucher for Filing Fee Under Sec. 170(f)(13)*.

Planning Tips

To make the donation of an easement on your property, you may need to pay an attorney to handle the legal work involved.

Donations are deductible up to 50% of the contribution base (which is essentially adjusted gross income), instead of the usual 30% limit (provided the use of the donated property does not prevent farming or ranching). Farmers and ranchers have a 100% limit. Unused contributions because of this limit can be carried forward for up to 15 years.

Pitfalls

Once you give away this interest, you can't change your mind and get it back. As explained earlier, the donation must be in perpetuity (forever). Here is a list of actions that run counter to the rule about perpetuity and can cost you a deduction for any conservation easement donation:

- Failing to subordinate a mortgage to the easement (making the interests of the lender secondary to those of the easement, which requires the consent of the lender)
- Making a conservation easement in North Dakota, which limits the term of an easement to 99 years
- Providing (even informally) that the property be returned if the IRS denies a tax deduction
- Retaining the right to substitute property (even though no property is ever returned to you)

The IRS has designated syndicated conservation easements, which allow investors to deduct more than their economic outlays, as a listed transaction. Anyone entering one in 2021 must disclose this on his or her tax return. The failure to make this disclosure can result in penalties.

Where to Claim the Deduction

For information about where to claim a deduction for your donation, see the rules under "Appreciated Property Donations," earlier in this chapter, including the rules on substantiation and filing Form 8283.

Bargain Sales

Taxpayers can have their cake and eat it, too—recoup their investments in property while obtaining tax deductions to boot—by making bargain sales of property to charity. It's a bargain because the charity is paying only a portion of the property's actual value, typically the donor's original cost for the property. It's a sale because the donor is receiving payment for the transaction and not merely donating the entire value of the property. Even so, a partial tax deduction is permitted under certain conditions.

Benefit ⬄

If you have appreciated property, you can recoup your investment while obtaining a tax deduction when you make a bargain sale to charity. In effect, the donation is viewed as 2 transactions: part sale and part gift.

You figure your gain on the sale by allocating the basis between the sale and the gift part as follows:

Step 1: Divide the sales proceeds by the fair market value of the property (include any outstanding debt as sales proceeds).

Step 2: Apply the percentage in Step 1 to the adjusted basis of the property to find the portion of the basis allocated to the sale.

Step 3: Subtract the resulting basis of Step 2 from the sales proceeds to find your gain.

Example

You sell property to your favorite charity for what you paid for it ($12,000). At the time of the donation, it is worth $20,000. Under Step 1, divide $12,000 by $20,000, which is 0.6 or 60%. Apply 60% to the adjusted basis of $12,000, which is $7,200, the basis allocated to the sale. Your gain is $4,800, the difference between your sales proceeds of $12,000 and this basis of $7,200. By making the donation, you have obtained a charitable contribution deduction of $8,000 (the appreciation on the property), while recouping your initial investment, so you are out-of-pocket nothing. Had you sold the property to someone other than a charity, you would have paid capital gains tax on the gain of $8,000 ($20,000 − $12,000), or $1,200 at a 15% capital gain rate (assuming you are not in the 37% tax bracket).

Conditions

The same conditions apply to bargain sales as to other charitable contributions (for example, the charity must be an IRS-approved organization). For conditions, see earlier in this chapter.

Planning Tip

A bargain sale can enable you to recover your cost (investment in the property) while also obtaining a deduction for any increased value in the property. Donating the property through a bargain sale saves you the time and expense of selling it to a third party in order to raise the funds to make the donation you would make if you keep your initial investment.

Pitfall

If the property you donate is not the type of property that entitles you to a donation of the appreciation (for example, you didn't own it for more than one year), then the bargain sale doesn't produce any charitable contribution deduction. Of course, the charity still obtains the item at a bargain price.

You must allocate the basis of the property on a bargain sale even if the annual AGI limit prevents you from claiming a charitable contribution deduction.

Where to Claim the Deduction

You report the bargain sale on 2 schedules accompanying Form 1040 or 1040-SR: Use Schedule D to report the sale portion and Schedule A to report the gift portion.

Details on reporting gifts of appreciated property are explained earlier in this chapter.

Volunteer Expenses

During natural disasters, the efforts of volunteers are widespread and dramatic. According to the federal agency governing AmeriCorps and Senior Corps, about 77.4 million Americans did some volunteer work in 2017 (there are no more recent statistics). While individuals bear the burden of the time and effort they put in, the government helps defray any actual out-of-pocket costs through a deduction that can be claimed if certain conditions are met.

Benefit ⊜

If you incur out-of-pocket expenses in serving your favorite charity, you can deduct these costs as part of your itemized deduction for charitable donations.

If you use your vehicle for charitable purposes, including attending meetings of organizations you serve, you can deduct your actual vehicle expenses for gas and oil or mileage at the rate of 14¢ per mile. The 14¢ per mile rate is fixed by law (unchanged since 1997); it cannot be increased by the IRS and so has remained constant for many years. Whichever method you select, you can also write off parking and tolls.

Conditions

As long as you incur out-of-pocket costs for a qualified charity (explained earlier in this chapter under "Cash Donations"), your costs are deductible.

EXAMPLES OF DEDUCTIBLE UNREIMBURSED EXPENSES

Materials and supplies you furnish (e.g., stamps)

Related costs of hosting a fund-raiser (e.g., invitations, food, and beverages)

Telephone calls

Travel expenses, including meals and lodging for overnight trips away from home to serve as an official delegate to a convention of a church, charitable, veteran, or other similar organization

Travel expenses to work for a charitable organization (such as Habitat for Humanity and Meals on Wheels)

Uniforms required in serving the organization

Planning Tip

Keep track of your mileage and out-of-pocket expenses on behalf of the charity. In a diary, logbook, or app, note the odometer readings for every charity-related trip for which your car is used.

Pitfall

Just because you are not compensated by the charity for your efforts doesn't automatically mean that every cost you incur on behalf of the charity is deductible. You *cannot* deduct:

- The value of your time and energy. Even if you perform work for the charity, you cannot deduct what you would have charged for your expertise.

Example

You are an attorney who does pro bono work for a local charity. You cannot deduct your usual hourly rate for the time spent on this charitable activity.

- The rental value of your home or vacation home that you allow the charity to use in its fund-raising activities.

- Babysitting expenses you paid to enable you to put in time for your charity.
- Travel costs to attend a convention for a nonprofit organization if you are not a delegate.
- Travel costs to work on a project for a nonprofit organization if there is a significant element of personal pleasure, recreation, or vacation involved.

You *must* substantiate your out-of-pocket expenses in order to deduct them. If total expenses are $250 or more, you must obtain a written acknowledgment from the charity for your activities. Without this substantiation, a deduction is limited to $249, provided there are credit card statements, canceled checks, or other documentation.

Where to Claim the Deduction

To claim a charitable deduction for your unreimbursed expenses, you must complete Schedule A of Form 1040 or 1040-SR.

Tickets to Fund-Raisers, Raffles, and Sporting Events

Who hasn't bought a ticket to a fund-raising event or activity, such as a raffle or dinner dance, to benefit a charity? Just because the check is written out to a charity doesn't automatically entitle taxpayers to a deduction. Special rules govern the extent, if any, to which the cost of fund-raising tickets may be deductible.

Benefit ⊜

You can deduct the purchase price for raffle tickets and charity-sponsored events in excess of the regular admission price or other benefit you receive.

Example

You pay $100 for a ticket to an evening sponsored by your favorite charity that includes dinner and a show. The value of the dinner and show (what you would have paid regularly) is $75. You can deduct $25 (the excess cost over the regular price). If you wind up not going (e.g., you are ill that evening), you can deduct $100.

Condition

If you pay more than $75, the charity must supply you with a written explanation of the value of the benefit you receive so that you can figure your deduction, if any.

Planning Tip

If your donation entitles you to a ticket to a charity event but you do not want to attend, you can refuse to accept the ticket. In this case you can deduct your entire contribution (provided you meet other conditions such as substantiation). Make sure that an acknowledgment you receive from the charity reflects your refusal to accept the ticket.

Pitfalls

You cannot deduct any of the cost of Girl Scout cookies you buy for your own consumption. The cost of the cookies is treated as their fair market value so you haven't made any gift. But if you leave the cookies with the troop, you may treat your payment as a deduction. Similarly, if you donate the cookies to a charity, you can deduct your cost (not the estimated retail value).

No deduction is allowed for a donation entitling you to receive the right to buy tickets or seating at college or university athletic events.

Where to Claim the Deduction

To claim a charitable deduction for your donations in connection with tickets, raffles, or other fund-raisers, you must complete Schedule A of Form 1040 or 1040-SR. You do not have to attach the written explanation for your donations to your return; save them for your records with the copy of your return.

If you do not make donations of property, you do not need any additional form or schedule other than Schedule A to report your charitable contributions.

Membership Fees to Nonprofit Organizations

Anthropologist Margaret Mead said, "Never doubt that a small group of thoughtful, committed citizens can change the world. Indeed it is the only thing that ever has." Perhaps that's why so many Americans belong to organizations of all kinds, including religious, civic, and fraternal organizations. Belonging is rewarded taxwise to a certain extent by permitting the cost of dues to be deductible, within certain limits.

Benefit ⊜

If you pay dues to nonprofit organizations, you can treat the payments as cash contributions subject to the rules discussed earlier in this chapter. Examples of membership fees that are deductible include payments to religious organizations (e.g., your church) and fraternal organizations operating under a lodge system (e.g., Elks Club).

You must reduce your deduction, however, by the value of any benefits (other than token amounts) you receive, such as monthly journals.

Example

You donate $100 to your local public broadcasting station during its annual fund drive. You receive a DVD of one of its programs. Your deduction is limited to the donation in excess of the value of the DVD (the station should supply you with this information).

You do *not* have to reduce your donation by these tokens distributed by the charity in gratitude for your gift:

- Items costing no more than $11.30 if your gift is at least $56 in 2021 (these figures are adjusted annually for inflation)
- Items worth no more than $2.26 (2% of $113) in 2021, regardless of the amount of your gift

If you pay $75 or less for membership that entitles you to benefits, you can fully deduct your dues if either of these alternatives applies:

- You receive membership privileges that can be exercised frequently (e.g., free or discounted parking or admission) or discounts on gift shop or mail order items.

- Your membership entitles you to admission to members-only events and the cost of each event is no more than $11.30 in 2021.

If you pay more than $75, you can exclude only those benefits that you would have excluded had you paid $75 or less; more expensive benefits are not excludable.

Student Exchange Program

Individuals who open their homes to students, serving as hosts under special programs, may be eligible for a tax break that helps to defray the cost of hospitality. To claim this tax benefit (which hasn't changed since 1960), certain conditions must be met.

Benefit

If you support a student in your home, you may deduct up to $50 per month as a charitable contribution deduction as long as you itemize your deductions and meet certain conditions. If the student is in your home for at least 15 days of a month, you can treat it as an entire month.

Conditions

To claim a deduction for supporting a student in your home, you must meet all 3 of these conditions:

1. The student must be in elementary or high school.
2. The placement in your home must be arranged under an educational program by a charitable organization and is documented by a written agreement.
3. You have records showing what you spend on the student's food, clothing, medical care, schooling, and recreation.

Planning Tip

Supporting a student in your home may entitle your child to spend time in another family's home. For example, if you accept a foreign exchange student into your home, you may not only obtain a tax deduction for that foreign student, but in addition, your child may be able to go abroad and there is no tax cost to this benefit—to you or to your child. While you may have to pay out-of-pocket for airfare, your child's living expenses abroad may be provided for free.

Pitfall

You usually cannot deduct any payments made where you receive money from the charity for the student's maintenance. For example, if the charity reimburses you for medical expenses you pay for the student, you cannot deduct the medical expenses you paid. However, you are permitted to deduct your prepayment of a one-time expense, such as a medical bill or vacation for the student at the request of the student's parents or sponsoring organization for which you are later reimbursed for part of the cost.

Where to Claim the Deduction

See under "Cash Donations" earlier in this chapter.

Special Inventory Donations

Business owners may enjoy an enhanced charitable contribution deduction for donations by sole proprietors and any other businesses to public charities. The food must be apparently wholesome and meet all federal quality and labeling standards. The deduction is the lesser of (1) the item's basis in inventory plus ½ of its appreciation, or (2) 2 times the item's basis.

Donor-Advised Funds

You've heard the old saying "buy now, pay later." Well, you can donate now and deduct the contribution now, even though money is not disbursed to a charity until later. Using a donor-advised fund, you make contributions to the fund and *suggest* which charity should benefit from them. The fund usually follows your recommendation, although it is not required to. You claim the deduction when money or property goes into the fund.

Benefit ⊜

You can deduct the money and property donated to the fund (see earlier in this chapter for rules on cash donations and donations of appreciated property).

Conditions

You cannot *require* the fund to disburse the money to a charity of your choice. You can only make suggestions. For example, if you have $15,000 in your fund account, you can ask that $5,000 be disbursed to the American Red Cross; the fund will usually follow your request, but does not have to.

Planning Tip

Wealthy individuals can set up private foundations or use other charitable vehicles to direct funds to the charities of their choice. If you do not have sufficient funds to create a private foundation, you can use a commercial fund (minimum contributions start at $5,000), such as:

- Fidelity Investments Charitable Gift Fund (www.fidelitycharitable.org/) ($5,000 initial contribution)
- Schwab Charitable Fund (www.schwabcharitable.org/public/charitable/home) ($5,000 initial contribution)
- The Vanguard Charitable Endowment Fund (www.vanguardcharitable.org/) ($25,000 initial contribution)

Some large charities and trusts offer donor-advised funds, which you can find through a web search.

Pitfalls

No deduction can be claimed for a contribution to a donor-advised fund if the sponsoring organization is a war veterans organization, a fraternal society, or a nonprofit cemetery company.

Donations to donor-advised funds in 2021 are limited to 60% of AGI even though cash donations given directly to qualified charities are deductible to the extent of 100% of AGI if this limit is elected.

Where to Claim the Deduction

See "Cash Contributions" earlier in this chapter.

Sophisticated Charitable Giving Arrangements

Wealthy individuals have a number of options for giving away substantial amounts of money and property. The reason they're essentially restricted to these individuals is the costs of setup and administration.

A full discussion of these options is beyond the scope of this book, but they include:

- *Private foundation.* This is an organization set up to further the charitable goals of the donor. The foundation must distribute annually at least 5% of the previous year's average net assets for charitable purposes. Contributions to the foundation are deductible, although cash contributions usually are limited to 30% of AGI and long-term capital gain property to 20% of AGI.

- *Charitable lead trust.* This type of donation enables the charity to receive income from the trust for the life of the donor or joint lives of the donor and spouse, or for a term of years. At the end of this period, the property remaining in the trust passes to a beneficiary named by the donor (it can revert to the donor, but this option typically isn't used). The contribution deduction is based on the charity's income interest, which is figured using a factor determined by the IRS.
- *Charitable remainder trust.* This type of donation enables the donor to retain the right to receive income for life or a term of years not exceeding 20 years. At the end of this period, the property remaining in the trust belongs to the charity. There are 2 types of charitable remainder trusts: a charitable remainder unitrust (CRUT), where annual income is a fixed percentage of the value of the trust determined each year, and a charitable remainder annuity trust (CRAT), where income is a fixed annual amount similar to a commercial annuity. The contribution deduction is based on the charity's remainder interest, which is figured using a factor determined by the IRS.

Again, setting up and managing these arrangements requires substantial professional fees. They must comply with IRS rules to avoid penalties or other tax problems. Again, such arrangements should be undertaken only with professional assistance.

IRA Transfers to Charity

Individuals age 70½ and older may make direct transfers from their IRAs to public charities up to $100,000, called qualified charitable distributions (QCDs). No charitable contribution deduction may be claimed for the transfer, but the distribution is not taxable. The rules for QCDs are explained in greater detail in Chapter 5. This transfer option may be especially appealing to seniors who want to benefit their favorite charity but who do not itemize their deductions and could not claim a charitable deduction in any event. For details about doing this, see Chapter 5.

Leave-Based Donation Programs

Your employer may offer a leave-based donation program that is used to help co-workers who need help when out because of illness or other event. You give up your vacation, sick, or personal leave that other employees may use as needed. Usually, you are taxed on your contributed compensation. However, in 2021, if your employer makes a timely cash donation to a charity for COVID-19 relief, your donation isn't taxable. It doesn't even appear on your Form W-2. But you

TABLE 6.2 Record Keeper for Your Cash Donations

Date	Name of Charity	Amount of Donation
		$
		$
		$
		$
		$
		$
		$
		$
		$
		$
		$
		$
		$
		$
		$
		$
		$

can't deduct the charitable contribution. It's up to your employer to complete donations before January 1, 2022; the employer claims the charitable contribution deduction.

Record Keeper for Your Charitable Giving

Use the record keeper in Table 6.2 to note cash contributions you make throughout the year. Include in this record your weekly donations in the church plate and similar donations. Obtain a written acknowledgment from the charity for these donations.

Your Car

Americans love their cars. According to Hedges & Company, there were 286.9 million vehicles registered in the United States as of 2020. Cars can be expensive to buy or lease and to operate, especially with today's high fuel prices. But the tax law provides some relief for your car use by way of tax write-offs.

This chapter explains the tax breaks you can take for your car (the term may also cover light trucks and vans for certain purposes as explained later). Deducting the use of your car for medical-related travel is discussed in Chapter 2. Deducting the use of your car when working as a volunteer for charity is discussed in Chapter 6.

For more information, see IRS Publication 463, *Travel, Gift, and Car Expenses* and IRS Publication 535, *Business Expenses*.

Business Use of Your Personal Car

According to the U.S. Department of Transportation's Federal Highway Administration, Americans drive their cars on average 13,500 miles each year, although this didn't hold true in 2020 and perhaps in 2021 due to COVID-19-related restrictions. The cost of driving can be high when you factor in gasoline, insurance, and other costs. But the tax law lets a portion of the cost of this mileage be deductible under certain circumstances.

Benefit

If you use your personal car for business and you are self-employed, you can deduct expenses related to the business use of your car. For example, if you are an independent contractor (not an employee) and use your car to drive for Uber or Lyft, you are eligible for a deduction.

There is a choice of methods for claiming your deduction: You can deduct your actual expenses, including an allowance for depreciation if you own your car or lease payments if you lease it ("actual expense method"), or you can claim the IRS standard mileage rate.

The IRS standard mileage rate is 56¢ per mile for business driving in 2021. Whichever method you select, you can also deduct parking and tolls that are business expenses (and not for personal commuting).

There is no dollar limit on what you can deduct for your car use each year. However, if you own your car and use the actual expense method, there are dollar limits on how much you can deduct for depreciation or first-year expensing (unless your car weighs more than 6,000 pounds).

If your employer reimburses you for business use of your car under an "accountable plan," you do not have to report the reimbursements as income (the reimbursements are not even included on your Form W-2). Ask your employer if reimbursements are made under an accountable plan, or check your W-2 form.

Conditions

To claim write-offs for business use of your personal car you merely have to keep good records, as explained later. However, *what* you can deduct may be limited by certain conditions.

STANDARD MILEAGE RATE

You can use the IRS standard mileage rate whether you own or lease your car. The standard mileage rate takes the place of separately deducting gas, oil, repairs, new tires, vehicle registration fees, insurance, and depreciation if you own the car, or lease payments if you lease the car.

However, you cannot base your car deduction on the standard mileage rate if you have depreciated your car or claimed first-year expensing. This would have occurred if you owned your car in a previous year and claimed the actual expense method.

DEPRECIATION

If you own your car and use the actual expense method, you can claim an allowance for depreciation (including bonus depreciation) or elect first-year expensing. Cars are treated as 5-year property; for depreciation purposes they have a 5-year recovery period. Because of a special rule, however, a part of the depreciation allowance is limited in the first year so that the balance must be claimed in a sixth year if you still own the car at that time. (Remember, you apply depreciation only to the business-use portion of the car, and you can use accelerated depreciation only if the car is used more than 50% for business; if business use is 50% or less, you are limited to straight-line depreciation.)

If you use accelerated depreciation (and are not subject to a special rule called the midquarter convention, which applies if you place more than 40% of all of your depreciable property in service in the last quarter of the year), your depreciation rates are:

- Year 1 (the year the car is placed in service): 20%
- Year 2: 32%
- Year 3: 19.2%
- Year 4: 11.52%
- Year 5: 11.52%
- Year 6: 5.76%

Example

In January 2021, you buy a car for $28,000 and use it 60% for business and 40% for personal purposes. You do not use first-year expensing or bonus depreciation. Assume that your business-personal use percentages remain constant so that the business-use portion of the car for depreciation purposes is $16,800 ($28,000 × 60%). Here is your depreciation amount for each year (subject to the dollar limits discussed later).

Year 1: $3,360

Year 2: $5,338

Year 3: $3,226

Year 4: $1,935

Year 5: $1,935

Year 6: $968

Instead of depreciating the business-use portion of your car, you can elect to expense it in the year it is bought and placed in service. However, like depreciation, this option may be restricted to a dollar limit, explained next.

DOLLAR LIMIT

Unless your car weighs more than 6,000 pounds, if it is a "luxury vehicle" (the cost depends on the year it was placed in service), your allowance for depreciation or first-year expensing is limited to a dollar amount fixed by the IRS. Table 7.1 shows the dollar limits for gas-powered cars, light trucks, and vans.

Example

In November 2021, you buy a car costing $90,000 and use it 80% for business and 20% for personal purposes. Your dollar limit is $14,560 (80% of $18,200).

For 2021, the same dollar limits for passenger cars listed in Table 7.1 apply to light trucks and vans. In prior years, these vehicles had slightly higher dollar limits than passenger cars.

The full amount of the dollar limit on depreciation applies only if the car is used 100% for business. If the car is used partly for business, you must allocate the dollar limit.

If the vehicle weighs more than 6,000 pounds but not more than 14,000 pounds, as is the case for a heavy SUV used in business, you can elect to expense its cost up to $26,200; the dollar limits in Table 7.1 do not apply in this case. In addition, you can claim normal depreciation for the vehicle without applying the dollar limits. Normal depreciation rates are 20% for the first year, 32% for the second year, 19.2% for the third year, 11.52% for the fourth and fifth years, and 5.76% for the sixth year.

TABLE 7.1 Dollar Limit on Depreciation of Passenger Cars

Date Car Placed in Service	1st Year	2nd Year	3rd Year	4th and Later Years
2021	$18,200*	$16,400	$9,800	$5,860
2019–2020	18,100*	16,100	9,700	5,760
2018	18,000*	16,000	9,600	5,760
2012 through 2017	11,160**	5,100	3,050	1,875

*$8,000 less if you elect not to use bonus depreciation.
**$3,160 if the car does not qualify for bonus depreciation (i.e., it is a used car).

Safe harbor method when claiming bonus depreciation. If you claim bonus depreciation for a vehicle, you can continue to claim depreciation on it only if you follow the rules set forth in Rev. Proc. 2019-13. Essentially, this means figuring depreciation for years following the placed-in-service year using the percentage found in Appendix A of IRS Publication 946 (https://www.irs.gov/pub/irs-pdf/p946.pdf). Use Table A-1 of Appendix A if the half-year convention applies (the usual situation) or Table A-2 if the mid-quarter convention applies. The depreciation claimed each year is the lower of the amount figured using the applicable table or the dollar limit in Table 7.1.

Example

In 2020, you placed in service a car costing $60,000 for which 100% bonus depreciation was used (assume no Section 179 deduction was claimed and the mid-quarter convention does not apply). As a result, $18,100 was deducted in 2020, leaving a remaining adjusted depreciable basis for the car of $41,900 ($60,000 − $18,100). For 2021 through 2025, figure depreciation using the annual rate in Appendix A of IRS Publication 946. Assume that the rates in Table A-1 apply here. Thus, for 2021, the depreciation allowance is $13,408 (32% × $41,900), which is less than the dollar limit of $16,000 for 2020 (from Table 7.1 in this chapter). Total depreciation allowed for the vehicle through its recovery period will be $51,616, as follows:

Taxable Year	Dollar Limit (Table 7.1 of This Chapter)	Depreciation under Table A-1 of Publication 946
2020	$18,100	$18,100
2021	$16,100	$13,404 ($41,900 × 32%)
2022	$ 9,700	$ 8,045 ($41,900 × 19.2%)
2023	$ 5,760	$ 4,827 ($41,900 × 11.52%)
2024	$ 5,760	$ 4,827 ($41,900 × 11.52%)
2025	$ 5,760	$ 2,413 ($41,900 × 5.76%)
TOTAL		$51,616

For 2026, the depreciation deduction is $5,760, which is the lesser of the adjusted depreciable basis of $8,384 ($60,000 − $51,616) or the dollar limit of $5,760. The remaining basis of $2,624 is deducted in 2027, assuming the vehicle is still owned at that time.

Non-personal use vehicles. Vans and trucks that are not suitable for personal use (e.g., they have permanent shelving, a front jump seat, or a permanent business sign) can be depreciated or expensed without any dollar limit.

SUBSTANTIATION

You *must* keep good records to back up your deduction for business use of your car. If you fail to do so, you can lose some or all of your deduction. Here's what your records should show:

- Mileage (your odometer reading at the start and end of each trip for business purposes). A court has indicated that you cannot merely note the length of the trip (e.g., 10 miles) but must record the actual odometer readings for the trip.
- Date, destination, and purpose for the trip (when you used your car, the customers or clients you visited, and the reason for taking the trip).
- Costs for gas, oil, and other car-related expenses. *Note:* If you claim the standard mileage rate, you do not have to keep track of these costs.

Planning Tips

At the start and end of the year, note your odometer reading in your records. Then use a diary, logbook, handheld computer, or other device to record your business mileage throughout the year. Knowing your annual mileage and what part of it represents your business mileage will allow you to properly allocate your car expenses.

You can simplify your recordkeeping for car use with a method called "sampling." This allows you to keep records for only a part of the year and then extrapolate the business mileage for the entire year. You can use this method *only* if the portion of the year in which you kept records (e.g., the first quarter of the year) is representative of car use throughout the year.

For more details and strategies for deducting the expenses of using your car for business, see *J.K. Lasser's Small Business Taxes 2022*.

Pitfalls

If you are an employee and drive your vehicle on company business, you cannot take any deduction for your costs. This is so, whether you own or lease your vehicle.

If you own your car and you want to use the IRS standard mileage rate, you must elect to do so in the first year of use. Otherwise you are limited to deducting your actual expenses. For example, if you bought and used your car for business in 2020 and used the actual expense method for claiming a deduction for business use, you cannot use the IRS standard mileage rate in 2021 for this car.

If you lease your car and claim a deduction under the actual expense method, you may have to include a phantom amount in income. This is called

TABLE 7.2 Sample Inclusion Amounts for Cars First Leased in 2021*

Fair Market Value		Tax Year during Lease				
Over	Not Over	1	2	3	4	Later
$ 51,000	$ 52,000	0	0	1	0	1
55,000	56,000	2	3	5	6	6
60,000	62,000	3	7	11	13	15
70,000	72,000	7	14	22	26	30
80,000	85,000	11	23	34	41	48
90,000	95,000	14	30	45	55	62
100,000	110,000	18	40	58	71	81

*Figures for all inclusion amounts are at https://www.irs.gov/pub/irs-drop/rp-21-31.pdf.

the inclusion amount and is designed to equate write-offs for leased cars with those that are purchased. The inclusion amount is generally a modest figure that you take from an IRS table created for this purpose. You include only the portion of the inclusion amount related to your car use. For example, if you use your car only 25% for business, you include only 25% of the applicable inclusion amount. Table 7.2 shows you some sample inclusion amounts for passenger cars (for 2021 the same amounts apply to light trucks and vans that you lease).

Inclusion amounts for vehicles leased prior to 2021 can be found in IRS Publication 463, *Travel, Gift, and Car Expenses.*

Where to Claim the Benefit

As a self-employed person, if you use your car for both business and personal purposes, you can deduct expenses related to your business use on Schedule C of Form 1040 or 1040-SR.

If you own your car and are required to file Form 4562, *Depreciation and Amortization* (you are claiming depreciation on property placed in service in 2021), complete Part V of the form. Be sure to answer the question about whether you have written evidence of your claimed use.

If you are not required to file Form 4562, you must answer the questions about your car use in Part IV of Schedule C. These questions concern your mileage for business and personal use and whether you have written evidence to support your deduction.

Employer-Provided Car

Perhaps one of the most helpful employee benefits is the so-called company car, which means that the business pays for a car you are allowed to use not only for business travel but also for personal purposes. The extent, if any, to which you are taxed on use of a company car depends on several factors, including *how* you are using the car.

Benefit ⊗

If you use a company-owned car *only* on company business, you are not taxed on this use of the company car because it is for business (it is tax-free income to you). Similarly, if you use a certain type of company vehicle for personal use, you are not taxed on this benefit because the IRS views you as having limited personal use (it is tax-free income to you). Such vehicles include: ambulances; hearses; flatbed trucks; dump, garbage, and refrigerated trucks; one-passenger delivery trucks (even if there is a folding jump seat); tractors and other farm equipment; and forklifts. The same exclusion from income applies to vehicles where personal use is restricted or authorized only by a government authority: school buses, passenger buses, moving vans, and police and fire vehicles (including unmarked cars).

Unfortunately, if you are given unfettered use of a company-owned car that you use for personal purposes, you are taxed on this personal use. The value of this use is reported on your Form W-2.

Example

In 2021, your employer allows you to use a company car for personal purposes and you do so 25% of the time the car is used (the rest of the use is strictly for business). Assuming the car's value is $20,000, your employer includes in your income $1,400 (based on the annual lease value method for determining the value of personal use: $5,600 annual lease value of the car × 25%). If you are in the 24% tax bracket, this added income results in additional tax of $336. In effect, it costs you just $336 to use your company's car for personal purposes for the year.

If you are a full-time car salesperson who is allowed to use demonstration cars for personal use, you are not taxed on this benefit (it is tax-free income to you), provided there are restrictions on personal use. For example, personal use after normal business hours might be restricted to a 75-mile radius of the dealer's sales office or you might not be allowed to drive family members or use the car for vacation trips.

In 2018 through 2025, if you are an employee you can't claim any deduction for business driving of your personal vehicle. Similarly, if your employer provides you with a vehicle and chooses to include all of its use by you (business and personal) as compensation, you cannot deduct the business driving on your return.

Condition

To fully exclude the value of using a company car, your personal use must be restricted or the company vehicle must be one of those listed earlier.

Planning Tip

Your employer is *not* required to withhold income taxes on your personal use of a company car. If there is no withholding for car use and you have not paid enough taxes throughout the year by means of withholding or estimated tax payments, you may wind up owing taxes at the end of the year. You may wish to voluntarily increase your withholding if you know that your employer will not withhold taxes for your car use to avoid the problem. Complete a new Form W-4 and give it to your employer to increase your withholding.

Pitfalls

As mentioned earlier, for 2018 through 2025, you cannot deduct any business driving on your personal tax return.

Where to Claim the Benefit

If you are not taxed on using the company car (i.e., your employer does not report it on your Form W-2), you do not have to report anything on your return.

If your employer reports only the actual value of your personal use of a company car, again you do not have to do anything on your return. This income is included in your compensation and reported as such on your return.

Vehicle Registration Fees

One way in which states raise revenues is through the fees they charge for certain activities, including registering cars and other vehicles. The cost of registration, however, may be deductible under certain conditions.

Benefit ⊜

The state registration fees you pay for your vehicle may be deductible. If your car is used only for personal purposes, you can deduct auto registration fees based on the value of the car as a state personal property tax if certain conditions are met. You must itemize your deductions to be able to deduct this expense and your overall deduction for state and local taxes is subject to a $10,000 overall cap ($5,000 if you're married filing separately).

Conditions

To deduct auto registration fees as a state personal property tax, you must meet all 3 requirements:

1. The fee is an ad valorem tax. This means the fee is based on a percentage of the car's value, for example, 1% of the value. Table 7.3 lists the states that satisfy this requirement.

2. The fee is imposed on an annual basis, even though it is collected more or less frequently.

3. The fee is imposed on personal property.

4. The fee, plus your other state and local taxes, does not exceed $10,000 ($5,000 if you are married filing separately).

If the tax or fee is based on weight, model, year, or horsepower, it is not deductible. But if the tax is based on *both* value and another factor, the portion based on value is deductible.

Example

Your vehicle registration fee is 1% of the car's value, plus 40¢ per hundredweight. You can deduct the 1% portion as a personal property tax.

TABLE 7.3 States with Ad Valorem Taxes*

Alabama	Michigan
Arizona	Minnesota
Arkansas	Mississippi
California	Missouri
Colorado	Montana
Connecticut	Nebraska
Georgia**	Nevada
Indiana	New Hampshire
Iowa	North Carolina
Kansas	Rhode Island
Kentucky	South Carolina
Louisiana	Virginia
Maine	West Virginia
Massachusetts	Wyoming

*In Louisiana, Missouri, and Virginia there may be county-imposed ad valorem taxes.
**One-time title ad valorem tax.

Planning Tip

If you have questions about whether your state's registration fee is deductible in whole or in part, contact your state tax authority.

Pitfall

There is no downside to deducting auto registration fees as a personal property tax if you are eligible to do so. However, it is subject to the $10,000 overall limit for itemizing state and local taxes (the SALT cap).

Where to Claim the Benefit

If you are deducting auto registration fees on your personal car as a state personal property tax, you must file Schedule A of Form 1040 or 1040-SR.

Car Accidents and Other Car-Related Problems

According to the U.S. Department of Transportation, there were about 6.7 million motor vehicle accidents in the United States in 2018 (the most recent year for statistics). Whether a car is partially damaged or totaled, an owner may have out-of-pocket costs. These may be limited to the deductible or may be a greater amount. The tax law may allow for a write-off, even if the car is used exclusively for personal reasons and not at all for business.

For 2018 through 2025, you cannot deduct any property loss from a car accident or as a result of a basic casualty event, such as a fire or storm. But if your car is damaged or destroyed in a federally-declared disaster, you may have a deductible loss (see Chapter 12).

Donating Your Car

If you donate your car to a tax-exempt organization, you may be entitled to claim a deduction for the car's fair market value. For more details, see Chapter 6.

Credit for Plug-In Electric Drive Vehicles

You can claim a tax credit for buying a plug-in electric drive vehicle. The credit applies whether you use the vehicle for personal driving, business driving, or a combination of both. One credit applies to 4-wheel vehicles; another credit applies to 2-wheel vehicles.

Benefit ✚

You can reduce your tax bill by claiming a tax credit of between $2,500 and $7,500 for the purchase of a 4-wheel plug-in electric vehicle. The amount of the credit does not depend on the weight of the vehicle. Instead, it depends on battery power. (The credit is reduced for certain vehicles; see *Planning Tips* below.) A minimum credit of $2,500 applies to a vehicle with a battery capacity of 4 but less than 5 kilowatt hours. The base credit amount of $2,500 is increased by $417 for a vehicle drawing propulsion energy from a battery with at least 5 kilowatt hours of capacity, plus $417 for each additional kilowatt hour of capacity in excess of 5 kilowatt hours, up to a maximum of $5,000 (for a total credit limit of $7,500).

For a 2-wheel plug-in electric vehicle (motorcycle), the credit is based on the cost of the vehicle. The credit is 10% of the cost, up to a maximum credit of $2,500.

Conditions

The credit applies to vehicles with a minimum of 4 wheels manufactured for use on public streets (i.e., have a speed of at least 35 mph and require state tags) and roads that are propelled by a battery having a capacity of at least 4 kilowatt hours. The vehicle must weigh less than 14,000 pounds. Two-wheel vehicles must have a minimum top speed of 45 mph (if the credit is extended).

Planning Tips

The tax credit can be used to offset both the regular tax and the alternative minimum tax.

In addition to this federal income tax credit, you may be eligible for state-level tax breaks on sales and income taxes. Check with your state tax department for details or go to www.afdc.energy.gov/laws/ and click on your state.

When a manufacturer sells more than 200,000 4-wheel plug-in vehicles for use in the United States after 2009, the credit limit will be phased out (50% credit in the 2 quarters after the 200,000 vehicle limit is reached and 25% in the next 2 quarters). Thus, anyone interested in purchasing a plug-in electric vehicle should monitor these sales figures (the dealer should be able to provide information) and not miss the opportunity to claim the full credit. For example, both Tesla and GM passed the 200,000-vehicle mark. As a result, there is no credit allowed for the purchase of either type of vehicle in 2021.

For links and resources for plug-in electric vehicles, go to FuelEconomy.gov (www.fueleconomy.gov/feg/taxevb.shtml).

Pitfall

The credit for 2-wheel plug-in electric drive vehicles expires at the end of 2021 unless Congress again extends this break.

Where to Claim the Credit

If the vehicle is used for personal driving, then the credit is reported on Form 8834, *Qualified Electric Vehicle Credit*, and entered on Schedule 3 of Form 1040 or 1040-SR.

If the vehicle is used for business driving, then the credit is part of the general business credit and subject to limitations. The same form used for personal driving is used to figure the credit and then the business portion is entered on Form 3800, *General Business Credit*; the net general business credit is then entered on Schedule 3 of Form 1040 or 1040-SR.

Car Insurance Rebates

During the pandemic, because people were under stay-at-home orders and there were fewer vehicle accidents, many insurance companies rebated some portion of car insurance premiums (e.g., 15%). The rebates are not taxable. They are simply a reduction of the premiums paid.

Investing

Putting money aside for that proverbial rainy day is an admirable and necessary goal but it can be a difficult proposition, especially when your paycheck doesn't seem to stretch far enough. Still, savings and investing are essential to your financial well-being, and Americans are saving at a growing rate. According to Federal Reserve Bank, the personal savings rate (the ratio of personal savings to disposable personal income) in the United States, which is typically 6% to 7%, increased substantially during the pandemic, and was 9.6% in July 2021. Fortunately, the tax laws can help you to make the most of your efforts. It also provides tax breaks if your investments don't work out.

However, for 2018 through 2025, investment-related expenses that were previously deductible as miscellaneous itemized deductions are not deductible. These include safe deposit box rental fees; subscriptions to investment newsletters, online services, and apps; computers and tables used for investments; and fees for financial advice.

This chapter deals with tax breaks for so-called *taxable accounts* and other investments that are not held in tax-favored retirement accounts. The tax breaks for IRAs and qualified retirement accounts, which are tax-deferred accounts, can be found in Chapter 5. For more information, see IRS Publication 514, *Foreign Tax Credit for Individuals*; IRS Publication 525, *Taxable and Nontaxable Income*; IRS Publication 544, *Sales and Other Dispositions of Assets*; IRS Publication 550, *Investment Income and Expenses*; IRS Publication 551, *Basis of Assets*; IRS Publication 564, *Mutual Fund Distributions*; and IRS Publication 575, *Pension and Annuity Income*.

Penalty on Early Withdrawal of Savings

Time deposit accounts and certificates of deposit are fixed for a set term. These savings vehicles, which have been paying very low interest rates in recent years, still generally pay a higher rate of interest than money-market and passbook accounts. But if they are cashed in before maturity, a bank penalty is imposed. The penalty usually is forfeiture of some interest and, in some cases, even principal. The penalty is tax deductible.

Benefit 🔼

If you cash in a certificate of deposit (CD) or savings account before its fixed maturity date for any reason (such as you need the money to pay personal expenses or you can obtain a higher interest rate if you move the money), you may be forced to pay a penalty. The penalty is subtracted from the funds you receive.

You can deduct this penalty, which may be a forfeiture of interest and/or principal (if the penalty exceeds the interest), even though you do not itemize your other deductions. In the case of savings certificates with fixed maturities of longer than one year, your deduction is based on the forfeiture of original issue discount (which is nothing more than a way of figuring interest). Regardless of the maturity involved, this deduction is called a penalty on early withdrawal of savings. There is no dollar limit on this deduction.

Conditions

There are no conditions or requirements to meet. As long as you take money out of a savings certificate before the specified maturity date and are subject to a penalty, you can deduct the penalty in full.

Planning Tip

When putting money into time-savings vehicles, such as certificates of deposit, don't extend the investment period beyond the time you *may* need the funds so that you can avoid early withdrawal penalties if you *do* need the money then. Consider splitting your savings into multiple savings certificates with different maturity dates so that you can readily have access to some funds penalty free.

Example

You have $10,000 for savings. Instead of putting $10,000 into a single CD for 5 years, consider putting only $5,000 in for 5 years and putting the other $5,000 into a renewable 12-month CD. Each year you know that you can obtain at least $5,000 penalty free. This will also allow some of the funds to be reinvested for higher interest rates should rates rise (but, conversely, you may lose out on your interest rate if rates decline).

Pitfalls

You cannot net the penalty against the interest you receive and eliminate the need to separately deduct the penalty. You must report all of the interest on the savings certificate and then separately deduct the early withdrawal penalty.

The above-the-line deduction for the penalty on early withdrawals from savings accounts does not apply to the 10% early distribution penalty usually imposed on withdrawals from qualified retirement plans and IRAs before age 59 ½.

Where to Claim the Benefit

The forfeited amount is reported to you (and the IRS) on Form 1099-INT if the certificate of deposit is for one year or less, or on Form 1099-OID if the certificate of deposit is for longer than one year. You deduct this amount on Schedule 1 of Form 1040 or 1040-SR.

Loss on Bank Deposits

During the Great Depression, there was a run on the banks; depositors rushed to withdraw their money, forcing many banks to go under. Today, there are many protections in place (such as state-mandated funding requirements and Dodd-Frank, a federal law) to ensure the integrity of banks. But despite these protections, some banks still fail. Losses suffered by depositors of failed banks that are not insured by the Federal Deposit Insurance Corporation (FDIC) or funds not covered by FDIC protection may be tax deductible under certain conditions.

Benefit

If your bank goes under and your account is not covered in whole or in part by FDIC insurance, you can deduct your loss.

Historically, there have been different ways to treat your loss (each of which is explained in the next section):

- Bad debt deduction
- Casualty loss, but this option doesn't apply for 2018 through 2025
- Ordinary loss, but this option is also barred for 2018 through 2025

For 2021, your only option is to claim a bad debt deduction.

Conditions

The conditions for deducting your loss on bank deposits are simple: The bank must be insolvent or bankrupt so that there is no reasonable prospect of recovering your money, and your deposits must not be covered by FDIC or state insurance. Additional conditions and limits, however, may apply to the deduction method you select.

BAD DEBT

You can opt to treat your loss as a bad debt, which is classified for tax purposes as a short-term capital loss (regardless of how long your money was on deposit). This means you can deduct your loss against capital gains. If you do not have capital gains or if these losses are greater than your capital gains, you can only deduct up to $3,000 against your ordinary income. Any unused amount of the loss can be carried forward and used in a future year.

There is one condition for selecting this deduction method: There must be no reasonable prospect of recovery from the insolvent or bankrupt bank. You must wait until the year in which your nonrecovery becomes clear.

The rules for bad debts are explained more fully in Chapter 11.

CASUALTY LOSS

Before 2018, you could opt to treat your loss as a casualty loss, which means you itemized deductions to claim the loss. The amount of your loss was reduced by $100 right off the top—the $100 subtraction is a feature in the tax law for claiming a casualty loss deduction. Other limitations applied. This option does not apply for 2018 through 2025.

ORDINARY LOSS

Prior to 2018, you could opt to deduct up to $20,000 ($10,000 if you are married and file a separate return) as a miscellaneous itemized deduction, which is subject to the 2%-of-AGI floor. Because miscellaneous itemized deductions subject to the 2%-of-AGI floor are suspended for 2018 through 2025, this option cannot be used for 2021.

Planning Tip

Why rely on tax write-offs to make you whole? The best option is to make sure that your deposits are adequately covered by FDIC insurance. Understand your FDIC limits so you don't expose your savings to potential loss, especially when you have accounts in separate institutions that have merged or been taken over.

The rules on FDIC coverage and a listing of the banks with this insurance protection may be found at www.fdic.gov. You can also use the Electronic Deposit Insurance Estimator (EDIE) at www.fdic.gov/edie/ to see where you stand in terms of FDIC coverage for your checking and savings accounts, money market accounts, and certificates of deposit.

Pitfall

The biggest problem with bank losses is knowing exactly what your losses really are. You may recover something when the bank's finances are settled, even if it is only pennies on the dollar. Generally the trustees of a troubled bank will give you an estimate of your expected recovery and loss.

Where to Claim the Benefit

A bad debt is reported on Form 8949, *Sales and Other Dispositions of Capital Assets*. Be sure that your loss is entered in parentheses to indicate a loss amount. This is then entered on Schedule D, the amount of which is then reported on page 1 of Form 1040 or 1040-SR.

Capital Losses

Wouldn't it be great if every investment turned out to be profitable? Unfortunately, this isn't the way things work—despite our best efforts, investments may decline in value. A mere drop in an asset's value isn't a tax loss; there must be an actual transaction that fixes the loss. If a sale produces a loss, it may be tax deductible.

Benefit ⬆

In today's volatile stock market, as well as trading in cryptocurrencies, it's not uncommon to have losses. Capital losses are deductible in full (there is no dollar limit) as an offset to your capital gains for the year. If your capital losses exceed your gains, up to $3,000 of capital losses can be used to offset ordinary income, such as salary and interest income. If your capital losses are more than this $3,000 limit, you can carry the excess forward indefinitely to be used in a future year. The $3,000 limit has not been increased since 1978.

Understand what capital losses are so that you can plan wisely to get the greatest tax benefit from your losses. Capital losses generally arise on the sale or other disposition of capital assets, such as stocks, collectibles, or real estate. Your loss is the difference between what you receive on the sale and your adjusted basis in the property (usually what you paid for it).

Example

In 2018, you bought 100 shares of X Corporation for $10,000. In December 2021, you sell those shares for $6,000. You have a $4,000 capital loss ($10,000 basis – $6,000 proceeds on the sale). If this is your only capital transaction for the year, you can deduct $3,000 in the current year as an offset to ordinary income and carry forward $1,000 ($4,000 – $3,000) to the next year.

There are 2 classes of capital losses: short-term losses resulting from assets held one year or less and long-term losses resulting from assets held more than one year. As a practical matter, while complex rules govern the order in which capital losses are used to offset different categories of capital gains, in the end capital losses can be used to fully offset capital gains.

Conditions

You must sell or otherwise dispose of an asset to have a deductible loss. A mere decline in the value of an asset you continue to hold does not entitle you to claim a loss. There are exceptions to the disposition requirement (e.g., a bad debt is treated as a short-term capital loss even though the debt is not sold or otherwise disposed of).

As mentioned earlier, the loss must be with respect to a capital asset. And this asset must be held for investment or business purposes. You cannot deduct a capital loss on an asset held primarily for personal purposes (such as your home, personal car, or boat).

Planning Tips

Don't overlook basis adjustments that may increase your loss (by increasing your basis). Take into account:

- Stock dividends you reinvested in the same company
- Brokers' commissions
- Acquisition costs (e.g., attorney's fees to handle the purchase of real estate)
- Selling costs (e.g., real estate broker's fees)

At year-end, review your investment portfolio to see if there are capital losses you want to harvest for tax advantage. But always temper your tax planning with investment considerations. Don't sell only to generate losses; let your investment decisions be driven primarily by economics (e.g., you think the investment will never recover or there are better places to put your investment dollars).

Pitfalls

While you may have an economic loss on a transaction, do not automatically assume it qualifies for capital loss treatment for tax purposes. Certain pitfalls may trip you up.

WASH SALE RULE

You cannot claim a loss if you acquire substantially identical securities within 30 days before or after the date of sale. Under this "wash sale rule," you do not lose the loss entirely. Instead, you adjust the basis of the newly acquired securities to reflect the loss you could not take. This will enable you to claim the loss when you later sell the newly acquired securities in a transaction that is not subject to the wash sale rule.

What is a substantially identical security? If you sold shares in GameStop at a loss on March 14, 2021, and purchase shares in GameStock on April 10, 2021, you are subject to the wash sale rule. But if you sold shares in GameStop at a loss on March 14 and bought shares in Sony on April 10, the wash sale rule does not apply because these are different companies and their stocks are not substantially identical securities.

If you sell a Netflix bond at a loss on March 14, 2020, bearing an interest rate of 4.625% payable in 2025, and purchase a Netflix bond on April 10, 2021, bearing an interest rate of 3.625% payable in 2029, you are *not* subject to the wash sale rule. The differences in the coupon rates and maturities of these bonds make them different securities.

Also, if you sell stock at a loss in your personal investment account and then you cause your IRA or other tax-advantaged account to buy the identical stock within the wash sale period, you cannot take the loss.

OTHER PITFALLS

You cannot claim a capital loss on the sale or other disposition of all property. Some types of property are not classified as capital assets so they do not qualify for capital loss treatment:

- Business inventory and property held for sale to customers
- Depreciable business property and rental property
- Copyrights, literary compositions, letters, or other such property that you created, that you acquired by gifts from the persons who created them, or that were created for you
- Government publications

If a spouse incurs the capital loss and dies, it can be used only in the year of death. Excess capital losses cannot be carried forward and used by a surviving spouse in a later year.

Also, as mentioned earlier, you may not claim a loss on your personal property, such as on the sale of your residence, vacation property, or personal car. You can claim a loss only on assets held for investment and which are not otherwise excluded from capital loss treatment. While you may view your home as an investment (perhaps your greatest investment), the tax law does not.

INHERITED PROPERTY

As explained earlier, the capital losses you can deduct are the difference between what you receive on the sale or other disposition and your tax basis (usually what you paid for the items). In the case of inherited property that was part of an estate that filed a federal estate tax return, your tax basis for an item of property is reported to you on Form 8971. If you don't receive this form (e.g., the estate is too small to be required to file a federal estate tax return), your tax basis is the value of the property on the date of the decedent's death.

Where to Claim the Loss

To claim capital losses, you must file Form 8949, *Sales and Other Dispositions of Capital Assets*, and Schedule D to figure the deductible amount. Short-term transactions are entered in Part I of Form 8949; long-term transactions are entered in Part II of Form 8949. The form has 3 different ways to determine basis: transactions listed on Form 1099-B with basis included, transactions listed on Form 1099-B without basis included, and transactions not reported on Form 1099-B. You must use a separate Form 8949 for each type of basis determination. Gains and losses are netted in each of these parts and then short-term gains or losses are carried over to Parts I and II of Schedule D and then netted against long-term gains or losses in Part III of Schedule D. Make sure that the amount of any loss entered in column (f) of Schedule D is within parentheses to indicate a loss amount.

You enter the amount of your net capital loss from Part III of Schedule D onto Form 1040 or 1040-SR.

Capital Gains and Qualified Dividends

During the tough economy, investments may not necessarily have paid off. However, you may still have realized some capital gains or received a capital gains distribution from a mutual fund; you may also have received dividends from stocks and equity mutual funds. Normally, net capital gains, capital gains distributions, and qualified dividends are taxed at a top rate of 15%. However, those with taxable income below a threshold amount that depends on filing status have a *zero* capital gains tax rate. And those with taxable income above a threshold amount that depends on filing status have a 20% capital gains tax rate. *Note: Pending legislation would hike the capital gains rate for transactions after September 13, 2021; check the Supplement for any update.*

Benefit ⬤

If you qualify, you pay *no* tax on net capital gains (net long-term capital gains in excess of net short-term capital losses), capital gain distributions from certain mutual funds, and qualified dividends.

Conditions

To qualify for the zero tax rate, your taxable income must be below a set amount. Table 8.1 shows the upper limit for taxable income that you can receive and still have zero tax on capital gains. In the past, this threshold was based on being in the bottom two tax brackets, but now it's a specific dollar amount. The potential zero-tax income (e.g., qualified dividends) is taken into account in determining whether you fall within this threshold.

Taxable income is adjusted gross income reduced by the standard deduction or itemized deductions, limited cash contributions to charity, net disaster

TABLE 8.1 2021 Ceiling on Taxable Income for Zero Tax Rate

Filing Status	Taxable Income Limit
Single	$40,400
Head of household	54,100
Married filing jointly and surviving spouse	80,800
Married filing separately	40,400

losses, and the 20% qualified business income (QBI) deduction for owners of pass-through entities; it does not take tax credits into account.

The gains must be from property held long term (usually more than one year). Capital gains distributions and qualified dividends are identified as such on Form 1099-DIV.

Planning Tip

Just because taxable income is above the threshold amount for your filing status does not mean you lose out entirely on the zero tax rate. Depending on your filing status, taxable income, and qualified dividends and capital gains, you may be able to use the zero rate for some of your dividends and capital gains.

Pitfalls

Receiving too much income in capital gains can push you into a higher tax bracket and void the use of the zero tax rate. For example, say you are single and you estimate that your taxable income for the year will be $35,000. You sell property you've held for years at a profit of $10,000. This gain will put you over the $40,000 threshold for your filing status, preventing your gain from being fully tax free.

If your taxable income exceeds the threshold in Table 8.1, you pay a tax rate of 15% on your capital gains. But if your income exceeds the threshold in Table 8.2, the applicable tax rate is 20%.

Where to Claim the Benefit

Dividends and capital gains must be reported on the return, even though they may be tax free because of the zero tax rate. Dividends are reported directly on Form 1040 or 1040-SR. Capital gains distributions and capital gains must be reported on Schedule D and then on Form 1040 or 1040-SR.

Worthless Securities

Investments in a corporation—stocks or bonds—are made with the intention of collecting income and/or making a profit. But some corporations go under and investors are left holding the bag. The tax law allows a deduction for worthless

TABLE 8.2 2021 Taxable Income Triggering 20% Tax Rate

Filing Status	Taxable Income Limit
Single	Over $445,850
Head of household	Over $473,750
Married filing jointly and surviving spouse	Over $501,600
Married filing separately	Over $250,800

securities. Special rules for losses resulting from Ponzi schemes are discussed later in this chapter.

Benefit ⬆️

If you hold stocks or bonds issued with coupons or in registered form that become worthless, you can deduct your investment. Worthless securities are treated as becoming worthless on the last day of the year in which they actually become worthless. This date governs whether the loss is treated as a short-term loss (if you held the security no more than one year prior to December 31) or a long-term loss (if you held the security more than one year prior to December 31).

The loss is treated as a capital loss (discussed earlier in this chapter), even though there is no sale involved. However, if the loss relates to Section 1244 stock (discussed later in this chapter), the loss is treated as an ordinary loss up to $50,000 ($100,000 on a joint return).

Conditions

There are 2 conditions you must meet to write off your investment in worthless securities:

1. The security must have had some value at the end of the prior year.
2. The security must have become *totally* worthless.

VALUE IN THE PRIOR YEAR

To claim a loss in 2021, you must show that the stock or bond had some value on December 31, 2020. Generally, you can learn whether the stock has any value by checking your year-end statements from brokerage firms holding your investment. If you hold publicly traded stock in your own name rather than in the brokerage firm's name ("street name"), check newspapers for December 31 to see if the stock is listed in the financial section (only stock with a value is listed in the papers). For example, Enron stock officially became worthless on November 17, 2004 (so the loss was claimed on December 31, 2004), even though the corporation filed for Chapter 7 bankruptcy in 2001. (Chapter 7 bankruptcy is a liquidation process used to go out of business forever.) Due to COVID-19, there have been a slew of bankruptcy filings, but most of them as Chapter 11 reorganizations, which do not make their securities worthless.

TOTALLY WORTHLESS

The stock or bond must have *no* value by the end of the year in which you claim the loss. Just because a bond has stopped paying interest or a stock has been delisted does not mean it is totally worthless. If you claim a loss, be prepared to present facts showing your security is worthless. You can assume that it is worthless if the company issuing it:

- Goes into bankruptcy that results in a liquidation of the company
- Ceases to do business
- Becomes insolvent

However, don't assume that a security is worthless if the company has plans to reorganize in bankruptcy. Due to COVID-19, there have been numerous Chapter 11 filings, but these are reorganizations where companies can emerge from bankruptcy and the stock has value.

Planning Tips

If you hold a security that is partially but not wholly worthless, sell it to nail down your loss. For example, if you think a company is on the brink of bankruptcy, try to sell the security so that you can fix the loss. Typically, your brokerage firm will buy it for a nominal amount, enabling you to claim a loss for the difference between your basis (usually what you paid for it) and what you received for it. Or you can abandon the security, which means that you permanently surrender and relinquish all rights in the security and receive no consideration in exchange for the security.

Bonds not issued with interest coupons or in registered form that become worthless result in a bad debt deduction (discussed earlier under "Loss on Bank Deposits").

You can claim a loss only in the year in which the security becomes totally worthless, but you have 7 years to discover that a security has become worthless. This is because the statute of limitations on amending your return to claim the loss for a worthless security is 7 years rather than the usual 3 years from the due date of your return.

Example

In 2021, you discover that a stock you held became completely worthless in 2014. You have until April 18, 2022, to file an amended return for 2014 (which was due on April 15, 2015) to report the loss.

If you are unsure in which year to claim the loss, it is generally advisable to report it in the earliest year you suspect that the worthlessness occurred and then to renew your claim in each subsequent year when the earliest year proves to be incorrect. This requires that you file amended returns to eliminate the loss from the earliest return and report it on a subsequent return.

Pitfalls

Don't let time pass you by. Once the 7-year period for filing an amended return has passed, your loss can never be claimed. Each year, make sure to check on the status of any questionable securities to make sure you don't overlook a loss write-off you are entitled to claim.

The amount you can write off for worthless securities is limited to your basis in the stocks or bonds. Even though you may have witnessed soaring prices only to be followed by the wipeout, you cannot benefit in any way from those record highs; your tax loss is limited to your basis, which is usually what you paid for the securities.

Where to Claim the Loss

You report worthless securities on Form 8949, *Sales and Other Distributions of Capital Assets* (in Part I if the securities were held for no more than one year; Part II if they were held more than one year). In columns (c) and (d) write "Worthless." Then, in column (f), be sure to enter the amount of your loss in parentheses. Amounts from Form 8949 are then carried over to Schedule D and then Form 1040 or 1040-SR.

Loss on Section 1244 Stock

Typically, losses on stock are treated as capital losses, which are deductible to the extent of capital gains for the year, plus up to $3,000 of ordinary income. But losses on a special type of stock, called Section 1244 stock after the section in the Internal Revenue Code defining it, can be treated as ordinary losses within set limits.

Benefit ⬆

If you own stock that qualifies as Section 1244 stock, you can claim an ordinary loss on the sale or worthlessness of the stock. The ordinary loss is limited to $50,000 ($100,000 on a joint return).

Conditions

To be able to treat your loss as an ordinary loss, you must meet the following 2 conditions:

1. The stock must qualify as Section 1244 stock.
2. The amount of your loss cannot exceed the dollar limit.

SECTION 1244 REQUIREMENTS

The issuing corporation can be a C or an S corporation. The stock can be common or preferred (provided the preferred stock was issued after July 18, 1984). But all 4 of these conditions must be met:

1. The corporation's equity cannot be greater than $1 million at the time the stock is issued (including amounts received for the stock).
2. The stock must be issued for money or property (other than securities). If you inherited the stock or acquired it for services rendered to the corporation, you cannot treat your loss as an ordinary loss.
3. The corporation must have derived more than half of its gross receipts during the 5-year period before your loss from business operations (and not from passive income such as investments, rents, or royalties). If the corporation is in business less than 5 years, then it must have derived more than half of its gross receipts from business operations in all of its years in existence.
4. You must be the original owner of the stock (you cannot have purchased it from the original owner or someone else).

DOLLAR LIMIT

You can treat only the first $50,000 of the loss as an ordinary loss. The limit on a joint return is $100,000, even if one spouse owned the stock in his or her sole name. Losses in excess of this dollar limit may be treated as capital losses (discussed earlier in this chapter).

Planning Tip

You can claim a Section 1244 loss regardless of how you suffer the loss. Whether you sell your stock at a loss or the company goes under, ordinary loss treatment applies if you meet the conditions discussed earlier.

You (and the corporation) must keep certain records and make them available for IRS inspection, if requested. The records should show that the corporation met the qualifications for the stock to be classified as Section 1244 stock. The corporation should keep records on its gross receipts data for 5 years, and you should keep records on what you paid for the stock. If you don't keep these records, you risk losing your ordinary loss deduction.

Pitfall

If you own stock in an S corporation that holds small business stock, the portion of any loss on such stock passed through to you does *not* qualify as an ordinary loss on Section 1244 stock. Under the technical language of the tax law, only individuals and partnerships can claim Section 1244 losses. Even though S corporations are pass-through entities like partnerships, they are not eligible to claim Section 1244 losses.

Where to Claim the Loss

An ordinary loss on Section 1244 stock is reported on Form 4797, *Sales of Business Property*, which you attach to Form 1040 or 1040-SR. This form is used whether the loss arises from the sale of the stock or from its becoming worthless so that no sale takes place. The amount from Form 4797 is entered on Schedule 1 of Form 1040 or 1040-SR.

If the amount of the loss exceeds your dollar limit, you treat the excess loss as a capital loss (discussed earlier).

Margin Interest and Other Investment-Related Borrowing

Interest paid to borrow money for the purpose of making investments is viewed as "investment interest." The tax law sets strict limits on when and the extent to which investment interest may be deductible.

Benefit ⊜

You can deduct interest on borrowing from a brokerage firm that uses your brokerage account as collateral if the money is used for investment purposes. This is called margin interest, and the brokerage firm sets the limits on borrowing, interest rate, and other terms of the loan. You can also deduct interest on other loans used to make investments as an itemized deduction to the extent of your net investment income. If your investment interest is more than your net investment income for the year, you can carry the excess interest forward indefinitely and use it in a future year.

Conditions

There are 2 important conditions:

1. The funds borrowed must be used for investment purposes.
2. For full deductibility of the interest, you must have net investment income to offset it.

BORROWING FOR INVESTMENT PURPOSES

It is not the source of the borrowing that determines the treatment of the interest but the purpose for which you use the proceeds from the loan. For example, margin interest is not automatically deductible. If you use the loan to buy a personal car, you cannot deduct the margin interest even though the loan arises from your investment account.

If you borrow money to buy stock in a business, interest on the loan is treated as investment interest, not business interest. In contrast, if you buy the assets of a business, the interest is treated as a fully deductible business interest, not investment interest limited to the extent of net investment income.

NET INVESTMENT INCOME

Your investment interest is deductible only to the extent of your net investment income for the year. Investment income includes:

- Interest income
- Annuities
- Royalties

Interest from passive activities that is not classified by the activities as "portfolio income" is not treated as investment income. This includes interest on rental real estate or interest passed through to you from investments in limited partnerships or other pass-through entities in which you do not materially participate. Property subject to a net lease is not treated as investment property (it is treated as a passive activity). As a practical matter, you simply look at the Schedule K-1 (and K-3 if applicable) sent to you by the entity to see how to classify the passed-through interest.

You must reduce investment income by investment expenses for the year to arrive at your net investment income. Investment expenses are expenses directly connected with the production of investment income. Examples of other investment expenses are found throughout this chapter.

Planning Tip

You can opt to treat capital gains and/or qualified dividends as investment income. If you make this election, your capital gains and/or dividends are not eligible for preferential tax rates and are instead included as ordinary income.

Generally it is *not* advisable to make this election because doing so effectively converts income that would otherwise be taxed at no more than 15% or 20% to income taxed at up to 37% (the taxable income thresholds for the 20% rate are listed in Table 8.2 earlier in this chapter). But the election can make sense in some situations; only running the numbers can determine when this is so.

Example

You are in the 32% tax bracket and have $3,000 of capital losses for the year and $6,000 of capital gains. You also have investment interest of $3,000 and no other investment income. If you don't make the election, $3,000 of your capital gains is taxed at 15%, but you can't deduct any of your investment interest this year. If you do make the election, then your capital losses become deductible against ordinary income so that only $3,000 of your capital gains is exposed to ordinary income, while all of your investment interest becomes deductible.

Pitfall

You cannot deduct interest, regardless of the source of the loan, if you use the money to buy or carry municipal bonds (for example, you need to raise cash and you sell your taxable investments while holding on to your municipal bonds).

Where to Claim the Deduction

You figure your investment interest limitation on Form 4952, *Investment Interest Expense Deduction*. You then enter the deductible amount on Schedule A, which is filed with Form 1040 or 1040-SR.

Amortization of Bond Premium

If you buy a bond at a price greater than its stated principal (or face) amount, the excess is called bond premium. You may opt to amortize the premium on taxable bonds; in some cases you *must* amortize bond premium (you don't have any choice).

Benefit ⬤

If you buy a taxable bond, such as a corporate bond, you can elect in the year of the purchase to begin amortizing the bond premium. This means that each year you own the bond, you can offset the taxable interest received on the bond by the amortizable premium amount.

Example

In 2021, you buy a $5,000 corporate bond for $5,500. Your bond premium is $500. Assuming the bond has 5 years left to maturity, you can amortize the $500 premium over 5 years. This means you can use $100 ($500 ÷ 5 years) to offset interest from the bond.

If you opt to amortize bond premium, reduce the bond's basis by the amount of amortization.

If you buy a tax-exempt bond, such as a municipal bond, at a premium, you *must* amortize the bond premium. But you cannot deduct the amortized premium amount. Instead, you reduce the basis of the bond by the amortization for the year.

Example

Same as the preceding example except the bond is a tax-free municipal bond. If you sell the bond at the end of the third year, the basis in the bond is $5,200 ($5,500 − $300). If the sale price of the bond is $5,200, you have no gain or loss on the transaction. If the price is higher than $5,200, you have a taxable gain; if the price is lower, you have a taxable loss.

Conditions

To amortize the bond premium on a taxable bond, you must meet the following 2 conditions:

1. You elect amortization.
2. You figure amortization using the constant yield method for bonds issued after September 27, 1985 (other amortization methods apply for earlier bond issues). This is a 3-step process under which you determine your yield, the accrual periods to use in figuring amortization, and the bond premium. The computation is rather complicated. For more details, see Chapter 3 of IRS Publication 550, *Investment Income and Expenses*.

Planning Tips

It is usually advisable to elect amortization so you can offset current interest income from the bond. If you do not make the election, you will probably realize a capital loss when the bond is redeemed at par or you sell it for less than you paid for it.

You do not have to elect amortization for taxable bonds held in IRAs or qualified retirement plans. Since the interest is not currently deductible, no offset is necessary.

Pitfall

If you want to amortize bond premiums on taxable bonds, you generally must elect to do so by attaching your own statement to the return indicating this choice. The election applies to all taxable bonds you own and to those you buy in later years.

Once you have made your choice, you can't change it unless you receive the written approval of the IRS. To request a change, you must file Form 3115, *Application for Change in Accounting Method*.

Where to Claim the Deduction

The amortizable amount of a premium is not a separate deduction. Instead, it is an adjustment to the interest reported on Schedule B of Form 1040 or 1040-SR.

Report the bond's interest and then subtract the amortization, noting "ABP Adjustment" next to it.

If the amortization exceeds the amount of interest reported, the excess can be deducted as a miscellaneous itemized deduction on Schedule A of Form 1040 or 1040-SR. This deduction is not subject to the 2%-of-adjusted-gross-income floor, so it is deductible in 2021 even though deductions subject to the 2%-of-AGI floor are not.

Municipal Bonds

States, local governments, and their agencies raise money to operate through the sale of bonds. They pay interest on the bonds as inducements to investors to buy the bonds (i.e., lend them money). The federal government generally exempts this interest from taxes; there may or may not be any state income tax breaks as well.

Benefit ⊗

Interest on municipal bonds is not subject to federal income tax. You may fully exclude this interest from income. There is no dollar limit.

The exclusion applies to both interest on individual bonds and interest from mutual funds holding municipal bonds.

Conditions

Interest is classified as municipal bond interest only if the bond is issued by a state or local government or government agency.

Planning Tip

Interest on municipal bonds may also be exempt from state income taxes. Table 8.3 shows you how the states treat municipal bond interest. The U.S. Supreme Court has decided that it is permissible for a state to tax the interest earned on out-of-state bonds while exempting the interest from in-state bonds.

Pitfalls

Municipal bond interest can affect the amount of taxes you pay on your Social Security benefits. Municipal bond interest, while exempt from federal income tax, is taken into account in determining your provisional income, the figure used to fix the taxable portion of Social Security benefits at 85%, 50%, or zero.

Interest on private activity bonds issued after August 6, 1986, while excluded from income for regular tax purposes, is subject to the alternative minimum tax (AMT) (the interest on such bonds issued in 2009 and 2010 continues to be exempt from AMT). These bonds generally pay a slightly higher interest rate

TABLE 8.3 State Income Tax Treatment of Municipal Bond Interest

State	State Income Tax Treatment
Alaska, Florida, Nevada, South Dakota, Tennessee, Texas, Washington, and Wyoming	No state income tax (so interest on municipal bonds is not taxed).
Alabama, Arizona, Arkansas, California, Colorado, Connecticut, Delaware, Georgia, Hawaii, Idaho, Indiana, Kentucky, Louisiana, Maine, Maryland, Massachusetts, Michigan, Minnesota, Mississippi, Missouri, Montana, Nebraska, New Hampshire, New Jersey, New Mexico, New York, North Carolina, North Dakota, Ohio, Oregon, Pennsylvania, Rhode Island, South Carolina, Vermont, Virginia, and West Virginia	Interest is exempt from state income tax if the bond is issued by the state in which you file your return (or by Puerto Rico, U.S. Virgin Islands, or American Samoa).
District of Columbia and Utah	Interest is tax free regardless of the state of issuance (in Utah interest on out-of-state bonds is tax free only if the other state does not tax interest on Utah bonds).
Illinois, Iowa, Kansas, Oklahoma, and Wisconsin	Interest is fully taxable for state income tax purposes regardless of the state of issuance.

than other municipal bonds. However, if you know you will be subject to AMT, it is advisable when making bond investments to forgo the additional interest in favor of municipal bonds not subject to AMT.

Even though interest on municipal bonds is tax free, gain on the sale of the bonds is taxable. For instance, you purchase a bond at par value and sell it 2 years later for $2,000 more than you paid. You have a $2,000 gain that is taxable.

Where to Claim the Exclusion

Even though the interest is fully excludable, you are required to report tax-exempt interest on your return. You report this interest on line 2a of Form 1040 or 1040-SR.

Savings Bonds

United States savings bonds were first sold by the federal government in World War I and again in World War II as a way to raise money. Today, these bonds have become a permanent savings vehicle for the millions of Americans who own them. They can be purchased only online at www.treasurydirect.gov.

Benefit

Tax on the interest on series E, EE, and I bonds can be deferred until the bonds are cashed in or reach their final maturity dates.

Conditions

Deferral is automatic; you don't have to take any action to receive this tax treatment. You simply do not report the interest annually on your return.

Planning Tips

You can opt to report interest on these savings bonds annually instead of using deferral. This option may make sense when the bondholder has little or no other income so that the interest is taxed at a low rate, if at all.

Example

A child receives a series EE bond at her birth with a face value of $1,000. Since these bonds are sold at a 50% discount (the $1,000 bond costs only $500), any increase in the bond's value over $500 is treated as interest. If the child has no other income, the interest is effectively tax free provided that an election is made to report the interest annually. This election is made simply by including the interest on a tax return filed for the child. File a return to establish this reporting even though the child is otherwise not required to file because his or her income is below the filing threshold.

The U.S. Treasury has changed the way in which interest on series EE bonds is computed. Rather than adjusting the interest semiannually, bonds sold on or after May 1, 2005, now pay a fixed rate until redemption or maturity (e.g., 0.10% for bonds purchased from May 1, 2021, to October 31, 2021). As a result, Series I bonds may be a better option because their interest rate still adjusts semiannually for inflation. For example, I bonds purchased from May 1, 2021, through October 31, 2021, pay a variable rate of 3.54% plus a fixed rate of 0.00%, for a total rate of 3.54%.

Interest *may* be tax free if bonds are redeemed to pay certain higher education costs and other conditions are met (see Chapter 3).

Interest is *never* subject to state and local income taxes.

You can use a federal tax refund to purchase up to $5,000 in series I savings bonds. Purchases must be made in multiples of $50. You can request up to 3 different savings bond registrations (e.g., in your name, in your spouse's name, or for someone else). See the instructions to Form 8888, *Allocation of Refund (Including Savings Bond Purchases)*, for details.

Pitfalls

Do not continue to hold a bond beyond its final maturity date. No interest is paid after this date. Bonds reach final maturity in 30 years for series EE and I bonds. E bonds used to have maturies of 30 years or 40 years; the last E bond reached its final maturity in June 2010.

In the past, you could have continued deferral beyond a bond's maturity date by rolling it over into a series HH bond. However, these bonds ceased being issued as of August 31, 2004 (previously issued series HH bonds continue to earn interest).

You cannot redeem an EE or I bond until 12 months after its purchase *unless* your county has been declared a disaster area. There is a 3-month interest penalty for bonds redeemed before 5 years.

Where to Claim the Benefit

You do not have to report interest if you want to defer it; no special form or schedule needs to be filed.

Gain on the Sale of Small Business Stock

The government wants to encourage investments in small businesses. To do so, it has created certain tax breaks should these investments turn out to be profitable.

Benefit ⊗

If you have a gain on the sale of small business stock, you can exclude a percentage of the gain from income (called a Section 1202 exclusion). The portion of the gain that is not excluded is subject to a 28% capital gain rate (unless your tax bracket is below this rate so that the tax rate is limited to your bracket, which is what you would pay on ordinary income). The amount of the exclusion depends on when the stock was acquired. The exclusion is 50% of the gain on stock acquired before February 18, 2009; 75% of the gain for stock acquired after February 17, 2009, and before September 28, 2010; and 100% for stock acquired after September 27, 2010.

Conditions

To qualify to exclude a percentage of the gain from income, the stock must qualify as small business stock and you must meet a holding period requirement.

SMALL BUSINESS STOCK

There are 5 conditions for qualifying as a small business stock:

1. The issuing corporation must be a C corporation (an S corporation cannot issue small business stock for purposes of rollover or exclusion treatment).
2. The stock must have been originally issued after August 10, 1993.
3. The gross assets of the business cannot be more than $50 million when the stock is issued.
4. The corporation must be an active business (and not a holding or investment company). This requires that at least 80% of the corporation's assets are used in the active conduct of a qualified business. A qualified business is one involved in other than the practice of law, medicine, architecture, engineering, health, performing arts, consulting, actuarial science, financial services, brokerage services, banking, insurance, leasing, farming, hotel or motel management, restaurants, or similar businesses. This means that eligible businesses are in such fields as technology, manufacturing, retail, and wholesale.
5. You must have acquired the stock for cash or other property or as pay for services. You cannot treat inherited or gifted stock as small business stock.

HOLDING PERIOD

For rollover treatment, you must have held the stock more than 6 months before the date of sale.

For the special exclusion, you must have held the stock more than 5 years before the date of sale.

Planning Tips

If you acquired qualified small business stock from a C corporation at different times, be sure to track your holding period for each as well as your cost basis in the stock. Then when selling qualified small business stock, you can identify which shares you are selling to optimize your tax position in the year of the sale.

If you don't qualify for the 100% exclusion, you can defer tax on the gain from the sale of Section 1202 stock by reinvesting the proceeds in other Section 1202 stock within 60 days of the sale.

Pitfall

If you deferred gain on the sale of small business stock, understand that eventually you may pay tax on the gain. You had to reduce the basis in the small business stock acquired during the 60-day period by the amount of the deferred gain. When you sell this stock, the reduction will effectively increase your gain.

In 2019, you sell small business stock and acquire new stock within 60 days. The gain from the sale is $10,000. You pay $25,000 for the new stock. Your basis in the new stock is $15,000 ($25,000 – $10,000 deferred gain). In 2021, when the value of the new stock has increased to $35,000, you sell and keep the proceeds. You have a taxable gain of $20,000 ($35,000 – $15,000).

Where to Claim the Exclusion

To exclude a portion or all of your gain, report the entire gain on Form 8949, completing all the columns on that line. Then immediately below the line on which you reported gain in column (a) write "Section 1202 exclusion" and in column (g) enter the amount of the exclusion as a loss (in parentheses).

Gain on DC Zone Assets

In the past, there were about 180 empowerment zones (EZs) in the United States; urban EZs fall under the jurisdiction of the U.S. Department of Housing and Urban Development (HUD). While these zones continue to apply for certain tax breaks (e.g., a special employment tax credit), they no longer entitle those who invested in these zones to defer gain on the sale of their assets by rolling them over. However, certain prior investments in DC Zones may result in tax-free treatment upon a sale in 2021.

Benefit

If you have a gain on the sale of DC Zone assets, you can exclude all of the gain from the sale of assets held more than 5 years in the District of Columbia Enterprise Zone for assets if they were acquired after 1997 and before January 1, 2012. In effect, you are not taxed when you sell these qualified assets.

Conditions

There are 3 conditions for excluding gain on property acquired before January 1, 2012:

1. The property must be a District of Columbia Enterprise Zone (DC Zone) asset, which includes DC Zone business stock, DC Zone partnership

interest, and DC Zone business property (including real or other property integral to a DC Zone business).

2. You must have acquired the DC Zone assets before January 1, 2012, and held them for more than 5 years before the sale. Obviously, any sale in 2021 meets this time condition.

3. The gain may not be otherwise treated as recapture income or gain from a sale to a related party.

Planning Tips

To determine whether you own property in a DC Zone, see IRS Publication 954, *Tax Incentives for Distressed Communities*.

If you own a business that employs people in a qualified empowerment zone, you may be eligible for a special employment tax credit (see Chapter 14).

Pitfall

The election to postpone gain from empowerment zone assets by making a rollover no longer applies; it expired at the end of 2020.

Where to Claim the Benefit

Report the sale of DC zone stock in Part II of Form 8949 as if you weren't electing the exclusion. Enter "X" in column (f), with the amount of the exclusion reported as a negative number in column (g). Report the sale of DC Zone business property on Form 4797, *Sales of Business Property*.

Gain on Reinvestments in Opportunity Zones

The U.S. Treasury, on states' recommendations, has designated low-income communities as qualified opportunity zones. If you sell property and reinvest your gain in one of these zones within 180 days of the sale, you can opt to defer the gain from your income. The deferred gain is reported on the earlier of the date you sell the investment or December 31, 2026.

Benefit

You can postpone gain on the sale of any property as long as you reinvest it in a qualified opportunity zone through an investment fund. There is no dollar limit on how much gain your can defer; in effect it is limited only by your reinvestment. This deferral opportunity applies only through December 31, 2026.

Conditions

There are 2 conditions:

1. You usually must make the reinvestment within 180 days of the sale that produces your gain. But due to COVID-19, the IRS provided an automatic extension, so any reinvestment period ending after March 31, 2020, was extended to March 31, 2021.
2. The sale must be to an unrelated party.

Planning Tip

There are now more than 200 qualified opportunity zone funds (called "O Funds") for investors. As with any investment, check on fund managers, investment fees, and the location in which the funds are invested.

Pitfall

Investing in an investment fund in a qualified opportunity zone presents an investment risk and a tax risk. While you get to defer your gain, you must settle up with the government when selling your investment in a qualified opportunity zone fund, or December 31, 2026, whichever is earlier. Your basis in the investment in the fund is deemed to be zero, so all of your resulting gain is taxable. However, if you hold it for at least 5 years, your zero basis is increased by 10% of the gain originally deferred. If you hold it for another 2 years (at least 7 years in total), your basis is increased by another 5% of the gain originally deferred.

Example

On March 1, 2021, you sell property to an unrelated party for a gain of $100,000 and on July 1, 2021, you reinvest it in an investment fund. You opt to defer $100,000 gain. If you sell your shares in the fund on March 1, 2024 (3 years after investing), your basis in the shares is zero, so all of the sale is taxable gain. If you hold until December 26, 2026, your basis is $15,000 (10% of $100,000 + 5% of $100,000); your recognized gain in 2026 is $85,000 ($100,000 deferred gain − $15,000 basis).

Even though you have to recognize gain no later than December 26, 2026, if you continue to hold the investment fund beyond this date there's a special election for a sale of your shares in the investment fund. You can elect to use a basis for an investment held at least 10 years equal to the fair market value of the property on the date of sale.

> ### Example
>
> Same facts as the example above, except that you sell your shares in the investment fund in April 2029 (more than 10 years) for $150,000. You already recognized gain in 2026. Your basis in the shares when you sell in 2029 is $150,000 ($85,000 gain previously recognized + $65,000 balance of fair market value of the shares when sold).

Where to Elect Deferral

The election to defer gain is reported on Form 8949, *Sales and Other Dispositions of Capital Assets*. Form 8997, *Initial and Annual Statement of Qualified Opportunity Fund (QOF) Investments*, must be filed each year you hold any investment in a qualified opportunity fund.

Foreign Taxes on Investments

Investors in foreign companies may pay taxes overseas to other governments. To provide a break so that these investors aren't taxed twice, for federal income tax purposes a deduction or tax credit can be claimed if certain conditions are met.

Benefit ⊜ ⊕

If you hold investments in foreign countries, including stocks or mutual funds, you may pay taxes abroad. You can write off foreign taxes you pay in one of 2 ways:

1. Deduct the taxes as an itemized deduction.
2. Claim a tax credit for the foreign taxes.

Either way, there is no dollar limit to the benefit you can claim.

Conditions

The foreign tax must be a tax on income similar to U.S. tax. However, you cannot write off any tax imposed by a country designated by the U.S. government as engaging in terrorist activities. These countries are listed in IRS Publication 514, *Foreign Tax Credit for Individuals*.

Planning Tips

Generally, claiming the credit is more valuable than deducting the foreign taxes. The credit reduces your tax liability dollar for dollar. You do not have to be an itemizer if you claim the credit.

If you opt to claim the credit and the amount of the credit you can use in the current year is limited because of your tax liability, you can carry the excess credit back to the 2 preceding years and then forward for up to 5 succeeding years until it is used up. You can only use a carryback or carryover in a year in which you have income from foreign sources.

You have 10 years in which to change your choice from deduction to credit or credit to deduction. You can file an amended return for a period of up to 10 years to change the treatment of the write-off on your return.

Example

For the past 15 years, you have been claiming a deduction for foreign taxes you paid with respect to a mutual fund. In March 2022, you discover that it would have been preferable to claim the credit. You can amend returns from 2011 onward. The 10-year period for the 2011 return ends on April 18, 2022, 10 years from the due date of that 2011 return.

Pitfalls

You cannot elect to treat some foreign taxes as a deduction while treating others as a credit within the same year. You must opt to use one write-off method for all your foreign taxes. But you can change your choice from year to year.

You get no benefit for foreign taxes paid on investments held by an IRA. Since the IRA is not a taxpayer, it cannot claim a deduction or credit for the foreign taxes paid by it. This means the funds in your IRA are reduced by these taxes with no offsetting benefit. You may wish to reconsider investments subject to foreign taxes being held in an IRA.

If you are subject to the alternative minimum tax (a shadow tax system to ensure that taxpayers who successfully reduce their regular tax will at least pay some income tax), you lose the benefit of an itemized deduction for foreign taxes, which are not deductible for AMT purposes.

If you have an ownership interest in a foreign corporation with earnings from intangibles (patents, trademarks, copyrights), you may have global intangible low-taxed income (GILTI), which is included in the corporation's income for the year. As an individual, if you make a special election (called a Section 250 election), you are treated as a corporation for purposes of the tax and can claim a foreign tax credit (subject to an 80% limitation). These rules are highly complex and should be discussed with a tax expert.

You may have to complete Form 8938, *Statement of Specified Foreign Financial Assets*, and file it with your personal tax return if the value of foreign accounts exceeds certain thresholds (e.g., more than $50,000 at the end of the year if you're single). This is referred to as FATCA because the reporting obligation was created by the Foreign Account Tax Compliance Act. Check the instructions to this form and IRS guidance at www.irs.gov/Businesses/Corporations/Basic-Questions-and-Answers-on-Form-8938 for more details about the foreign assets to which the form applies.

If you own or have authority over a foreign financial account, including a bank account, brokerage account, mutual fund, unit trust, or other type of financial account, with a value exceeding $10,000 at any time during the year, you may be required to file a Report of Foreign Bank and Financial Accounts (FBAR) annually. FinCEN Form 114 is used for this purpose and must be filed for 2021 by April 18, 2022 (the same deadline as the one for your federal income tax return) with a 6-month filing extension (this extension is automatic). Filing Form 8938 does not relieve you of the obligation to file the FBAR form.

Where to Claim the Deduction or Credit

Foreign taxes you pay on investments are reported to you (and the IRS) on Form 1099-INT or Form 1099-DIV. Use this figure for claiming your deduction or credit.

If you are claiming a deduction for foreign taxes, you must file Schedule A. Your deduction is part of your itemized deductions entered on Form 1040 or 1040-SR.

If you are claiming the foreign tax credit related to your investments, you may qualify to report it on Schedule 3 on Form 1040 or 1040-SR (without having to complete Form 1116). This simplified filing option applies if the amount of the foreign tax credit is not more than $300 ($600 on a joint return).

If your foreign tax credit is more than this limit, you must complete Form 1116, *Foreign Tax Credit (Individual, Estate, or Trust)*, and then follow the filing instructions given earlier.

Exercise of Incentive Stock Options

Employees may receive special options, called incentive stock options (ISOs), to buy company stock at attractive prices. The exercise of ISOs is not taxable for regular tax purposes, although the spread between the exercise price and stock price is an adjustment for the alternative minimum tax (AMT) and can result in AMT liability.

Benefit ⊕

There is no regular tax on the exercise of incentive stock options.

Conditions

Incentive stock options (ISOs) are a type of compensation that must be granted in connection with employment. An ISO gives an employee the right to buy employer stock at a set price (called the strike price) within a set time period, after the ISO vests (i.e., cannot be taken from the employee unless he or she leaves employment). If the strike price is less than the market price, an employee exercising the option buys the stock at a bargain; the spread between the strike price and market price at the time the ISO is exercised is not subject to regular income tax if the following 2 conditions are met:

1. You must hold the stock acquired through the ISO for more than 2 years from the date the ISO was granted and more than one year after the ISO was exercised.

2. You must have been continuously employed by the employer granting the ISO from the date of the grant up to 3 months prior to the date on which you exercise the ISO.

If the stock acquired through the ISO is sold prior to the required holding period, then there is taxable compensation and immediate capital gain or loss recognition. The rules are complex; see IRS Publication 525, *Taxable and Nontaxable Income*.

Planning Tip

If you hold ISOs, determine how many to exercise this year, factoring in their expiration date and the impact on alternative minimum tax.

Pitfall

While there is no *regular* tax on the exercise of an ISO if certain conditions are met, the spread between the strike price and market price is treated as an adjustment for the alternative minimum tax (AMT). Thus, exercising ISOs can generate or increase AMT liability.

Where to Claim the Benefit

The exercise of the ISO is not reported on Form 1040 or 1040-SR, except to the extent it is included on Form 6251, *Alternative Minimum Tax—Individuals*.

Losses from Investment Ponzi Schemes

During the financial meltdown in 2008 and 2009, some investors discovered that their money had been lost through Ponzi schemes. Unscrupulous financiers collected funds from investors and used new investments to pay off old investors; this worked until they were unable to bring in new investors and the scheme was exposed. While Bernard Madoff, a Ponzi scheme king, was sentenced to a 150-year prison sentence for these crimes, new schemes continue to come to light.

Under a safe harbor deduction, an investor in a Ponzi scheme can deduct 95% of the "qualified investment" if he or she isn't pursuing any third-party recovery, or 75% if pursuing or intending to pursue a third-party recovery. The "qualified investment" is the sum of cash and the basis of property invested in the arrangement over the years, plus income (even so-called phantom income) derived from the arrangement that was included for federal tax purposes in the investor's income, minus any cash or property withdrawn by the investor from the arrangement. After applying the 95%/75%, the deductible amount is then reduced by any actual or potential insurance or SIPC recovery. The deduction is claimed as a miscellaneous itemized deduction not subject to the 2%-of-AGI floor. Find more details in Revenue Procedure 2009-20.

Deferral of Income in Commercial Annuities

Annuities are contracts with insurance companies to pay income for life or a term of years. They may be used to ensure you never run out of money during your lifetime. According to U.S. Individual Annuities, there was more than $241.7 billion invested in annuities in the U.S. at the end of 2019.

There are 2 basic types of annuities: fixed and variable. Fixed annuities guarantee a set payout at regular intervals (e.g., monthly) based on a minimum interest rate and the company's projections for its returns. Variable annuities allow you to put your funds in certain types of investment, with the payout dependent on investment performance and, in some cases, cost-of-living adjustments. Annuities can be immediate—investing your after-tax dollars and commencing distributions—or deferred—waiting to receive distributions at some time in the future (e.g., when you retire). Generally, annuities end upon the death of the owner or last joint owner, but some may have a guaranteed payout that will be distributed to heirs if the owner(s) dies before this payout has been made.

Benefit

Income that builds up in the annuity over the years is not currently taxed; earnings are deferred until distributions are taken. Usually this occurs when you "annuitize" at a certain age to commence regular distributions for the remainder of the contract. This may be a set number of years or over your life ("single life annuity") or joint life with a named beneficiary such as a spouse ("joint and survivor annuity").

Conditions

To defer tax on the investment earnings in the contract, you must adhere to the terms of the contract imposed by the insurance company.

Planning Tips

If you need money before you want to start annuity payouts, you may be able to take a loan from your contract; this is tax free. Such borrowing is limited of course by the value of the annuity. You must pay interest on the loan and meet repayment terms to avoid taxation.

Once annuity payments commence, only the earnings portion is taxable. Amounts representing a return of your investment cost in the contract (your total investment as of the annuity starting date) are not taxed. The information needed to report the taxable amount of payments is provided to you on Form 1099-R, *Distributions from Pensions, Annuities, Retirement or Profit-Sharing Plans, IRAs, Insurance Contracts, Etc.*

Usually, there is automatic federal income tax withholding on annuity payments, but you may choose not to have withholding or to have additional withholding by completing Form W-4P, *Withholding Certificate for Pension or Annuity Payments,* and submitting it to the insurance company.

Pitfalls

If you take distributions (not loans) from an annuity before age 59½ or surrender the contract, you may be subject to a 10% early distribution penalty. What's more, there may be surrender charges imposed by the insurance company for canceling the contract.

If the annuity guarantees a certain payout and you die before receiving it, your heirs must report the income portion of the payout as income in respect of decedent.

Where to Claim the Benefit

While you are deferring earnings, you do not have to report anything on your tax return. Once distributions commence, earnings are reported directly on Form 1040 or 1040-SR.

Travel

We live in a highly mobile age—we are always on the go for work, play, or other activities. We travel by car, airplane, train, ship, bus, and taxi. We spend a lot of money annually on getting around. Of course, the coronavirus severely depressed travel in 2020, but it picked up somewhat in 2021. The tax laws can help to defray some of your travel costs in certain situations.

This chapter explains the types of travel expenses you can deduct. You will find an explanation of recordkeeping rules for travel expenses as well as some forms you can use to comply with these rules.

Prior to 2018, if you entertained customers, clients, or other business associates, you could claim a deduction for entertainment costs (subject to certain limits). However, this write-off opportunity has been eliminated.

For more information, see IRS Publication 463, *Travel, Gift, and Car Expenses*; and IRS Publication 1542, *Per Diem Rates*.

Business Travel

Americans travel quite a lot for business. According to the U.S. Travel Association, U.S. residents logged 464.4 million person-trips (one person one way on a trip away from home) for business in 2019 (statistics for 2020 and 2021, the years of the pandemic, have not yet been released and business travel isn't expected to return to pre-COVID-19 rates until 2024). The costs of travel, including transportation, lodging, and meals, that are related to business may be fully or partially tax deductible if certain conditions are met.

Benefit ⊗ ⊜ ①

If you are self-employed, business travel is a deductible expense. There is no overall dollar limit on what you can deduct. As an employee, you cannot deduct the business travel that you pay for. But if your employer reimburses you under an accountable plan, you aren't taxed on the reimbursements. An accountable plan is a reimbursement arrangement under which you are required to account for your expenses to your employer within a set time and refund to your employer any excess advances or reimbursements.

If, however, your employer has an accountable plan that reimburses you for travel expenses, you are not taxed on the reimbursements (your employer claims the deduction).

Conditions

Business travel costs are deductible if they are ordinary and necessary business expenses. In other words, the travel costs must be business-related and not for personal reasons.

Also, as a condition for claiming a deduction, you must maintain good records (discussed later).

EXAMPLES OF BUSINESS TRAVEL EXPENSES

Airfare

Bus fare

Car expenses (explained in Chapter 7)

Cab fare

Convention costs (explained later in this chapter)

Educational travel, if work-related (explained later in this chapter)

Fax and Internet charges

Job-hunting travel costs in the same line of work

Laundry and dry cleaning during trips

Lodging

Lodging taxes

Meals away from home

Out-of-town expenses while working on a temporary job assignment (explained later in this chapter)

Subway and train fare

Telephone calls

You cannot deduct travel expenses if you are looking for your first job or changing your line of work. For example, if you fly from Los Angeles to Houston to interview for a new position in your same line of work, you can deduct your airfare and local transportation costs as a business expense. But if this travel is for your first job out of college, it is not deductible.

LOCAL OVERNIGHT STAYS

As long as this is not a compensatory benefit but done for a business purpose, you are not taxed on the overnight stay(s) paid by your employer. If you paid the cost and you are self-employed, you can deduct it. For example, your company requires you to stay at a local hotel for the bona fide purpose of facilitating training or team building directly connected with the employer's trade or business.

PART-BUSINESS TRIPS WITHIN THE UNITED STATES

If you combine business with pleasure, you can deduct your travel costs, such as airfare, as a business expense if the *primary* purpose of the trip is for business. But you can deduct hotel costs only for the business portion of the trip.

Example

You live and work in New Haven and fly to San Francisco for a 5-day business trip. You extend your stay for 2 extra days to sightsee. You can fully deduct your airfare as a business expense since the primary purpose of your trip is business. Your lodging is deductible only for the 5 days on business (the cost of lodging for your 2 personal days are nondeductible).

If you extend your stay over the weekend to obtain more favorable airfare that requires a Saturday night stay-over, this time is treated as business time, not personal time, even if you spend the weekend on personal activities.

If the primary purpose of your trip is for personal activities, you can deduct only local transportation costs to and from business locations as a business expense.

Example

You live and work in New Haven and fly to San Francisco to attend your niece's wedding. Family activities take up 4 days of your trip. On the 5th day you see a client and then fly home. Only local transportation costs from your hotel to the client and from the client to the airport are deductible.

PART-BUSINESS TRIPS ABROAD

If you combine business with pleasure on a trip outside the United States, different rules apply to determine if and the extent to which airfare can be treated as a deductible business expense.

If you are a more than 10% owner of the business or a self-employed person with control over scheduling, you can deduct airfare, lodging, and 50% of meal costs only if you fall within one of these categories:

- The trip lasts a week or less (not counting the day you left the United States but counting the day of your return).
- The trip lasts more than one week, but less than 25% of time (counting both the day of departure and arrival) is spent on personal activities.
- In planning the trip, major emphasis was not placed on personal activities.

If a trip lasts more than one week and you spend 25% or more on personal activities (and cannot show that major emphasis was not placed on these activities), then you can deduct only the portion of expenses related to business. This requires that you allocate costs between business and personal time. Divide the total number of days of the trip by the days spent on business activities to find the deductible portion of your costs.

Example

On Sunday you fly from New York to London for a 10-day stay. You spend Monday through Friday on business and the balance of the trip sightseeing. You can deduct ½ of your airfare, lodging, and meal costs as a business expense (5 ÷ 10).

If you have business meetings scheduled before or after a weekend or holiday, you can treat the days in between the meetings as business days, even though you spend the time on personal activities.

PER DIEM RATES

Instead of keeping track of your actual costs for lodging, meals, and incidental expenses away from home on business, you can rely on government-set standard rates. (Incidental expenses include tips for porters, baggage carriers, bellhops, and hotel maids.) You have 2 options for rates:

1. *Maximum federal per diem rate*—an allowance for lodging and for meals and incidental expenses (M&IE) for travel within the continental United States (CONUS). The rate you use depends on the location you are in and the time of travel. Federal per diem rates may be found at www.gsa.gov (click on Per Diem Rates).

2. *High-low substantiation rate*—an IRS-set rate for lodging and for meals and incidental expenses for business travel within CONUS. One rate applies for IRS-designated high-cost areas while the other rate applies to all other areas in CONUS. The rates for October 1, 2020, through September 30, 2021, may be found in IRS Notice 2020-71. The rates starting on October 1, 2021, may be found in IRS Notice 2021-52.

Even though you use a standard per diem rate, you must still apply a 50% limitation to the M&IE portion of the allowance.

If you incur incidental expenses on any travel day for which you do not have deductible meals, you can deduct these expenses at a flat $5 per day.

Planning Tips

If you plan a business trip that is canceled, you can deduct the costs you can't recoup. These costs may include a hotel charge that is nonrefundable or an airline fee to reschedule a flight.

You *must* keep good records of your business travel in order to claim a deduction. The tax law requires substantiation of business travel expenses as a condition of claiming the deduction. You generally need 2 types of records: written information and documentary evidence such as receipts or credit card statements.

You must note certain information in a diary, logbook, account statement, app, or other record keeper. The type of information to record and a sample weekly travel expense form that you can use for this purpose are included at the end of this chapter.

If you are an employee whose employer has an accountable plan, you are required to provide recordkeeping information to your employer. If not, you should generally retain these records along with copies of your tax return for at least 3 years from the date you filed the return on which you claimed a deduction for business travel. This will allow you to back up your deduction if your return is questioned by the IRS.

You do not have to retain receipts for travel costs (other than lodging) of less than $75. Thus, for example, you do not need receipts for taxi fares under $75.

If you fail to maintain the necessary records or if they are destroyed by events beyond your control, such as a flood or fire, you *may* be able to prove your entitlement to a deduction through your own written or oral statement and other supporting evidence. But it may be difficult to establish the full amount of expenses, and you can lose out on a deduction you are otherwise entitled to claim.

In some situations, especially when records are destroyed through no fault of the taxpayer, courts have allowed taxpayers to estimate their expenses. This is called the *Cohan rule*, named after the famous entertainer George M. Cohan, who convinced a court of his entitlement to a business deduction despite the lack of records.

Pitfalls

Generally the cost of commuting to and from work is not deductible; it is a personal expense. This is so even if you are forced to use your car because there is no public transportation or you must travel great distances. You cannot convert nondeductible commuting costs to deductible expenses merely by using your cell phone on business or putting a sign with your business logo on the side of your car. Nondeductible commuting costs include:

- Carpooling expenses, even if you discuss business with your fellow passengers
- Emergency travel between home and work
- Travel from a union hall to a job site

However, there are certain situations in which commuting costs can be treated as deductible business expenses by self-employed individuals.

- If you incur additional costs to transport tools to and from work you can treat the added cost as a deductible expense.
- You commute to a temporary work location.
- You work from home and claim a home office deduction. The cost of travel between your home and any business location, such as customers' offices, is deductible.

- You work at temporary locations. For example, if you are an accountant or other professional who travels to client work sites for a few days or a week or 2, you can deduct the costs of travel between home and these sites as business travel, *provided* you have a regular work office.

If you are an employee, you cannot deduct your business travel. No deduction for unreimbursed employee business expenses can be claimed in 2018 through 2025.

Where to Claim the Deduction

If you are an employee whose job-related travel costs are covered by an employer's accountable plan, you do not have to do anything. Reimbursements for this travel are *not* included on your Form W-2.

If you are self-employed, you deduct your business travel costs on Schedule C.

Temporary Work Assignments

Not everyone who works does so from a fixed location. Some people are stationed at various work locations for a few days, a few months, or even longer. Living away from home means paying for additional housing and travel expenses between home and work. In recognition of the burden these additional costs can place on workers, the tax law allows what might be viewed as personal expenses to become deductible if certain conditions are met.

Benefit ⊜

If you are self-employed and work at a temporary location, your travel costs between home and this location are deductible.

If the temporary location is out of town, you can deduct not only your travel costs but also your living expenses, including lodging and 50% of meals (100% for meals provided by restaurants in 2021). There is no dollar limit on what you can deduct.

Conditions

There are 2 key conditions for deducting expenses related to temporary work assignments:

1. The assignment must be temporary.
2. You must have a regular place of business to deduct travel costs between home and work or be away from home on business to deduct travel and living costs.

DEFINITION OF TEMPORARY WORK ASSIGNMENTS

For travel expenses to be deductible, the work assignment must be temporary. This means that the assignment is expected to last no more than one year and does in fact end within this time. A work assignment is *not* considered temporary if it is expected to last:

- For more than one year even if it in fact ends within the year
- For no more than one year but runs beyond this time (although expenses for the period up to one year are deductible in this case)

REGULAR PLACE OF BUSINESS

You must maintain a regular place of business outside of your home, or have a home office that is your principal place of business.

If all of your work takes place at temporary assignments outside of the metropolitan area in which you live, you do not have a regular place of business and cannot deduct your travel costs.

AWAY FROM HOME

You must maintain a tax home from which you are away on business to deduct travel and living costs. Your tax home is your place of employment or business, regardless of where you or your family live. It may be one and the same place if you live and work in the same area.

Example

You live and work in Trenton, New Jersey. You travel to Boston for 2 weeks of business. You can deduct your travel and living expenses on this trip.

Example

You live in Trenton, New Jersey, and work in Washington, D.C. Washington, D.C., not Trenton, is your tax home. You cannot deduct your travel costs between Trenton and D.C. But if you travel for 2 weeks to Dallas, Texas, you can deduct your travel costs between D.C. and Dallas, as well as your living costs in Dallas.

If you are constantly on the road, moving from job to job so that you do not work within any particular locality, you may not deduct your living costs. The reason: You are not away from home on business.

Your residence can be treated as your tax home so that if you travel away from home on business your costs are deductible if you meet 3 conditions:

1. You do *some* work in the vicinity of your residence.
2. You have mortgage expenses or pay rent for the residence while you are on the road.
3. You or a member of your immediate family has lived in the area of your residence for a long time.

If you meet 2 of the 3 conditions, you *may* be able to use your residence as your tax home, but if you meet only one condition, you cannot do so. A member of the armed forces who maintains a home cannot treat the home as his or her tax home if he or she has a permanent duty station elsewhere.

If you regularly work in 2 or more locations, your tax home is the area of your *principal* work location. This is usually determined by the time spent in each location, the degree of business activity in each place, what income you receive from each place, where you have your home, and whether either location is temporary. You can't use any single factor to decide which of the 2 locations is your tax home.

Planning Tips

When you travel away from home, be sure to keep accurate and complete records of your travel and living expenses.

If you are in the armed forces and your ship or squadron is away from your home port or base, you may be able to deduct travel expenses while away. However, you are not treated as being "away" if you are at your permanent duty station or you are a naval officer assigned to permanent duty aboard a ship.

Pitfalls

Spouses who live and work in different cities can have different tax homes. Just because they are treated as domiciled within the same place and may vote or file their taxes together, they may be restricted in deducting travel expenses between these locations.

Example

A couple maintains a home in Baltimore, where the husband resides. One spouse has a business in New York City during the week and travels to Baltimore each weekend. Even though Baltimore is the city she considers home, she cannot deduct her travel costs between Baltimore and New York City, nor her living expenses in New York City. Her tax home is New York City, not Baltimore, and she is not traveling on business when she returns to Baltimore each weekend.

Pitfalls

If you work in another state, you may be responsible for paying state income taxes there. Check the rules in the state in which you temporarily work.

Where to Claim the Benefit

As a self-employed individual, you deduct your business travel costs on temporary work assignments on Schedule C.

Conventions

Conventions and trade shows are a key way in which businesses can show off their wares, make new connections, and learn about industry developments. To find the best shows to market your products or services, visit www.expodatabase .com/trade-shows-america/usa/. Whether you are an exhibitor or a visitor, your attendance costs may be deductible.

Benefit

You can deduct the cost of attending business conventions, including travel, lodging, 50% of meal costs, and attendance fees, even though there is an element of pleasure associated with such activities.

There are restrictions, however, if you attend a convention held outside the North American area or on a cruise ship.

Conditions

You must be able to show that your attendance at the convention has some benefit to your trade or business. This can be shown by comparing the purpose of the convention as stated in its program or agenda with your official job duties or work.

The fact that you are appointed or elected as a delegate to the convention does not, by itself, establish a business benefit.

FOREIGN CONVENTIONS

If the convention is held outside the North American area, you must show that:

- The meeting is directly related to your trade or business.
- It is as reasonable to hold the meeting outside the North American area as in it. Reasonableness is based on the purpose of the meeting and activities taking place, the sponsoring group or organization, and the homes of active members. The North American area includes all of the locations detailed in Table 9.1.

CONVENTIONS ON CRUISE SHIPS

If you attend a business convention held on a cruise ship, your business deduction is limited to $2,000 per year (a limit in place since the Tax Reform Act of 1986 and not adjusted annually), regardless of the cost of the cruise or the

TABLE 9.1 North American Area for Convention Deduction

American Samoa	Jarvis Island
Antigua and Barbados	Johnston Island
Aruba	Kingman Reef
Bahamas	Marshall Islands
Baker Island	Mexico
Barbados	Micronesia
Bermuda	Midway Islands
Canada	Netherlands Antilles
Costa Rica	Northern Mariana Islands
Curacao	Palau
Dominica	Palmyra
Dominican Republic	Panama
Grenada	Puerto Rico
Guam	Saint Lucia
Guyana	Trinidad and Tobago
Honduras	United States
Howland Island	U.S. Virgin Islands
Jamaica	Wake Island

number of convention cruises you take. And even this limited deduction can *only* be claimed if all 5 of these conditions are met:

1. The convention is directly related to your business.
2. The ship is a vessel registered in the United States.
3. All of the ports of call on the trip are in the United States or U.S. possessions.
4. You attach a signed statement to your return that includes the number of days for the cruise, the hours you spent each day devoted to scheduled business activities, and a copy of the program showing the scheduled business activities.
5. You also attach a signed statement by an officer of the organization or group sponsoring the meeting that shows the schedule of business activities each day and the number of hours you attended.

Planning Tip

Keep good records of your expenses at the convention, including a copy of the convention program with notations of the sessions you attended. If the convention has a sign-in book, be sure to sign in at every session.

If the convention is held on a cruise ship, follow the recordkeeping requirements discussed earlier.

Pitfall

If your spouse or other person accompanies you to the convention, you cannot deduct the expenses of your companion. This is so even if your companion is helpful to you.

However, as a practical matter, there may be no added cost for a second person in your room, so the only extras for your companion are meals and travel. And if you drive to the convention, even extra travel costs are eliminated.

Where to Claim the Deduction

If you are an employee whose job-related travel costs are covered by an employer's accountable plan, you do not have to do anything. Reimbursements for attendance at a business convention are *not* included on your Form W-2. Your employer claims the deduction for your travel costs.

If you are self-employed, you deduct your business convention costs on Schedule C.

Medical Travel

The days of doctors' house calls are all but over. To obtain medical assistance, you must go to the providers' sites—doctors' offices, hospitals, clinics, and other facilities. The tax law lets you treat your travel costs for medical purposes as a deductible medical expense.

Benefit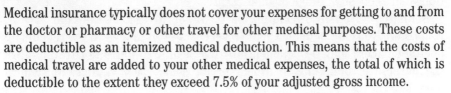

Medical insurance typically does not cover your expenses for getting to and from the doctor or pharmacy or other travel for other medical purposes. These costs are deductible as an itemized medical deduction. This means that the costs of medical travel are added to your other medical expenses, the total of which is deductible to the extent they exceed 7.5% of your adjusted gross income.

Conditions

To be treated as qualified medical expenses, the costs of travel must be related to obtaining a diagnosis, cure, mitigation, treatment, or prevention of disease or any treatment that affects a part or function of your body.

Deductible expenses include those paid not only for yourself, but also for a spouse and dependents. Who qualifies as a dependent is explained in Chapter 1.

EXAMPLES OF MEDICAL TRAVEL COSTS

- Ambulance hire
- Autoette (auto device for a handicapped person)
- Bus, cab, or train fare to see doctors, obtain treatment (including attendance at AA meetings, or to the gym if you are obese), or pick up prescriptions
- Car use to see doctors, obtain treatment (including attendance at AA meetings or to the gym if you are obese), or pick up prescriptions at 16¢ per mile for driving in 2021
- Medical conferences (travel costs and admission fees) on an illness or condition suffered by you, your spouse, or a dependent
- Lodging to receive outpatient care at a licensed hospital, clinic, or hospital-equivalent facility, up to $50 per night ($100 per night if you accompany a sick child)

Planning Tips

Keep good records of your expenditures for medical-related travel.

- For use of your car, note the date, purpose, and odometer reading at the start and end of each trip, as well as related parking and tolls
- For other travel costs, retain receipts of all expenses

Pitfall

You cannot deduct the costs of trips taken for general good health. For example, your car mileage to and from the gym is not deductible if you are there to improve your appearance or maintain general good health rather than to treat a condition such as obesity or high blood pressure.

Similarly, if you fly to Florida each winter to escape the cold of New Hampshire, you cannot deduct your travel costs, even though the warm climate or other factors may be beneficial to your health. You are not traveling for the purpose of obtaining treatment or for some other deductible medical purpose.

Where to Claim the Deduction

Medical travel costs, which are part of itemized medical expenses, are reported in the "Medical and Dental Expenses" section of Schedule A of Form 1040 or 1040-SR.

Charitable Travel

Volunteering for your favorite cause may cost you money; just getting to and from your volunteer activity can be an expense. The tax law lets you deduct your out-of-pocket travel costs incurred for charitable pursuits.

Benefit ⬟

If you use your car for charitable purposes, including attending meetings of organizations you serve, you can deduct either your actual car expenses for gas and oil or mileage at the rate of 14¢ per mile. Whichever method you select, you can also write off parking and tolls.

You can also deduct travel expenses, plus meals and lodging, for overnight trips away from home to serve as an official delegate to a convention of a church, charitable, veteran, or other similar organization.

Conditions

You qualify to deduct your car expenses to the extent that the use of your car is for a tax-exempt organization or governmental unit. To see whether the charity you work for is tax exempt, see Chapter 6.

You qualify for convention-related expenses that you are not reimbursed for if you serve as an official delegate on behalf of a religious, charitable, veteran, or other similar organization.

Planning Tip

Keep track of your mileage and out-of-pocket expenses on behalf of the charity. In a diary or logbook, note the odometer readings for every charity-related trip for which your car is used, as well as any related parking and tolls.

Pitfalls

You cannot deduct travel costs to work on a project for a nonprofit organization if there is a significant element of personal pleasure, recreation, or vacation involved.

You cannot deduct travel costs to attend a charity-related convention if you do not serve as an official delegate.

Where to Claim the Benefit

To claim a charitable deduction for your charity-related travel expenses, you must complete Schedule A of Form 1040 or 1040-SR. Enter your deduction for charity-related expenses in the "Gifts to Charity" section of Schedule A.

Education-Related Travel

Unless you're taking classes online or via television from home or listening to teleconferences, you must travel to a classroom to learn. If the education is work-related and you are self-employed, your travel costs may be deductible.

Benefit

Whether you drive across town to take college credits or fly across the country for a continuing education course, you can deduct your travel costs as a business expense. For example, if you go to night school to take a computer course to keep you up-to-date for your business, which is working with computers, your travel from work to school and from school to home is deductible.

Conditions

For educational travel to be treated as a deductible expense, the education you are traveling for must be work-related. This means that:

- You are self-employed. For example, you cannot deduct as work-related expenses the cost of an undergraduate education because you are not already working at your business.
- You already meet the minimum requirements for your position, based on the laws and regulations of your state.
- The courses maintain or improve your current business skills.
- The courses do not lead to qualification for a new profession.

EXAMPLES OF EDUCATIONAL TRAVEL COSTS

- Car expenses from work to school. You can deduct your actual costs or use the standard mileage rate for business travel (56¢ per mile in 2021), plus parking and tolls.
- Car expenses or local transportation expenses (bus, subway, cab, train, ridesharing, or other fare) of going from your place of business to school and from school to home, *provided* you are regularly employed and going to school is a temporary endeavor (courses are expected to last no more than one year and do, in fact, end within this time).
- Travel costs away from home to attend a course (transportation to and from the course, lodging, and 50% of meals).

Example

Your business is in New York City, and every night for 6 weeks you take a refresher course. Since the course is temporary, you may deduct your travel expenses between work and school and school and home. It does not matter whether you go directly from work to school; your travel costs from home to school, in either or both directions, are deductible. The same is true if you take the refresher course on Saturday.

Planning Tip

If you are taking a course out of town and spend some time on personal activities, be prepared to prove that the primary purpose of the out-of-town travel was business-related education. This can be done by showing that you spend most of your time attending the course and only a relatively small amount of time on sightseeing or other personal activities.

Example

You travel from Boston, your place of business, to Las Vegas for a 2-day continuing education program. If your total travel is 3 days, you can confidently show that the primary purpose of your trip is for the education so that your airfare to and from Boston is a deductible travel expense.

Example

Same facts except your trip to Las Vegas lasts 7 days. In this case, it may be difficult to show that the primary reason for the trip was work-related education since you spend 5 of the 7 days on personal activities. However, even if the airfare is not deductible, local transportation costs to and from the 2-day course are deductible.

Pitfalls

You cannot deduct travel that is educational in nature, even though it may be beneficial to your work. For example, an architect may not deduct the cost of travel to a foreign country to look at the architecture. However, if the architect takes courses abroad, then the travel costs become deductible even if the courses are not taken for credit. Decide whether it will save you money to pay for and take a course in order to deduct your travel costs.

If you are away from home for education purposes, you may not deduct travel costs for sightseeing, social visiting, or entertaining while taking the course.

You cannot deduct the cost of traveling to and attending investment seminars, despite how educational and beneficial they may be. The tax law specifically bans this deduction.

You cannot deduct education expenses in 2018 through 2025 if you are an employee. The reason: No deduction is allowed for miscellaneous itemized expenses subject to the 2%-of-adjusted-gross-income floor, which include employee-related education costs.

Where to Claim the Benefit

As a self-employed individual, you enter your education-related travel on Schedule C.

National Guard and Military Reservist Travel

According to the U.S. Department of Defense, in the government's 2020 fiscal year (the most recent year for statistics), there were approximately 807,800 members of the National Guard and the Reserves. If you're one of them, you likely have service-related costs and you may be able to deduct them.

Benefit ⬆

You can deduct your overnight travel costs as an adjustment to gross income.

Conditions

To claim the deduction, besides the obvious requirement of being a member of the National Guard or in the reserves, you must meet the following 3 conditions:

1. You must incur the costs to attend a meeting more than 100 miles away from home. You are considered to be away from home if you are away from the permanent duty station long enough to require rest or sleep in order to complete your duties. For naval personnel of a drydocked submarine, your tax home is the area or vicinity of your principal place of employment or shore assignment (not the submarine itself).
2. The costs must relate to overnight transportation, meals, and lodging.
3. The amount of the deductible expenses cannot exceed the general federal per diem rate applicable to the locality to which you travel. You can find these per diem rates at www.gsa.gov (click on Per Diem Rates).

Planning Tips

Keep good records of your travel mileage and expenses to be able to substantiate the deduction you claim.

Pitfalls

Only 50% of the cost of meals not provided at restaurants is deductible. Service-related travel expenses that cannot be deducted as an adjustment to gross income are nondeductible. This is because in 2018 through 2025 no miscellaneous itemized deduction is allowed for unreimbursed employee business expenses.

Where to Claim the Deduction

The deduction for travel expenses that meet these qualifications is claimed on Schedule 1 of Form 1040 or 1040-SR.

Frequent Flier Miles

Whether you travel on business or for pleasure, you can build up frequent flier miles that can be cashed in for fares or upgrades. You can also earn frequent flier miles by charging goods and services to special credit cards that award mileage. Fortunately, there may be no tax cost to you for using frequent flier miles.

Benefit ⊗

You are not taxed on the value of frequent flier miles you earn on business travel and use for personal travel. For example, you earn enough points on your business travel throughout the year to receive free tickets for your summer vacation. You are not taxed on the frequent flier miles as they accrue, and you are not taxed when you use them for travel benefits—business or personal. The IRS, for the moment, has given up trying to tax this benefit because it is too difficult to assign a value to it. There is no dollar limit to the amount of this benefit that you can exclude from income.

Condition

To be excludable from income, frequent flier miles can be used only for in-kind benefits, which include free airline tickets or seat upgrades.

Planning Tips

Check on the expiration date of frequent flier miles you have earned so that you can use them up before it is too late.

Consider donating your frequent flier miles to charity. While you can't claim a tax deduction (there is no way to value the miles, and the donation is viewed as having been made to the user of the miles rather than to the organization), you'll benefit someone. For instance, Make-A-Wish Foundation needs over 2.8 billion miles annually to grant wishes to children with life-threatening medical conditions.

Pitfalls

If you convert frequent flier miles to cash, the cash value of the benefits must be reported as income in this case.

If you receive frequent flier miles as a bonus or gift, the miles *may* be taxable. For example, a number of years ago Citibank ran a special promotion offering frequent flyer miles for opening deposit accounts and reported on a Form 1099 frequent flier miles at 2.5¢ per mile for those who opened new accounts. There has been no similar reporting since this one.

> **NOTE**
> A number of years ago, the IRS has said it may devise a way to tax frequent flyer miles, but to date no further information has been announced; see the Supplement for any development.

Where to Claim the Exclusion

Since this employee fringe benefit is excluded from income, you do not have to report anything on your tax return. Frequent flier miles earned as an employee are not reported on your Form W-2.

Recordkeeping for Travel Expenses

The tax law requires you to keep records of your travel expenses as a condition for claiming a deduction. Your travel expense records must include the following information:

- *Amount.* The cost of each separate expense for travel, lodging, and meals. Incidental expenses can be totaled in any reasonable category (such as taxi fares). However, if you rely on a per diem rate for lodging, meals, and incidental expenses, you need not record these expenses nor retain receipts for them.
- *Time.* Record the dates you leave and return for each trip and the number of days spent on business.
- *Place or destination.* Note the area of your travel (the name of the city, town, or other destination).
- *Business purpose.* Record the reason for the expense or the benefit to be gained, or expected to be gained, from the trip.

You can use the recordkeeper in Table 9.2 to record the amount of your travel expenses each week. You can also use a variety of apps for your smartphone or tablet to keep required records for deductible travel expenses.

TABLE 9.2 Sample Weekly Travel Expense Record Keeper

Date: From:_____ To:_____

Expense	Sunday	Monday	Tuesday	Wednesday	Thursday	Friday	Saturday	Total
Airlines								
Excess baggage								
Bus								
Train								
Cab/limo								
Tips								
Other costs								
Hotel: Name City								
Breakfast								
Lunch								
Dinner								

In addition to your diary or logbook (created on paper or electronically), you also need documentary proof of your expenses. This usually means retaining receipts, canceled checks, or other proof of what you paid for your travel expenses. However, you do not need receipts for expenses under $75 (except in the case of lodging, where proof is required regardless of the amount).

Real Estate

The vast majority of Americans own real estate, with 65.4% owning their own homes. (Tax write-offs for your main home are discussed in Chapter 4.) But owning a principal residence isn't the only way to invest in real estate. Many individuals also own second homes or invest in rental properties to generate income. These investments produce important tax breaks. If real estate activities are your business, see Chapter 14.

This chapter covers tax breaks related to real estate other than your principal residence. For more information, see IRS Publication 527, *Residential Rental Property (Including Rental of Vacation Homes)*; IRS Publication 587, *Business Use of Your Home (Including Use by Day-Care Providers)*; and IRS Publication 946, *How to Depreciate Property*.

Vacation Home

The rich have traditionally maintained more than one residence, summering in Newport, skiing in Aspen, escaping winters in Miami. But today, second homes aren't limited to the very rich; they are increasingly common among an ever-broadening populace. The tax law offers some tax breaks that help to make ownership of vacation homes more affordable.

Benefit

If you use your vacation home solely for your own personal enjoyment (you don't rent it out at any time during the year), you can deduct all of your real estate taxes and home mortgage interest (if the vacation home is designated as your second home under the home mortgage interest rules in Chapter 4). But, like your personal residence, you can't write off any of the costs of utilities, insurance, or upkeep.

If you rent out a home that you use for part of the year yourself, you may be entitled to certain tax benefits over and above those allowed for pure personal use of the home. The rules that apply to you depend on your rental period and the time that you use the home.

Conditions for Vacation Home with No Rentals

The conditions for deducting real estate taxes and home mortgage interest are explained in Chapter 4.

Conditions for Vacation Home with Rentals

The conditions you must meet and the benefits you are entitled to depend on how long you rent out the home and how long you use it for yourself during the year. There are 3 categories into which you can fall.

1. Rental of no more than 14 days during the year.
2. Rental of 15 days or more but personal use is for less than 14 days or 10% of the days of rental.
3. Personal use is more than 14 days or 10% of the total days the home was rented for a fair rental price.

TAX-FREE RENTAL INCOME

If you rent out your home for no more than 14 days during the year, you do not have to report the rental income. There's no dollar limit on this exclusion.

Example

In February 2021, because of your proximity to Super Bowl LV, you rented your home in Tampa, Florida, for 3 days. You receive a rental payment of $1,900 per night, for a total of $5,700. None of the $5,700 is taxable.

You cannot, however, deduct any expenses related to maintaining the home, depreciation, or any rent you pay. Of course, if you itemize your deductions, you can deduct your mortgage interest, if you designate the home as your second residence, and your real estate taxes (there is no limit on the number of homes for which you can deduct real estate taxes).

BUSINESS DEDUCTIONS

If you rent out your home for 15 days or more but you personally use the home for less than 14 days or 10% of the days of rental, your rental activities are viewed as a business.

Example

You rent out your home for 3 months and use it for only 1 week during the year. Since the rental period is more than 15 days (it is actually 92 days) and your personal use is less than 14 days or 10% of the days of rental (9 days), you fall within this rule for figuring your deductions from the rental activity.

As such, you must report all of the rental income, but you can deduct from rental income only the mortgage interest, real estate taxes, operating expenses, and depreciation prorated for rental use. If your prorated expenses, including depreciation on a home you own, exceed your rents for the year, you can use the loss to offset your income from other purposes (subject to the passive loss limitations discussed further on).

Personal use of your home includes any day the home is used by:

- You or any member of your family (unless a family member pays a fair rental price)
- Anyone else who pays less than a fair rental price
- Anyone under a reciprocal agreement who lets you use his or her home
- Any other person who owns a part of the home (unless it is rented to that person under a shared equity agreement)

You do not have to count your personal use during the year if your home is rented for at least 12 consecutive months.

Example

You move from your home in March 2021 and start renting it in April 2022. Assuming your rental lasts at least until through March 2022, you do not have to count your personal use in 2021.

However, your actual write-offs for the year may be limited by the passive activity loss rules discussed later.

LIMITED BUSINESS DEDUCTIONS

If your personal use is more than 14 days or 10% of the total days the home was rented for a fair rental price, you must report all of the rental income. Your deductions are limited to the amount of rents you receive. And the order in which you claim your deductions is carefully orchestrated:

1. Mortgage interest, real estate taxes, and casualty losses are fully deductible. You can claim them even if they exceed your rental income. But you must apply them first against your rental income to determine how much of your other deductions to claim.

2. Operating expenses, such as utilities and maintenance costs, are deductible only to the extent of your rental income after reduction for mortgage interest and so on.

3. Depreciation and other basis adjustments are deductible only to the extent that rental income has not yet been fully offset by the aforementioned deductions.

Example

You own a condo at the shore. You rent it out for June and July. You use it for August. Since your rental is 61 days and your personal use is 31 days, you must figure your deductions using this ordering rule. Assume you receive $6,000 for the 2 months of rental, and your deductions for the year are $2,000 for interest and $3,000 for taxes. In this case, you can deduct up to $1,000 of operating expenses. Assuming you have at least $1,000 of operating expenses, then you cannot claim any depreciation. Your deductions, in effect, fully offset your rental income so you have no taxable income from your rental activity.

PASSIVE LOSS LIMITATIONS

If the rental of your vacation home is treated as a rental activity (your personal use is fewer than 15 days but the rental period is more than 2 weeks), you are subject to the passive loss rules. Generally, your deductions related to the rental of your home cannot exceed all of your passive activity income from the year (income from this rental activity plus any other passive activities). (The law calls them passive "losses" but really means deductions in excess of rental income.)

Example

The rental of a vacation home is your only passive activity. Rental income for the year is $6,000, while deductions are $8,000. You can deduct only $6,000 this year.

Passive activity losses in excess of passive activity income can be carried forward and used in a future year when there is passive activity income to offset it. There is no limit on the carryforward period.

There are 3 key exceptions to the ban on deducting passive losses in excess of passive activity income.

1. You can deduct all carryover losses from a passive activity in the year in which you dispose of your passive activity (e.g., sell your vacation home).

2. You can deduct up to $25,000 of passive activity losses in excess of passive activity income from a rental activity in which you actively participate (e.g., approve new tenants, decide on rental terms, and authorize capital expenditures and repairs). The $25,000 limit is phased out when your modified adjusted gross income exceeds $100,000 and is completely phased out when MAGI reaches $150,000. MAGI for this purpose means AGI without taxable Social Security benefits, the exclusion for interest from U.S. savings bonds used for higher education, the exclusion for employer-paid adoption expenses, and the deductions for IRA contributions and student loan interest. If you're married, filing a separate return, and lived apart from your spouse for the entire tax year, the special allowance is up to $12,500. If you lived with your spouse at any time during the year and are filing a separate return, you can't use the special allowance.

Example

You are single with MAGI of $135,000. You actively participate in the rental of your condo at a ski resort. Your rental loss in excess of passive activity income is limited to $7,500: $25,000 − 50% of ($135,000 − $100,000).

3. You are a "real estate professional" who meets certain tests in the tax law. In this case, your losses from rental realty are not subject to the passive activity loss rules. This is explained in greater detail later in this chapter under "Rentals."

Planning Tip

If you rent out your vacation home for more than 15 days and use it for less than 14 days or 10% of the days of rental, you are *not* subject to the passive activity loss limitations on your deductions if you are considered a "real estate professional." This means:

- More than 50% of your personal services during the year are performed in real estate trades or businesses in which you materially participate (e.g., work more than 500 hours for the year, which is 10 hours a week for 50 weeks, or your participation is substantially all of the participation for the activity during the year and this is more than the time you spend in a job or on a non-real estate business).
- You perform more than 750 hours of service in real estate trades or businesses in which you materially participate.

Pitfalls

Getting help with home renovations through an HGTV show may be taxable even if the show uses the home for fewer than 15 days. The value of the home improvements is not tax-free rental, but rather taxable income.

If you rent out your home for more than 15 days but use it for less than 14 days or 10% of the rental days, you cannot deduct the portion of home mortgage interest disallowed under the rental loss rules discussed earlier. In this case, since your home ceases to be treated as a personal residence, you cannot itemize any portion of the mortgage interest.

When you sell your vacation home, don't be surprised by the tax impact that can result. Your gain probably does not qualify for the home sale exclusion (see Chapter 4) because the vacation home is not your principal residence. As long as you own the home for more than one year, your gain is a long-term capital gain.

However, if you rented the home at any time and claimed depreciation on it, you must recapture the depreciation on the sale. This means that gain to the extent of your depreciation is taxed at 25% (assuming you are in a tax bracket at or above this rate).

Example

In 2021, you sell your vacation home for a profit of $100,000. You had bought the home in 2014 and claimed depreciation deductions for the rental of the home totaling $2,800. Of the $100,000 gain, $2,800 is taxed at 25%, while $97,200 is taxed at 15% (20% if your taxable income exceeds a certain threshold for your filing status).

If you realize a loss on the sale of your vacation home, your ability to claim the loss depends on whether or not the home was used for rental.

- If the home was used solely for personal purposes, no loss can be claimed on the sale.
- If the home was used some of the time for rental activities, you cannot claim a loss on the sale.
- If the home was converted solely to rental, you can then claim a capital loss on the sale. The loss is limited to the decline in value after the conversion.

Example

If the home was purchased for $150,000 and has declined in value to $125,000 when you decide to sell it, you can convert it to rental at this time and figure your deductible loss with reference to the $125,000 value. Assume you sell the home after a year on the market for $100,000. Your actual loss is $50,000 ($150,000 − $100,000), but your deductible loss is $25,000 ($125,000 − $100,000). Converting the home to rental means holding the property out for rental, even if you are unsuccessful in your efforts.

Where to Claim the Benefit

If you use your vacation home solely for personal purposes, you deduct your mortgage interest and real estate taxes on Schedule A of Form 1040 or 1040-SR (as explained in Chapter 4).

If you rent out your vacation home, you report your rents and expenses in Part I of Schedule E of Form 1040 or 1040-SR (unless rental income from your vacation home is tax free).

If you are subject to the passive activity loss limitations, you must complete Form 8582, *Passive Activity Loss Limitations*, to determine your deduction limit for the year.

If you have income from rental activities and you are not a real estate professional, this income is taken into account in determining the net investment income (NII) tax figured on Form 8960, *Net Investment Income Tax—Individuals, Estates, and Trusts*.

Home Office

The president of the United States works from home, but since he doesn't pay for the costs of the Oval Office, he can't claim any deduction for his home office. But if you work from your home and are self-employed, you may qualify for write-offs if certain conditions are met.

Benefit 🔼 ⬇

If you use a part of your home for business, you may qualify to deduct costs related to the home office, including rent (if you lease your residence) or depreciation (if you own your home), maintenance and utilities, and other expenses. In effect, the personal expenses you are already paying become deductible business expenses, so the home office deduction is a write-off that doesn't require you to pay anything other than what you are already paying. Alternatively, you can opt to use an IRS-set standard amount for your home office deduction.

Generally, you figure your home office deduction by apportioning expenses to that space. The IRS generally wants you to make the apportionment based on square footage. If you use the IRS-set simplified method, you can take into account your square footage up to 300 square feet to figure your deduction.

Example

If your home is 2,500 square feet and you use 250 square feet of it for a home office, then generally 10% of your home's expenses are part of your home office deduction if you figure your deduction based on your actual expenses.

If all your rooms are about the same size, you can opt to make your allocation based on the number of rooms. For example, if you have 8 rooms in your home and one is used for business, then one-eighth of your home's expenses are part of your home office deduction. If you use the IRS's simplified method, your deduction is $5 per square foot of up to 300 of square feet, for a maximum deduction of $1,500. If you base your deduction on your actual costs, the computation is more complex. There are 2 general categories of deductible expenses—those directly related to the home office and those indirectly related to the home office. The first category includes only costs for the office itself, and these costs are fully deductible; the second category includes costs related to the home in general, and these are deductible to the extent of your allocation.

Example

If you paint the office, it is a direct expense and is fully deductible. If you paint the outside of your home, it is an indirect expense and is deductible to the extent of your allocation. For example, if your allocation to the home office is 10%, then 10% of the outside paint job is part of your home office deduction.

If you own the home, you can claim depreciation on the portion of the house or other unit (not the land) used as a home office (see later in this chapter under Rentals). Usually, depreciation is figured using a 39-year recovery period on a straight line basis. However, if the office is within property qualifying as residential rental property (e.g., you use one room in your apartment within an 8-unit building you own), then depreciation is figured using a 27.5-year recovery period.

Conditions

To be eligible to treat costs related to a home office as a deductible business expense (regardless of how you figure the deduction), you must first show that the office is one of the following:

- Your principal place of business
- A place to meet or deal with patients, clients, or customers in the normal course of your business
- A separate structure (not attached to your residence) that is used in connection with your business

Then you must show that you use the home office regularly and exclusively for business. Assuming you meet this condition, you must have sufficient income from your home office activity.

PRINCIPAL PLACE OF BUSINESS

The home office must be the prime location for running your business. The business itself need not be your prime activity; you can claim a home office deduction for a sideline or moonlighting business. Usually, prime location means the place where you earn your money. For example, a freelance writer's prime location is his home office.

Your home office is treated as your prime location if it is used for substantial managerial or administrative activities and there is no other fixed location for these activities. For example, an electrician's prime location is the customers' homes where her fees are earned. But if she uses a home office to keep her books, schedule appointments, and order supplies, and she does not have another office, then the home office is treated as her prime location.

PLACE TO MEET OR DEAL WITH CUSTOMERS

You don't have to use your home office as your prime location. You merely have to use it on a regular basis to meet or deal with customers, clients, or patients. For example, an attorney with a downtown office who uses a home office several times each month to meet with clients qualifies as having a deductible home office. Merely using a telephone from a home office to talk with clients or customers is *not* considered meeting or dealing with them on a regular basis.

SEPARATE STRUCTURE

If you have a freestanding garage, barn, greenhouse, or studio that you use in connection with your business, it qualifies as a deductible home office. It does not have to be used as an office or qualify as a principal place of business or a place to meet or deal with customers. For example, a florist with a store in the city who uses a greenhouse on her property to grow orchids can treat the greenhouse as her home office.

EXCLUSIVE USE TEST

Whether you figure the deduction based on actual expenses or the IRS-set rate, you must show that you use the home office space regularly and exclusively for business. There is no minimum amount of time that the office must be used to show regular use. Regular use means more than just occasional use.

For purposes of showing exclusive use, you can't, for example, use the family den as an office by day and a family room by night. A piano teacher was able to show that her living room containing her baby grand piano was her home office; her family never used the room for personal reasons. However, incidental use, such as walking through the office to get to personal space because of necessity does not violate the exclusive use test.

You do not have to use an entire room as your office; a portion of a room can qualify. You don't even need to make a physical partition for the space. Just be sure it is used only for business. Furnish it appropriately for your business activity (e.g., a desk, and so on if you run a travel agency business from home).

There is a special rule if you run a day-care business from home. There is another special rule for storing inventory and samples if you have a retail or wholesale business and no other fixed location for the business. These special rules are explained in IRS Publication 587, *Business Use of Your Home*.

GROSS INCOME LIMITATION

Your home office deduction cannot be more than your gross income from the home office activity whether you use the actual expense method or the IRS's simplified method. If you use your home office for a profitable business, this limitation should pose no problem. But if your business is merely a sideline generating modest income or a struggling business, you must check whether this limitation applies to you.

Gross income for purposes of the home office deduction means income from the business activity you run from home, reduced by business deductions unrelated to the qualified use of the home.

If you find that gross income is less than your home office deduction, the deduction becomes limited. Under the actual expense method, your deduction for expenses that would otherwise be nondeductible (such as depreciation and utilities) cannot exceed gross income from the home office activity, reduced by the business portion of otherwise deductible expenses. Some expenses (real estate taxes, mortgage interest, and casualty losses) may or may not be subject to the gross income limitation. It's very complicated and depends on whether you claim the standard deduction, or if you itemize whether other limitations apply for personal itemized deduction purposes.

If, after going through the computation, you have an unused home office deduction, you can carry it forward indefinitely. (There is no carryover if you use the IRS's simplified method.) The carryforward can be used in any future year in which there is gross income from the same home office activity to offset it. Using the carryforward is permissible even if you are no longer in the same home office.

Example

At the end of 2021 you relocate to a larger home. You have a carryover from 2020. You continue to conduct your sideline business from your new home but cannot use the 2020 carryover in 2021. In 2022, you can use the carryover from 2020 (assuming your sideline business has sufficient gross income).

Planning Tips

If you were unable to claim the full home office deduction in a prior year due to income limitations, be sure to include any carryover of the home office deduction in your computations for the current year.

If you qualify for a home office, there is an ancillary benefit to consider. Travel to and from your home on business is deductible business travel. In effect, there is no such thing as nondeductible commuting when you have a home office.

Pitfalls

If you are an employee who was forced to work from home due to business closures related to COVID-19 or has remained a remote worker even though safe to return to the company office, you cannot claim a home office deduction. As explained earlier, even though you meet the requirements for the deduction, you're barred from claiming it due to the suspension of miscellaneous itemized deductions (which include unreimbursed employee business expenses) subject to the 2%-of-adjusted-gross-income floor in 2018 through 2025.

You cannot claim a home office deduction if you are an employee who leases the space to your corporation. The tax law specifically bars a home office deduction in this case. However, like any homeowner, you can continue to claim your regular deductions, such as mortgage interest, real estate taxes, and casualty and theft losses.

If you use the IRS's optional method and cannot claim a current deduction because of the gross income limitation, you *cannot* carry over the unused deduction to a future year. And, the year you use the optional method, you cannot claim any carryover of an unused home office deduction from a year in which the actual expense method was used.

When figuring the deduction using actual expenses, all expenses related to your home office are deductible. The cost of landscaping is not part of a home office deduction. Similarly the expenses of a telephone to a home office are not part of your home office deduction. You cannot deduct the basic service charge for the first line to your home. But the cost of a second phone line or even extra charges on the first line are separately deductible as a business expense that is not part of your home office deduction.

Claiming a home office deduction has often been called a red flag, a signal to the IRS to look closely at the deduction. However, if you are entitled to claim the deduction, then by all means do so; just be prepared to back up the position you take on your tax return.

If you own your home, then any depreciation claimed with respect to a home office after May 6, 1997, must be recaptured when your home is sold. Recapture means that this portion of your gain is taxed at a 25% rate (assuming you are in a tax bracket at or above this level). You must report your depreciation even if you qualify to exclude gain on the sale of your home; you cannot use the exclusion to offset depreciation recapture.

Where to Claim the Deduction

As a self-employed individual, you figure your home office deduction using actual expenses on Form 8829, *Expenses for Business Use of Your Home*. The deduction using the IRS's simplified method is figured on a worksheet in the instructions to Schedule C.

Timeshares

Owning a timeshare entitles you to use your furnished unit in a resort location for a set period of time each year. In many cases, you can exchange yours for one in another resort or change your fixed time for another. According to the American Resort Development Association, in 2019 approximately 9.6 million households in the U.S. owned one or more timeshares.

Owned for personal use. Timeshares owned for personal reasons are treated in the same way as vacation homes. Thus, the tax breaks available for such ownership include:

- Deducting mortgage interest as long as the debt is secured by the property.
- Deducting real estate taxes. The taxes are deductible whether you are billed directly (as is the case in California) or the tax is separately identified on the timeshare maintenance bills (as is the case in Florida).

As in the case of other realty owned for personal use, you cannot deduct homeowners insurance, maintenance fees, or special assessments. Gain cannot qualify for the home sale exclusion (see Chapter 4) because the timeshare can never be your principal residence. Thus, gain on the sale of your timeshare is taxed as capital gain; any loss is not deductible.

The rules for timeshares owned for investment purposes are explained under the topic of Rentals, which follows.

Rentals

Becoming a landlord by acquiring real estate and renting it out can be a sound financial activity. There is the possibility of making money both from rental income as well as property appreciation upon an eventual sale. The tax law helps to underwrite the cost of being a landlord, allowing for certain tax deductions. But there are limits on and special rules for write-offs associated with rental properties.

Benefit

If you rent out property, directly to tenants or through an online platform such as airbnb, you can deduct your expenses against the rental income. Net income from rentals may entitle you to claim a qualified business income (QBI) deduction. Any loss resulting from having expenses in excess of rental income can effectively be used to offset your other income, such as salary or dividends.

However, losses from rental activities are subject to the passive loss rules that may restrict your deductions for the current year.

Conditions

If you own realty—a single-family home, a condo unit, a multifamily home in which you live and rent out a portion, an office building, a strip mall, or any other property—you can deduct expenses related to the property.

EXAMPLES OF DEDUCTIBLE RENTAL EXPENSES

- Advertising to find tenants
- Car expenses to and from the property
- Cleaning and maintenance
- Commissions to real estate brokers when finding tenants
- Depreciation
- Insurance
- Legal and professional fees (but not attorney's fees to buy the property)
- Management fees
- Mortgage interest on rental property
- Repairs
- Security system monitoring fees
- Supplies
- Taxes
- Utilities

PASSIVE LOSS LIMITATIONS

When you rent out property, you usually fall within the passive loss rules (exceptions to these rules are discussed later). Then, generally, your deductions cannot exceed all of your passive activity income from the year (income from this rental activity plus any other passive activities). (The law calls them passive "losses" but really means deductions in excess of rental income.)

Example

The rental of a single-family home in which you do not live during the year is your only passive activity. Rental income for the year is $6,000, while deductions are $8,000. You can deduct only $6,000 this year (unless you meet any of the 3 key exceptions in the list following).

Passive activity losses in excess of passive activity income can be carried forward and used in a future year when there is passive activity income to offset them. There is no limit on the carryforward period.

There are 3 key exceptions to the ban on deducting passive losses in excess of passive activity income.

1. You can deduct all carryover losses from a passive activity in the year in which you dispose of your interest in the realty in a taxable disposition (e.g., sell your rental property).
2. You can deduct up to $25,000 of passive activity losses in excess of passive activity income from a rental activity in which you actively participate (e.g., approve new tenants, decide on rental terms, and authorize capital expenditures and repairs). The $25,000 limit begins to phase out when your modified adjusted gross income exceeds $100,000 and is completely phased out when MAGI reaches $150,000. MAGI for this purpose means AGI without taxable Social Security benefits, the exclusion for interest from U.S. savings bonds used for higher education, the exclusion for employer-paid adoption expenses, deductions for IRA contributions, the deduction for contributions to Archer medical savings accounts, and student loan interest. If you are married filing separately, see the limitation discussed earlier in this chapter.

Example

You are single with MAGI of $135,000. You actively participate in the rental of your beachfront condo. Your rental loss in excess of passive activity income is limited to $7,500: $25,000 − 50% of ($135,000 − $100,000).

3. You are a real estate professional exempt from the passive loss rules. If you are in the real estate business and want to check whether you are treated as a real estate professional exempt from the passive loss rules, see the instructions to IRS Form 8582. Just know that if you have a full-time job in addition to your real estate activities, it's highly unlikely that you'll qualify as a real estate professional.

QUALIFIED BUSINESS INCOME DEDUCTION

Regardless of whether you are actively or passively involved with your real estate rentals, if you show a profit you may be eligible for a deduction of up to 20% of your qualified business income (QBI). The QBI deduction, which is a personal deduction based on your rental income and can be taken whether you itemize or claim the standard deduction, is discussed in more detail in Chapter 14.

The IRS has provided a safe harbor under which a rental real estate enterprise is treated as a trade or business for purposes of the QBI deduction. All of the following conditions must be met:

1. You must keep separate books and records to reflect income and expenses for each rental real estate enterprise.

2. For rental real estate enterprises that have been in existence less than 4 years, 250 or more hours of rental services are performed per year with respect to the rental real estate enterprise. For rental real estate enterprises that have been in existence for at least 4 years, in any 3 of the 5 consecutive taxable years that end with the taxable year, 250 or more hours of rental services are performed per year with respect to the rental real estate enterprise.

3. You must maintain contemporaneous records, including time reports, logs, or similar documents, regarding the following: (i) hours of all services performed; (ii) description of all services performed; (iii) dates on which such services were performed; and (iv) who performed the services. If services with respect to the rental real estate enterprise are performed by employees or independent contractors, you can provide a description of the rental services performed by such employee or independent contractor, the amount of time such employee or independent contractor generally spends performing such services for the enterprise, and time, wage, or payment records for such employee or independent contractor. These records are to be made available for inspection at the request of the IRS.

4. You or the relevant pass-through entity (RPE), such as a limited liability company in which you have an interest, attaches a statement to a timely filed original return for each taxable year in which you or RPE relies on the safe harbor. An individual or RPE with more than one rental real estate enterprise relying on this safe harbor may submit a single statement but the statement must list the required information separately for each rental real estate enterprise.

Planning Tips

Depreciation is a no-cost deduction (you don't spend any dollars to claim the write-off, other than buying the property). How do you figure this valuable write-off called depreciation? It is a deduction *only* for the building (you can't depreciate land), so you must allocate the cost of the property between the building and the land.

> **Example**
>
> You buy a single-family home for rental, paying $180,000. According to your county assessor's assessment for improvements (buildings), you allocate $155,000 to the house. This is your basis for depreciation.

If you convert personal property to rental property (for example, you move from your home and rent it out), your basis for depreciation purposes is your basis (as figured earlier) or the fair market value of the home at the time of conversion, whichever is less (exclusive of the land).

> **Example**
>
> You bought your home (exclusive of the land) for $200,000 in 2008. In 2020, you move from it and rent it out indefinitely. The value of the home in 2020 is $300,000. Your basis for depreciation is $200,000, which is the lower of basis or fair market value at the time of conversion.

The amount you claim for depreciation is based on the month in which you place the property into service as a rental and the type of realty involved:

- Residential rental property is depreciated over a period of 27.5 years using the straight-line method and a midmonth depreciation convention. Residential rental property is a building for which 80% or more of the gross rental income for the year is rental income from dwelling units. So, if you own an apartment building with stores at street level, you must see whether the property meets the 80% test.

- Nonresidential property is depreciated over a period of 39 years.

Depreciation is simply your basis in the home or building (but not the land) multiplied by the depreciation rate from the IRS table. Table 10.1 shows depreciation rates for residential property. Table 10.2 shows depreciation rates for nonresidential property.

If you sublease property—you are a tenant who leases the property to someone else—you cannot claim a depreciation deduction. Depreciation for the cost of the building can only be claimed by the owner of the property.

Leasehold improvements that you make can be deducted separately from depreciation on the building. Write-offs for leasehold improvements are explained later in this chapter.

TABLE 10.1 Depreciation Rates for Residential Rental Property

| Year | | | | | | Month | | | | | | |
	1	2	3	4	5	6	7	8	9	10	11	12
1	3.485%	3.182%	2.879%	2.576%	2.273%	1.970%	1.667%	1.364%	1.061%	0.758%	0.455%	0.152%
2–9	3.636	3.636	3.636	3.636	3.636	3.636	3.636	3.636	3.636	3.636	3.636	3.636
10	3.637	3.637	3.637	3.637	3.637	3.637	3.636	3.636	3.636	3.636	3.636	3.636

For years 11–28, see IRS Publication 946, *How to Depreciate Property*.

TABLE 10.2 Depreciation Rates for Nonresidential Rental Property (Placed in Service after May 13, 1993)

Year	Month											
	1	2	3	4	5	6	7	8	9	10	11	12
1	2.461%	2.247%	2.033%	1.819%	1.605%	1.391%	1.177%	0.963%	0.749%	0.535%	0.321%	0.107%
2–39	2.564	2.564	2.564	2.564	2.564	2.564	2.564	2.564	2.564	2.564	2.564	2.564

If your landlord activities rise to the level of being a business, you may be eligible for the qualified business income deduction (see Chapter 14).

Pitfall

Depreciation claimed on your rental realty is subject to a special capital gain rate for recaptured depreciation. This means that the gain you realize on the sale is taxed at 25% to the extent of depreciation deductions you have claimed. Gain in excess of this amount is taxed at no more than 20%, or 15% for most taxpayers (assuming you owned the property for more than one year).

Example

On July 5, 2016, you bought an office building for $250,000 (exclusive of the land). You sell it on July 5, 2021, for $350,000. Depreciation deductions total $31,665. Your gain is $131,665 ($350,000 − $218,335). Of this gain, $31,665 is taxed at the 25% rate; $100,000 is taxed at 15% (assuming your taxable income does not exceed a threshold amount triggering a 20% rate). Your total tax is $22,916 ($7,916 + $15,000).

Where to Claim the Deduction

You report your rents and expenses in Part I of Schedule E of Form 1040 or 1040-SR. If you own a multifamily home in which you live, the portion of mortgage interest and real estate taxes is allocated between Schedule E (for the rental portion) and Schedule A of Form 1040 or 1040-SR (for the personal portion of the home, assuming you itemize deductions).

Example

You own a 3-family house and live in one unit. Subject to applicable limits, two-thirds of your mortgage interest and property taxes and all of your rent-related expenses are reported on Schedule E; one-third of your mortgage interest and property taxes are reported on Schedule A (subject to applicable limitations for these itemized deductions).

If you own an interest in rental realty through a partnership or limited liability company that files a partnership return, you report your share of rental income or losses on Schedule E (you obtain the amount you must report from a Schedule K-1 that is given to you by the entity).

You must also complete Form 8582, *Passive Activity Loss Limitations*, to determine your deduction limit for the year under the passive activity rules.

Low-Income Housing Credit

The federal government wants to encourage investments in housing to accommodate low-income individuals. To make such investments attractive to investors, special tax credits have been made available. These credits effectively operate to replace the rental income investors do not receive because of the rent reductions or breaks provided to certain renters because of their income levels.

Benefit ✚

If you invest in low-income housing—to build it or substantially renovate existing structures—you may be eligible for a tax credit each year for a period of 10 years, generally starting with the year the building is placed in service. The amount of the credit depends on whether the building is new and whether any federal subsidies were used for construction or rehabilitation purposes.

The credit is based on 70% of the qualified basis of each new low-income housing building placed in service after 1986 or 30% of the qualified basis in the case of federally subsidized new or existing buildings. The credit itself is the present value of the 10 annual credit amounts determined as of the last day of the first year of the credit period. However, there is a minimum 9% for newly constructed nonfederally subsidized buildings.

Conditions

You can invest in low-income housing directly, by building the units or rehabilitating existing ones, or by putting money into a limited partnership that does the building or rehabilitating for you. Either way, to qualify for a credit, the building must be considered a low-income housing building.

LOW-INCOME HOUSING BUILDING

Low-income housing does not mean the property must be located in the slums or that the building itself is a tenement. Rather, the tax law requires only that the building offer a certain percentage of the rental units to tenants with income below fixed levels. For example, in the case of housing in suburban areas and smaller towns, the building is considered to be low-income housing if the tenants earn no more than 60% of the local median income. How do you know if your building qualifies? You must receive certification from an authorized housing credit agency. The agency allocates the credit to you on Form 8609, *Low-Income Housing Credit Allocation Certificate*.

The building must have been constructed after 1986; older buildings don't qualify.

Planning Tip

Generally, the first year of the credit is the year in which the building is placed in service for low-income housing. However, you can elect to start claiming the credit in the following year just by indicating your election on Form 8609. You may wish to do so if you cannot fully benefit from the credit in the year the building is placed in service (see "Pitfalls" that follow) or if you will have more income to offset in the following year.

Pitfall

If you dispose of your interest before the end of a set period, you are subject to recapture. This means that part of the benefit you received from claiming the credit is reported as an additional tax you owe in the year of recapture. The building must continue to meet certain requirements for a 15-year period. If not, then your recapture is figured on Form 8611, *Recapture of the Low-Income Housing Credit*.

Where to Claim the Credit

You figure your credit on Form 8586, *Low-Income Housing Credit*. The credit is part of the general business credit, which is figured on Form 3800, *General Business Credit*.

You may also need to figure whether the passive activity restrictions apply to your claiming the credit in the current year. You do this by completing Form 8582-CR, *Passive Activity Credit Limitations*.

The amount of the credit that can be claimed this year is then entered on Schedule 3 of Form 1040 or 1040-SR.

Rehabilitation Credit

Fix it up or tear it down? The tax law provides a key incentive for restoring certain older properties. The incentive is a tax credit that may be claimed if certain conditions are met.

Benefit ⊕

If you spend money fixing up an old building, you may be eligible to claim a tax credit. The credit is 20% for qualified rehabilitation expenditures for a certified historic structure. The credit is taken ratably over 5 years.

There is no overall dollar limit on the credit. However, there are certain limitations that may restrict the amount you can claim in the current year.

Conditions

There are 2 conditions:

- The building must be a historic structure
- The costs must be qualified rehabilitation expenditures that exceed a certain amount

HISTORIC STRUCTURES

The credit applies to both residential and nonresidential buildings (such as industrial and commercial buildings). The only criterion is that the building is a historic structure that has been recognized by a national or state registry (placed on the National Register of Historic Places or located in a registered historic district and certified by the Secretary of the Interior as being of historic significance to the district).

The National Park Service must certify that your planned rehabilitation of the building is in keeping with its historic status designation.

MINIMUM REHABILITATION

You can't claim the credit simply for adding a doorbell or making other minor renovations. The credit is limited to expenses of at least a certain amount: $5,000 or your adjusted basis in the building, whichever is greater.

Example

You buy an old building for a cost of $50,000 (exclusive of the land). To claim the credit, you must spend at least $50,000 on renovations (since your basis of $50,000 is greater than $5,000).

The expenditures must be made within a 24-month period. This period is extended to 60 months if the rehabilitation is undertaken pursuant to a written architectural plan and specifications are completed before the rehabilitation begins.

Planning Tips

When shopping for real estate to purchase for investment or business, consider the impact that claiming the credit may have on your fix-up costs. Also explore any federal or state grants that may be available for restoring historic structures.

Check to see if there are state income tax credits or other incentives (such as real estate tax abatements) for rehabilitating certified historic structures.

The rehabilitation credit can offset both regular tax and the alternative minimum tax.

Pitfalls

The tax credit for rehabilitating an old building falls under the passive loss rules. This means that the credit you are otherwise entitled to claim may be limited by passive activity restrictions. For more details, see the instructions to Form 8582-CR, *Passive Activity Credit Limitations*.

If you want to make a donation of a conservation easement, such as a façade easement (see Chapter 6), the amount of the contribution must be reduced by any rehabilitation credit claimed in the prior 5 years.

Where to Claim the Credit

You figure your credit on Form 3468, *Investment Credit*. The credit is part of the general business credit, which is figured on Form 3800, *General Business Credit*.

You may also need to figure whether the passive activity restrictions apply to your claiming the credit in the current year. You do this by completing Form 8582-CR, *Passive Activity Credit Limitations*.

The amount of the credit that can be claimed this year is then entered on Schedule 3 of Form 1040 or 1040-SR.

Like-Kind Exchanges

If you swap real property held in business or for investment purposes and meet certain requirements, gain on the exchange can be deferred. You may see like-kind exchanges being referred to as "tax free," but this is a misnomer; you're merely postponing having to pay tax on your gain.

Benefit ⬤

When you trade realty for other realty that is "like kind," gain or loss on the trade is deferred. So if you have a gain, you don't pay tax on it now; you pay tax on it when you dispose of the property you got in the exchange, assuming that disposition is a taxable transaction and not another like-kind exchange. This is accomplished by reducing your basis in the property acquired by the amount of gain not recognized on the trade. However, if you also receive cash or other non-like-kind property on the trade, you must report your gain to the extent of this other property (called "boot"), which is explained later.

> **NOTE**
> Proposals have been made in Congress to cap the value of property for which like-kind exchange tax treatment may be used. Check the Supplement for any update.

Conditions

The main condition for deferring gain on a trade of realty is that the property given up and the one acquired in the trade are like kind. If the trade is not simultaneous, you must meet certain time limits.

LIKE-KIND PROPERTY

Most realty held for business or investment purposes is like kind even though one property may be very dissimilar to another. Examples of like-kind realty swaps:

- Commercial property for residential rental property
- A lease that still has at least 30 years to run for an ownership interest in realty
- Improved property for unimproved property
- Lots in urban areas for lots in rural areas

> ### Example
>
> On March 1, 2021, you trade a factory for an apartment building, each worth $1 million. If you'd sold the property, you would have had a $300,000 profit. You don't have to report this profit in 2021, but the basis of the property you acquired is $700,000 ($1 million − $300,000). When you sell the apartment building, the gain not recognized on the trade increases the gain reported on this sale.

Not all property can be exchanged to produce tax deferral. Nonqualifying property includes:

- Main home
- Real property located outside the United States *cannot* be part of a like-kind exchange. You can't swap a building in Canada for one in the U.S. and defer your gain.
- Vacation homes and second homes unless an IRS-set safe harbor is met (see Rev. Proc. 2008-16).
- Fixer uppers and newly built homes (these are considered "stock in trade" that cannot be exchanged for tax deferral).

You can trade multiple properties, as long as they are all like kind.

You trade a strip mall for 2 office buildings or 5 residential rental properties for 3 vacant lots, all of which are in the United States. These qualify for like-kind exchange treatment. However, if the trades are not simultaneous, see the time limits that follow.

NON-SIMULTANEOUS EXCHANGES

You don't have to trade properties simultaneously. But if you give up property (the "relinquished property") and receive the replacement later on (a "deferred exchange"), or receive a replacement but don't give up property for a while (a "reverse exchange"), you must watch for certain time limits in order for the trade to enjoy like-kind exchange treatment. And you may use a qualified intermediary, such as an escrow company, to facilitate the trade without you collecting sales proceeds, which is an action that kills like-kind exchange treatment.

There are 2 key time limits:

- You have 45 days from the date you sell the relinquished property to identify potential replacement properties. The identification must be a legal description (e.g., street address or distinguishable name) in writing, signed by you and delivered to a person involved in the exchange, such as the seller of the replacement property or the qualified intermediary. Notice to your attorney, real estate agent, accountant, or similar persons acting as your agent is not sufficient. You can identify up to 3 potential properties of any value or more than 3, but there are value limits on the identified properties.

- The replacement property must be received and the exchange completed no later than 180 days after the sale of the exchanged property or the due date (with extensions) of the income tax return for the tax year in which the relinquished property was sold, whichever is earlier. The replacement property received must be substantially the same as property identified within the 45-day limit.

For reverse exchanges, the IRS has created a safe harbor that essentially uses the same time limits. For more information, see Rev. Proc. 2000-37.

RECEIVING BOOT

If you receive anything over and above the property, such as cash or the payment for you of certain closing costs, the additional property is called "boot." You must report taxable gain to the extent of boot received.

If you pay additional cash on the exchange, it becomes part of your tax basis for the acquired property.

Example

You trade your unimproved land worth $100,000 that you bought for $60,000 for unimproved land worth $85,000 plus $15,000 cash. Of your $40,000 gain, you must report $15,000 as taxable gain in the year of the exchange; you can defer the balance of the gain ($25,000).

Planning Tip

Watch out for tax scams that pitch the use of "tax-free exchanges" for vacation homes or second homes used solely for personal purposes. These do not qualify for tax deferral of gain on the trade.

Pitfalls

If you have a loss, it is advisable to sell the property so you can take the loss for tax purposes. If you exchange the property, you cannot take the loss now; the same deferral rule for gains applies to losses.

Monitor the time limits for non-simultaneous exchanges carefully. You cannot get an extension of time other than if you're delayed by a federally-declared disaster.

Where to Report the Like-Kind Exchange

You report the like-kind exchange on Form 8824, *Like-Kind Exchanges,* and file it with Form 1040 or 1040-SR. If you have to report gain on the exchange (e.g., you receive boot), it is reported on Form 4797, *Sales of Business Property*.

Deduction for Energy-Efficient Commercial Buildings

It has been estimated that commercial buildings use one-quarter of all domestic energy consumption. To encourage owners and lessees of commercial property to make certain energy improvements, there is a special deduction.

Benefit ⬆

The cost of energy-efficient property can be deducted up to $1.80 per square foot. A reduced deduction of 60¢ per square foot can be claimed for a building that achieves only partial energy savings. These dollar amounts may be adjusted for inflation after 2021.

Conditions

To qualify for the full deduction, the addition of energy-efficient property must help a commercial building achieve a 50% energy savings as compared with similar property that meets benchmarks set by the Reserve Standard 90.1 of the American Society of Heating, Refrigerating, and Air Conditioning Engineers and the Illuminating Engineering Society of North America published 2 years prior to the start of construction. The savings is measured by the reduction in cost (not in the actual units consumed). Cost is determined on a fuel-neutral basis (e.g., without regard to whether the building is heated by gas, oil, or electricity) by reference to the Standard and not on the basis of the owner's actual costs.

The partial deduction (60¢ per square foot) is allowed for a building that fails the 50% energy-savings requirement but meets a lesser standard.

The deduction applies to improvements made to:

- The interior lighting system
- The heating, cooling, ventilation, and hot water systems
- The building envelop (exterior)

The building owner must obtain certification of a plan to reduce overall energy costs before installing the property. There are various ways to satisfy the certification requirement, including use of approved software to calculate energy consumption.

Planning Tip

Check for state tax incentives for making energy improvements. Many states provide deductions and/or tax credits for these improvements.

Pitfall

The basis of the property must be reduced by the amount of any deduction claimed. This will have the effect of reducing allowable depreciation for the property.

Where to Claim the Deduction

The deduction is a business expense reported by the building's owner or lessee on the proper tax return.

Qualified Improvement Property

If you make capital improvements to the interior of these commercial facilities, a deduction for your outlays is not tied to depreciation over 39 years for the cost of the building. Instead, you may be able to take significant write-offs in the year you make the expenditures and put the property into service.

Benefits 🔼

Capital improvements (not repairs) made to qualified improvement property can be written off using:

- Section 179 deduction (first-year expensing), up to $1,050,000 in 2021.
- Bonus depreciation (another first-year depreciation allowance) of 100% of expenditures.
- Regular depreciation. Qualified improvement property has a 15-year recovery period. This comes into play, however, only if costs are not fully written off using first-year expensing and/or bonus depreciation.

Conditions

The deductions apply only to qualified improvement property. Qualified improvement property is an improvement to the interior of a commercial building that has already been placed in service (i.e., not new construction). However, certain improvements are specifically excluded from this definition:

- Improvements that enlarge the building
- Improvements that change the internal structural framework of the building
- An elevator or escalator

The rules for first-year expensing, bonus depreciation, and regular depreciation are covered in Chapter 14 under "Equipment Purchases."

Planning Tips

Capital improvements that cannot be treated as qualified improvement property are nonetheless deductible. The cost may have to be recovered through depreciation or may qualify for more immediate write-offs. It's advisable to conduct a cost segregation study to analyze improvements to a building structure and each key building system to determine maximize write-offs. The IRS has a Cost Segregation Audit Technique Guide at https://www.irs.gov/businesses/cost-segregation-audit-techniques-guide-table-of-contents, which details how such an analysis works. The key building systems are the plumbing system, electrical system, HVAC system, elevator system, escalator system, fire protection and alarm system, gas distribution system, and the security system.

There is a special safe harbor election for small taxpayers that allows improvements to be treated as ordinary repairs, which are currently deductible (i.e., not capitalized and deducted using expensing, bonus depreciation, and regular depreciation). This safe harbor applies if you are in business with average annual gross receipts less than $10 million and you own or lease property with an adjusted basis of $1 million or less. The safe harbor deduction can be claimed if the total amount paid for improvements does not exceed the lesser of 2% of the building's basis or $10,000.

Pitfall

Deductions related to qualified improvement property are limited to those "made by the taxpayer." If the landlord gives the tenant an allowance for improvements, the tenant claims the deduction (various conditions apply).

Where to Claim the Deduction

Deductions for first-year expensing, bonus depreciation, and regular depreciation are reported on Form 4562, *Depreciation and Amortization*. Total deductions from this form are then reported on the applicable business form (e.g., Schedule C for self-employed individuals, Schedule E for landlords).

Conservation Easements

You can benefit from your realty without disposing of it if you're willing to share. You can enjoy a current tax deduction if you donate a conservation easement to a charity, such as a local land trust. Find details in Chapter 6.

CHAPTER 11

Borrowing and Interest

With the prices of things rising, jobs tight or gone as a result of the coronavirus, and investments performance unsteady, it seems that every paycheck is stretched to the limit. We often choose or are forced to rely on credit to pay for the things we want or need. Fortunately, interest rates are at historic lows. And whether you are a borrower or a lender, you may be eligible for tax breaks with respect to certain loan activities.

While interest on credit cards for consumer purchases is not deductible, interest on certain other borrowing is tax favored, as explained in this chapter. For more information, see IRS Publication 550, *Investment Income and Expenses*, and IRS Publication 4681, *Canceled Debts, Foreclosures, Repossessions, and Abandonments*.

Home Mortgage Interest

If you are a homeowner repaying a mortgage, you can deduct the interest portion of your payments. There is no dollar limit on how much interest you can deduct.

However, the law limits the amount of borrowing you can take into account in figuring your deductible interest on loans taken after October 14, 1987.

- For acquisition indebtedness obtained before December 15, 2017, to buy, build, or substantially renovate your home: $1 million ($500,000 for a married person filing separately)
- For acquisition indebtedness obtained on or after December 15, 2017, to buy, build, or substantially renovate your home: $750,000 ($375,000 for married persons filing separately)

Mortgage insurance premiums may also be treated as home mortgage interest in 2020.

Home mortgage interest is deductible only as an itemized deduction; you cannot deduct the interest if you use the standard deduction.

For more details on deducting home mortgage interest, see Chapter 4.

Student Loan Interest

When you are repaying student loans, you may be able to deduct up to $2,500 of interest annually. The deduction is an adjustment to gross income, so you can claim it even if you do not itemize your other deductions and simply use the standard deduction.

The ability to deduct student loan interest depends on your modified adjusted gross income (MAGI). If your MAGI is too high, you cannot claim this benefit.

Due to the pandemic, interest on federal student loans between March 13, 2020, and January 31, 2022, does not have to be paid; the interest rate on these loans for this period became zero. Because this is not debt forgiveness, there is no income created by this interest rate change. It may impact the amount of student loan interest that can be deducted.

For more details on deducting student loan interest, see Chapter 3.

Borrowing from Retirement Plans

A 401(k) or other qualified retirement plan may allow you to borrow from your account. The loan proceeds from a qualified retirement plan are generally not taxable to you. No tax-free borrowing is allowed for IRAs and IRA-based plans, such as SEPs and SIMPLE-IRAs.

Benefit ⊗

Proceeds you receive when borrowing from your 401(k) or other qualified retirement plan are not taxable. The plan must allow for borrowing by participants; a plan is not *required* to offer this option. Assuming your plan does, then the maximum loan is usually limited to 50% of your vested account balance or $50,000, whichever is less. However, for plan loans because of COVID-19 that were taken from March 27, 2020, through December 31, 2020, the borrowing limit was 100% of your vested account balance up to $100,000 for loans taken within a specified period. The same rule applies to plan loans taken by victims of federally-declared disasters from January 1, 2020, through February 25, 2021.

Interest on the loan used for personal purposes (other than acquisition indebtedness explained earlier), such as paying off credit card debt or college tuition, is generally not deductible. Interest on the loan used for investment purposes is deductible under the investment interest rules (discussed later in this chapter), assuming you are not a "key" employee (a more-than-5%-owner, a more-than-1%-owner-employee earning more than $130,000, and a corporate officer with compensation over $185,000). Interest on the loan to buy a first or second residence is deductible if (1) you are not a key employee, (2) the account balance is not used to secure the loan, and (3) the residence is collateral for the loan.

Conditions

The loan can be taken for *any* reason; you don't even have to tell the plan administrator why you want to borrow money. However, the reason impacts the repayment term. If you use the loan to buy a principal residence for yourself, the repayment period can be any time frame that is reasonable (e.g., 15 years). If you borrow for any other purpose, you must repay the loan in substantially equal ("level") amounts that include interest and principal within 5 years. Repayment is made at least quarterly, and there may be a processing fee charged for the loan. For COVID-19-related loans taken during the period described earlier, the normal 5-year repayment period is extended to 6 years. However, interest continues to accrue during this suspension period.

If you are married, your spouse must consent to the loan.

Planning Tip

The interest rate charged by the plan is usually very low compared with commercial loans. What's more, it is easy to arrange a plan loan. Just ask your plan administrator, complete a short form (you do not have to disclose any personal financial information), and the money is paid to you quickly (usually within days of your request).

Pitfalls

Because retirement plans are designed to build savings for your retirement, borrowing will limit your savings for the future. The money taken as a loan is no longer invested for growth. However, the interest you pay on the loan is repaid to your account. You are permitted to continue making contributions to the plan, but most people who borrow in this fashion use their wages for loan repayment and other purposes and effectively suspend making contributions until the loan is repaid, which means another missed opportunity for retirement savings.

If you fail to repay the loan, it is treated as a taxable distribution to you (immediately taxable and, depending on your age, subject to a 10% early distribution penalty). If you leave the company before repaying the loan, you usually will have to repay the loan immediately or have a taxable distribution. The amount that is taxable is reported to you on Form 1099-R, *Distributions From Pensions, Annuities, Retirement or Profit-Sharing Plans, IRAs, Insurance Contracts, etc*. However, for repayments due that are treated as distributions, you have until the extended due date of your return to deposit the balance to an IRA and avoid taxation. This rule applies if you are terminated or leave the job voluntarily with an outstanding loan balance.

There is a distinction between loans that you take because you have a financial emergency and "hardship distributions." Hardship distributions, which may be allowed for certain severe financial hardships (e.g., facing foreclosure), are always fully taxable and, if you are under age 59 ½, subject to a 10% early distribution penalty (unless there is an exception, such as a qualified coronavirus distributions).

Where to Report the Loan

The loan is not reported on your tax return because it is not taxable income.

Investment-Related Interest

You can deduct interest paid on loans used to buy or carry investments to the extent of your net investment income received (such as interest income). If your investment interest paid is more than your net investment income for the year, you can carry the excess interest forward indefinitely and use it in a future year. There is no overall dollar limit on this deduction.

You can deduct investment-related interest only if you itemize your deductions. You cannot claim a deduction if you use the standard deduction.

You cannot deduct interest on a loan used to buy tax-exempt securities, such as municipal bonds or muni-bond funds.

For more details on deducting investment-related interest, see Chapter 8.

Business Interest

Business in many cases runs on other people's money. Loans are used to start up a company, buy equipment, and pay operating expenses. Loans used for business come in all sizes—fixed loans for a set term, revolving lines of credit, or even basic credit card charges for purchases made. Fortunately, whatever type of business loan is involved, interest on the loan may be fully deductible. (There is a limit on deducting business interest in 2021 for companies with average annual gross receipts in the 3 prior years exceeding $26 million; this rule is not discussed here.)

Benefit ⬆

If you borrow money for business—by taking out a loan or charging a business purchase to a credit card on which you finance the payments—you can deduct the interest in full against your business income. There is no dollar limit on this deduction.

Condition

The source of the loan does not govern the treatment of the interest. Deductibility depends on what you use the proceeds for. If you use the proceeds for business—for example, to acquire a sole proprietorship—then interest is considered fully deductible business interest.

Interest on a loan used to buy shares in a corporation is viewed as investment interest, not business interest. Interest you pay on tax deficiencies related to your business (for example, a deficiency related to Schedule C of your sole proprietorship) is not deductible. This interest is treated as personal interest, not business interest.

Planning Tip

If you guarantee a loan made to your corporation, you can deduct interest on the loan as business interest, but only when and to the extent you are called upon to do so because the corporation cannot make the payment.

Pitfalls

You cannot deduct business interest that is otherwise required to be capitalized, such as construction period interest. In effect, you cannot deduct interest during the construction period. Construction period interest is added to the basis of the property.

If you borrow money from your corporation, the interest you pay back to the corporation is *not* automatically business interest just because of your relationship to the lender. Again, the treatment of interest depends on what you use the proceeds for. For example, if you borrow money from your corporation to take a vacation, the interest is nondeductible personal interest.

Where to Claim the Deduction

Self-employed individuals who pay business interest deduct these payments on Schedule C of Form 1040 or 1040-SR.

Accrued Interest on Bond Purchases

In the financial world, bonds are bought and sold in the secondary market: After an initial offering, they trade among investors at their current values. But when trades are made between interest payment dates, which is common, bond buyers pay for the interest that is actually received by the bond sellers; the interest is included in the cost of the bond. The tax law allows for a correction of this situation by allowing bond sellers a deduction.

Benefit

If you buy a bond between its interest payment dates, some interest may be included in the purchase price that doesn't belong to you. That interest is payable to the bond seller even though it is reported as payable to you. To correct this inequity, you can effectively deduct the accrued interest. This is not a tax deduction in the true sense of the word. Rather, you are allowed to make a subtraction that amounts to the same thing.

Condition

This subtraction applies only if you are a bond purchaser and there is accrued interest on the bond you buy. This occurs only when the purchase takes place between the bond's interest dates (typically twice a year).

Planning Tips

When purchasing a bond, you can ask your stockbroker about interest dates on the security. Knowing the interest dates will apprise you of whether there will be any accrued interest to deal with when you file your return.

If you *sell* a bond with accrued interest, you do not subtract it from interest income. Instead, you reduce the sales proceeds by the amount of accrued interest belonging to the purchaser (which reduces your gain or increases your loss).

Example

If you sell a bond for which you paid $9,500 at $10,000 and have accrued interest of $180, you reduce the proceeds by this amount. As a result, your gain is $320 ([$10,000 proceeds − $180 accrued interest] − $9,500 basis).

Pitfall

Do *not* simply subtract from the interest reported to you on Form 1099-INT the accrued interest you paid when you purchased a bond. Netting the interest in this manner can trigger an examination of your return because your reporting does not match the information sent to the IRS on Form 1099-INT. Instead, follow the reporting instructions that follow.

Where to Claim the Benefit

Accrued interest is netted against taxable interest reported on Form 1040 or 1040-SR.

Below-Market Loans

In today's low-interest environment—the federal funds rate at which banks borrow dropped to zero following the onset of COVID-19—it's hard to imagine that borrowers would bother to devise strategies for avoiding interest payments. But when rates were higher, it was common for business owners to borrow from their companies and for children to borrow from parents at little or no interest, realizing a considerable economic benefit. The tax law took note of this benefit, creating the below-market interest rate rules. Under these rules, phantom interest may be created for lenders and phantom interest deductions for borrowers. While the interest may be phantom, the income from this interest can be very real. As interest rates rise, as they have begun to do in 2021, watch for below-market loans.

Benefit

If you lend money to or borrow from a relative, friend, or your business at no interest or at highly favorable low interest rates, there may be some tax issues to consider. Depending on who the parties are, the amount of the loan, and the interest rate charged, these results can ensue:

- *Gift loans up to $10,000.* Gift loans, compensation-related loans, and shareholder-corporation loans up to $10,000 have no consequences to the parties. No interest deduction can be claimed with respect to any interest that is not actually paid.

- *Gift loans in the range of $10,000 to $100,000.* No interest deduction can be claimed with respect to any interest that is not actually paid if the borrower's investment income is no more than $1,000.

- *All other loans.* In addition to interest actually paid, a deduction can be claimed for below-market interest (assuming that it is deductible interest). This is the interest that should have been charged, based on the government's applicable federal rate (AFR) for the term of the loan. The lender must report a like amount of income. However, the lender may be able to offset the income by deducting the forgiven interest in some way.

Example

You borrow $20,000 from your corporation interest free for 5 years. Assuming the AFR for this term is 1% at the time the loan originates, your annual interest deduction is $200 for each of the 5 years that the loan is outstanding (21% of $20,000). If the corporation treats the forgiven loan as compensation, you must report $4,200 as compensation. From the corporation's standpoint, it picks up $200 interest and deducts $200 compensation.

Keep in mind that even if you have imputed interest from a below-market loan, it may not necessarily be deductible. It depends on what you use the loan proceeds for. If you use the funds to buy stocks, for example, you can treat the imputed interest as investment interest (discussed earlier in this chapter). But if you use the funds to pay off your personal credit card debt or take a vacation, you cannot deduct the imputed interest; it is nondeductible personal interest.

Condition

Whether a loan falls within the below-market loan rules depends on the rate of interest, if any, fixed when the loan originates. Loans fall into 3 basic categories:

1. Short-term: 3 years or less.
2. Mid-term: over 3 but not over 9 years.
3. Long-term: over 9 years.

If the loan is payable on demand (there is no fixed term), then the interest rate used for a loan outstanding for the entire year is a blended rate announced by the IRS each July. For 2021, the blended rate is 0.13%.

Each month the IRS publishes AFRs. You can find an index of the AFRs monthly at https://apps.irs.gov/app/picklist/list/federalRates.html.

Planning Tip

When arranging loans between family or other related persons, keep the below-market loan rules in mind. With today's historically low interest rates, it is easy to keep loans from falling subject to the rules by charging the minimum AFR. But even if lower or no interest is charged so that income results, the arrangement may still be desirable.

Pitfall

If you are the lender of a below-market loan that does not meet the gift loan or other exemption rules, you have to report interest income even though you do not actually receive any payments.

Where to Claim the Benefit

If you are exempt from the below-market loan rules, do not report anything on your return. If you are a borrower subject to the below-market loan rules, you can deduct your interest payments if such interest is otherwise deductible. For instance, if the interest qualifies as investment interest, deduct it on Schedule A of Form 1040 or 1040-SR (more details about deducting investment interest are discussed earlier in this chapter).

Bad Debts

Lenders never loan money with the expectation they won't be repaid. They expect to collect interest during the term of the loan and recoup the amount of principal in the loan. But reality shows that some borrowers default. Taxwise, lenders may be able to write off these bad loans under certain conditions.

Benefit 🔼

If you loan money to someone who fails to repay you, you can claim a loss for the outstanding balance. The conditions for writing off the loss and the manner in which the loss is treated for tax purposes depend on the type of bad debt involved. There are 2 types:

1. Business bad debts, which are debts arising in the course of business. For example, your business is on the accrual method of accounting and fails to receive payment on an accounts receivable; this is a business bad debt. Loans made to protect your salary are treated as business bad debts. Business bad debts are fully deductible as ordinary losses against business income.

2. Nonbusiness bad debts, which are any other type of debt. For example, you loan money to your friend to buy a car and your friend fails to repay the loan; this is a nonbusiness bad debt. Nonbusiness bad debts also include loans that you make to protect your investments and uninsured bank deposits (explained in Chapter 8). Nonbusiness bad debts are deductible as short-term capital losses.

Condition

You must satisfy 4 conditions in order to deduct a bad debt loss:

1. It is a valid debt.
2. There was a debtor-creditor relationship.
3. The loan was made from your after-tax income or capital.
4. You must show that the debt has become worthless.

VALID DEBT

Your right to repayment must be enforceable and cannot depend on some future occurrence. For example, if the loan violates state usury laws, the debt cannot be deducted when it goes unpaid.

If you own a corporation and make loans to it, be sure that the arrangement is truly a loan and not merely an advance of capital. If the corporation is thinly capitalized (there is just too much debt compared with equity), the IRS may view a supposed loan to the corporation as an advance of capital.

DEBTOR-CREDITOR RELATIONSHIP

You must prove that there was a debtor-creditor relationship. In the context of a business loan, there is usually no issue.

But when you lend money to family or friends, there is the question of whether you are truly lending the money or really making a gift of it.

If you guarantee a loan made to someone else who defaults, you can claim a bad debt deduction when you make the payment *if* it is a business bad debt or a nonbusiness bad debt made to protect an investment. No deduction can be claimed for making good on your guarantee of a loan for personal reasons, such as a favor to a relative or friend.

LOAN FROM AFTER-TAX INCOME OR CAPITAL

If, like most individuals, you are on the cash basis of accounting, you cannot treat nonpayments of salary, rents, or fees owed to you as bad debts. Since you never reported the income (under the cash method you report as income only what you receive), you cannot claim a bad debt deduction for nonpayment.

Example

You are a consultant on the cash method of accounting. You complete a job for which you are owed $2,500. You never recover your fee because the client has gone out of business. You cannot deduct this amount as a bad debt because you never reported the consulting fee as income. While this may seem unfair because of the time and effort you put into the work, the tax law does not view you as having sustained a loss.

WORTHLESSNESS

You must show that the debt will never be repaid. If the debtor has gone out of business or filed for bankruptcy, this is a good indication that there is little hope of recovery. Show any steps you have taken to recover on the debt, such as suing for it in court or turning it over to a collection agency. You do not actually have to sue if this action would be futile because you would be unable to collect on a judgment.

In the case of nonbusiness bad debts, you must show that the debt is entirely worthless; a partially worthless bad debt cannot be claimed in this case.

To fix the year of worthlessness, show that the debt had some value on December 31 of the year prior to the year in which you believe the debt became worthless. Then show the identifiable event that leads you to conclude the debt is worthless.

You do not have to wait until the debt is due in order to claim a bad debt deduction if you know that it has already become worthless. You claim the deduction in the year it becomes worthless, not the year in which it is due.

Planning Tips

Whenever you make a loan, be sure to put all of the terms of the loan in writing. This will accomplish a couple of things: It will make the borrower aware of when and how much you expect to be repaid, and, in the case of default, you will have the proof that the arrangement was truly a loan and not a gift.

It's not always easy to tell when a debt has gone bad. You have 7 years in which to file an amended return for the year in which the bad debt became worthless in order to make a claim for a refund. The filing period generally runs 7 years from the due date of the return for the year of worthlessness.

Example

In June 2021, you discover that a loan you made to a friend became totally worthless in 2018. You have until April 15, 2026 (7 years from the original due date of the 2018 return, or April 15, 2019), to file an amended return for 2018 to report the nonbusiness bad debt.

Pitfalls

You cannot claim a bad debt deduction for unpaid child support. For example, if your former spouse owes you $10,000 in back child support, you cannot write this off as a bad debt. The reason: You do not have any basis in the debt so, for tax purposes, you do not have a loss (even though you surely have an economic loss).

Also, you cannot take a nonbusiness bad debt for any debt owed to you by a political party or committee.

If you deducted a bad debt in a prior year and to your amazement you receive repayment now, you must include the amount in income. But inclusion is required only to the extent that the deduction in a prior year reduced your tax in that year.

Where to Claim the Benefit

A business bad debt that you make in the course of your business is reported as a deductible item on Schedule C of Form 1040 or 1040-SR. But if you are a shareholder-employee with a loan to your corporation that has gone sour, determine whether it is a business bad debt or a nonbusiness bad debt. A business bad debt in this situation is not deductible due to the suspension of the deduction for miscellaneous itemized deductions in 2018 through 2025.

A nonbusiness bad debt is reported as a short-term capital loss on line 1 of Part 1 of Form 8949. In column (a), enter the name of the debtor and "Statement attached." On your own statement, which you attach to your return, include:

- A description of the debt, including the amount, and the date it became worthless.
- The name of the debtor and any business or family relationship between you.
- The efforts you made to collect the debt.
- Why you believe the debt is now worthless.

Debt Forgiveness

In some situations, lenders may be willing to accept less than the full amount owed in order to get your loan or other obligation off their books. Usually, income from the cancellation of debt (COD) is fully taxable. However, there are certain exceptions to this rule that allow you to exclude COD from your income. Thus, a bad economic situation may have a good tax result.

Benefit ⊗

COD income is tax free if you can qualify under any category described next.

Conditions

To be nontaxable, the cancellation of debt must fall within a specific category:

- You are bankrupt.
- You are insolvent at the time the debt is canceled. Insolvency means that your debts exceed the fair market value of your assets immediately before the discharge.
- The debt is on your main home and you meet certain requirements. Cancellation of mortgage debt is explained in Chapter 4 and is not discussed further in this chapter.
- The debt is qualified farm indebtedness.
- The debt is qualified real property business indebtedness.
- The debt is a student loan made by a qualified lender. Cancellation of these student loans is explained in Chapter 3 and is not discussed further in this chapter.
- The debt is cancellation of a loan under the Paycheck Protection Program (PPP) and certain other COVID-19-related government programs.

Planning Tip

If you're excluding COD income because you are insolvent, be sure to retain good records of your assets and liabilities at the time of the debt forgiveness. This will be helpful in case the IRS questions your return.

Pitfalls

If you exclude COD income, you must reduce certain tax attributes (described next) by the amount of the excluded COD income (but not below zero). There is a set order to the reduction of tax attributes, depending upon the reason for the cancellation of debt. When excluding COD income, you must usually reduce tax attributes so that you effectively increase your income in other ways (e.g., losing deductions or reporting greater gain on the sale or property). The order of reduction is as follows unless a special election (beyond the scope of this book) is made:

- Net operating losses (including carryovers)
- General business credit carryover
- Minimum tax credit
- Net capital losses (including carryovers)
- Basis of property
- Passive activity losses and credits (including carryovers)
- Foreign tax credit

If the cancellation of debt is because of bankruptcy or insolvency and is not because of qualified principal residence indebtedness, the basis of personal-use property (e.g., a home, home furnishings, a car) is made if there is no tax attributes to be reduced.

When you pay less than the full amount of the money owed on a loan or other obligation (e.g., credit card debt), this adversely affects your credit rating (FICO score). However, the sooner you settle up, the sooner you can begin to rebuild a good credit rating.

Where to Claim the Benefit

Forgiven debt is reported to you by the lender on Form 1099-C, *Cancellation of Debt*. If you are excluding cancellation of debt income, you must complete Form 982, *Reduction of Tax Attributes Due to Discharge of Indebtedness*. There is no income to report on your return; just attach the completed Form 982 to the return.

CHAPTER 12

Insurance and Catastrophes

No one likes to think about bad things happening, but happen they do. The COVID-19 pandemic impacted people and businesses in every state in 2021. Natural disasters, accidents, building collapses and explosions, rioting and terrorist activities, and war all present serious personal and financial threats that can become reality. When faced with such catastrophes, insurance may carry you just so far, with economic losses outstripping your insurance recoveries. If the losses to personal-use property occur in federally-declared disaster areas, you may be able to deduct them.

This chapter explains the tax rules related to insurance and certain catastrophes. Mortgage insurance is covered in Chapter 4. Losses to your bank deposits are discussed in Chapter 8. For more information, see IRS Publication 547, *Casualties, Disasters, and Thefts (Business and Nonbusiness)*; IRS Publication 584, *Casualty, Disaster, and Theft Loss Workbook (Personal-Use Property)*; and IRS Publication 2194, *Disaster Resource Guide for Individuals and Businesses*.

Casualty, Theft, and Disaster Losses

Things happen beyond human control, such as hurricanes and wildfires, that damage or destroy property. If there is insurance, it may only partially cover the loss. For 2018 through 2025, you cannot deduct casualty and theft losses to personal-use property; only losses from *federally-declared disasters* are deductible.

Benefit

If you suffer damage to personal-use property due to a casualty or theft, any insurance proceeds you recover are tax free. If you have a loss in a federally declared disaster area that is not fully covered by insurance or other reimbursements, you may be able to take a deduction for your loss. Depending on the type of disaster loss, you may be able to deduct it even if you claim the standard deduction; other disaster losses are only deductible by those who itemize. There is no overall dollar limit on the amount you can deduct.

The amount of your disaster loss, however, is limited to the decrease in the value of property from the casualty or its adjusted basis (usually your cost), whichever amount is smaller. *Rule of thumb:* For property that appreciates in value, your loss is usually based on your adjusted basis; for property that declines in value, your loss is usually based on the decrease in value.

Example

You bought a painting several years ago for $2,500 that was valued at $25,000 before it was destroyed in a storm in a federally declared disaster area (you did not have any insurance). Your loss is limited to your adjusted basis of $2,500, which is lower than the loss in value of $25,000.

Conditions

To deduct a loss relating to your personal-use property, such as your home or car, you must meet all 4 of these conditions:

1. The loss must result from a federally declared disaster.
2. You must have proof of the loss.
3. You must reduce your loss by any insurance or other reimbursements.
4. The amount of your loss must exceed certain limits if the loss is exclusive to personal items (there are no such limits for business losses).

TYPES OF DISASTERS

There are 3 types of losses related to personal-use property that may give rise to a deduction. All 3 types of losses refer to federally declared disasters, but the requirements for each loss vary. A federally declared disaster is a disaster determined by the President to warrant assistance by the federal government under the Robert T. Stafford Disaster Relief and Emergency Assistance Act (Stafford Act). A federally declared disaster includes (a) a major disaster declaration, or (b) an emergency declaration under the Stafford Act.

1. *Federal casualty loss.* A federal casualty loss is an individual's casualty or theft loss of personal-use property that is attributable to a federally declared disaster. The casualty loss must occur in a state receiving a federal disaster declaration. If you suffered a federal casualty loss, you are eligible to claim a casualty loss deduction.

2. *Disaster loss.* A disaster loss is a loss that is attributable to a federally declared disaster and that occurs in an area eligible for assistance pursuant to the Presidential declaration. The disaster loss must occur in a county eligible for public or individual assistance (or both). Disaster losses are not limited to individual personal use property and may be claimed for individual business or income-producing property and by corporations, S corporations, and partnerships. If you suffered a disaster loss, you are eligible to claim a casualty loss deduction and to elect to claim the loss in the preceding tax year.

3. *Qualified disaster loss.* A qualified disaster loss is an individual's casualty or theft loss of personal-use property that is attributable to a major disaster subject to a special declaration. This includes an individual's casualty and theft of personal-use property that is attributable to a major disaster (other than COVID-19) that occurred in the period beginning January 1, 2020, and ending February 25, 2021. If you suffered a qualified disaster loss, you are eligible to claim a casualty loss deduction, to elect to claim the loss in the preceding tax year, and to deduct the loss without itemizing other deductions on Schedule A (Form 1040 or 1040-SR) (explained in Where to Claim the Deduction).

PROOF OF YOUR DISASTER LOSS

You must show all 4 of these conditions for a disaster loss:

1. The damage or destruction of your property occurred in a federally declared disaster area. You can find disaster designations from FEMA at www.fema.gov/disasters.

2. The date of the disaster.

3. The connection between the disaster and your loss (that is, that your loss is the direct result of the disaster).

4. That you are the owner of the property. If you lease property, you cannot claim a loss; this right belongs only to the owner unless you are contractually obligated to return the property in the same condition (in effect, you bear the risk of loss).

INSURANCE REIMBURSEMENTS

If you carry property insurance coverage, you may have little or no loss for tax purposes. You cannot create a tax loss by not submitting an insurance claim to which you are entitled. If you do not submit a claim for a covered loss, you cannot claim a deduction, even for the portion of the loss not covered by insurance.

> **Example**
>
> You have insured an item for $10,000 for which you paid $12,000; it is now worth $15,000. If the item is destroyed in a disaster and you do not submit an insurance claim because you do not want the premiums increased on your other property or for any other reason, you cannot deduct any loss. You cannot even deduct the $2,000 that you would have been entitled to had you made the claim and received the full coverage.

What if you have made a claim but have not received any reimbursement from the insurance company by the end of the year? File your return using an estimate of what you expect for reimbursement.

If you receive more in a later year than you had estimated, report the additional insurance recovery as "Other income" on your return for that later year (do not file an amended return for the year of the disaster) to the extent you received a tax benefit from the deduction you should not have claimed. (Whether you realized any tax benefit is a difficult determination for which you may need to consult a tax expert.)

> **Example**
>
> In 2020, you suffered a casualty in a federally-declared disaster and figured your loss deduction based on the assumption you will receive $10,000 from the insurance company. In 2021, you receive a check from the insurance company for $12,000. On your 2021 return, report $2,000 as "Other income."

If you later receive *less* than you had estimated, you need to file an amended return to increase your loss deduction.

$100 OR $500 LIMIT

Generally, you must reduce each loss from a disaster by $100. The dollar reduction applies per event (not per item lost or damaged in the event). Thus, you figure your loss separately for each item but then apply only one $100 reduction per event.

If you are unfortunate enough to suffer losses from 2 different disasters in the same year, you must reduce your loss for each event by $100 (effectively, your total losses are reduced by $200).

If you do not itemize deductions and the loss is a "qualified disaster loss," then the reduction is $500. However, if the $500 reduction is applicable, then the 10%-of-adjusted-gross-income floor described next does not apply.

10%-OF-AGI LIMIT

You deduct disaster losses (other than "qualified disaster losses") only to the extent that the total of all such losses for the year exceeds 10% of your adjusted gross income.

Example

You determine that the unreimbursed damage to your home from a tornado is $8,400, after reducing your loss by the $100 limit (assume you are in a disaster area). If your adjusted gross income for the year is $75,000, you can deduct $900 ($8,400 − 10% of $75,000). If your adjusted gross income is $84,000 or more, you cannot claim any disaster loss deduction.

Losses that cannot be claimed because of the 10% limit are lost forever; you cannot carry forward the unused amount.

TIMING OF DISASTER LOSS DEDUCTION

Usually, you claim the loss on the return for the year of the disaster, which gives you plenty of time to amass the information needed to establish your loss when completing your return.

But if you want to claim the loss on a return for the prior year, you must act no later than 6 months after the original due date of the return for the year of the disaster. This 6-month period applies whether or not you obtain a filing extension for your return.

> ### Example
>
> On February 1, 2021, you experience a natural disaster in an area declared eligible for federal disaster assistance through FEMA. The due date for the 2021 return is April 18, 2022. You have an additional 6 months from April 18 to make the election to deduct the disaster loss on a 2020 return; this extends the election period through October 17, 2022.

You have 90 days after the due date for making the election to change your mind and revoke your choice by returning to the IRS any refund or credit you received. If you revoke your choice before receiving a refund, you must return the refund within 30 days after receiving it in order for the revocation to be effective.

Planning Tips

How do you determine the decrease in value? There are a few alternatives:

- Obtain an appraisal. Use a qualified appraiser to determine the value of the property before and after the casualty (the tax treatment of appraisal fees is discussed later in this chapter).
- Use the cost of repairs or restoration as the measure of loss. You can rely on this cost if the repairs are necessary to bring the property back to its precasualty condition, the amount spent is not excessive, and the value of the property after the repairs is not more than it was before the casualty.
- If the loss involves your car, you can use various online valuation services to determine the value of your car, including Kelley Blue Book (www.kbb.com) and NADA Appraisal Guides (www.nadaguides.com).

If you are married and one spouse suffers a casualty loss (for example, an expensive uninsured piece of jewelry is lost in a disaster), it may be advisable to file separate returns. This is so where the spouse with the lower AGI suffers the loss. The lower AGI may entitle the spouse to a deduction that would otherwise be blocked because of the couple's combined AGI. Of course, other factors must be taken into account when filing separate returns, such as eligibility to claim other tax benefits that require filing a joint return.

Review your insurance coverage carefully to understand what it does and does not cover. You may be able to expand the coverage under your existing policy; or you may need to obtain other coverage (for example, flood insurance if you are located within a flood zone). In some cases, you may not be able to obtain coverage because it is just not sold or the premiums are prohibitive. For example, even though federal legislation has provided underwriting guarantees to carriers for claims due to terrorist attacks, many major carriers are simply not covering such events.

Which year should you claim the loss—the year of the disaster or the prior year? Generally, choose the year in which you have a lower adjusted gross income threshold for figuring your loss.

Example

In 2021, you have a $22,800 disaster loss (after the $100 reduction). Your adjusted gross income (AGI) for 2021 is $86,000. Your AGI for 2020 was $75,000. If you take the deduction on your 2020 return, your AGI threshold is $8,600, so only $14,200 of your loss is deductible. If you take the deduction on your 2020 return, your AGI threshold is $7,500, allowing you to deduct $15,300. In this situation, claiming the disaster loss deduction on the prior year's return provides a greater tax benefit.

If your home and its contents are damaged or destroyed in a disaster, figure the loss separately for the home and for the furnishings.

If you are living in a federal disaster area, you may be entitled to certain tax breaks, even if you don't qualify to claim a disaster loss (you might be fully compensated by insurance or might not have had any loss). For example, you may be eligible for a 6-month postponement of tax deadlines. The IRS may also abate the interest and penalties on underpayment of income tax for the length of any postponement of tax deadlines.

If you have a loss that isn't from a disaster, you can use it to offset gain from a casualty or theft. Such gain results when insurance proceeds exceed the adjusted basis of the damaged or destroyed property.

Pitfalls

Not all losses related to a disaster are deductible. You cannot deduct your personal living expenses in temporary housing when a disaster forces you out of your home. You cannot deduct cleanup costs from the disaster.

Your deduction is limited to your economic loss. You cannot recoup anything related to sentimental value.

Example

Your wedding album is ruined during a disaster. The pictures cost a few hundred dollars, which is the limit of your tax loss, even though their value to you may have been priceless.

Where to Claim the Deduction

You must file Form 4684, *Casualties and Thefts*, to report the loss and figure the amount of the deduction. The deduction is then entered on Schedule A of Form 1040 or 1040-SR.

If you are itemizing deductions, the disaster loss is entered on line 15 of Schedule A. If you do not itemize but have a net qualified disaster loss, you enter the amount on line 16 of Schedule A, with adding on the dotted line "Net Qualified Disaster Loss." Also, on Line 16, list your standard deduction amount (see the Introduction) and add "Standard Deduction Claimed with Qualified Disaster Loss." Combine the 2 amounts (net qualified disaster loss and standard deduction amount), which is then entered on Form 1040 or 1040-SR.

If you are claiming a disaster loss for the prior year for which you have not yet filed a return (for example, in January 2022 you have a casualty loss that you report on your 2021 return to be filed by April 18, 2022), note at the top of the return "DISASTER LOSS." If you are claiming a disaster loss for the prior year for which you have already filed a return, you must file an amended return, Form 1040-X. At the top of the return note "DISASTER LOSS."

Economic Impact Payments

To help with economic recovery following the pandemic, the American Rescue Plan Act created a third round of Economic Impact Payments (EIP3). These payments were sent in advance to eligible taxpayers in the Spring of 2021. They are, in fact, refundable tax credits. They are tax free.

Benefit

The maximum EIP3 is $1,400 per individual ($2,800 for a married couple filing jointly). There is an additional EIP3 for up to $1,400 per eligible dependent, with no limit on the number of dependents. The benefit is reduced or phased out entirely, depending on adjusted gross income (AGI). If the full payment has not been received, you may claim a refundable recovery rebate credit on your 2021 income tax return.

Conditions

There are only 4 conditions for receiving EIP3:

1. Having adjusted gross income (AGI) below a set limit.
2. Being a U.S. citizen or resident alien.
3. Not being a dependent of another taxpayer on a 2020 tax return.
4. Having a valid Social Security number.

TABLE 12.1 Phaseout Range for the Economic Impact Payment

Filing Status	Phaseout Begins when AGI in 2021 Exceeds:	Full phaseout AGI in 2021 Reaches:
Married filing jointly	$150,000	$160,000
Head of household	$112,500	$120,000
Single/married filing separately	$ 75,000	$ 80,000

Income limitation

The full economic impact payment applies for individuals with adjusted gross income (AGI) not exceeding $75,000 for singles and married persons filing separately, $112,500 for heads of households, or $150,000 for married persons filing jointly. The amount phases out for those with AGI above the initial phaseout threshold. Table 12.1 shows the point at which the credit begins to phase out and is fully phased out. The phaseout also applies to the additional amounts paid per dependent.

Example

The phaseout rate for a single person is 28% (a reduction of $280 for every $1,000 over the initial threshold amount). Assume a single person has AGI of $77,000. The EIP3 payment for this person is $840 ($1,400 – [28% of $2,000 excess AGI]).

Reconciliation

The EIP3 was based on 2019 or 2020 AGI, depending on whether the income tax return for 2020 had been filed when the EIP3 payments were sent. You are not required to report your EIP3 on your 2021 return, but doing so may entitle you to an additional amount. That may result if, for example, you now have a dependent that the IRS did not know about when it issued the payments. Use the IRS notice you received at the time of the EIP3 payment to figure whether you are eligible for a recovery rebate credit.

If you received more than what you were entitled to based on your actual AGI, you do not have to repay this amount.

Planning Tips

If you had a child born or adopted in 2021, you may be eligible for an additional payment by claiming a recovery rebate credit on your return.

Taxpayers who had previously provided their bank information to the IRS received their payments quickly via direct deposit. In some cases, this was weeks—or months—before those for whom the IRS had no bank information. This suggests that, going forward, taxpayers should include their bank information on income tax returns. There is no downside to doing this, and should additional payments be authorized in the future, make sure the IRS has direct deposit information that will expedite any new payment to you.

Any taxpayer eligible for an EIP3 who did not receive it because of relocating and the IRS not having bank or contact information or being a new non-dependent taxpayer may receive a payment by figuring the recovery rebate credit.

Pitfall

There is no downside to receiving the refundable recovery rebate credit. It is not taxable.

Where to Claim the Recovery Rebate Credit

If EIP3 has already been provided to you, there is no need to "claim the tax credit" unless you are entitled to an additional amount. Taxpayers should reconcile their 2021 AGI with their 2019 or 2020 AGI (the amount used to figure the payment) to determine whether any additional credit is allowed. The recovery rebate credit is claimed on line 30 of Form 1040 or 1040-SR.

Disaster Relief Payments

When disaster strikes, the federal government may provide needed assistance. The Federal Emergency Management Agency (FEMA) steps in to provide grants and other assistance to affected individuals and businesses. (For more information about disaster assistance, check www.fema.gov.) To avoid adding insult to injury, certain government assistance can be received tax free.

Benefit ⊗

You are not taxed on disaster relief payments you receive from federal agencies or charitable organizations to cover personal expenses. There is no dollar limit on the amount you can exclude from income. Your exclusion does not depend on your income or need.

Conditions

Only "qualified disaster relief payments" are excludable. These include payments, regardless of the source, for the following reasonable and necessary expenses:

- Personal, family, living, or funeral expenses incurred as a result of a presidentially declared disaster.
- Expenses incurred for the repair or rehabilitation of a personal residence due to a presidentially declared disaster (whether you own the home or rent it as a tenant).
- Expenses incurred for the repair or replacement of the contents of a personal residence due to a presidentially declared disaster.

Grants under the Disaster Relief and Emergency Assistance Act are excludable from income, but you cannot deduct a disaster loss to the extent you are reimbursed for it by the grants. Cancellation of all or part of a federal disaster loan is also considered reimbursement for a loss (it reduces your casualty loss deduction).

Disaster relief mitigation payments are also excludable from income. These are payments made under the Robert T. Stafford Disaster Relief and Emergency Assistance Act or the National Flood Insurance Act for hazard mitigation of your property, such as to elevate or relocate flood-prone homes.

Planning Tip

If you are the victim of a disaster, be sure to check with your local authorities as well as with FEMA to see whether there are any grants or relief payments you may be entitled to.

Pitfall

Disaster relief payments for business-related expenses, lost wages, or unemployment compensation may not be excluded from income and are fully taxable.

Where to Claim the Benefit

Since qualified disaster relief payments are not taxable, you do not have to report them on your return.

Damages

According to the National Center for State Courts, in 2018 (the most recent year for statistics), there were more than 83.5 million cases in state courts in the United States to redress wrongs, such as medical malpractice claims and breach of contract (and there were over 300,000 civil cases in federal courts in 2020). The tax law allows only certain types of damages to receive favorable tax treatment.

Benefit

If you receive compensatory damages for personal *physical* injury or illness, you can exclude your recovery. For example, if you recover damages for a medical malpractice incident that affected your body, the damages are tax free. There is no dollar limit on the amount you can exclude from income.

There is a special exclusion for persons who were persecuted by the Nazis. They can exclude *all* amounts received as restitution payments for their ordeal. The exclusion applies to:

- Heirs or estates of such persons who suffered on the basis of their race, religion, physical or mental disability, or sexual orientation.
- Restitution payments for assets that were lost or stolen before or during World War II.
- Life insurance issued by European insurance companies immediately before and during the war.
- Interest earned on escrow accounts and funds established in settlement of Holocaust victim claims.

There is a special exclusion for restitution for victims of human trafficking. Even though the restitution payments are not limited to physical injury, the payments are fully excludable.

There is also a special exclusion for compensation paid to the wrongfully incarcerated even though the payments do not relate to physical injury. All of the payments received for wrongful incarceration are tax free.

Damages arising out of the purchase of property are treated as a recovery for injury or damage to a capital asset. As such, damages are tax free to the extent of your basis in the property.

Example

You buy land for $100,000. After the sale you learn it is contaminated and sue the seller, who settles with you for $25,000. You are not taxed on these damages. They serve to reduce your basis in the land to $75,000.

If you receive damages for any other reason, including punitive damages for physical injury or any type of damages for personal injury that is not physical, the damages are fully taxable. Nonphysical personal injuries for which damages are taxable include injury to reputation, discrimination, and back pay.

Conditions

To claim the exclusion for damages, the award must relate to some physical injury or sickness. Damages for emotional distress are excludable only if they are attributable to a physical injury or sickness.

"Soft injuries," such as headaches, weight loss, and insomnia, arising from a work-related case (e.g., discrimination, sexual harassment) are viewed as emotional distress and not as physical injuries for which damages are tax free. However, any awards for these soft injuries are excludable to the extent they compensate for medical costs.

The damages must be compensatory, meaning that they aim to make you whole from your loss (covering medical expenses, etc.). Punitive damages are not tax free, even if they relate to physical injuries.

The damages award can be a negotiated settlement or an award fixed by a court.

Planning Tip

If an action involved both physical and nonphysical injury aspects, be sure that the complaint allocates the degree of injury to each part.

Example

Suppose you are injured in a car accident in a state that does not have a no-fault law. You sue for $75,000 for personal injuries and $25,000 for damage to your car. You settle with the other party for $40,000. Of this amount, three-quarters, or $30,000, relates to personal injuries and is tax free; $10,000 relates to property damage and is taxable.

Pitfalls

If you receive interest on an award for physical damages, you are taxed on the interest even though the award itself is tax free.

If you obtain a recovery under a contingent fee agreement with your attorney, you must include the *entire* award in income if such awards are taxable (e.g., defamation actions). How you treat the attorney's fees depends on the nature of the action (see Chapter 15).

Where to Claim the Benefit

Since damages for personal physical injury are excludable from your income, you do not have to report them on your return.

If you receive damages for personal injuries that are not physical (for example, for libel), they are taxable and must be reported as "Other income" on Schedule 1 of Form 1040 or 1040-SR.

Disability Coverage

The statistics about disability are startling. According to Cornell University's Disability Statistics, 12.6% of the U.S. population have a disability. Disability can happen at any time during a person's life. To protect against this possibility during your working years, it is advisable to carry disability insurance. The tax law does not treat disability coverage in the same way as medical insurance; special rules apply that *may* allow a deduction for premiums.

Benefit ⊗

Disability benefits you receive under a policy on which you paid the premiums are tax free. There is no dollar limit on the amount of disability benefits you can exclude from income. If your employer paid the premiums on a policy that you are now collecting on, the benefits are taxable to you. If you and your employer shared the cost of premiums, you must allocate the benefits accordingly; you can exclude only the portion that relates to *your* payments.

Disability coverage under Social Security is treated for tax purposes in the same way as Social Security retirement benefits—they may be wholly excludable or included in income in the amount of 50% or 85% of benefits, depending on your filing status and income. Generally, the payment of disability benefits under Social Security ends once you attain your full retirement age (for example, 66 years old for someone born in 1943 through 1954; the age increases gradually until it reaches 67 for those born after 1959). At that time you start receiving Social Security retirement benefits.

Condition

Tax-free treatment applies to benefits paid under a policy for which you paid the premiums with after-tax dollars. Tax-free treatment also applies to these types of disability payments:

- Disability pensions from the Department of Veterans Affairs
- Pensions for combat-related injuries or injuries from a terrorist attack
- Disability pensions for anyone who has injuries resulting from terrorist attacks after September 10, 2001

Planning Tips

If your employer gives you the choice between accepting employer-paid disability coverage or paying for such coverage yourself, you may prefer to pay for it so that benefits will be tax free if you become disabled. While your employer's payment of disability insurance premiums may be tax free to you, the price for this benefit is taxability of any disability payments you later receive.

If you are totally and permanently disabled and receive little or no Social Security benefits, you may be eligible for a tax credit called the credit for the elderly and disabled.

Pitfall

If you retire on disability and receive a lump-sum payment for accrued annual leave, you cannot exclude this payment; it is fully taxable as additional compensation.

Where to Claim the Benefit

If you are entitled to exclude disability payments you receive, you do not have to report them on your return.

Taxable disability pension payments shown on Form 1099-R are reported on your return as compensation if you have not reached the minimum retirement age set by your employer (use the same line you would for reporting salary, wages, etc.). Once you have attained the minimum retirement age, the disability pension payments are reported on lines 5a and 5b of Form 1040 or 1040-SR.

To determine the portion of Social Security disability payments that are excludable from income, complete the worksheet for Social Security benefits in the instructions to Form 1040 or 1040-SR. Social Security disability payments are reported on lines 6a and 6b of Form 1040 or 1040-SR.

Accelerated Death Benefits

A life insurance policy may provide more than just death benefits. In some cases, it can be used to provide funds during the insured's lifetime. The tax law treats the proceeds during life, called accelerated death benefits, the same as post-death payments (that is, tax free), if certain conditions are met.

Benefit ⊗

Accelerated death benefits are an insurance company's payment of some or all of the death benefits under a life insurance policy on account of terminal or chronic illness of the insured. Viatical settlements involve the selling of a cash-value life insurance policy to a company in the business of buying such policies. Accelerated death benefits and viatical settlement proceeds received by a terminally ill individual are tax free.

Such payments to a person who is chronically ill can be excluded in full to the extent used to pay long-term care costs; per diem payments in excess of care costs are excludable only up to a set dollar limit per day ($400 in 2021).

Conditions

Tax-free treatment of accelerated death benefits and viatical settlement proceeds apply for someone who is terminally ill. This means you have a condition or illness that is expected to result in death within 24 months of certification by a physician. The exclusion applies without regard to the use of the benefits or proceeds.

To qualify for favorable treatment as a chronically ill individual, you must be certified by a licensed health-care practitioner that, within the preceding 12 months, you are unable to perform for a period of at least 90 days 2 or more of the following activities:

- Eating
- Toileting
- Bathing
- Dressing
- Continence
- Transferring (such as getting in and out of bed)

A person also qualifies as chronically ill if certified as requiring substantial supervision for one's own health and safety because of cognitive impairment (for example, the person has Alzheimer's disease).

For a chronically ill individual, excludable amounts must be used to pay long-term care expenses. These are necessary diagnostic, preventive, therapeutic, curing, treating, mitigation, and rehabilitative services, as well as personal care services. The services must be provided under a plan of care prescribed by a licensed health-care practitioner (which includes a doctor, registered nurse, or licensed social worker).

Planning Tip

When shopping for life insurance, inquire about accelerated death benefit options under the policy. You want to have as many options as possible, even if you never need to use them.

Pitfall

Generally, it is not advisable for someone who is terminally or chronically ill to use life insurance proceeds to cover lifetime care expenses. The purpose for which the policy was originally purchased, such as the care of surviving family members or the payment of funeral expenses and estate taxes, is frustrated by such use. Thus, using a life insurance policy for lifetime needs is usually a last resort for paying care expenses.

Where to Claim the Benefit

If accelerated death benefits or viatical settlement proceeds are excludable, they are not reported on the return.

Legal Fees

In most cases, there is no requirement that a lawyer be used to bring a lawsuit or conduct other types of business. But it is usually advisable to use an expert to protect your rights. Of course, this assistance may not come cheaply. Whether you can deduct legal fees depends on the type of activities involved.

Legal fees are discussed in Chapter 15.

Identity Theft Losses

Identity theft is all too common in the United States today. According to the Javelin 2020 Identity Fraud Survey, 5.1% of individuals in the U.S. had their personal identities stolen in 2019, with total fraud amounting to $16.9 billion (these are the most recent statistics). If you become a victim, you can experience damage to your FICO score, delays in tax refunds, and various financial losses.

Financial losses as a result of identity theft may be tax deductible because it usually constitutes a theft under state law (see the rules for deducting theft losses earlier in this chapter, which generally limit such losses to those occurring in federally-declared disaster areas). However, the time and effort you expend to fix problems caused by identity theft (e.g., contacting credit bureaus; talking with creditors) are not tax deductible. Neither is the cost of identity theft insurance or similar coverage to protect your personal identity.

However, identity theft protection services that you receive (as a consumer or an employee) as a result of a company's data breach are not taxable. Such services include credit reporting and monitoring services, identity theft insurance, identity restoration services, and other similar services.

Tax Identity Theft and Relief

The IRS has been working to combat the growing number of identity theft cases where taxpayer information is used to obtain tax refunds, often preventing the legitimate person from receiving his or her refund on a timely basis. The IRS has a landing page for information and assistance on identity theft at https://www.irs.gov/identity-theft-central. Here you'll find a link to the Taxpayer Guide to Identity Theft.

If you think you may be a victim of identity theft, you can protect yourself with respect to your tax return by filing Form 14039, *Identity Theft Affidavit*, with the IRS. This will help to ensure that you receive any tax refund you're entitled to. You must obtain an IP PIN if you receive a notice from the IRS (CP01A) giving you a new IP PIN or because you should have had one because your return was rejected without it. You may choose to get an IP PIN, which may be advisable if you suspect your identity may have been compromised. Find details at www.irs.gov/getanippin.

Your Job

Your job not only is what occupies the majority of your time during the greater part of each week and, hopefully, provides satisfaction; it also gives you a paycheck and perhaps other benefits. While your earnings are taxable in most cases, some of the fringe benefits may be tax free.

In order to earn that paycheck, you may have to expend your own dollars on various things. Unfortunately, for 2018 through 2025, you cannot deduct most of your unreimbursed employee business expenses (unless you are a performing artist with certain income, a reservist, a state or local government official paid on a fee basis, or have impairment-related work expenses). You may want to talk with your employer about covering some or all of your job-related expenses (e.g., driving your car on company business). If your employer sets up an "accountable plan" for reimbursing your business expenses, you aren't taxed on the reimbursements (your employer gets to deduct the costs, and the reimbursements aren't subject to employment taxes).

For more information, see IRS Publication 3, *Armed Forces' Tax Guide*; IRS Publication 535, *Business Expenses*; and IRS Publication 587, *Business Use of Your Home*.

Educator Expenses

There are about 3.7 million teachers in grades K–12, according to the National Center for Education Statistics. Most teachers spend money from their own pockets to pay for classroom expenses. The tax law lets them deduct their costs, up to a limit, regardless of whether they itemize deductions.

Benefit ⬚

If you are an educator, you can deduct up to $250 of what you spend out-of-pocket for classroom expenses and professional development courses related to curriculum as an adjustment to gross income; you do not have to itemize deductions to claim this benefit. The $250 limit may be adjusted annually for inflation, but because of low inflation, there is no increase in the limit for 2021.

Conditions

You must be an educator in grades K–12. This includes not only teachers, but also principals, guidance counselors, and aides. The Tax Court allowed a high school coach to deduct his costs for sports over IRS objections that only classroom expenses counted; the track was his classroom.

You must work at least 900 hours a school year in a school that provides elementary or secondary education.

You must pay qualified expenses. This includes:

- Supplies, books, computer equipment, and other materials used in the classroom (including health and physical education courses).
- Professional development expenses, which are courses related to the curriculum that the educator teaches.
- Personal protective equipment (PPE) and other materials and supplies designed to stem the spread of COVID-19. These include:
  - Face masks
  - Disinfectant for use against COVID-19
  - Hand soap
  - Hand sanitizer

- Disposable gloves
- Tape
- Paint or chalk used to guide social distancing
- Physical barriers (e.g., clear plexiglass)
- Air purifiers
- Other items recommended by the Centers for Disease Control and Prevention (CDC) to be used for the prevention of the spread of COVID-19

Planning Tip

Keep receipts to support any claimed deduction for classroom expenses.

Pitfall

If you homeschool your child, you cannot claim this deduction.

Where to Claim the Deduction

Enter the amount of your out-of-pocket expenses up to $250 on Schedule 1 of Form 1040 or 1040-SR.

Prizes and Awards

Recognition for a job well done is always appreciated. When it is accompanied by a monetary item, it may be valued even more. Taxwise, a prize or award may be tax free under very limited circumstances.

Benefit

If you receive certain prizes or awards *other than cash*, you can exclude the amount you receive from income. These include awards of tangible personal property, such as the proverbial gold watch, given as awards for length of service or safety achievements, and your employer is permitted to deduct the cost of those awards. However, other prizes and awards are fully taxable.

Conditions

Generally, your ability to exclude employment-related prizes and awards depends on your employer's ability to deduct the payments. But you don't have to be the company's comptroller to determine this; the company will report to you the tax treatment of the award on your Form W-2.

Just to give you some idea of the extent of what you can exclude, your employer's deduction depends on whether the award is part of a qualified award plan. If yes, then up to $1,600 may be given to the same employee during the year. If the award is not part of a qualified award plan, then the annual limit per employee is $400.

Planning Tip

If you receive a valuable prize or award that is *not* tax free, your employer will automatically withhold income taxes on the payment (at the flat rate of 22%). If this withholding is not enough to cover your estimated tax requirements, ask your employer to withhold an additional amount.

Pitfall

If you win a sales or other contest on the job and receive a prize, such as a vacation, you can decline the award to avoid taxation on the benefit. If you accept the prize, you are generally taxed on the value of the benefit.

Where to Claim the Benefit

Prizes and awards that are tax free need not be reported on your tax return.

Performing Artists

Actors, singers, dancers, comedians, and other performing artists can deduct the same job expenses as any other worker. But the tax law provides a special rule on *how* to claim deductions.

Benefit

If you are a performing artist with income below a set amount, you can deduct your employment-related expenses as an adjustment to gross income (AGI).

Conditions

You must meet all of the following 3 conditions to treat your job-related expenses as an adjustment to gross income rather than as an itemized deduction:

1. You have 2 or more employers in the performing arts during the year with at least $200 of earnings from at least 2 of them.
2. Your expenses from acting or other services are more than 10% of your gross income from such work. For example, you spend $8,000 during the year on voice lessons and earn $22,000 doing voice-overs and other jobs in the performing arts. Since $8,000 is more than 10% of $22,000, you meet this condition.
3. Your adjusted gross income from all sources (not just performing arts) is no more than $16,000.

SPECIAL RULE FOR MARRIED INDIVIDUALS

You must file a joint return if you are married, unless you live apart from your spouse for the entire year.

If both you and your spouse work in the performing arts, you figure the two-employer requirement and the 10% requirement separately for each of you. Compare your personal employment-related expenses to the money you earn from performing arts jobs.

For purposes of your adjusted gross income, the $16,000 applies to your *combined* AGI.

Planning Tip

As with any other type of expense, it is vital to keep good records of your job-related outlays. Retain receipts for lessons you take. Use a diary or other record keeper to note travel expenses and other items.

Pitfall

Even $1 of adjusted gross income over the $16,000 limit means your expenses cannot be deducted. If you anticipate AGI of about this amount, weigh carefully the after-tax cost of accepting work that puts you over the limit.

Example

You earn $15,000 from your work in acting, have expenses of $7,000, and meet the other conditions for treating your expenses as an adjustment to gross income. This means your AGI after the deduction becomes $8,000. But if you have $1,000 more of AGI, your expenses are deductible in excess of $320, so your write-off is limited to $6,680. The $1,000 of additional income nets you only $680 ($1,000 − $320 lost deduction).

Where to Claim the Benefit

You figure your deductible work-related expenses on Form 2106. Your total amount is then entered on Schedule 1 of Form 1040 or 1040-SR.

State or Local Government Officials Paid on a Fee Basis

Not every bureaucrat is a regular employee on the government's payroll. Some government employees are paid under a contract arrangement. Those who are can write off their related employee expenses in a special way.

Benefit

If you are an employee of a state or local government and are paid in whole or in part on a fee basis, you can deduct the business expenses related to these services as an adjustment to gross income rather than as a miscellaneous itemized deduction.

Conditions

The only conditions for treating your business expenses as an adjustment to gross income are:

- You are an employee of a state or local government.
- You are paid in whole or in part on a fee basis.

Planning Tip

If you are a state or local government employee, ask to arrange partial compensation on a fee basis (for example, related to a specific government project) to create an above-the-line deduction for your job expenses.

Pitfall

There is no downside to treating these business expenses as an adjustment to gross income.

Where to Claim the Deduction

You figure your deductible work-related expenses on Form 2106. Your total amount is then entered on Schedule 1 of Form 1040 or 1040-SR.

Repayment of Supplemental Unemployment Benefits

While unemployed, you may receive benefits in addition to regular state unemployment benefits. These "supplemental" benefits may have to be repaid once you obtain employment. If so, you may be able to write them off, either as a deduction or as a tax credit, if certain conditions are met.

Benefit

If you are required to repay supplemental unemployment benefits in order to qualify for trade readjustment allowances, you can claim a deduction for the repayment as an adjustment to gross income.

In some cases, you may even be eligible for a tax credit (instead of a deduction) for your repayments.

> **Example**
>
> In 2020, you received supplemental unemployment benefits and your tax bill was $3,800. In 2021, you repay $5,000. You recompute your 2020 tax, eliminating the $5,000 from income. Without this income, you would have paid $2,774. Therefore, your credit is $1,026 ($3,800 – $2,774).

Conditions

To claim the deduction, you must be required to repay supplemental unemployment benefits that you included in income in a prior year. The deduction is designed to wipe the slate clean; you already paid tax on the benefits when you received them and now you are entitled to a deduction to reduce your income, effectively backing out the benefits.

To claim a credit, your repayment must exceed $3,000. Then figure your credit by recomputing the tax you would have paid had you not received the repaid amount in the initial year, and compare the tax with what you actually paid.

Planning Tip

If you repaid supplemental unemployment benefits in the same year in which they were received, you do not have to do anything; the benefits were never reported as income, so there is no offsetting deduction necessary.

Pitfall

You cannot choose to file an amended return for the year in which the supplemental unemployment benefits were originally paid to subtract your later repayment. Your only choice in handling the repayment is to deduct it or, if eligible, claim a tax credit in the year of repayment.

Where to Claim the Benefit

If you are claiming the deduction, enter the amount of your repayment on Schedule A of Form 1040 or 1040-SR (it is a miscellaneous itemized deduction that is not subject to the 2%-of-AGI floor).

If you opt to treat repayments exceeding $3,000 as a tax credit, enter the credit on Schedule 3 of Form 1040 or 1040-SR. Write in "IRC 1341" on Schedule 3 to indicate the type of credit you are claiming.

Jury Duty Pay Turned Over to Your Employer

Jury duty is a civic duty that is hard to avoid. If you are called to serve, you are paid a nominal amount that is taxable income. But if you also receive your regular wages from your employer and must hand over your jury duty pay, you may claim a deduction for the income you don't get to keep.

Benefit ⬚

If you receive your regular pay while serving on jury duty and turn over your jury duty pay to your employer, you may claim a deduction for this action as an adjustment to gross income. This deduction is intended to offset your having to include the jury duty pay in income. There are no dollar limits on this deduction.

Condition

You must be required by your employer to turn over jury duty pay as a condition of receiving your regular compensation.

Planning Tip

Ask your employer whether you can keep your jury duty pay and simply receive your ordinary compensation in excess of this amount so that you reduce your FICA taxes (and your employer saves a like amount in FICA taxes).

Example

Your regular daily pay in 2021 is $150. Assume you serve on a jury for 5 days and receive $40 per day. If your employer pays you only $110 and allows you to retain the $40, you save $15.30 in taxes ($40 × 5 days × 7.65% rate for Social Security and Medicare taxes).

Pitfall

Don't overlook this deduction for jury duty pay, especially if you receive it early in the year. It's easy to forget about it since payments of less than $600 are not reported to you on an information return from the government.

Where to Claim the Deduction

If you are claiming a deduction for jury duty pay turned over to your employer, enter the amount on Schedule 1 of Form 1040 or 1040-SR.

Impairment-Related Expenses

Having a disability may necessitate certain additional expenses in order to work. The tax law recognizes this added cost and allows these work-related expenses to be deductible under a special rule.

Benefit

If you suffer from a physical or mental impairment and you must incur special expenses to enable you to work, you can deduct these impairment-related expenses as an itemized deduction. This miscellaneous itemized deduction is *not* subject to the 2%-of-AGI floor, so it remains deductible in 2018 through 2025 even though other job-related expenses subject to the 2%-of-AGI floor are not.

There is no dollar limit on this deduction. The deduction may be claimed without regard to the amount of your income.

Conditions

To be eligible for the deduction, you must meet both of the following conditions:

1. You have a physical or mental disability that results in a functional limitation of employment that substantially limits one or more major life activities.
2. You must pay the expenses in order to work. For example, if you require an attendant at work so you can perform your job, your cost for these services is a qualified expense.

EXAMPLES OF IMPAIRMENTS

Any one of these impairments entitles you to deduct job-related expenses without regard to the 2%-of-AGI limit:

- Blindness
- Deafness
- Impairment limiting your ability to perform manual tasks
- Inability to speak or walk

Planning Tip

You may be able to avoid paying some or all of your work-related expenses due to your impairment (no cost to you is better than a deductible one). Under the Americans with Disabilities Act (ADA), your employer must provide reasonable accommodations to enable you to perform your job duties. This may include special equipment or assistance. For more information about benefits to which you may be entitled by the ADA, visit www.usdoj.gov/crt/ada/adahom1.htm.

Pitfall

You cannot claim a double deduction for the same expense, so if you treat some impairment-related costs as a job expense, you cannot also deduct them as a medical expense. For example, Braille books for your work are an impairment-related job expense and also qualify as a deductible medical expense, but if you treat them as a job expense, you cannot also deduct them as a medical expense.

Where to Claim the Deduction

You must complete Form 2106, *Employee Business Expenses* to report your impairment-related expenses along with other unreimbursed employee business expenses. The total amount is then entered as a miscellaneous itemized deduction not subject to the 2%-of-AGI floor on Schedule A of Form 1040 or 1040-SR.

Military Benefits

Serving your country in the military won't make you rich, but it may entitle you to a variety of benefits and other assistance. The tax law looks favorably on those in the service by allowing tax-free treatment for a long list of benefits.

Benefit ⊗

If you are a member of the armed forces, including the National Guard and the reserves, you may be entitled to certain benefits because of your job status.

EXAMPLES OF TAX-FREE BENEFITS

- Adjustments in pay to compensate for losses resulting from inflated foreign currency
- Benefits under the Servicemembers' Group Life Insurance
- Combat pay
- Death allowance for burial services, gratuity payments to survivors up to $5,000, and travel of dependents to burial sites
- Death benefit payable to family members of those killed in combat
- Defense counseling payments
- Disability pay
- Dislocation allowance (intended to partially reimburse expenses such as lease forfeitures, temporary living costs in hotels, and other expenses incurred in relocating a household)
- Dividends on GI insurance

- Education, training, or subsistence allowances paid under any law administered by the Veterans Administration (VA) (deductible education costs must be reduced by the VA allowance)
- Family allowances for education expenses of dependents, emergencies, evacuation to a place of safety, and separation
- Housing allowances (Basic Allowance for Housing, Variable Housing Allowance, temporary lodging expense allowance, and a moving-in allowance intended to defray costs such as rental agent fees, home security improvements, and supplemental heating equipment associated with occupying leased space outside the United States)
- In-kind moving and storage expenses for relocation pursuant to a military order and incident to a permanent change of station
- Interest on dividends left on deposit with the VA
- Living allowances (Basic Allowance for Subsistence)
- Medical or hospital treatment
- Payments to former prisoners of war
- ROTC educational and subsistence allowances
- State and local payments of bonuses to active or former military personnel or their dependents by reason of such personnel's service in a combat zone
- Survivor and retirement protection plan premium payments
- Travel allowances for annual round-trip for dependent students, leave between consecutive overseas tours, reassignment in a dependent-restricted area, and transportation for you or your dependents during ship overhaul or inactivation
- Uniform allowances

Condition

There are no specific conditions for claiming these benefits; you are entitled to them if you are a member of the armed forces.

Planning Tips

If you receive a Basic Allowance for Housing (BAH), you can still deduct your mortgage interest and real estate taxes on your home, even though you pay these expenses with your BAH.

Military personnel can treat tax-free combat pay as earned income for purposes of making contributions to a traditional or Roth IRA.

Military personnel can also treat tax-free combat pay as earned income for purposes of the earned income credit (see Chapter 1).

For purposes of the home sale exclusion for gain on the sale of a principal residence, military personnel have a 10-year period (in place of a 5-year period) in which to have owned and used the home as their main home (see Chapter 4).

Pitfall

Nearly half the states tax military retirement pay, so check with your state for details.

Where to Claim the Benefit

Benefits that are excludable are not to be reported on your return.

Contributions to State Benefit Programs

You may deduct mandated employee contributions to state unemployment, disability, and family leave programs as an itemized deduction. This deduction is explained in Chapter 15 under State and Local Income Taxes.

Dependent Care Assistance

Your employer may pay for your dependent care costs up to a set amount, or enable you to pay them on a pre-tax basis. The arrangement used to allow you to use your wages for these personal expenses without being taxed on them is called a flexible spending account (FSA).

Benefit

You are not taxed on dependent care assistance—paid by your employer or you through a dependent care FSA—up to $10,500 ($5,250 for a married person filing separately) in 2021. Even if both spouses work for an employer offering a dependent care plan, the same dollar limit applies to the couple (i.e., $10,500 per couple).

Looking Ahead

In 2022, the dollar limit is set to be $5,000 unless Congress extends the 2021 limit. The $5,000 limit is what applied prior to 2021.

Conditions

Employee salary reduction contributions made on a pre-tax basis and reimbursements of expenses tax free or employer-paid reimbursements have the following conditions:

1. There must be a plan set up by an employer for this purpose.
2. You must have a dependent under age 13 (or spouse or other dependent incapable of self-care). However, because the age limit was raised for 2020

to 14, reimbursements can be made in 2021 for a child who aged out in 2020 from any carryovers of unused 2020 amounts.

3. Any reimbursements must be for qualified dependent care expenses. These are the same benefits applicable to the dependent care credit (Chapter 1).

4. No reimbursements may be made for services provided by a child who is under age 19 at the end of the year or any other person who is your dependent.

Planning tip

Usually, salary reduction contributions are made on a use-it-or-lose-it basis, so if your contributions aren't used up, you forfeit them. But due to COVID-19, if you have any used amounts from 2021, they may be carried over to 2022.

Pitfall

You must reconcile any dependent care FSA with the dependent care credit (Chapter 1). In effect, you cannot take the credit to the extent you use the dependent care FSA.

Where to Claim the Benefit

Because this is a tax-free opportunity, you do not report the employer payment or the salary amount contributed to the FSA. You can see this amount reflected on Form W-2. For example, the amount for dependent care appears in box 10.

Fringe Benefits

Wages, or salary, are only one aspect of remuneration for working. Your job may entitle you to a wide range of benefits, called perquisites ("perks") or fringe benefits, that your employer pays for. (Employer-paid dependent care assistance was discussed earlier in this chapter.) Many of these benefits are fully or partially tax free.

Benefit ⊗

If your employer pays for certain benefits, you may be able to exclude from your income some or all of these items. In many cases, however, tax-free treatment does not apply if you are an employee of an S corporation in which you own more than 2% of the stock.

There are various limitations and conditions for different fringe benefits, many of which are discussed in other chapters in this book (see Table 13.1).

TABLE 13.1 Fringe Benefits in 2021

Type of Benefit	Dollar Limit on Exclusion	Other Limitations	For More Details, See Chapter
Accident and health plans	None (except for long-term care benefits)		2
Achievement awards	Up to $1,600 ($400 for nonqualified awards)		
Adoption assistance	$14,440	Income limitations	1
Athletic facilities	None		
De minimis (minimal) benefits			
Dependent care assistance	$10,500		1
Educational assistance	$5,250		3
Employee discounts			
Employee stock options			
Free parking	$270/month		
Group term life insurance	$50,000		
Lodging on business premises			
Meals on business premises for convenience of employer			
Meals—de minimis			
No-additional-cost services			
Transit passes	$270/month		
Vanpooling	$270/month		
Working condition benefits			

You may be unaware of certain fringe benefits because you do not have to sign up for them as you would for, say, health coverage or a retirement plan, and they are not reported on your annual Form W-2. These fringe benefits include:

De minimis (minimal) fringe benefits. These are items so modest that accounting for them would be an administrative burden on your employer. For example:

- Birthday cakes
- Doughnuts, coffee, and soda
- Flowers or fruit for special occasions
- Occasional lunch or dinner money
- Photocopying
- Postage on personal items once in a while
- Use of employer's car if not more than once a month

Caution: Some companies have a policy against personal use of company property (e.g., photocopying) and such use can be considered a theft, so ask about your employer's policy on this matter.

Employee discounts. Typically, these are limited to 25% to 30% of the cost of goods such as store merchandise (usually 20% of the cost of services such as dry cleaning).

No-additional-cost services. These are items for which your employer does not incur any additional cost when you use them. For example:

- Flights for airline employees and their families on a standby basis
- Hotel rooms for hotel workers when there is a vacancy

Moving expenses. Reimbursements for moving expenses incurred after 2017 are not tax free (unless you're in the military and meet certain conditions).

Working condition fringe benefits. These include expenses that would be deductible as an unreimbursed employee business expense on your return if you, rather than your employer, had paid for them and if the deduction for miscellaneous itemized deductions subject to the 2%-of-AGI floor had not been suspended for 2018 through 2025. For example:

- Clothing and uniforms to wear on the job
- Dues to professional or trade associations
- Subscriptions to work-related publications
- Travel and meals
- Work-related continuing education courses

Transportation fringe benefit. This includes free parking, transit passes, and vanpooling of $270 per month in 2021. You can receive all transportation benefits each month. But the $20 per month in effect before 2018 for bicycle commuting does not apply in 2021.

Conditions

Different fringe benefits have different conditions and limitations. Table 13.1 contains a survey of various fringe benefits that are excludable, including any other limitations that may apply, and references, where appropriate, to the chapter in which you will find an additional explanation.

Planning Tips

Congress may increase the types of tax-free benefits that employers can provide to workers, so check with your employer for benefits for which you may be eligible.

If a fringe benefit is tax free, it may also be exempt from Social Security and Medicare (FICA) taxes. Table 13.2 shows which benefits are exempt from Social Security and Medicare taxes.

Pitfalls

Employees in an S corporation who own more than 2% of the stock cannot exclude the following types of fringe benefits from income:

- Accident and health benefits.
- Achievement awards.
- Adoption assistance.
- Lodging on the business premises.

TABLE 13.2 Benefits Exempt from Social Security and Medicare (FICA) Taxes

Benefit	FICA Taxes
Accident and health benefits	Exempt (except for S corporation shareholders owning more than 2% of the stock)
Achievement awards	Exempt up to $1,600 ($400 for nonqualified awards)
Adoption assistance	Not exempt
Athletic facilities	Exempt
De minimis benefits	Exempt
Dependent care assistance	Exempt up to $10,500

- Meals furnished for the employer's convenience.
- Transportation benefits (free parking and transit passes). However, transit passes up to $21 per month can be excluded if the value of the passes is not more than this amount (if more, then all of the benefit is taxable; you cannot exclude the $21 per month).

Certain benefits payable to highly compensated employees (generally executives and other highly paid workers, even those who are not S corporation shareholders) are not excludable. These benefits include:

- Self-insured medical reimbursement plans
- Dependent care assistance if the program favors these employees
- Employee discounts
- No-additional-cost services

Where to Claim the Benefit

Tax-free fringe benefits are not reported on your return. Many fringe benefits are listed on your Form W-2, with any necessary reporting requirements included in the instructions to the form.

Income Earned Abroad

Working abroad does not relieve citizens of their obligation to file U.S. tax returns and pay taxes here. But to make things easier for those working overseas, the tax law lets a limited amount of income be received tax free each year as long as certain conditions are met.

Benefit

If you live and work abroad, you are not taxed on up to $108,700 of foreign earned income. If you are married and both you and your spouse have foreign income, you may each be eligible for an exclusion. If your foreign earned income is more than $108,700, you are taxable only on amounts in excess of $108,700.

This exclusion is not automatic; you must elect it.

Conditions

To qualify for the foreign earned income exclusion, you must meet 3 conditions:

1. Your tax home is in a foreign country.
2. You meet either a foreign residence test (you live abroad for an uninterrupted period that includes one full year) or a physical presence

test (you live abroad for 330 days during a 12-month period). This eligibility requirement is waived for certain countries. Check the Supplement for any relief in 2021 specific to a region or due to COVID-19.

3. You do not work for the U.S. government or a government agency.

You can apply the exclusion only to foreign earned income, not to other types of foreign income.

FOREIGN EARNED INCOME

You must have income from the performance of personal services. This includes:

- Allowances from your employer for housing or other expenses
- Bonuses
- Business profits tied to the performance of services
- Commissions
- Professional fees
- Rents and royalties tied to the performance of services
- Salaries
- Value of an employer-provided car or housing
- Wages

The earned income must be received no later than the year after the year in which you performed the services.

Once you have established bona fide residence in a foreign country for an uninterrupted period that includes an entire tax year, you are a bona fide resident of that country for the period starting with the date you actually began the residence and ending with the date you abandon the foreign residence.

If you receive payment this year for foreign earned income earned last year, you can exclude this amount this year to the extent that you did not use up your exclusion in the prior year.

Example

In 2020, you earned $75,000 but were paid only $65,000, which you excluded. In 2021, you earn $120,000 and receive the $10,000 for 2020 services. In 2021, you can exclude a total of $118,700 ($10,000 for 2020 pay because you did not use up your 2020 exclusion of $107,600, plus $108,700 exclusion for 2021). You are taxable on $2,400 of your 2021 earnings.

Not all foreign income is eligible for the exclusion. Nonqualified payments include:

- Alimony
- Annuity income
- Capital gains
- Dividends
- Gambling winnings
- Interest income
- Pensions
- U.S. government pay (if you work for the government and are stationed abroad, your pay is not tax free)
- Value of tax-free meals or lodging

If you work in Antarctica, you cannot exclude your income (Antarctica is not considered a foreign country by the IRS).

Planning Tips

What happens if you haven't met the foreign residence or physical presence test by the time your return is due? You cannot claim the exclusion before you have met either test, but you have a choice: You can ask for a filing extension if you expect to meet either test within the extension period.

Example

Your return for 2021 is due June 15, 2022, but you request a filing extension to October 17, 2022, because you expect to satisfy the 330-day test in July 2021, so that you can claim the exclusion on your 2021 return.

Alternatively, you can file your return to report the foreign earned income and then file an amended return to claim the exclusion once you satisfy either test.

Example

Same as the preceding facts except that you won't satisfy the 330-day test until after October 17, 2022. You file your 2021 return and pay tax on the foreign income. Once the test is met, you file an amended return to receive a refund.

Once you make the election to exclude foreign earned income, it remains in effect for subsequent years unless you revoke it. You revoke the election by attaching a statement to your return indicating revocation.

Weigh carefully whether you want to revoke the election to claim the foreign earned income exclusion. Following a revocation, you may not use the exclusion for 5 years unless the IRS grants you permission to do so. The IRS may grant permission under these circumstances:

- You return to the United States for a period of time.
- You move to a different foreign country that has different tax rates.
- You change employers.
- There is a change in the tax law of the foreign country in which you reside.

If you are eligible to exclude foreign earned income, you may also qualify to exclude housing. The basic limit on housing expenses in areas that are not designated as high-cost areas in 2021 is $32,610 (30% of $108,700) ($89.34 per day). The maximum exclusion for areas where the basic limit applies is $15,218 (the basic housing expense minus the basic housing amount, which is $17,392 [16% of the foreign earned income exclusion of $108,700]).

Pitfalls

If you elect to exclude your foreign earned income, you may not deduct any expenses related to such income.

You cannot base a contribution to an IRA or a Roth IRA on excludable foreign earned income.

You cannot claim the foreign tax credit or a deduction for foreign taxes related to excludable foreign earned income. In fact, if you had claimed the foreign earned income exclusion in the past and claim a foreign tax credit this year, you have effectively revoked your election to claim the exclusion. You cannot claim the exclusion for at least 5 years unless the IRS grants you permission to claim the exclusion.

Under a "stacking rule," excluded foreign income is taken into account in figuring the tax rate you pay on income that is taxable.

You cannot claim the foreign earned income exclusion for work in Antarctica, in international waters, or in international airspace.

You cannot claim the foreign earned income exclusion with respect to earnings from any country subject to U.S. government travel restrictions. Countries subject to travel restrictions may be found at www.state.gov/travel and in IRS Publication 54, *Tax Guide for U.S. Citizens and Resident Aliens Abroad*.

Where to Claim the Benefit

To elect the foreign earned income exclusion, file Form 2555, *Foreign Earned Income*, which you attach to Form 1040 or 1040-SR.

Your Business

The United States is an entrepreneurial country—it is the American dream to own your own business, and millions already do. It has been estimated that there are over 30 million small businesses, 80% of which have no employees. During the COVID-19 crisis, many businesses shut down and, unfortunately, some went under. But given the entrepreneurial spirit, the number of new business license applications are impressive and now a recovery is well under way.

Most expenses related to running a business are deductible, but timing issues and limitations may come into play. This chapter deals primarily with business deductions for a sole proprietor, independent contractor, or freelancer who files Schedule C (or, for farming, Schedule F). Of course, many rules discussed in this chapter apply to partnerships, limited liability companies (LLCs), and corporations.

This chapter explains the tax rules for various business-related deductions and other tax breaks. These rules apply whether your business is full time or part time (e.g., you do freelance work in the "gig" economy). If your activity isn't a business but rather a hobby (because you lack a profit motive), then in 2018 through 2025 you cannot deduct any expenses for the activity even though all of the income from it must be reported. The rules for claiming a home office deduction are in Chapter 10. Retirement plans for self-employed individuals are discussed in Chapter 5. Health insurance is covered in Chapter 2.

For more information, see IRS Publication 15, *Circular E, Employer's Tax Guide*; IRS Publication 225, *Farmer's Tax Guide*; IRS Publication 334, *Tax Guide for Small Business*; IRS Publication 535, *Business Expenses*; IRS Publication 536, *Net Operating Losses*; IRS Publication 587, *Business Use of Your Home*; and IRS Publication 946, *How to Depreciate Property*. Also see *J.K. Lasser's Small Business Taxes 2022* by Barbara Weltman.

Start-Up Costs

The term "start-up" has a very specific meaning for tax purposes. When you think of the start-up phase of a business, you typically think about the first few years of operation when the business gets going. But for tax purposes, start-up means that period of time just *before* you actually focus on the business you then begin. It is the period in which you are looking for a business to go into.

Benefit 🔼

When you decide to start a business, you may incur certain costs. Usually, these costs are viewed as capital expenditures that are not currently deductible. But you can deduct up to $5,000 of start-up costs in the year the business begins. If start-up costs exceed $5,000, the balance can be amortized (deducted ratably) over 180 months.

If start-up costs exceed $50,000, the $5,000 deduction limit is reduced dollar for dollar by the excess over $50,000. If start-up costs exceed $55,000, no immediate deduction is allowed; such costs can be amortized over 180 months.

Example

You've been looking into a business to start and have incurred expenses for research, travel, and other related costs of $5,900. You begin business in December of 2020. You can deduct $5,000, plus 1/180 of $900, or $5 for a total of $5,005 in 2020. In 2021 and for the next 13 years, you'll deduct 12 x 1/180 of $900, or $60 each year. In the 15th year, you'll deduct 11 x 1/180 of $900 or $55. If your start-up costs had been $54,000, you could have deducted $1,000 ($5,000 − [$54,000 − $50,000]), plus 1/180 of $53,000 in the first year. If your costs had been $55,000 or more, then all of the costs would be deducted ratably over 15 years (1/15 each year).

Conditions

Start-up expenses include ordinary and necessary business costs related to deciding *whether* to go into business and which business to buy or start. This is referred to as the "whether and which" test.

EXAMPLES OF START-UP COSTS

- A survey of potential markets
- Advertisements for the opening of the business
- An analysis of available facilities, labor, and supplies
- Salaries and fees for consultants and executives
- Travel and other expenses incurred to get prospective distributors, suppliers, and customers

Expenses incurred after the start-up phase that relate to starting the business cannot be amortized; they must be capitalized (added to the cost of the business).

Example

You find a business you want to purchase and ask your accountant to review the company's books. Then you ask your attorney to draw up a contract of sale. Since you have already identified a particular business, you are beyond the start-up phase for tax purposes and accountant's and attorney's fees cannot be currently deducted or amortized as part of start-up expenses; they are simply part of the basis (cost) of your business, along with the purchase price of the company.

Planning Tips

Remember to keep track of your annual deductible amount so you don't overlook the write-off opportunity in the coming years if you do not write them off in full in your first year of business.

If you sell your business before the end of the amortization period (assuming your start-up costs were not initially fully deducted), you can deduct any unamortized amount in the final year of business.

A separate $5,000 deduction limit and 180-month amortization period applies to certain other expenses you may incur in forming a business: incorporation costs and partnership organizational costs. Like start-up costs, make sure that the items fit within the write-off category and then apply the $5,000 deduction limit and 180-month amortization rule.

Pitfall

Start-up costs are limited to expenses incurred *before* you begin operations. Once you have passed the start-up phase, which means you've identified the business or type of business you'll start, you can no longer include expenses in your pot of start-up expenses.

Where to Claim the Benefit

Report the amortizable amount of your start-up costs on Schedule C (or Schedule F) as "Other expenses." If you have more than one expense, you must list each of them in the space provided for this on Schedule C (or Schedule F).

Qualified Business Income Deduction

As the owner of a pass-through business, there is a "qualified business income deduction" that you can use to reduce taxable income if you're profitable. It is also referred to as the Section 199A deduction (the section in the Tax Code that governs it). There is no extra outlay required to enjoy the deduction; you claim it if you are eligible. There are many more rules for this QBI deduction than are covered in this section; see *J.K. Lasser's Small Business Taxes 2022* for more details.

Benefit ◉

The deduction is 20% of qualified business income, to the extent you qualify for it. The deduction is not a business write-off on Schedule C, E, or F; and it is not a reduction of gross income to reduce adjusted gross income. The deduction is taken into account in figuring taxable income on which your applicable tax rate applies. It can be taken whether or not you itemize personal deductions. The 20% deduction is increased by 20% of qualified REIT dividends and income from publicly-traded partnerships (PTP); this is not discussed here.

Conditions

There are various conditions and several limitations on this write-off. The 20% deduction is figured on "qualified business income" (QBI). This is income from a business in the United States, including Puerto Rico. Qualified business income is determined for each of an owner's separate businesses. Only items of income, gain, deduction, and loss allowed in determining taxable income are taken into account for qualified business income.

QBI does not include capital gains (including Section 1231 gains) and losses, certain dividends, and interest not allocable to a trade or business. QBI does not include reasonable compensation to S corporation shareholders or guaranteed payments to partners for services rendered to the business. Any net loss is carried over and treated as a loss generated by the business in a subsequent year.

QBI must be reduced by business-related deductions, including those claimed as adjustments to gross income. These include the self-employed health insurance deduction, the deduction for contributions to owners' qualified retirement plans, and the deduction for a portion of self-employment tax.

Rental real estate activities may amount to a trade or business, making you eligible for the QBI deduction. There's no bright line test for determining whether rental real estate activities are a trade or business. There is a safe harbor for treating a "real estate enterprise" as a trade or business.

Again, there are many more rules for this QBI deduction than are covered in this section; see *J.K. Lasser's Small Business Taxes 2022* for more details.

INCOME THRESHOLD

If your taxable income (not just business income) in 2021 does not exceed $329,800 for joint filers, $165,925 for married persons filing separately, and $165,900 for all other filers, then the deduction is simply 20% of QBI. If your taxable income is over these threshold amounts, then limitations apply. For specified service businesses (discussed later), there is a phaseout of QBI taken into account. The phaseout amounts are in Table 14.1.

W-2 LIMITATION

If your taxable income is over the applicable thresholds noted above, the deduction is limited to the *lesser* of (1) 20% of qualified business income, or (2) the greater of (a) 50% of W-2 wages, or (b) 25% of W-2 wages *plus* 2.5% of the unadjusted basis immediately after acquisition of qualified property (there are time limits on what property can be taken into account). This is referred to as the "W-2 limitation."

TABLE 14.1 2021 Taxable Income Phaseout for the QBI Deduction

Filing Status	Taxable Income over	Fully Phased Out
Married filing jointly	$329,900	$429,800
Married persons filing separately	$165,925	$215,925
Other filers	$165,900	$215,900

Example

You are single with taxable income over the applicable amount and are the sole owner of an S corporation in the construction business. You receive wages from the business of $500,000 and QBI of $600,000. The business has W-2 wages (other than what is paid to you) of $300,000 and $1 million unadjusted basis in qualified property. Your QBI deduction is $120,000 because it is the lesser of:

- 20% of QBI (20% of $600,000 = $120,000), or
- The greater of 50% of W-2 wages ($150,000), or 25% of W-2 wages ($75,000) plus 25% of $1 million unadjusted basis of qualified property ($25,000) = $150,000.

SPECIFIED SERVICE TRADES OR BUSINESSES

There's another rule that effectively limits or bars the 20% QBI deduction for specified service trades or businesses (SSTBs), which are those involved in the performance of services in the fields of health, law, consulting, accounting, actuarial science, performing arts, athletics, financial services, brokerage services, or any business where its principal asset is the reputation or skill of one or more of its owners or employees.

If you fall into this category and your taxable income exceeds the applicable threshold, the amount of QBI that can be taken into account phases out over the next $100,000 for joint filers or $50,000 for other filers. In other words, if you are in an SSTB and have taxable income within the phaseout range, only a percentage of qualified business income can be used to figure the W-2 limitation as explained above. If you are in an SSTB and your taxable income in 2021 exceeds $429,800 if married filing jointly, $215,925 if married filing separately, or $215,900 if you are any other filer, you cannot take any deduction.

OTHER LIMITATIONS

Even after you jump through all of these hoops, the deduction cannot be more than 20% of taxable income minus net capital gains. And if you have a loss from one or more businesses, it's carried forward to the following year; any 20% deduction allowed in the following year is reduced by the carryover loss.

Planning Tip

While an S corporation owner-employee cannot include compensation in QBI, the compensation is part of W-2 wages for purposes of the W-2 wages limitation.

Usually businesses are treated separately, but you can elect to aggregate them under certain conditions (aggregation isn't allowed for SSTBs).

The IRS has questions and answers on the QBI deduction at https://www.irs.gov/newsroom/tax-cuts-and-jobs-act-provision-11011-section-199a-qualified-business-income-deduction-faqs.

Pitfalls

If your business is a partnership or S corporation, the limitations apply at the owner level. This means that you may or may not be eligible for the qualified business deduction even though your co-owner(s) is or is not.

If you have negative QBI for 2021, it is carried forward to offset positive QBI in 2022. This may mean that even if you become profitable in 2022, you may not be eligible for a QBI deduction if you suffered a loss in 2021. And if you had a loss in 2020, it impacts your 2021 QBI deduction.

If you erroneously claim the qualified business income deduction, you may be subject to a 20% accuracy-related penalty. This penalty applies if the deduction causes an understatement of tax that is greater than 5% of the tax required to be shown on the return for the year, or $5,000.

Where to Claim the Deduction

The deduction is taken on line 10 of Form 1040 or 1040-SR.

Equipment Purchases

It usually takes more than just your brains and hard work to make a business run. You need equipment, from technology-based items (e.g., computers, tablets, and smartphones), to furniture (e.g., desks, file cabinets, and chairs), to industry-specific items (e.g., carpentry tools and heavy machinery). For tax purposes, all of these items are viewed as "equipment" for which special tax treatment may be claimed. Today, the tax law encourages investments in equipment as a means of spurring the economy by allowing an immediate deduction for purchase costs if certain conditions are met.

Benefit ⬆

You can deduct amounts you pay for equipment used in your business as an ordinary business expense. However, tax law dictates when and how much of your cost you can deduct. Four sets of rules come into play:

1. *First-year expensing.* Up to a set dollar limit can be deducted in the year the equipment is placed in service. Higher dollar limits apply for equipment placed in service in certain distressed areas; a lower dollar limit applies for vehicles weighing more than 6,000 pounds. The limit for 2021 is $1,050,000. This is also known as the Section 179 deduction.

2. *Bonus depreciation.* The full cost of equipment (100%) is allowed to be deducted if purchased and placed in service in 2021. There is no dollar limit on bonus depreciation.

3. *Depreciation.* A percentage of the equipment's basis is deducted over a set term (a recovery period fixed for various types of assets). There is no dollar limit on depreciation.

4. De minimis *safe harbor rule.* If you don't capitalize the cost of an item (i.e., you don't add it to your balance sheet), you can immediately deduct up to $2,500 per item or invoice if you make such an election on your tax return.

Conditions

Equipment purchases are not limited to machinery; the term "equipment" includes just about any type of property other than most real estate.

EXAMPLES OF EQUIPMENT

- Answering machines
- Bookshelves
- Cars (see Chapter 7)
- Computers
- Copiers
- Credit card readers
- Desk accessories
- Desk chairs
- Desks
- Farming equipment (see later in this chapter)
- Fax machines
- File cabinets
- Floor models and displays
- Machinery
- Musical instruments for musicians
- Printers
- Qualified improvement property
- Scanners
- Signs
- Smartphones
- Software purchased off the shelf

- Tablets
- Telephones
- Tools of your trade
- Trucks (see Chapter 7)
- Vacuum cleaners

Slightly different rules apply to the different write-off methods. For example, a particular item may qualify for the Section 179 deduction but not for bonus depreciation.

The rules on depreciation are quite complex, and a complete discussion is well beyond the scope of this chapter. Here you will gain an overview of the rules that apply. To learn more, see IRS Publication 946, *How to Depreciate Property* or *J.K Lasser's Small Business Taxes 2022*.

Conditions for First-Year Expensing

There are 3 basic conditions for claiming first-year expensing:

1. You must elect it.
2. Your total equipment purchases for the year cannot exceed a set dollar amount.
3. Your taxable income must at least equal your expense deduction.

ELECTION

You must elect to claim first-year expensing (also referred to as a Section 179 deduction because of the section in the Internal Revenue Code governing the deduction).

EQUIPMENT PURCHASES

To qualify for the election, your total equipment purchases for the year cannot exceed a set dollar amount. For 2021, you can claim the expensing deduction only if your total purchases are no more than $3,670,000. The dollar limit phases out on a dollar-for-dollar basis for total purchases over $2,620,000.

CERTAIN IMPROVEMENTS TO COMMERCIAL SPACE

Qualified improvement property (certain improvements to the interior space of a commercial building and roofs; heating, ventilation, and air-conditioning property; fire protection and alarm systems; and security systems in nonresidential realty) can qualify for first-year expensing up to $1,050,000 in 2021. They also qualify for bonus depreciation discussed later. Write-offs for these properties are explained in Chapter 10.

TAXABLE INCOME

Your first-year expensing deduction cannot be more than the taxable income from the active conduct of a business. Taxable income for this purpose means your net income (or loss) from all businesses you actively conduct. If you are married and file a joint return, your spouse's net income (or loss) is added to yours. Taxable income also includes Section 1231 gains and losses (from the sale of certain business property) and salary or wages from being an employee. Taxable income must be reduced by the deduction for the employer portion of self-employment tax and net operating loss carrybacks and carryforwards.

Example

You own a sole proprietorship that shows a $5,000 profit for the year, and your deduction for the employer portion of self-employment tax is $353. Your spouse works as an employee with a salary of $50,000. Your taxable income for purposes of figuring your first-year expensing deduction is $54,647 ($5,000 − $353 + $50,000).

Condition for Bonus Depreciation

The property must qualify for this special deduction. Qualified property includes:

- Tangible property depreciated under the modified accelerated cost recovery system (MACRS) with a recovery period of 20 years or less
- Off-the-shelf computer software
- Certain improvements to commercial space as explained earlier.
- Certain plants planted or grafted

Conditions for Depreciation

Depreciation is a method for recovering your investment in property over a period of time fixed by law, called a recovery period. You apply a set percentage (based on the property's recovery period) to the property's basis (generally, its cost) to arrive at your annual deduction. These percentages may be found in IRS Publication 946.

Example

In 2021, you place in service a copier machine (5-year property) for which you do not claim any first-year expensing because you are not profitable and you

> elect out of bonus depreciation. Assume the cost of the machine is $8,000. Your depreciation percentage for the year that 5-year property is placed in service is 20%, so your depreciation deduction is $1,600 ($8,000 × 20%).

Different types of property are classified by their recovery periods:

- 3-year property, such as taxis, tractors, racehorses, and breeding hogs
- 5-year property, such as cars, trucks, copiers, assets used in construction, and breeding and dairy cattle
- 7-year property, such as office fixtures and furniture, fax machines, assets used in printing, assets used in recreation (e.g., billiard tables), and breeding horses and workhorses

There are also 10-year, 15-year (e.g., qualified improvement property), and 20-year types of property as well as realty (27.5 years for residential realty and 39 years for nonresidential realty such as office buildings, strip malls, and factories).

CONVENTIONS

Special depreciation rules, called conventions, come into play to determine your write-offs for the year.

- For property other than realty, a mid-year convention makes a hypothetical assumption that the property has been placed in service in the middle of the year. As a result of the mid-year convention, 5-year property is depreciated over 6 years.
- For property other than realty, a mid-quarter convention applies. If you place in service more than 40% of all your equipment purchases for the year in the final quarter of the year, a special rule dictates the amount of depreciation you can claim for each item placed in service during the year. This special rule is called a mid-quarter convention and generally operates to limit write-offs (although in some cases it may enable you to take greater deductions than under regular depreciation rules).
- For realty, a mid-month convention assumes that the property has been placed in service in the middle of the month it is actually placed in service. The mid-month convention is built into the depreciation rate tables applied to realty.

Conditions for De Minimis *Safe Harbor Rule*

You must be consistent in your treatment of the items, which means that if you use the *de minimis* rule to treat items as materials and supplies, you can't treat them as an asset on your balance sheet. You must attach your own statement that you are electing to use this safe harbor rule. The statement must make reference to Reg. Sec. 1.263(a)-1(f).

Planning Tips

The amount of your write-offs does not depend on whether you pay cash for the equipment or finance your purchase in whole or in part. If, for example, you finance your purchase, you may wind up deducting more in the first year than you pay out of pocket.

> **Example**
>
> In December 2021, you buy a machine for $25,000, financing it over 5 years at 8% interest. In 2021, you can claim a first-year expensing deduction of $25,000, even though you have not yet paid a penny.

Decide whether to make the first-year expensing election and/or forgo bonus depreciation. Generally, if your current income is modest but you expect it to increase in coming years, it may be preferable to forgo the deduction now in favor of using it against future income that would otherwise be taxed at higher rates.

Bonus depreciation can be used to create or increase a net operating loss (NOL). Thus, even if you do not have sufficient current taxable income to use bonus depreciation, the write-off can be taken into account in figuring an NOL.

Pitfalls

Special rules apply to so-called listed property, which includes cars, other property used as means of transportation, and property of a type used for entertainment, recreation, or amusement. You cannot use first-year expensing or accelerated depreciation *unless* business use of a listed property item is more than 50% of total use.

> **Example**
>
> You buy a boat that is used 75% for business and 25% for personal purposes. Since business use exceeds 50%, you can use first-year expensing or accelerated depreciation for the portion of the boat (75% of its purchase price) used for business.

If you sell or cease using property for which first-year expensing has been claimed, you *may* be subject to recapture. This means you're required to report a portion of the previous write-off as income in the year of the disposition of the property. Discuss this rather complicated matter with a tax adviser.

Where to Claim the Deduction

You figure your deduction for equipment purchases on Form 4562, *Depreciation and Amortization.* You enter the amount of your deduction on the line provided for this write-off on Schedule C (or Schedule F).

If you are claiming depreciation this year on an item placed in service in a prior year and you do not have any new items to report, you do not have to file Form 4562. Simply attach your own schedule to the return showing the amount of depreciation you are claiming this year.

Payment for Services

You may not be able to do it alone and may therefore need to hire employees to work for your business. The costs of wages, salaries, bonuses, and other payments are deductible if certain conditions are met.

Benefit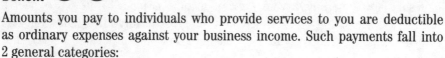

Amounts you pay to individuals who provide services to you are deductible as ordinary expenses against your business income. Such payments fall into 2 general categories:

1. Wages and compensation to employees.
2. Fees and payments to independent contractors or to third parties (e.g., temp employment agencies) providing workers to you.

There are no dollar limits on the amount you can deduct for payments for services.

In addition to a deduction for wages and compensation to employees, you may be eligible to claim a tax credit for a portion of these payments.

Conditions

There are several conditions for determining how much to deduct for payments to workers:

- It must be determined whether the worker is an employee or independent contractor.
- Amounts paid must be reasonable.

- Payment must relate to work actually performed.
- Payments must be made in a timely fashion.

WORKER CLASSIFICATION

First, you must determine whether workers are your employees or independent contractors. The key reason for making the distinction is the obligation to pay employment taxes—Social Security and Medicare (FICA) taxes, federal unemployment insurance (FUTA), and state unemployment and other payroll taxes. If you are the employer, you are responsible for the employer's share of taxes as well as withholding income taxes and the employee's share of FICA. If your worker is an independent contractor, then he or she is responsible for employment taxes.

Generally, worker classification as an employee or independent contractor is based on control. If you control when, where, and how work is to be performed, the person is your employee regardless of what label you may attach. If the person is in his or her own business and provides services to you, the person is usually treated as an independent contractor. Worker classification is a perennial "hot" IRS audit issue, so work with a knowledgeable tax adviser to get it right.

REASONABLE PAYMENTS

Compensation paid to your employees must be "reasonable." There's no set dollar amount. Reasonable depends on many factors, including job responsibilities, education level, and location of the business. Payments to yourself as a sole proprietor are not treated as deductible compensation because you are not an employee.

Payments paid to independent contractors must also be reasonable.

PERFORMANCE OF WORK

You can deduct only payments for work actually performed. Generally, this poses no problem for your rank-and-file employees. But if you put family members on the payroll, the IRS may look closely at the relation between their wages and work performed. Keep track of the hours they worked and the tasks they performed as proof that they earned the compensation you paid.

TIMELINESS OF PAYMENT

You may deduct only payments you actually make (if you are on the cash method of accounting for your business). If you are on the accrual method (which is unusual for self-employed individuals and most small businesses), payments to rank-and-file employees must be made no later than $2\frac{1}{2}$ months after the close of the year (e.g., by March 15, 2022, for compensation earned in 2021) to be deductible in 2021. (Different rules apply to payments to shareholders in C and S corporations.)

Planning Tips

Compensation paid to certain employees may entitle you to claim an income tax credit (more details may be found later in this chapter). These include:

- Work opportunity credit
- Credit for paid family and medical leave (not COVID-19-related payments for sick and family leave)
- Empowerment zone credit for workers within designated areas
- Indian employment credit for workers on Indian reservations
- Social Security tax credit on certain tips for workers in restaurant and tavern businesses
- Employer wage differential payment credit
- Employee retention credit related to federally-declared disasters

There are also some credits that reduce your payroll taxes for employees. They are not reported on your income tax return; they are claimed on Form 941. For 2021, these include:

- Employee retention credit to keep workers on your payroll despite closures or business reductions through December 31, 2021 (different rules apply for different quarters in 2021). This credit is different from the credit with the same name—employee retention credit—which only applies to employers impacted by federally-declared disasters.
- Paid sick leave and paid family leave for COVID-19-related reasons through September 30, 2021.
- COBRA premium assistance from April 1, 2021, through September 30, 2021.
- Research credit up to $250,000 (see instructions to Form 8975, *Qualified Small Business Payroll Tax Credit for Increasing Research Activities*.

Pitfalls

If your workers are employees, you are responsible for employment taxes. This requires you to withhold federal and, if applicable, state income taxes from their wages, as well as the employee share of FICA tax. You must also pay the employer share of FICA as well as FUTA and state employment taxes. If you fail to pay over these taxes in a timely fashion, you may be personally liable for them.

If you opted to defer your employees' Social Security taxes from September 1, 2020, through December 31, 2020, the deferred amount must be repaid in 2022. For more information, see IRS Notice 2021-11.

Where to Claim the Deduction

You report the deduction for compensation to employees on the line designated as "Wages" on Schedule C of Form 1040 or 1040-SR. Wages are reduced by employment tax credits you claim (listed earlier in "Planning Tip"). You report payments to independent contractors on the line marked "Commissions and fees" of this schedule.

For farming-related activities, the deduction for wages to employees is reported on the line marked "Labor hired" on Schedule F of Form 1040 or 1040-SR. Wages are reduced by employment tax credits you claim. You report payments to independent contractors on the line marked "Customer hire" of this schedule.

Employment-related income tax credits to which you may be entitled are figured on the following forms (there are more credits that apply if you provide certain benefits to employees and they are not covered here):

- Work opportunity credit: Form 5884
- Credit for paid family and medical leave: Form 8994
- Empowerment zone credit: Form 8844
- Indian employment credit: Form 8845
- Social Security tax credit on certain tips: Form 8846
- Credit for employer wage differential payments: Form 5884-A

Supplies

To paraphrase Benjamin Franklin, for want of a paper clip, your business may be lost. Despite predictions of a paperless society, most businesses use reams of paper and other supplies every year. The tax law allows a full write-off for the cost of ordinary supplies as long as certain conditions are met.

Benefit 🔼

Office supplies (including paper, pens, tape, and toner replacements) and cleaning supplies (such as detergent, paper towels, and sponges) are deductible against your business income. There is no dollar limit on this deduction.

Supplies that are part of your inventory are *not* currently deductible; they are part of the cost of goods sold.

Conditions

For supplies to be currently deductible, they must be ordinary and necessary business expenses. They cannot be items with a useful life of more than one year. If they have a longer useful life, they are treated as equipment (discussed earlier in this chapter).

EXAMPLES OF DEDUCTIBLE SUPPLIES

- Binders and presentation material
- Boards and easels
- Business cards
- Cleaning supplies
- DVDs and thumbdrives
- Filing and storage material
- Ink cartridges and toners
- Labels, envelopes, and shipping material
- Paper clips, tape, and staples
- Paper, pads, and notes
- Pens, pencils, and markers
- Replacement parts (which are not part of inventory)
- Rubber stamps
- Small wares of restaurants and taverns (e.g., glassware, paper or plastic cups, dishes, pots and pans, and bar supplies)
- Stationery
- Trash bags

Planning Tips

From a nontax standpoint, it may not make economic sense to load up on supplies even though you can deduct them. You are incurring costs now that could be paid later.

While the cost of supplies is generally deductible, it is a good business practice to economize on purchases. Look for discounts and special business incentives from such office supplies companies as:

- Office Depot (www.officedepot.com) (Office Max is part of Office Depot)
- Staples (www.staples.com)
- The Ultimate Green Store (www.theultimategreenstore.com/s-3-office .aspx)

Pitfalls

Supplies that are part of your inventory are *not* separately deducted. Instead, they are included as part of your cost of goods sold.

Watch the timing of ordering supplies. A current deduction is allowed for supplies used within the year. A deduction for supplies *not* used within the current year but kept on hand may still be claimed as long as doing so does not distort income, no records are maintained to indicate when supplies are actually used, and no inventory is taken of the amount of supplies on hand at the beginning and end of the year.

Where to Claim the Benefit

Report supplies used in your business on the line provided for this item on Schedule C (or Schedule F) of Form 1040 or 1040-SR. You do not have to complete any additional form or schedule for this purpose.

Gifts

Gifts generally are given because of personal feelings without any expectations or strings attached. But business gifts are usually motivated by gratitude for some business activity or hope for future business activity. In recognition of this fact, the tax law allows a deduction for business gifts, but only in very limited amounts.

Benefit ⬆

You may wish to bestow some gratuitous benefit on employees, customers, dealers, distributors, or other business relations. You can qualify for a deduction for business gifts, but the amount you can deduct is limited. Generally, you cannot deduct more than $25 per gift for any person each year (the same dollar limit in place since 1962). The dollar limit applies even if you attempt to make an indirect gift (for example, you give the gift to a company that is intended for the eventual personal use of a particular person).

Conditions

To claim a deduction for business gifts, you must meet both of the following conditions:

1. Dollar limit
2. Substantiation

DOLLAR LIMIT

The deductible amount of the gift cannot exceed $25 per person per year. The dollar limit does not include incidental costs, such as wrapping, insuring, or shipping the gift.

Example

You give a new vendor a gift that cost you $60. You paid $10 more to insure and ship it. You can deduct $35 ($25 of the $60, plus incidental expenses of $10).

In determining your $25 annual limit, you do not have to count any gifts of nominal value ($4 or less) with your company name imprinted on them that you distribute to a number of clients or customers (e.g., calendars at Christmastime).

SUBSTANTIATION REQUIREMENTS

You must show the cost of the gift, a description of the gift, the date it was given, and to whom. You must also state the reason for the gift (such as the business to be gained from making it). This information should be recorded on an expense log or business diary.

In addition, you must have evidentiary proof of the expense, such as a canceled check or receipt for the item.

Planning Tip

Gifts to your employees are *not* subject to this $25 limit because payments to them are usually treated as compensation (discussed earlier in this chapter). As long as regular compensation plus any purported gifts are reasonable, the total is deductible as compensation.

Pitfall

You must substantiate your business gifts in order to support your deduction. If you fail to meet full substantiation requirements, your deduction is lost. For example, merely retaining a receipt for the gift is not sufficient; you need to note all the information listed earlier as full substantiation for the gift.

Where to Claim the Deduction

You report the gifts as "Other expenses" on Schedule C (or Schedule F) of Form 1040 or 1040-SR. If you have more than one such expense (for example, in addition to business gifts, you are deducting environmental cleanup costs), you must list each type of expense in the space provided (or on your own attachment if more space is required).

Self-Employment Tax Deduction

Self-employed individuals pay both the employer and employee share of Social Security and Medicare taxes. But self-employed persons are treated as their

own employers to the extent they are permitted to deduct the employer share of these taxes.

Benefit ⬆

If you pay self-employment tax on your net earnings from self-employment, you deduct one half of the tax as an adjustment to gross income, even if you do not itemize your other deductions.

Conditions

Self-employment tax is the employer and employee share of Social Security and Medicare taxes figured on your net earnings from self-employment. As long as you show a profit in your self-employment activities of at least $400, you owe self-employment tax and can deduct one half, which represents the employer share. The same is so if you opt to pay self-employment tax even if you had a loss or a small amount of income.

Planning Tip

To figure your deduction, simply look at Schedule SE, *Self-Employment Tax*, the form used to figure your self-employment tax. The last line in Part I of Schedule SE allows you to figure your deduction. You deduct the employer portion of 7.65% (6.2% of Social Security taxes on 92.35% of net earnings up to $142,800 in 2021, plus 1.45% of Medicare taxes on 92.35% of net earnings from self-employment with no limit).

Pitfalls

The deduction for one-half of your self-employment tax is *not* a business expense, but a personal one. It does not reduce your profits on which you pay income taxes. The deduction reduces qualified business income for purposes of the QBI deduction (explained earlier in this chapter).

If you opted to defer part of your 2020 self-employment tax, 50% of the deferred amount must be paid by December 31, 2021; the other 50% is due by December 31, 2022.

Where to Claim the Benefit

You figure self-employment tax, including the maximum deferral amount, on Schedule SE of Form 1040 or 1040-SR. You report the deduction on the line provided on Schedule 1 of Form 1040 or 1040-SR.

Home Office Deduction

According to the U.S. Small Business Administration, 60.1% of all firms without employees are home based, as are 23.3% of those with employees. While

many businesses were forced to close for some time in 2020, making owners and employees work from home, the recovery in 2021 still left many working remotely. The cost of operating an office from home may be deductible as long as certain conditions are met. The term "home office" isn't limited to clerical space; it can include a workshop, greenhouse, artist studio, or any other area of a home used for business. The rules for claiming a home office deduction are explained in Chapter 10.

Farming-Related Breaks

According to the U.S. Department of Agriculture, there were more than 2.02 million farms in the United States in 2017 (the data was released in April 2019). Farming is considered a type of business and is therefore entitled to deductions available to any other business. But the tax law provides special breaks just for farms.

Benefit 🔼 ⊗ ⊕

If you operate a farm or farming activity, many of your costs are deductible against your farming income. In addition to any business expense you could claim in a nonfarming business, you may be entitled to special write-offs. Generally, there are no dollar limits on your farming-related deductions.

Some benefits payable to farmers may be tax free, and some expenses paid by farmers may qualify for a tax credit.

Conditions

Like other business expenses, farming-related deductions must be ordinary and necessary expenses.

EXAMPLES OF FARMING-RELATED DEDUCTIONS

- Chemicals
- Conservation expenses for soil and water
- Custom hire (machine work)
- Enhanced deduction for donations of conservation easements (100% of the contribution base, which is essentially adjusted gross income)
- Feed purchased (there are limits on how much you can deduct for feed to be consumed beyond this year)
- Fertilizers and lime
- Freight and trucking
- Gasoline, oil, and other fuel

- Ginning
- Hired labor (reduced by any employment-related tax credits discussed earlier in this chapter)
- Insect sprays and dusts
- Seeds and plants purchased
- Storage and warehousing
- Tying materials and containers
- Veterinary and breeding fees and medicine

You may also be entitled to the 20% qualified business income deduction discussed earlier in this chapter. Special rules not covered here apply to patrons of cooperatives.

Planning Tips

Some payments to farmers may be tax free. These include:

- Cost-sharing payments under The Conservation Reserve Program (CRP)
- Soil and water conservation assistance payments under a special federal program, which may run as high as $50,000
- Agricultural management assistance program payments

In addition to deductions for farming expenses, you may be eligible for certain tax credits related to farming. These include:

- Credit for federal excise tax paid on kerosene used in your home for heating, lighting, and cooking
- Credit for federal excise tax paid on gasoline, special motor fuels, and compressed natural gas used on a farm for farming purposes
- Credit for federal excise tax on fuels used in running stationary machines, for cleaning purposes, or in other off-highway vehicles

You can claim the credits on your return or claim a refund of the excise taxes you already paid. The credits and your options on claiming them are explained in more detail in IRS Publication 225, *Farmer's Tax Guide*.

Pitfall

Not all farming-related expenses are deductible. You may not deduct your personal living expenses, such as taxes, insurance, and repairs to your home.

Where to Claim the Deduction

Report the deduction on the line provided for it on Schedule F of Form 1040 or 1040-SR. If there is no specific line for the type of deduction you are claiming, list it in the space provided for other expenses (attach your own explanation or description of the expense if not self-explanatory).

Other Business Deductions

Not every expense fits neatly into a business deduction category. The tax law provides a catchall deduction rule, referred to as the ordinary and necessary expense rule, under which an expense can be written off as long as certain conditions are met.

Benefit

A variety of miscellaneous expenses you incur in your business are currently deductible against business income.

Condition

The only condition for deductibility of miscellaneous expenses is that they are ordinary and necessary for your business. "Ordinary" means that they are usual. "Necessary" means they are helpful and appropriate.

EXAMPLES OF OTHER BUSINESS DEDUCTIONS

- Advertising costs—promotional costs as well as goodwill advertising to keep your name in the public eye.
- Asbestos removal.
- Banking fees.
- Depletion for certain oil, gas, and mineral as well as timber properties.
- Dues to professional and trade associations.
- Environmental cleanup costs—expenses to restore property to its precontamination condition.
- Insurance (for self-employed health insurance, see Chapter 2).
- Intangibles (e.g., goodwill and covenant not to compete) that are acquired (must be amortized over 15 years).
- Interest on borrowing by small businesses (for example, financing of equipment purchases).
- Leasing costs for equipment.
- Licenses and regulatory fees paid annually to state or local governments.

- Meals with customers, vendors, or other business associates if it is not lavish or extravagant and you or an employee are present at the furnishing of food or beverages (100% deductible in 2021 if provided at restaurants; 50% if not provided at restaurants).
- Merchant authorization fees for credit/debit card and electronic payments.
- Moving equipment and machinery.
- Rent for office and other business-related space.
- Repairs to keep property in working order (if repairs add to the value or usefulness of the property, the cost must be capitalized in most cases).
- Repayments of income reported in prior years if over $3,000. *Note:* You may be able to take a tax credit in lieu of a deduction to obtain a greater benefit from the write-off.
- Shipping and postage.
- Storage and warehousing.
- Subscriptions.
- Telephone. If you operate your business from a home office, the basic service charge of the first landline to your home is not deductible. But this ban does not apply to additional charges, such as business long-distance calls and the cost of a second business line. The monthly cost of cell phone use is deductible.
- Utilities. Gas, electric, water, and other charges are deductible. If you claim a home office deduction, the treatment of these charges is discussed earlier in this chapter.

Planning Tip

As with all business expenses, keep good records, including receipts, canceled checks, and bills of sale.

Pitfall

Not all expenses you incur in your business are deductible. The tax law specifically prevents you from writing off certain expenses, even though they may be ordinary and necessary to your business.

EXAMPLES OF NONDEDUCTIBLE EXPENSES

- Bribes and kickbacks—even if customary or common business practice, if they are in violation of the law. For example, an insurance broker who pays a "referral fee" to car dealers who refer customers to him cannot deduct the fee because the car dealers are not licensed to sell insurance.

- Club dues for clubs organized for pleasure, recreation, or any other social purpose.
- Demolition expenses to raze a building. These costs are added to the basis of the land on which the building was demolished.
- Entertainment costs.
- Fines and penalties.
- Interest on a business-related tax deficiency.
- Lobbying expenses to influence legislation.

Where to Claim the Deduction

Deductible miscellaneous business expenses are reported on Schedule C (or Schedule F) either on the line provided for the type of expense (e.g., "Advertising" on Schedule C) or as "Other expenses." If you have more than one such expense, you must list each type of expense in the space provided (or on your own attachment, if more space is required).

Business Credits

Not every business expense is treated as a deductible item. Some expenses qualify as tax credits that can be used to reduce tax liability on a dollar-for-dollar basis.

Benefit ⊕

Other expenses you incur in your business may entitle you to a tax credit, which reduces your taxes dollar for dollar. The offset usually is against federal income tax. Those that offset certain payroll taxes are explained under *Planning Tips*. In Table 14.2 you will see a listing of tax credits that offset income taxes, the forms you use to figure them, and where the credits are discussed in this book.

Conditions

Each credit has its own conditions. However, many of the credits are part of the general business credit, which acts as an overall limitation on these credits. The limit for the general business credit is your regular tax liability (after credits other than those that are part of the general business credit), plus any alternative minimum tax liability, minus whichever of the following is larger:

- Tentative AMT from Form 6251
- 25% of your regular tax liability (after other credits) over $25,000

TABLE 14.2 Tax Credits

Tax Credit	IRS Form	For More Information, See Chapter
Alcohol fuels credit	6478	14
Alternative fuel vehicle refueling credit	8911	
Alternative motor vehicle credit	8910	
Biodiesel and renewable diesel fuel credit	8864	
Credit for contributions to certain community development corporations	8847	
Credit for employer-paid FICA on certain tips received by employees of food and beverage establishments	8846	14
Credit for wages paid in an empowerment zone	8844	14
Disabled access credit	8826	
Distilled spirits credit	8906	
Employer-provided child care facilities and services	8882	
Employer credit for wage differential payments to activated military reservists	8932	
Employee retention credit related to federal disasters	5884-A	14
Energy efficient home credit	8908	
Indian employment credit	8845	14
Investment credit (including rehabilitation property credit)	3468	11
Low-income housing credit	8586	11
Low sulfur diesel fuel production credit	8896	
New markets credit	8874	
Nonconventional source fuel credit	8907	
Orphan drug credit	8820	
Paid family and medical leave credit	8994	
Plug-in electric vehicle credit	8834	
Railroad track maintenance credit	8900	
Renewable electricity production credit	8835	
Research credit	6765	
Small employer health credit	8941	
Small employer pension plan start-up costs and auto-enrollment credits	8881	
Work opportunity credit	5884	14

Planning Tips

Credits in excess of the general business credit limitation can be carried back one year and forward for up to 20 years until they are used up. Be sure to keep track of carryfowards so you do not fail to claim credits to which you may be entitled.

Certain tax credits are not part of the general business credit and do not offset federal income tax. Instead, they offset certain payroll taxes:

- *Employee retention credit related to COVID-19.* The offset is against the employer share of Social Security taxes (part of FICA).

- *Research credit.* Small businesses can choose to use up to $250,000 of the research credit as an offset to the employer share of Social Security taxes (part of FICA).

- *Paid sick leave refundable credit.* This credit for certain COVID-19-related sick leave that small businesses paid through September 30, 2021, is an offset to all employment taxes.

- *Paid family leave refundable credit.* This credit for certain COVID-19-related family leave that small businesses paid through September 30, 2021, is an offset to all employment taxes. This credit should not be confused with the basic paid family and medical leave credit listed earlier, which is an offset to federal income taxes.

- *COBRA premium assistance.* This credit applies for employer-paid amounts from April 1, 2021, through September 30, 2021, for employees who were involuntarily terminated (other than for gross misconduct) or who had their hours reduced.

Pitfall

A special limitation applies to tax credits related to passive activities. See Chapter 10 for more details.

Where to Claim the Credits

Figure the credits on the forms specified for each one. Then, if required, complete Form 3800, *General Business Credit*, to figure the overall limitation on certain credits.

The credits are entered on Schedule 3 of Form 1040 or 1040-SR. Credits that are offsets to employment taxes are not part of Form 1040 or 1040-SR; they are not discussed further here.

Net Operating Losses

Not every business can be profitable year in and year out. What happens if your business suffers a loss from its operations that effectively wipes out more than your tax liability for the year? You may then have what is called a net operating loss. You may be able to use this loss to reduce taxes in prior and/or future years.

Benefit ⓣ

If your business expenses for the year outweigh your income, your loss may give rise to a net operating loss (NOL) that can be used to offset income in certain other years. For NOLs arising in 2021, the loss is carried forward to offset income in future years. NOLs arising in prior years are carried forward to 2021; they offset taxable income for 2021. NOLs claimed in 2021 may offset 80% of taxable income. If the NOL is not used up, it can be carried forward.

The net operating loss deduction is not an additional loss deduction. Rather, it is the result of having deductions exceed your business income and applying this excess against income in other years.

Conditions

You must determine whether having a loss in your business for the year results in a net operating loss. You have an NOL if your adjusted gross income is a negative figure. But adjusted gross income for purposes of an NOL does not include certain deductions you are otherwise allowed to take. When figuring your NOL, increase your adjusted gross income by all of the following that apply to you:

- IRA deduction
- Alimony deduction for pre-2019 divorces and separation agreements
- Net capital losses (capital losses in excess of capital gains)
- Self-employed person's contribution to a qualified retirement plan

The qualified business income (QBI) deduction is not taken into account in figuring an NOL.

CARRYBACKS AND CARRYFORWARDS

Net operating losses arising in 2021 may not be carried back (there's an exception for farming businesses, which have a 2-year carryback). NOLs may only be carried forward indefinitely until they are used up. Any NOLs carried forward from prior years offset 80% of taxable income in 2021.

Example

In 2020, you have a net operating loss of $100,000 that you carried forward to 2021. You may use $80,000 as a net operating loss deduction on your 2021 return.

Planning Tip

Be sure to keep track of NOLs arising in different years, especially since they may be subject to different carryback and carryforward periods.

Pitfall

Be sure to limit your NOL deduction to 80% of taxable income (it had been 100% prior to 2021).

Where to Claim the Deduction

There is no special form required to be used in figuring a net operating loss. As a practical matter, you can figure your NOL on Schedule A of Form 1045.

A net operating loss is reported as a negative income item; it is not a direct offset to your business income. For example, if your net operating loss carryforward is $4,400, enter –4,400 on Schedule 1 of Form 1040 or 1040-SR.

COVID-19 Government Assistance

Due to the pandemic, the government has several programs designed to help companies and self-employed individuals stay in business. Some of the assistance is tax free. Here is a listing of some government programs and how benefits are treated for federal tax purposes:

- *Economic Injury Disaster Loans (EIDLs)*. SBA loan proceeds are not taxable.
- *Pandemic Unemployment Assistance (PUA)*. The program expanded the availability of unemployment benefits to self-employed individuals. Such benefits are fully taxable.
- *Paycheck Protection Program (PPP) loans*. Loan forgiveness is not taxable. Expenses covered by loan forgiveness are still deductible to the extent otherwise allowed.
- *Restaurant Revitalization Fund grants*. These are grants, not loans, although amounts not timely used for specified purposes must be repaid. The grants are not taxable income.

- *Shuttered Venue Operator grants*. These are grants, not loans, although amounts not used for specified purposes within one year must be repaid. The grants are not taxable income.
- *State grants to small businesses*. Many localities provided grants to help small businesses during the pandemic. As a general rule, grants are taxable income for federal income tax purposes, but rules may differ for state tax purposes.

Miscellaneous Items

There are some tax benefits that simply defy classification so they cannot be included in any other chapter. You may be entitled to claim them nonetheless.

This chapter explains a variety of miscellaneous tax breaks you may be entitled to claim. The standard deduction amount that can be claimed instead of itemizing personal deductions is explained in the introduction to this book. For more information see IRS Publication 525, *Taxable and Nontaxable Income*, and IRS Publication 529, *Miscellaneous Deductions*.

State and Local Income Taxes

Individuals in all but 8 states (Alaska, Florida, Nevada, South Dakota, Tennessee, Texas, Washington, and Wyoming) and the District of Columbia may be subject to income taxes (those in New Hampshire have an income tax on interest income and dividends only). There may also be income taxes on the local level. These taxes are deductible for federal income tax purposes up to a set limit if you itemize personal deductions.

Benefit ⊜

If you pay state and local income tax, through withholding or estimated tax payments, you can deduct the total amount as an itemized deduction. However, the total amount of state and local taxes that is deductible (including state or local income and real estate [SALT] taxes) cannot exceed $10,000 ($5,000 if you are married but file separately). This is referred to as the SALT cap or limitation.

Conditions

There are no conditions for claiming this deduction. Whatever amount you pay is deductible up to the SALT cap, provided you itemize your deductions and do not opt to deduct state and local sales taxes.

State income tax withholding reported on Form W-2 is deductible. Withholding includes not only state and local income taxes, but also mandatory contributions you make to state unemployment, disability, or family leave programs. States with one or more of these programs include Alaska, California, New Jersey, New York, Pennsylvania, Rhode Island, Washington, and West Virginia.

As mentioned earlier, you may not deduct your state and local income tax if you opt to deduct state and local sales taxes, explained next.

Planning Tips

You may increase your deduction for state income tax for 2021 by prepaying the fourth installment of estimated tax. Generally, the fourth installment for 2021 is due on January 15, 2022. This fourth installment would normally be deductible for federal income tax purposes in 2022. However, you can pay it before the end of the year to increase the deduction for 2021.

If you deduct state and local income taxes as an itemized deduction, do not forget to add any 2020 state and local estimated taxes that were paid in January 2021 to total payments for 2021.

If, in 2021, you receive a refund of your 2020 state income taxes and you itemized in 2020, all, some, or none of the refund is taxable to you. This is explained later in this chapter under Tax Refunds.

Some states, such as Connecticut, Louisiana, New Jersey, Oklahoma, Rhode Island, and Wisconsin, have created a way for owners of pass-through entities to get around the SALT cap with respect to state and local income taxes. This move involves having the business—sole proprietorship, partnership, limited liability company, or S corporation—elect to pay an entity-level tax on the owner's distributive share. The owners then claim an offsetting refundable income tax credit based on the net income passed through to them.This effectively allows such owners to sidestep the SALT cap with respect to taxes on their distributive shares.

Pitfalls

Some states have enacted or are considering workarounds to enable their residents to benefit on their federal income tax returns from their state tax payments. For example, New York created a charitable contribution mechanism that converts real property taxes into charitable contributions. The IRS has nixed a workaround using charitable contributions. A taxpayer who makes payments or transfers property to an entity eligible to receive tax deductible contributions must reduce their federal charitable deduction by the amount of any state or local tax credit the taxpayer receives or expects to receive. But under a *de minimis* rule, a federal charitable contribution deduction is allowed for tax credits of no more than 15% of the payment amount or of the fair market value of the property transferred.

If you do not deduct state and local taxes (you do not itemize, or if itemizing, you opt to deduct state and local sales taxes) or your taxes exceed $10,000 ($5,000 if you are married and file separately), you lose any tax benefit from contributions you make to state unemployment, disability, or family leave programs. Such amounts are withheld from your pay nonetheless.

Do not prepay state income tax if you are subject to the alternative minimum tax (AMT). State income tax is not deductible for AMT purposes, so prepaying effectively wastes the deduction.

Where to Claim the Deduction

The deduction is claimed on Schedule A of Form 1040 or 1040-SR. There is no special form or worksheet needed to figure your deduction.

State and Local Sales Taxes

There are more than 10,000 state and local sales tax jurisdictions throughout the United States. The amount of tax you pay depends on how much you buy each year and the state (or states) in which you live. The deduction for state and local sales taxes up to a set limit can be claimed only if you itemize deductions and you do not deduct state and local income taxes.

Benefits

You can deduct state and local sales taxes paid during the year as an itemized deduction. You can claim your actual payments based on receipts for purchases or rely on an IRS table in the instructions to Schedule A of Form 1040 or

1040-SR. However, the total amount of state and local sales tax (SALT) that is deductible (including these sales taxes) cannot exceed $10,000 ($5,000 if you are married but file separately). The SALT limitation applies to these taxes.

Conditions

There are no conditions for claiming this deduction. Whatever amount you pay (or the figure for your state of residence, income level, and number of your dependents) subject to the overall SALT cap can be deducted. "Income" for purposes of the IRS tables is based on total available income, which is taxable income increased by nontaxable items such as tax-exempt interest; veterans' benefits; nontaxable combat pay; workers' compensation; nontaxable part of Social Security and Railroad Retirement benefits; nontaxable part of IRA, pension, or annuity distributions (but no rollovers); and public assistance payments.

As mentioned, you may not deduct state and local sales taxes if you opt to deduct state and local income taxes.

Planning Tips

You can increase the deduction from the IRS tables by state and local general sales taxes paid on the following items *only*:

- Car
- Motorcycle
- Motor home
- Recreational vehicle
- Sport utility vehicle
- Truck
- Van
- Off-road vehicle
- Leased motor vehicle

You can also add in sales taxes paid on an aircraft, a boat, a mobile home, a prefabricated home, or home building materials as long as the tax rate is the same as the general sales tax rate.

If you live in more than one state, you must allocate the deduction found in the IRS tables for the number of days you lived in that state.

> ### Example
>
> If you lived in Arizona for 6 months and New Jersey for the other 6 months, your total deduction for state and local sales taxes is one-half of your amount from the table for Arizona and one-half of your amount from the table for New Jersey.

Just because you live in a state in which you pay income taxes, do not assume that that deduction will be larger than the one for state sales tax. You may have a higher sales tax deduction if you fall into any of the following situations:

- A retiree whose income is primarily from Social Security benefits, certain types of annuities and pensions, and interest on Treasury securities.
- A self-employed individual who had a bad year.
- A person who was laid off from a job.
- A disabled worker who receives nontaxable state disability and workers' compensation payments.

Pitfall

State and local sales taxes that are itemized are not deductible for alternative minimum tax (AMT) purposes, so claiming the deduction in this manner can trigger or increase your AMT liability.

Where to Claim the Deduction

The deduction is claimed on Schedule A of Form 1040 or 1040-SR. Be sure to check the appropriate box on the schedule to indicate that you are claiming a deduction for general sales taxes.

Certain Federal Taxes

Most federal taxes you pay, such as income taxes, are not deductible. But there are some deductible federal taxes:

- Employer equivalent portion of self-employment tax (see Chapter 14)
- Estate tax paid on income in respect of a decedent (see later in this chapter)

Tax Refunds

The IRS reported in June 2021 that it had thus far issued more than 104.3 million refunds out of the nearly 152.4 million returns for 2020 received thus far, with an average refund of $2,775. Certain refunds, such as refunds of federal income taxes, are fully tax free; state tax refunds may be taxable or tax free in the year in which you receive them, depending on the situation. You don't have to amend any prior year's return if some or all of your refund is taxable.

Benefit ⊜

The receipt of a tax refund may be taxable, or partially or fully tax free. Federal tax refunds are *always* tax free (because you are not allowed to deduct your federal income taxes). State and local tax refunds may be partially or fully taxable or tax free, depending on whether you itemized your deductions in the year in which the taxes were paid and certain other factors.

Conditions

If you receive a refund of state (and/or local) income tax for the year in which you claimed the standard deduction, none of the refund amount is taxable to you. For example, suppose you claimed the standard deduction on your 2020 federal income tax return. In 2021, you receive a check for $946 from your state representing a refund of state income tax that you overpaid for 2020. You do not have to report this refund on your 2021 federal income tax return.

If you itemized deductions on your 2020 federal income tax return and receive a refund of 2020 state income taxes in 2021, figure whether none, some, or all of the refund is taxable to you in 2021, based on the tax benefit rule (the benefit that the tax deduction afforded you). If you receive a refund of state income tax, the portion that is taxable and the portion that is tax free depends on the amount of your total itemized deductions as well as what you could have deducted for state and local sales tax instead of deducting state and local income tax after factoring in the SALT cap.

You include in gross income the lesser of:

- The difference between your total itemized deductions taken in the prior year and the amount of itemized deductions you would have taken in the prior year had you paid the proper amount of state and local tax, or
- The difference between your itemized deductions taken in the prior year and the standard deduction amount for the prior year (assuming you were not precluded from taking the standard deduction in the prior year).

Example

You are single and paid state and local taxes in 2020 totaling $9,000 ($5,000 of state income taxes and $4,000 of property taxes). You itemized deductions in 2020. In 2021, you receive a refund of $1,500 of state income taxes due to an overpayment. Because all of the refund in 2021 gave you a tax benefit in 2020 (total state and local taxes were below the SALT cap), all of the refund is includable in gross income in 2021.

Example

Same as the previous example except that state income taxes were $7,000 and property taxes were $5,000. Of the total $12,000, only $10,000 was deductible because of the SALT cap. Thus, a tax refund of $1,500 is not taxable to you; it did not produce a tax benefit (i.e., it would not have changed your deduction in 2020).

Example

Same as in the previous example, except that property taxes were $4,000, so that of the $11,000 total state and local taxes, only $10,000 was deductible in 2020 because of the SALT cap. A refund of $1,500 produces a partial inclusion. Here $1,000 is not taxable; it would merely have reduced total payments to the amount of the SALT cap. But $500 of the refund is includable in gross income.

You cannot use this worksheet, and your computations become more complex, if your refund is more than the excess of the deduction you claimed for state and local taxes over what you could have deducted for state and local sales taxes. Generally, the full amount of the refund is taxable if it is less than the excess of the deduction claimed for state income tax in the prior year over what could have been deducted for sales tax, but you'll need to complete a separate worksheet found in IRS Publication 525.

Planning Tip

Many taxpayers look forward to receiving their federal income tax refunds, but this is poor tax planning. If you are entitled to a refund, then you've made an interest-free loan to the government. A better way is to adjust wage withholding and/or estimated tax payments so you more closely approximate your actual tax bill for the year. Given today's relatively low interest rates, it may make sense to err on the side of underpaying (so you'll owe the government money and some interest), rather than overpaying. The IRS interest rate on underpayments was 3% for 2021, although it may change in 2022.

Pitfalls

Whether you actually receive a refund check of state income taxes or apply it to your next year's state income tax bill, you'll have to determine whether none, some, or all of it is taxable, as explained earlier.

If you are owed a federal tax refund or rebate check, the government can apply it to any outstanding federal tax liability, delinquent child support payments, outstanding student loan payments, or certain other payments. The government will inform you by letter of how it applied your refund or rebate amount.

Where to Claim the Benefit

You do not have to report your federal tax refund and/or rebate check on your federal income tax return. Refunds of state income taxes are reported to you on Form 1099-G, *Certain Government Payments*. If the state income tax refund is tax free, you do not have to report it on your return.

If any portion of a state income tax refund is taxable, it is reported on Schedule 1 of Form 1040 or 1040-SR. Where appropriate, be sure to enter your refund as a *negative* number on Form 6251 so you reduce the income reported for purposes of the alternative minimum tax (AMT).

Legal Fees

William Shakespeare said, "Let's kill all the lawyers." But when a person today wants to right a perceived wrong, he or she usually turns to a lawyer for assistance. The cost of this help, which can be very steep, can be deducted only in certain circumstances.

Benefit

Legal fees you pay for actions that include discrimination are deducted as an adjustment to gross income. Legal fees for certain other personal matters, such as personal injury cases, cannot be deducted in 2018 through 2025.

Legal fees related to your business that meet deductibility conditions are ordinary and necessary business expenses that offset business income. Legal fees to acquire property (e.g., to buy a home) are added to the basis of the property and serve to reduce the amount of gain (or increase loss) when you sell it.

Condition

To be deductible, legal fees must relate to certain discrimination actions in connection with a whistleblower award, or your business. To deduct legal fees as an adjustment to gross income, the claim must be for unlawful discrimination (such as age discrimination on the job), claims against the federal government under Subchapter III of Chapter 27, Title 31, of the U.S. Code, and a private cause of action under the Medicare Secondary Payer statute.

Planning Tip

When engaging an attorney for representation, be sure you fully understand the fee arrangement. For example, even in a contingency fee arrangement (in which you owe no money if you do not recover anything), you may owe the attorney money to cover expenses, such as photocopying and postage, in addition to any portion of the award. And you may have to report the entire award even though you can't deduct the legal fees.

Pitfall

If you pay legal fees to buy property, don't forget to add them to your basis. If you overlook this addition, you'll wind up with a bigger gain than you need to have.

Example

You buy investment property for $100,000 and pay $5,000 in legal fees. You cannot deduct the fees, but you can add them to the basis of the property. Assume that a few years from now you sell the property for $150,000. Your gain is $45,000 ($150,000 − [$100,000 + $5,000]). In effect, you have reduced your gain for tax purposes by the $5,000 in legal fees you added to the property's basis.

Where to Claim the Benefit

You report legal fees related to discrimination claims up to the amount of the award on line 24h Schedule 1 of Form 1040 or 1040-SR. You report legal fees paid in connection with an award from the IRS for information provided to help the IRS detect tax law violations ("whistleblower award") up to the amount of the award on line 24i Schedule 1 of Form 1040 or 1040-SR.

You report deductible legal fees related to your business or investment properties on the appropriate form: Schedule C, Schedule E, or Schedule F of Form 1040 or 1040-SR.

Gifts You Receive

Whether your birthday gift is a tie, a set of golf clubs, or a check for $25,000, you usually can treat the gift as tax free for income tax purposes. The gift doesn't have to relate to a special occasion, such as Mother's Day or an anniversary, and it doesn't have to come from a relative. All you need is for the transfer to be a true gift and not something else (such as disguised compensation).

Benefit

Gifts you receive from just about anyone are tax free. Gifts can be in cash or property. There is no dollar limit on the amount of gifts you can exclude from income each year.

Important: Your income tax treatment is separate and distinct from the gift tax rules imposed on the gift's giver (the donor). Thus, the fact that a donor can make gifts free from gift tax only up to a set dollar amount per person per year ($15,000 in 2021) does not affect your receipt of the gift. Even if the donor exceeds this limit, your receipt is still entirely tax free for income tax purposes.

Condition

To be treated as a tax-free gift, the transfer must be made with donative intent (a substantive view toward making a gift) and the recipient cannot pay any consideration for receiving it. In most cases, it is entirely clear that a transfer of property is intended as a gift. There are 2 key situations, however, in which the transfer may not be entirely clear and tax-free treatment is not assured:

1. When money is really intended as a loan rather than a gift (see Chapter 11 for rules on distinguishing between a gift and a loan, especially when the parties are related).
2. When money or property is given to employees (see "Pitfalls").

Planning Tip

When you receive a gift of property, be sure to obtain from the donor the following information needed to determine your gain or loss when you later dispose of the property:

- *The donor's basis.* If the basis of the property at the time of the gift was at least equal to its value at that time, then your basis becomes the donor's basis. If the gift's value was less than its basis at the time of the gift (the property had declined in value), then your basis for purposes of determining gain is the donor's basis, but your basis for determining loss is the value of the gift at the time it was made to you. It is possible under the right circumstances that because of these special basis rules, you may realize neither a gain nor a loss when you sell the gift.

- *The donor's holding period.* You can add to the time you own the property all of the donor's holding period. For example, assume the donor purchased stock on July 1, 2017, and gives you the shares on May 1, 2021. If you sell those shares on May 15, 2021, your gain or loss is *long-term* gain or loss because the shares are considered to have been held for more than one year (the holding period begins with the donor's holding period).

A donor who is required to file a gift tax return must provide you with the following information within 30 days after the gift tax return's due date (generally April 15 of the year after the year of the gift):

- The name, address, and telephone number of the person required to file the tax return.
- The information specified in the gift tax return (a description of the gift and its value at the time of the gift).

Pitfalls

Money or items received from your employer that are labeled as gifts may, in fact, be nothing more than additional compensation. Small items, such as a holiday turkey or ham, are tax-free gifts to you. But gifts of *any* cash or cash equivalents (such as gift certificates and gift cards) and more expensive items (such as golf clubs) are considered taxable compensation, not tax-free gifts.

Income earned on a gift is taxable (unless such income is also tax-free income).

Example

You receive a gift of $10,000. The receipt of the gift is tax free to you. You use the money to buy a Treasury bill: Interest on the investment is taxable to you. If you use the money to buy a municipal bond, however, the interest on the investment is tax free (because municipal bond interest is tax free).

There is no income tax deduction for *making* a gift. While some gifts may be free from gift tax, there is no break for income tax purposes when you make a gift to an individual. Charitable contributions to IRS-approved organizations are another matter; they are discussed in Chapter 6.

Where to Claim the Benefit

Since gifts are tax free, you do not report them on your return.

Inheritances

Whether you inherit your uncle's gold watch or your mother's entire million-dollar estate, you are not taxed on this inheritance. There are no limits to the amount you can inherit tax free.

While the receipt of an inheritance is always tax free, some inheritances may produce taxable income later on. For example, if you inherit a $100,000 traditional IRA, you are not immediately taxed on the inheritance; there's no tax as long as the funds remain in the IRA. However, as you start to withdraw funds from the IRA, you are taxed on this amount. Fortunately, you are entitled to claim a tax deduction for any federal estate tax attributable to this taxable income, called income in respect of a decedent (IRD), which is explained later in this chapter.

Benefit

Inheritances you receive are tax free. There is no dollar limit on the amount of an inheritance you can exclude from income.

Condition

There are no conditions on the tax-free receipt of an inheritance other than the fact you receive the inheritance on account of the death of a person. Inheritances include amounts paid to you under a will, or by the state's rules of intestacy (if the person died without a will), jointly owned property you receive in full when your co-owner dies, and other amounts you receive as a named beneficiary (for example, a person's pension benefits left to you as the designated beneficiary).

Planning Tips

When you inherit property, your basis usually becomes the value of the property for estate tax purposes (generally, the property's value on the date of death). This is called a "stepped-up basis." Also, you automatically have a long-term holding period, regardless of how long the decedent owned the property before death or how long you hold it after you inherit it.

Example

On December 20, 2020, you inherit 100 shares of X Company from a decedent who purchased them on November 15, 2014, at $10,000. On the date you inherit them, they are worth $12,000. Two weeks later in 2021, you sell them for $13,000. You have a long-term capital gain of $1,000 ($13,000 − $12,000).

However, for inheritances from certain decedents dying in 2010, there was a modified carryover basis rule (very few estates opted to use this rule). If the estate elected to use the zero estate tax rule, then the basis to an heir is the same as the basis that the decedent had in the property. However, the stepped-up basis rule continues to apply to the first $1.3 million of an estate, with an additional $3 million passing to a surviving spouse; this amount is allocated by the executor to property passing from the decedent.

Pitfalls

If you inherited property from a person whose estate tax return was required to be filed after July 31, 2015, and received Schedule A of Form 8971 from the estate, you must use the basis specified on this schedule. This is the same amount that the estate used on the decedent's estate tax return. If you use a basis for inherited property that is inconsistent with the amount reported on this schedule, you may be subject to a 20% accuracy-related penalty.

If you anticipate an inheritance and sell your right to receive it, the proceeds you receive are taxable as ordinary income. This is so even though you would have received tax-free income had you waited for the inheritance itself.

If you are named as the executor, administrator, or personal representative of an estate, payment of fiduciary fees to you are *not* tax-free inheritances (even if you are also an heir to the estate).

Income earned on an inheritance is taxable (unless the income is also tax-free income—see the earlier example under "Gifts"). Income includes amounts on assets that previously have gone untaxed, such as traditional IRAs and annuities.

Example

You are named as the beneficiary of your father's IRA. When he dies, there is $100,000 in the IRA. Your inheritance of this IRA is tax free. However, since your father never paid income tax on the funds, you must do so under the required minimum distribution (RMD) rules for IRAs (explained in IRS

Publication 590-B, *Distributions from Individual Retirement Arrangements*).
The IRA proceeds are taxable when and to the extent you take withdrawals from
the IRA.

Where to Claim the Benefit

Since inheritances are tax free, you do not report them on your return.

Life Insurance Proceeds

The beneficiary of a life insurance policy generally can receive the proceeds free
from income tax. There is no requirement that the beneficiary be related to the
insured (the person on whose life the insurance is based), and there is no limit
on the amount of proceeds that can be received tax free.

Benefit ⊗

Life insurance proceeds you receive on account of the death of the insured are
tax free to you. There is no dollar limit on the amount you can receive tax free.

Condition

To be tax free, life insurance proceeds must be payable on the death of the
insured. The insured may be the same person as the owner of the policy or may
be someone else.

Planning Tip

Life insurance proceeds can be used during the insured's life on a tax-free
basis under certain conditions. The treatment of accelerated death benefits is
explained in Chapter 2.

Pitfalls

If you leave insurance proceeds with the insurance company, interest you
receive is taxable. (Only surviving spouses of someone who died before October
23, 1986, can exclude the first $1,000 of interest each year.)

If you paid any consideration for the life insurance policy, then you
are taxable on the proceeds. You are treated as having paid consideration
if you become the policy owner and there is an outstanding loan on the
policy.

Example

A mother has a $100,000 life insurance policy against which she has borrowed $10,000. She gives the policy to her daughter (receipt of the policy is a tax-free gift to the daughter). Shortly thereafter, the mother dies and the daughter collects $90,000 ($100,000 face value of the policy minus the outstanding loan of $10,000). The daughter is taxed on the $90,000.

Where to Claim the Benefit

Where life insurance proceeds received on account of the death of the insured are tax free, you do not have to report them on your return.

Gambling Losses

Legal gambling in casinos and other venues, such as racetracks and online sites, and illegal gambling, such as office pools, mean a lot of money is being wagered each year. Everyone knows that the odds always favor the house, whether it is a casino, race track, or state lottery. The chances of losing far outweigh those of winning. The tax law allows gambling losses to be deductible within limits under certain conditions.

Benefit ⬆ ☰

You can deduct gambling losses, plus the costs of wagering (e.g., traveling to a casino) to the extent of your gambling winnings for the year. The losses do not have to result from the same gaming activities that produce the winnings.

If you are not a professional gambler, then gambling losses are claimed as miscellaneous itemized deductions, which are allowable because they are *not* subject to the 2%-of-adjusted-gross-income floor.

If you are a professional gambler who devotes full time to this activity, you can treat your losses as a business expense. But even in this case gambling losses are limited to the extent of your winnings.

Example

During 2021, you spend $20 every week to play bingo ($1,040 for the year) and you do not win anything. But in December 2021, you win $500 on a state-sponsored scratch-off game. In 2021, you can deduct $500 of your bingo losses; the other $540 of your gambling losses is not deductible, and cannot be carried forward to offset winnings in a future year.

Conditions

You must report the gambling winnings that equal or exceed your claimed losses for the year. And you must have adequate records or receipts to prove your gambling expenses.

The Tax Court says that gambling winnings can include "comps" given to high rollers by a casino, such as a car, jewelry, and tickets to sporting events.

Planning Tips

Keep track of the amount you gamble throughout the year, since you don't know when in the year you will win. For example, retain all losing lottery tickets as proof of your gambling expenses so you can claim these losses when and to the extent you have winnings for the year. If you play the slots, whether you win or lose is calculated with reference to your wager for the day. If you wager $100 in slot tokens, for example, and at the end of the day redeem $60, you have a $40 loss even though you may have had a winning spin of $1,000 during the day.

For the slot machines, determine "losses" carefully. The IRS says your losses are determined as of the end of a calendar day or the casino's gaming day (at the casino's option). Compare what you start the day with against the amount you have at the end to determine your loss (or gain). For example, if you start with $100 and at the end of the day you have only $50, you have a $50 gambling loss even though you may have hit jackpots throughout the day of $200 or $2,000, or had losing spins of more than $50. The casino must report winnings of $1,200 or more on Form W-2G, with no reduction for the amount of the wager.

Pitfalls

Gambling winnings may be reported to you (and the IRS) on Form W-2G, *Certain Gambling Winnings*. The reporting threshold depends on the type of gambling (e.g., horse racing, slot machines, lotteries). If you claim losses in excess of amounts reported to the IRS, be prepared to show you had other winnings and that you reported these other winnings as income on your return.

Be sure to pay sufficient taxes on winnings to avoid estimated tax penalties. Winnings of $5,000 or more are subject to income tax withholding, but this withholding may not adequately cover your liability; you are entirely responsible for estimated taxes on smaller winnings.

Where to Claim the Deduction

If you are not a professional gambler, you claim a deduction for gambling losses in the space provided on Schedule A of Form 1040 or 1040-SR. This miscellaneous itemized deduction is not subject to the 2%-of-adjusted-gross-income floor.

If you are a full-time professional gambler, you can treat your gambling losses as a business expense. The wages must be placed only for your own account. Gambling losses in this case are reported on Schedule C of Form 1040 or 1040-SR.

Estate Tax Deduction on Income in Respect of a Decedent

If you inherit something on which you must pay income taxes because the person who left you the inheritance never did, then you may be eligible for a special deduction related to federal estate taxes paid on certain types of assets left to you. To claim this special deduction, certain conditions must be met.

Benefit ⊜

If you inherit a traditional IRA, annuity, or other income in respect of a decedent (IRD) and must report income from this inheritance, you may be eligible for an itemized deduction for the portion of federal estate tax related to this property. This itemized deduction is *not* subject to the 2%-of-adjusted-gross-income floor. There is no dollar limit on this deduction.

Conditions

To claim this deduction, the IRA, annuity, or other income in respect of a decedent (any income that the decedent earned before death but was not taxable to him or her at that time) must have been part of an estate that was subject to federal estate taxes. State estate or inheritance taxes are not deductible.

Examples of IRD:

- Accounts payable to self-employed business owners on the cash basis
- Benefits from 401(k) and other qualified retirement plans
- Damage awards from lawsuits
- Deferred compensation
- Health Savings Accounts
- Interest on U.S. savings bonds that has been deferred
- Royalties
- Survivor annuities
- Traditional IRAs

Assuming there has been federal estate tax paid on income in respect of a decedent, then figure the portion of the estate tax deductible in the current year. If, for example, you withdraw all of the IRA funds, then all of the estate tax related to this asset is deductible this year.

Example

You inherit a $120,000 IRA from your brother, and your sister inherited an $80,000 IRA from him, so the total IRD from his estate is $200,000. The tax on your brother's estate is $94,600. The estate determines that without including the IRA and other income in respect of a decedent, the estate tax would have been $48,400. The estate tax that qualifies for a deduction is $46,200 ($94,600 − $48,400). This year you empty the inherited IRA, and thus include $120,000 in your gross income. You can take an itemized deduction of $27,720 for your share of the estate tax, figured as follows:

$$\frac{\text{Value included in your income}}{\text{Total value of IRD}} \times \text{Estate tax qualifying deduction}$$

$$\frac{\$120,000}{\$200,000} \times \$46,200 = \$27,720$$

The calculation on the portion of estate tax can become complex when only part of the IRA is withdrawn within the year. A full explanation of how to figure this deduction may be found in IRS Publication 559, *Survivors, Executors, and Administrators*.

Planning Tips

This deduction is often overlooked. If you inherited an IRA and have not been claiming the deduction every year in which you report a distribution from the account, consider filing amended returns for all open tax years. You generally have 3 years from the due date of the return to file an amended return. This means you may be able to file for the prior 3 years and obtain tax refunds for each year.

When you receive an inheritance of IRD, be sure to ask the executor for information about estate taxes so you can figure your deduction. Find out about the amount of federal estate tax, the total estate, and what portion of it is the IRD you inherited.

Pitfall

There is no downside to claiming this deduction where allowable.

Where to Claim the Deduction

Generally, you report this deduction as a miscellaneous itemized deduction on Schedule A of Form 1040 or 1040-SR. It is *not* subject to the 2%-of-adjusted-gross-income floor. However, when the income in respect of a decedent is long-term capital gain (such as an installment payment on a sale made before the dece-dent's death), the deduction is not claimed separately but rather treated as an expense of sale. This means you still get the benefit of the deduction, but in the form of a reduction of the gain you report.

Rebates and Discounts

Retailers may offer various rebates or discounts to induce you to buy their prod-ucts. You may receive an immediate price reduction or, if you submit paperwork, you can get a check in the mail. These rebates and discounts are not taxable to you.

Benefit

The receipt of a check representing a rebate for purchasing an item is not income. For instance, if you buy a car, you may be able to apply a $1,000 manufacturer's rebate to the purchase price of the car, saving you $1,000 on the spot. Or, if you purchase a computer within a certain time, you may be able to send in a copy of your receipt and proof of purchase to receive a check payable to you (you often have to wait 6 to 12 weeks for this check). Similarly, in 2020, a number of insurance companies rebated premiums for auto coverage; the rebates are not taxable because they are viewed as a reduction to the premiums.

Either way, the IRS says this rebate arrangement doesn't produce any taxable income for you. Instead, it's as if the rebate simply reduced the price of the item you purchased.

Planning Tips

While mail-in rebates have declined (and only 40% of these are redeemed correctly), the number of rebates offered through smartphones continues to increase. Check for rebates when you purchase goods.

If your credit card has a rebate program under which you have the option of receiving cash or donating your accrued benefit to charity, the IRS says you are *not* taxed on the benefit, whichever option you choose. What is more, if you itemize and apply your benefit to a charity, you can claim a charitable contribu-tion deduction as long as you meet substantiation requirements (i.e., obtain a written acknowledgment for a donation of $250 or more).

Pitfall

There is no downside to submitting rebate claims, other than the brief time it takes you to do this.

Where to Claim the Benefit

You do not report any rebates or discounts that qualify as tax free to you.

Government Benefits

Individuals may receive payments from the federal and/or state government for a variety of reasons. In many cases, these benefits may be received entirely tax free.

Benefit

Most government payments can be received tax free; they are excludable without regard to their amount or your income. This includes the Economic Impact Payments (discussed in Chapter 12).

Condition

As a practical matter, many types of government benefits are payable to individuals whose incomes are below the level at which a tax return must be filed and taxes are owed. Most government benefits or payments are fully or partially tax free. Any taxable amounts are usually reported to you on an information return:

- Form RRA-1099, Payment by the Railroad Retirement Board
- Form SSA-1099, Social Security Benefit Statement
- Form 1099-G, Certain Government Payments (for unemployment benefits, RTAA payments, agricultural payments, and taxable grants)

EXAMPLES OF FULLY TAX-FREE GOVERNMENT BENEFITS

- Black lung benefit payments.
- Crime victim payments from a state fund for this purpose.
- Disaster relief and disaster mitigation grants (see Chapter 12).
- Economic impact payments (EIPs).
- Energy conservation subsidies paid by public utilities.
- Federal Employees' Compensation Act (FECA) payments for personal injury or sickness (including death benefits to beneficiaries).
- Federal income tax refunds.
- Foster care provider payments (see Chapter 1).
- Foster Grandparents Program payments for supportive services or reimbursement for out-of-pocket expenses.
- Grants for homes designed for wheelchair living of disabled veterans.

- Grants for motor vehicles for veterans who have lost their sight or the use of their limbs.
- HFA Hardest Hit Fund payments to distressed homeowners.
- Historic preservation grants under the National Historic Preservation Act.
- Holocaust victims restitution (see Chapter 12).
- Interest on insurance dividends left on deposit with the Department of Veterans Affairs.
- Military benefits (see Chapter 13).
- Mortgage assistance payments under Section 235 of the National Housing Act (the homeowner cannot deduct interest paid by this assistance).
- Nutrition Program for the Elderly food benefits.
- Peace Corps payments for housing, food, utilities, and clothing.
- SCORE payments for supportive services or reimbursement for out-of-pocket expenses.
- Senior program payments for supportive services or reimbursement for out-of-pocket expenses.
- Social Security lump-sum death benefit of $255 payable to a surviving spouse.
- State income tax refunds if you did not itemize deductions in the year to which the payments relate.
- Supplemental Security Income (SSI) and Supplemental Security Disability Income (SSDI).
- Survivor benefits of deceased public safety officers (police and law enforcement officers, firefighters, chaplains, and rescue squad and ambulance crew members).
- Volunteer tax counseling for the elderly (TCE) reimbursements for transportation, meals, and other expenses.
- Volunteers in Service to America (VISTA) volunteers, living expense allowances.
- Welfare benefits.
- Winter energy cost reduction payments to qualified individuals.
- Workers' compensation benefits.
- Work-training program payments from state welfare agencies (as long as the payments, exclusive of extra allowances for transportation or other costs, do not exceed public welfare benefits otherwise receivable).
- Wrongful incarceration payments payable to those who were wrongfully incarcerated.

TABLE 15.1 Income Threshold for the Excludable Portion of Social Security Benefits

	100% Excludable	50% Excludable	15% Excludable
Married filing jointly	Up to $32,000	Over $32,000 but not over $44,000	Over $44,000
Married filing separately	—	—	Automatically applies
Other taxpayers	Up to $25,000	Over $25,000 but not over $34,000	Over $34,000

Planning Tips

Social Security benefits may be fully or partially tax free, depending on your filing status, the amount of Social Security benefits, and other income, including tax-exempt interest. (The same rules apply to equivalent Railroad Retirement benefits.) Table 15.1 shows the portion of benefits excludable from income. The income threshold includes total income plus tax-exempt interest and one-half of Social Security benefits.

Example

In 2021, you are single with income from wages and taxable interest of $18,000. You also receive $12,000 in Social Security benefits and $1,000 of tax-exempt interest, with no adjustments to gross income. Since total income ($18,000 + 50% of $12,000 + $1,000) does not exceed $25,000, none of your benefits are included in income; they are tax free.

This explanation of the taxation of Social Security benefits is a brief overview that does not include many nuances to be taken into account. For more complete information about excluding Social Security benefits, see IRS Publication 915, *Social Security and Equivalent Railroad Retirement Benefits*.

If Form SSA-1099 shows a negative number (the benefits you are required to repay for any reason exceed your annual benefits), you can't deduct the excess in 2018 through 2025, unless it is greater than $3,000. If the negative number exceeds $3,000, you may qualify to figure tax for the year in a special way (see "Repayment of Supplemental Unemployment Benefits" in Chapter 13).

Pitfalls

Disability payments from Social Security are taxed in the same way as Social Security retirement benefits.

Just because a payment comes from the government does not automatically mean it is tax free. Some government payments are taxable.

EXAMPLES OF TAXABLE GOVERNMENT BENEFITS
- Alaska Permanent Fund dividend income
- Election precinct officials' payments
- Jury duty pay
- Peace Corps payments for leave allowances, readjustment allowances, and termination payments
- State lottery winnings

Where to Claim the Benefit

Those government benefits that are tax free do not have to be reported on your return. Social Security benefits are reported on line 6a of Form 1040 or 1040-SR. The taxable portion is entered on line 6b of Form 1040 or 1040-SR.

Olympic Medals

American Olympians and Paralympians are not taxed on their winnings. This impacts winners in the Summer Olympics in 2021, and future Olympics. The exclusion applies to the cash payments (estimated to be $37,500 for gold, $22,500 for silver, and $15,000 for bronze) as well as the value of the medals (estimated to be $820 for the gold and $490 for the silver; the bronze has little value).

However, athletes with adjusted gross income exceeding $1 million ($500,000 for married persons filing separately) cannot exclude their winnings.

Alternative Minimum Tax

The alternative minimum tax (AMT) is a parallel tax system that exists to ensure all taxpayers pay at least some tax, even if they can reduce their regular tax through legitimate deductions. You pay AMT to the extent it exceeds your regular tax. Only about 200,000 pay ANT because of changes to the AMT exemption amounts and other rules. Throughout this book, you have seen many examples of items that receive different tax treatment for regular tax and AMT purposes.

Benefit ●

You can claim an AMT exemption that may eliminate or at least minimize your AMT liability. The 2021 exemption amounts are $114,600 for married filing jointly or a surviving spouse, $73,600 for single taxpayers and heads of households, and $57,300 for married persons filing separately.

TABLE 15.2 2021 Phaseout Thresholds for the AMT Exemption

Filing Status	AMTI
Married filing jointly and surviving spouse	$1,047,200
Other filers	523,600

Conditions

There are no conditions for claiming this exemption. Simply apply the correct one for your filing status.

Planning Tip

Even if the exemption amount does not eliminate AMT liability, you can use various personal tax credits to reduce this liability. All nonrefundable personal credits could offset AMT liability.

Pitfall

The AMT exemption is subject to a phaseout for those with alternative minimum taxable income (AMTI) over a set amount. The exemption is reduced by $1 for every $4 over the phaseout threshold. Table 15.2 shows the phaseouts for 2021.

Where to Claim the Exemption

The exemption is claimed on Form 6251, *Alternative Minimum Tax— Individuals*, which is attached to Form 1040 or 1040-SR. If any AMT is owed, it is entered on Schedule 2 of Form 1040 or 1040-SR.

Items Adjusted Annually for Inflation

Law changes are one important way in which write-off amounts and restrictions on them change each year. But another, less obvious way is adjustments to certain amounts and limits reflecting cost-of-living changes. The Tax Cuts and Jobs Act changed the benchmark for cost-of-living adjustments. They are now pegged to the Chained Consumer Price Index for All Urban Consumers (C-CPI-U). Without getting technical, this new benchmark means smaller increases for inflation as compared with the former benchmark. Not all items subject to adjustment actually change each year, but the list of the items subject to change continues to grow.

To help you plan your taxes for the future, it's helpful to know that certain limits affecting exclusions, deductions, and credits are raised in step with increases in the cost of living (although some items may be adjusted downward if the times demand it). The following exclusions, deductions, and credits are subject to annual adjustments for inflation:

401(k) 403(b), and 457 plan elective deferrals

accelerated death benefits daily dollar amount that can be paid tax free from a life insurance policy on account of chronic illness

adoption assistance programs the maximum dollar amount and AGI phaseout range

adoption credit the maximum dollar amount and the AGI phaseout range

affordable health coverage provided by an employer and which prevents eligibility for the premium tax credit

alternative minimum tax (AMT) exemption amount

alternative minimum taxable income for the 26% rate

Archer medical savings accounts the definition of a high-deductible plan (i.e., the range for an annual deductible) and the limit on out-of-pocket costs

attorney's fee recovery from the government

benefits limit for defined benefit plans the dollar limit on benefits under these plans for which contributions are figured on an actuarial basis

child tax credit the value used in determining the refundable credit after 2021

compensation on which qualified retirement plan deductions are based the amount of compensation or self-employment income taken into account in figuring deductions for plan contributions

contribution limit for profit-sharing and other defined contribution plans the dollar limit on deductible contributions to these plans

contribution limit for SEPs the dollar limit on deductible contributions to these plans

dollar limit for depreciation and first-year expensing on luxury cars the maximum deduction for depreciation or first-year expensing for cars and light trucks weighing no more than 6,000 pounds, as well as the $25,000 limit for heavy SUVs

earned income credit the earned income amount, the maximum amount of the credit, the AGI phaseout range, and the disqualifying investment income amount

educator deduction out-of-pocket costs for grades K–12

excepted benefit health reimbursement arrangement the $1,800 dollar limit on reimbursements

first-year expensing limit dollar limit on amount of equipment that can be expensed as well as the taxable income limit

flexible spending accounts for medical costs the employee salary reduction contribution limit and the carryover limit

foreign earned income exclusion the dollar amount that can be received tax free for performing services abroad

health savings accounts annual deductibles and contributions limits to HSAs for high-deductible health plans

insubstantial benefits from charities dollar limit on what constitutes insubstantial benefits (ignored when figuring charitable contribution deductions)

interest exclusion on savings bonds AGI phaseout range

interest on student loans AGI phaseout range

IRAs MAGI limit for active participants to make deductible IRA contributions

lifetime learning credit MAGI phaseout range

long-term care premiums dollar limit on annual contributions treated as deductible medical expenses

low-income housing credit amounts used to calculate the state housing credit ceiling

parking dollar limit on employer-provided tax-free parking

payments received under long-term care policies or accelerated death benefits daily dollar limit excludable without regard to long-term care expenses or terminal illness

premium tax credit income eligibility threshold

qualified business income deduction taxable income amounts

qualified longevity annuity contract the maximum contribution

qualified small employer health reimbursement arrangement amounts excludable

retirement savers credit MAGI limit on eligibility to claim a credit for making certain elective deferrals and IRA contributions

Roth IRAs MAGI limit on eligibility to contribute to this retirement savings plan

Social security wage base for FICA and self-employment tax limit on income taken into account in figuring the Social Security portion of FICA and self-employment tax

standard deduction dollar amount

standard mileage rate for business travel the cents-per-mile rate may be increased or decreased

standard mileage rate for medical the cents-per-mile rate may be increased or decreased

transportation fringe benefits dollar limit on excludable free parking, monthly transit passes, and van pooling

Not all of the dollar amounts covered in this book are indexed annually for inflation. There are certain dollar amounts set by law or the IRS that are not adjusted for inflation. In doing tax planning for future years, you can rely on these fixed amounts (unless Congress decides to change them). The following items are not adjusted annually:

achievement awards an exclusion for receiving these awards is limited to $1,600 for qualified awards and $400 for nonqualified awards.

alimony payments if alimony payments under pre-2019 divorces and separation agreements decline by more than $15,000 in the second or third year, some of the previously claimed deductions are recaptured.

business gifts these are deductible only up to $25 per recipient each year.

business travel substantiation no receipts are needed for travel costs under $75 (except for lodging).

capital losses up to $3,000 ($1,500 if married filing separately) of capital losses in excess of capital gains for the year can be used to offset ordinary income.

charitable contribution substantiation rules the dollar thresholds for certain types of substantiation are fixed by law. Donations of $250 or more require a written acknowledgment from the charity. Donations of cars or other vehicles valued over $500 require a special acknowledgment. Appraisals are needed for donations of property valued over $5,000. Additional appraisal rules apply to donations of art valued at $20,000 or more.

charitable distributions to charity the exclusion for transfers from traditional IRAs to a public charity (qualified charitable distributions) by those age 70½ and older is capped at $100,000 annually.

Coverdell education savings accounts (ESAs) the maximum annual contribution is capped at $2,000 per year for an eligible beneficiary, and the MAGI limit for making a full contribution is up to $95,000 for singles and $120,000 for joint filers.

cruise ship travel for business the deduction is limited to $2,000.

dependent care assistance employer assistance is tax free up to $5,000 annually (other than in 2021, when the limit is $10,500). If your employer offers a dependent care flexible spending account, you can contribute up to $5,000 annually from your compensation ($10,500 in 2021 only); the amount contributed is not taxed to you.

dependent care credit the maximum amount of eligible expenses taken into account in figuring the credit is $3,000 for one child and $6,000 for two or more children (other than in 2021, when it's $8,000 and $16,000, respectively).

disaster losses there is a $100 reduction in the amount of each disaster loss; it applies per event (not per damaged or destroyed).

education credits the income limits on eligibility for the American opportunity credit and lifetime learning credit are fixed.

foreign tax credit simplified reporting this is restricted to a foreign tax credit of no more than $300 ($600 on a joint return).

gift loans the below-market loan rules do not apply to gift loans up to $10,000 per recipient.

health savings account additional contribution limit those who are age 55 and older by year-end can add $1,000 to their applicable contribution limit for the year.

home sale exclusion up to $250,000 of gain ($500,000 on a joint return) on the sale of a principal residence can be excluded if certain conditions are met.

IRA catchup contributions the additional annual contribution by those age 50 or older is $1,000.

IRA early distribution penalty exception for first-time homebuyers there is a $10,000 cap on penalty-free IRA distributions.

loans from qualified retirement plans the maximum loan is 50% of your vested account balance or $50,000, whichever is less.

lodging for medical treatment lodging to receive outpatient care is deductible up to $50 per night ($100 per night if you are accompanying a sick child).

mortgage insurance the deduction for mortgage insurance is limited for those with adjusted gross income (AGI) below set limits. The full deduction applies for AGI up to $100,000 ($50,000 for married persons filing separately).

Olympic medals the adjusted gross income limit for claiming the exclusion for the medals is limited to $1 million ($500,000 for married persons filing separately).

performing artists the conditions for such individuals to deduct their job expenses from gross income rather than as an itemized deduction are fixed. Adjusted gross income from all sources (not just performing) cannot exceed $16,000.

recovering attorney's fees and administrative costs from the government there is a net worth cap on individuals seeking a recovery. The cap is $2 million.

rental losses you can deduct up to $25,000 of rental losses each year if you actively participate in the rental activity and your adjusted gross income is no more than $100,000 (special rules apply to married persons filing separately).

reporting payments to independent contractors only payments of $600 or more to an independent contractor must be reported to the IRS.

section 1244 losses you can treat losses on certain small business stock as ordinary (rather than capital) losses up to $50,000 ($100,000 on a joint return).

standard mileage rate for charitable driving the rate is 14¢ per mile.

student exchange program if you host an exchange student in your home under an agreement with a charitable organization, you can deduct $50 per month as a charitable contribution.

student loan interest the maximum annual deduction is $2,500.

Checklist of Tax-Free Items

When items are not included in income, and in some cases not even reported on the return, there are considerable tax savings. Here is a list of tax-free items for 2021 tax returns.

- 529 plan withdrawals to pay qualified education costs
- ABLE account withdrawals to cover qualified expenses for a disabled beneficiary
- Accelerated death benefits under a life insurance policy
- Adoption costs paid by employer up to $14,440 in 2021
- Awards to certain employees (usually up to $1,600)
- Bequests
- Black lung benefit payments
- Capital gains and capital gain distributions for those with taxable income below a set amount
- Charitable transfers of IRA distributions up to $100,000 by those age 70½ and older (reduced by post-70½ IRA contributions)
- Child support payments
- Coverdell education savings account withdrawals to pay education costs
- Crime victim payments from a state fund for this purpose
- Damages received for personal physical injury
- Damages received for wrongful incarceration

- Debt discharged during insolvency or bankruptcy
- Dependent care expenses paid by employer up to $5,000
- Disability payments under a policy in which you paid the premiums
- Disaster relief payments and disaster mitigation grants
- Discounts on purchases you make
- Dividends for those with taxable income below a set amount if the dividends are "qualified"
- Economic impact payment
- Education courses paid by employer (fully excluded if job-related; up to $5,250 if not job-related)
- Federal Employees' Compensation Act (FECA) payments for personal injury or sickness (including death benefits to beneficiaries)
- Federal income tax refunds
- Flexible spending arrangement contributions from salary for health care or dependent care
- Foreign earned income up to $108,700
- Foster care payments
- Foster Grandparents Program payments for supportive services or reimbursement for out-of-pocket expenses
- Frequent flyer miles you earn
- Fringe benefits from employers ("perks") if they are *de minimis*, an employee discount, working condition fringe benefits, or transportation fringe benefits
- Gifts
- Grants for homes designed for wheelchair living of disabled veterans
- Grants for motor vehicles for veterans who have lost their sight or the use of their limbs
- Health insurance tax credit for coverage months (the portion of premiums paid by the federal government)
- Health reimbursement arrangement (employer plan)—all reimbursements
- Health savings account distributions to pay for medical costs
- Higher Education Emergency Relief Fund grants related to COVID-19
- Historic preservation grants under the National Historic Preservation Act
- Home sale gain up to $250,000, or $500,000 on a joint return
- Inheritances

- Interest on insurance dividends left on deposit with the Department of Veterans Affairs
- IRA rollovers
- Life insurance proceeds
- Long-term care benefits under a policy to pay for the care of someone chronically ill ($400 per day limit in 2021 if benefits are paid under a per diem contract)
- Meals and lodging furnished on the employer's premises for the employer's convenience (accepting onsite lodging must also be a condition of employment)
- Military benefits, including combat pay and death benefits
- Minister's housing allowance
- Mortgage assistance payments under Section 235 of the National Housing Act
- Mortgage debt cancellation on a principal residence up to $750,000, or $375,000 for married filing separately
- Mortgage loan proceeds (including proceeds on refinancing)
- Municipal bond interest
- Nutrition Program for the Elderly food benefits
- Payment for wrongful incarceration
- Peace Corps payments for housing, food, utilities, and clothing
- Prizes to certain employees (usually up to $1,600)
- Public safety officers' survivor benefits
- Rebates on purchases you make
- Restitution payments for Nazi victims and victims of human trafficking
- Retirement planning advice paid for by an employer
- Roth IRA distributions (all contributions, plus earnings in the account for at least 5 years that are withdrawn after age 59½, or on account of disability, death, or first-time homebuying)
- Savings bond interest if used to pay qualified higher education costs of certain taxpayers
- Scholarships, fellowships, and grants covering tuition, fees, books, supplies, and equipment for a degree program
- SCORE payments for supportive services or reimbursement for out-of-pocket expenses

- Senior Companion program payments for supportive services or reimbursement for out-of-pocket expenses
- Senior Corps program payments for supportive services or reimbursement for out-of-pocket expenses
- Small business stock gain up to 50% (75% of the gain for stock acquired after February 17, 2009, and before September 28, 2010; 100% for stock acquired after September 27, 2010)
- Social Security benefits if your income is below a threshold amount
- Student loan debt cancellation by a qualified lender for those who work in certain professions or by any lender on account of death or disability
- Supplement Security Income (SSI) and Supplement Security Disability Income (SSDI)
- Transportation fringe benefits up to $270 per month in 2021
- Tuition reduction for employees of educational institutions
- Vacation home rental income if the rental is no more than 14 days during the year

Checklist of Nondeductible Items

Unfortunately, not everything you spend your money on gives rise to a tax deduction. Most of your personal expenses, such as food, clothing, and recreation, are nondeductible items. The tax law also specifically bans certain write-offs. Of course, in some cases, while a deduction may be banned as a general rule, there may be circumstances under which it becomes deductible (so check throughout the book for exceptions to the general rule).

The IRS has identified a number of scams (the IRS calls them the "Dirty Dozen") in which sharp promoters incorrectly advise taxpayers to claim certain types of write-offs. Here are some types of situations that the IRS has over the years cautioned taxpayers against:

- *Pandemic-related scams*. They include Economic Impact Payment thefts where scammers try through text messages, phone calls, or email to obtain bank account information.

- *Phishing*. Scammers purporting to be from the IRS send e-mails seeking to obtain personal information used for identity theft. *The IRS never contacts taxpayers by e-mail without prior notice of the communication; the IRS already has taxpayers' personal information.*

- *Pervasive telephone scams*. Callers pretend to be from the IRS in order to steal money or identities ("vishing"). If you know you don't owe money (i.e., you never received a bill from the IRS), don't respond. *Instead, call the Treasury Inspector General for Tax Administration at 800-366-4484 to report the call.*

- *Identity theft*. This has topped the list of scams in the past several years, despite considerable IRS efforts to thwart it where taxes are concerned. Thieves are looking for ways to use a legitimate taxpayer's identity and personal information to file a tax return and claim a fraudulent refund. *Avoid problems with obtaining your legitimate refund by safeguarding your tax information; contact the IRS Identity Protection Specialized Unit.*

- *Preparer return fraud*. Dishonest tax return preparers, often promising refunds too good to be true, can leave taxpayers owing taxes and penalties for underpayments. Or they may have client refunds directed to themselves, leaving clients with difficulty obtaining what they are owed. *Taxpayers remain liable for taxes owed on their returns.*

- *Fake charities*. Scam groups masquerading as charitable organizations may lure people into making donations. These donations aren't tax deductible. *Check the IRS's online list of approved organizations at* https://apps.irs.gov/app/eos/ *before making a donation.*

- *Inflated refund claims*. Scam preparers induce taxpayers (usually those with low income or poor English skills) to claim inflated or erroneous write offs (e.g., false claims for education credits or the earned income tax credit), often based on fake Social Security benefits. They may use phony W-2s and 1099s to create the illusion of income. *Only use a reputable return preparer, as explained earlier.*

- *Inflated deductions*. Some may pad deductions, such as charitable contributions and business expenses to which they are not entitled. *Only claim deductions to which you are entitled. If you pad deductions, you may be subject to significant penalties and even criminal prosecution.*

- *Frivolous tax arguments*. Some promoters encourage taxpayers to make unreasonable and outlandish legal claims to avoid paying their taxes. These arguments don't hold up. *Don't be talked into using a frivolous argument. Read the truth about frivolous tax arguments from the IRS at* www.irs.gov/privacy-disclosure/the-truth-about-frivolous-tax-arguments-introduction.

- *Hiding income offshore*. The IRS is working with some offshore banks to learn the identity of depositors who fail to report their offshore income on their U.S. returns. *The IRS continues to develop investigation procedures to catch nonreporters.*

- *Filing false documents to hide income*. This usually involves inflating earned income to maximize the earned income tax credit to which a taxpayer is not eligible (or at least not in the amount claimed). *Taxpayers can be subject to penalties, interest, and even criminal prosecution.*

- *Excessive claims for business tax credits.* Scammers induce taxpayers to claim credits that are meant for fuel used in off-highway vehicles (e.g., farm equipment) or the research credit designed for increasing research activities. *Taxpayers who agree to submit these claims may be liable to penalties of $5,000 for frivolous arguments as well as criminal prosecution.*

- *Abusive tax shelters, trusts, and conservation easements.* These are investment schemes, which are listed or reportable transactions requiring taxpayers to disclose them on their returns; the schemes promise write-offs greater than amounts invested. *These schemes can result in both civil and criminal penalties.*

- *Trust deductions for personal expenses.* Promoters tell taxpayers to transfer their assets to trusts and have the trusts deduct the cost of food, clothing, and other personal expenses. *Personal expenses, other than those explained throughout the book, are not deductible.*

- *"Abuse of charitable deductions."* These abuses include attempts by donors to maintain control over donated assets or income from donated property. They also include schemes involving the donation of noncash assets, including easements on property, closely held corporate stock, real property, and overvaluations of property donations. *No deductions are allowed for illusory donations, and there are penalties for significant overvaluations.*

- *"No gain realized" deduction.* Like the claim of right doctrine, promoters tell taxpayers to claim a miscellaneous itemized deduction on Schedule A equal to their adjusted gross income. *There is no such deduction.*

- *Zero returns.* Promoters instruct taxpayers to enter all zeros on the return (rather than reporting their actual income items). *Income must be reported unless there is a specific tax rule for exemption or exclusion.*

- *Slavery reparations.* Promoters suggest that African Americans can claim a deduction or credit for reparations. *There are no such reparations and no such allowable deduction or credit.*

- *Home-based businesses.* While there is a deduction allowed for legitimate home-based businesses, promoters tell taxpayers to fictitiously create a business run from home so that a deduction will be allowed. *Fake businesses do not support real deductions.*

- *Shared earned income credits.* Promoters tell taxpayers that they can "share" dependents in order for multiple taxpayers to claim the earned income credit with respect to the same dependents. *Only eligible taxpayers can claim the earned income credit and only one credit is allowed for each dependent.*

Nondeductible Items

Here is a listing of other items you may *not* deduct:

Additional Medicare taxes on earned income and net investment income for high-income taxpayers

Alimony payments under divorces or agreements executed after 2018

Attorney's fees on buying a home

Bank fees, such as monthly checking fees on a personal account

Bar examination fees

Blood donations

Bribes

Burial fees

Car expenses for personal use of the car

Child support payments

Club dues for recreational, social, and athletic clubs

Commuting expenses

Compensation to housekeepers and other domestic employees

Cosmetic surgery

Country club membership

Credit card interest incurred for personal expenditures

Debts belonging to another person that you pay

Demolition costs

Disability insurance premiums

Education costs for your child's primary and secondary school

Elective deferrals to 401(k) and similar plans

Employee business expenses (through 2025)

Entertainment costs

Estimated tax penalties

Expenses of earning tax-exempt income

Federal income tax

Fifty percent of meal costs for business (unless provided by a restaurant in 2021 and 2022)

Fines

Funeral expenses

Gambling losses in excess of winnings

Gift tax

Gifts you make to family and friends

Health spa expenses

Hobby losses

Interest on loans to buy or carry tax-exempt securities

Investment advisory fees (through 2025)

Investment seminars

IRA contributions by participants with AGI over set limits

Job-related expenses

Kickbacks

Life insurance premiums

Lobbying expenses (other than in-house expenses up to $2,000)

Losses from the sale of your home, furniture, car, and other personal items

Losses in excess of at-risk limits

Losses on sales to related parties

Lost or misplaced cash or property

Lunches with coworkers

Moving expenses

Organ donations (e.g., a kidney)

Over-the-counter medications for purposes of the itemized deduction (unless purchased with a prescription)

Partially worthless securities

Passive activity losses in excess of passive activity income

Penalties

Personal disability insurance premiums

Personal interest (such as credit card interest)

Personal living expenses (such as food, clothing, rent, and utilities)

Pet food (other than for Seeing Eye or therapy dogs, which may be a deductible medical expense)

Points paid to refinance a home mortgage

Political contributions

Professional accreditation fees

Property settlements when dissolving a marriage

Reimbursed expenses you receive under an accountable plan

Repairs to your home or personal car

Repayment of loans

Rollover contributions

Roth IRA contributions

Sales tax if you deduct state and local income taxes

Social Security and Medicare (FICA) taxes

Spousal travel costs

State inheritance taxes

Stockholder meetings, expenses of attending

Tax penalties

Tax return preparation costs

Telephone line (basic service charges of first residential line to home)

Title insurance

Toiletries

Travel as a form of education

Uniforms

Union dues

Vacations

Veterinary fees

Voluntary alimony payments

Voluntary unemployment benefit fund contributions

Wash sale losses

Index